Glocalized Security

Glocalized Security

DOMESTIC AND EXTERNAL ISSUES IN
INTERNATIONAL SECURITY

EDITED BY
ABU BAKARR BAH

INDIANA UNIVERSITY PRESS

This book is a publication of

Indiana University Press
Office of Scholarly Publishing
Herman B Wells Library 350
1320 East 10th Street
Bloomington, Indiana 47405 USA

iupress.org

© 2025 by Indiana University Press

All rights reserved

No part of this book may be reproduced or utilized in any form or by any means, electronic or mechanical, including photocopying and recording, or by any information storage and retrieval system, without permission in writing from the publisher.

First Printing 2025

Cataloging information is available from the Library of Congress.

ISBN 978-0-253-07288-7 (hdbk.)
ISBN 978-0-253-07289-4 (pbk.)
ISBN 978-0-253-07291-7 (e-book)
ISBN 978-0-253-07290-0 (web PDF)

CONTENTS

1. Introduction: *Glocalized Security and the Conundrums of Peace and Security* / ABU BAKARR BAH   1

2. Contemporary Nationalisms and Conceptions of National Security: *Military Power and the Reshaping of International Security* / ABU BAKARR BAH   24

3. The Taliban's Return, Terrorism, and Regional Security Policy Convergence on Afghanistan / HAQMAL DAUDZAI AND FAROOQ YOUSAF   69

4. Prestige Seeking and International Commitments: *Turkey's Involvement in the Nagorno-Karabakh Conflict* / ÜNSAL SIĞRI AND TAHA KALAYCI   94

5. Kenya's Collective Security Approach in a Glocalized Security Environment in Somalia / FRANCIS ONDITI AND JAMES YUKO   121

6. Shi'ism as Ideological Vector: *International and Domestic Security in Iranian Foreign Policy in Iraq* / MASSIMO RAMAIOLI   148

7. Communal Conflicts and Radicalization into Nonjihadi Violent Extremism in Nigeria: *The Case of Southern Kaduna* / GBEMISOLA ABDUL-JELIL ANIMASAWUN   172

8. The Yam between Two Boulders: *India, China, and the Glocalization of Contention in Nepal* / CHES THURBER   199

9. Conclusion: *Glocalized Security, Intersectionality, and a Sociology of International Peace and Security* /
ABU BAKARR BAH   222

Index   243

Glocalized Security

1

INTRODUCTION

Glocalized Security and the Conundrums of Peace and Security

Abu Bakarr Bah

Introduction: Issues in International Security

The chapters of this multiauthored collection, *Glocalized Security: Domestic and External Issues in International Security*, seek to examine the conundrums of international security through the dialectics of domestic and external issues and interests in international security matters. Since the end of the Cold War, numerous violent conflicts have emerged around the world. While some of them are largely domestic wars, others are international in nature whose outcomes have global implications. Violent conflicts ranging from the wars in the former Yugoslavia to the civil wars in Rwanda, Congo, Sierra Leone, Liberia, and Côte d'Ivoire, among others, destabilized the respective regions and took too long to resolve as the wars dragged on and too many people lost their lives.[1] In many cases, the drivers of these conflicts still linger in those countries. Other conflicts, such as those in Iraq, Syria, Afghanistan, Yemen, Libya, Mali, Somalia, and Nigeria, where terrorism has become a main method of warfare, have had wider-ranging effects. Domestic and geopolitical issues have also led to interstate wars in countries of the former Soviet Union, notably the Azerbaijan-Armenia and the Russia-Ukraine wars. While domestic discord has spurred all these conflicts, external factors have amplified many of them, causing them to proliferate from one country to another via global criminal and terrorist networks or the imposition of the wills of global and regional powers. The numerous international efforts to resolve these conflicts have too often led to international military interventions rooted in responsibility to protect (R2P), geopolitics, and national security doctrines, such as the war on terror, and the resolutions themselves have been problematic and offered limited success.[2]

The critical questions that arise from over three decades of international military interventions around the world are: How does the fusion of domestic issues and interests with external ones generate new security situations that further undermine international security? And, moreover, how can domestic issues and interests be disentangled from external ones in efforts to resolve violent conflicts? These questions require critical analyses of the broader nature of international security threats and the internal dynamics of countries plagued by prolonged conflicts that render them into ungovernable spaces, threats to regional and international security, and theaters of protracted war. By examining the dialectics of the domestic and external issues and interests in and around war-torn countries, this book sheds new insights into the problems of international security and why international military interventions have not been very successful in ensuring peace and security in conflict zones where domestic and external factors have created areas of terrorism warfare or regions of national interest among major world and regional powers. Ultimately, to ensure security, peacebuilding solutions must troubleshoot both the domestic and external contributors to glocalized security situations.

By probing the intersection of internal dynamics and external factors in glocalized security, this book ventures into what can be dubbed the sociology of international peace and security. Though international security and conflict studies have been heavily dominated by political science, the intricacies of the most common and persistent domestic drivers of violent conflicts are deeply sociological. Studies of peace and conflict, especially in the global south, often point to issues of ethnicity, religion, poverty, governance, corruption, human rights violations, and resource distribution as core causes of conflict.[3] All of these issues are deeply sociological as we see from studies of social inequality and discrimination in the United States and other Western countries as well as those that investigate the intersection of various forms of social inequality.[4] Although social inequalities in Western countries have not led to wars in the post–World War II era, they are frequently pointed to as drivers of violent conflicts in the global south and former communist counties. Sociology, which in the West has shied away from a rich historical tradition and become overly parochial,[5] has great potential not only to shed light on traditional peace and conflict studies by focusing on internal causes and dynamics of conflicts or micro conflicts but also to contribute to the more political terrain of international peace and security by tapping into the ideas of intersectionality and globalization as they relate to issues of domestic, regional, and international peace and security. Indeed, when sociologists study migration, for example, they seek to understand the intersection of identity and the global interconnections of people, families, countries, and cultures.[6] As we know, the globalization phenomenon goes well beyond migration as it permeates every aspect of modern life. Yet globalization, as traditionally understood in international and security studies, misses a critical sociological insight—a lacuna perpetuated by the parochial nature of Western sociology. Indeed, the global emanates from a local, too often the local of Westerners.[7] However, as the local is globalized so too is the global localized in a way that produces an intersectionality that can become a quantum reality in the sense that contradictory forces fuse to produce new glocal realities. In the context of international security, the fusion of the domestic and the external produces glocalized security situations. *Glocalization*, in this sense, refers to the fusion of domestic and external drivers of conflicts, generating new conflict dynamics that can be reduced to neither the local nor the global alone.

Indeed, the glocal nature of domestic, regional, and international security can also be approached through the classical notion of the sociological imagination, which captures the interconnections between the internal and the external and the symbiosis that emanates from that dialectic. As C. Wright Mills stated,

> the sociological imagination enables its possessor to understand the larger historical scene in terms of its meaning for the inner life and the external career of a variety of individuals. It enables him to take into account how individuals, in the welter of their daily experience, often become falsely conscious of their social positions. Within that welter, the framework of modern society is sought, and within that framework the psychologies of a variety of men and women are formulated. By such means the personal uneasiness of individuals is focused upon explicit troubles and the indifference of publics is transformed into involvement with public issues.[8]

The sociological imagination is a perspective that sees society through the intersection of the internal and the external, as evident in the notion of glocalization. Applied to a global understanding of society, the sociological imagination, as an idea of intersectionality, becomes a window into the concept of the glocal. In the realm of security studies, the connections between the domestic and global drivers of conflicts make security a truly glocalized phenomenon.

The cornerstone of this book is the notion of glocalized security and its connections to efforts to resolve violent conflicts. The notion of glocalized security is used to examine the intersection of domestic and external grievances and interests in and around war-torn countries. Glocalized security rests on the argument that the fusion of domestic and external matters produces new war dynamics that require both substantial domestic reforms and the realignment of external interests in order to achieve sustainable peace. Glocalized security draws on the lessons of the failures to resolve conflicts in countries where external interests have been integrally fused with domestic issues such as those in Somalia, Mali, Nigeria, Libya, Palestine, Yemen, Syria, Iraq, Afghanistan, and Ukraine. The key questions that animate the book are: What are the drivers of violent conflicts (namely, wars)? And how do domestic issues fuse with external issues? These questions raise related ones across the various cases studied in this work. These include questions about how conflict drivers are addressed, whose interests are protected through military interventions, why interventions fail, and what the acceptable forms of domestic solutions are. By addressing these questions, the book makes significant contributions to the extant literature and policy debates on international peace and security. Too often, these issues are fragmented in scholarly and policy debates, even though they are all addressing the issue of peace and security, albeit from different angles. A key issue in glocalized security is understating the intersection of the domestic and external drivers of conflicts.

Glocalized Security and Conceptions of Peace and Security

Studies on international security often evoke the question of how to achieve peace. However, they tend to bifurcate peace as that between countries and that within countries. In this book, the notion of glocalized security is used to weave together the various dimensions of security and peace from spatial and temporal lenses, akin to the way the notions of globalization and glocalization have been deployed to understand the intricacies of global homogenization and local resistances. The notion of glocalization often comes out as a critique of the spread and homogenization of Western values and practices that we often see under globalization. This flattening of the world, as captured in Thomas Friedman's *The World Is Flat*, masks a lot of the dialectics of local resistances as they encounter the global, not to mention the very glocalized nature of the environmental issues and environmentalism in our epoch of the Anthropocene.[9] Glocalization captures this dialectic and serves as a critique, and an adjustment, to the notion of globalization by accounting for the ways in which the global is localized and potentially influenced by the local as well. A key figure in the development of the notion of glocalization is Roland Robertson, who alluded to it in his article "Globality and Modernity" published in 1992 in *Theory, Culture & Society*.[10] Notably, Robertson was a sociologist. Working with others, Robertson continued to push the concept of glocalization in a series of articles that capture the ways local issues are connected to global processes and networks.[11] Other scholars, such as Ulrich Beck (a German sociologist) have also critiqued the homogenizing nature of globalization through a cultural relativism standpoint that accentuates the importance of the local, notably the non-Western local, through the notion of contextual universalism.[12] These kinds of critiques of globalization essentially point to the notion of glocalization, even when they do not explicitly use the term. Most of these initial critiques of globalization and framings of glocalization came from the realms of business, culture, and social movements, especially in the ways time and space are homogenized.[13] In fact studies of Japanese businesses have noted the idea of glocalization in the Japanese practice of *dochakuka*.[14] Glocalization, especially as used by sociologists, is akin to the sociological idea of intersectionality, albeit used in significantly different contexts—that is, the intersection of cultures instead of the intersections of modes of social inequality.

Though the concept of glocalization has been used in studies of social movements, culture, and globalization generally, it is hardly used in relation to international security issues. One notable effort in this direction is the study by Samuel Marfo and colleagues that sought "to make a case for a 'glocalized peace and security architecture,' a comprehensive peace and security design which is both domestically or inward-looking relevant and internationally or outside-looking practicable."[15] As they argue, a glocalized peace and security architecture "attempts to suggest an approach which can foster a peaceful co-existence among states without necessarily endangering domestic politics in a seemingly chaotic global environment."[16] Overall, the notion of glocalization is badly missing in international security despite the fact that studies of international relations have long noted the utility of using multiple levels of analysis, notably those formulated by Kenneth Waltz—individual, state, and international.[17] These three levels capture elements of the domestic and the external as well as the important influence of leaders. However, the domestic and the external do not necessarily exist as distinct factors in shaping international security. As we note from the more sociological notions of intersectionality, globalization, and glocalization, the multiple factors do not necessarily remain distinct or mere aggregated realities. Rather, their intersection breeds new realities in the sense of the Hegelian dialectic.[18] In the realm of international security, this is what we see in situations of glocalized security.

International security is often viewed through state-centric realist, liberal, constructivist, or more critical lenses.[19] Notably, the literature points to five central theoretical groups of arguments relating to the causes of insecurity: structural, political, economic, social psychological, and situational.[20] It is crucial to note that wars and peacebuilding are not exclusively domestic or international matters, even though scholars "treat individual nation-states as sovereign systems whose internal politics can be safely ignored."[21] However, international politics and external intervention play crucial roles in domestic politics and the security of countries. Hence, glocalized security is a useful lens into international security issues.

Perhaps, the connection between security and the core elements of peace, such as governance, finds its roots in the works of Charles Tilly as he tied "war making" and "state making" to forms of violence and transnational networks that are akin to organized crime.[22] Since the days of Tilly, international security has moved from classical state making, as experienced in Europe before World War II, to mostly wars within existing sovereign states and military interventions in states affected by civil wars. Contemporary international security has become glocalized both in terms of the root causes of conflicts and the nature of the conflicts, necessitating new ways of thinking of war and peace. As such, contemporary wars are best viewed as glocalized security situations. At the heart of glocalized security are three issues: geopolitics, national security, and governance—not to ignore the growing connections between environmental issues and security, especially at the regional and local levels.

Geopolitics is a critical factor in international security because of the way it transforms countries and regions into glocalized spaces where major powers claim preferential rights to influence based on historical ties or national interests. These spaces are typically peripheral countries that not only are internally volatile but also become sites of contestation for external powers.[23] Colonialism, national interests, and the balance of power typically shape which countries seek to exert influence and control in another country and how they do it. Notably, formerly colonized spaces in the Americas and Caribbean, Africa, South and East Asia, the Middle East, Europe, and the Caucasus have become highly contested geopolitical spaces where major world and regional powers, such as the United States, Britain, France, Russia, China, Turkey, and Iran, contest for influence and control. In the process, domestic political issues get fused with the interests of external powers, an intertwining that fuels wars. A critical issue for peace in geopolitically contested spaces is the balance of power, which rests on the interests of external powers.[24] However, the balance of power always shifts as countries seek to outmaneuver competitors, especially by interfering in the domestic affairs of vulnerable countries. While geopolitical conflicts do not necessarily lead to direct war among major powers, they do lead to proxy wars and direct military interventions under the guise of humanitarianism.[25] The wars in Ukraine, Nagorno-Karabakh, Syria, Iraq, Libya, and Mali are all examples of wars with significant geopolitics at work. During the Cold War, such spaces also included Vietnam, Cambodia, Cuba, Nicaragua, and El Salvador.

While geopolitics speaks to the ways countries seek influence and the balance of power, national security explains what motivates countries to intervene in external conflicts. Increasingly, national security has been broadened to mean not only the ability to repel attacks against a country but also to prevent them and the influx of unwanted refugees by taking preemptive action abroad.[26] As such, exaggerated notions of national security now encompass efforts to restore order in countries plagued by extreme violence so that they do not become sources of mass refugees or havens for terrorists. This framing of national security in relation to failed and failing states that generate ungoverned spaces is most evident in the global war on terror and the doctrine of R2P.[27] Both the global war on terror and R2P have led to massive military interventions in countries such as Afghanistan, Iraq, Syria, Somalia, Libya, and Mali. In some cases, such interventions are framed as peacekeeping and peacebuilding efforts. However, military interventions often face ethical and practical challenges relating to conflict of interests and the colonial legacies of Western humanitarianism.[28]

Governance issues are also critical in glocalized security in the sense that many conflicts revolve around domestic politics and governance problems. Too often these problems relate to human rights violations, ethnic discrimination, resource distribution, and the deficits of multiparty democracy.[29] At the same time, governance has become an issue of growing interest to Western powers as they tie it to the global liberal order rooted in neoliberal democracy and economics. Governance then becomes both a trigger of conflict and a motivating factor for external intervention, especially by Western powers. Such interventions may actually start before the outbreak of war through neoliberal conditionalities as well as continue into the postwar phase.[30] A key factor in governance is what Mark Duffield referred to as global liberal governance, which uncritically sets the standard for proper governance and the paths to achieve it.[31] Reyko Huang, for example examines the connection between civil wars and democratizations, most notably in Nepal, Tajikistan, Uganda, and Mozambique.[32] Robert Blair takes up the issue of governance by examining the role of the international community in building the rule of law in postwar settings, notably in Liberia.[33] Similar issues of liberalism are addressed by Roland Paris, who examined the efforts to build market democracies in numerous war-torn countries in Africa, Latin America, and

Asia.[34] The critical issue has been how to consolidate peace, a process that often gravitates toward economic and political liberalization along the lines of liberal peace. In all the cases, security is glocalized through the fight for neoliberal democracy.

Increasingly, environmental issues are becoming very critical to glocalized security. Global environmental degradation is causing significant stresses to local resources that are sources of livelihood, especially in poor countries. The decline of environmental resources generates tensions among local communities that can easily fuse with national and regional political conflicts. Such conflicts have been most prevalent among herders and farmers, especially in Africa.[35] In Nigeria, for example, there are numerous violent conflicts between Fulani herders seeking grazing lands and farming communities resisting encroachment on their ancestral lands. Similar conflicts over natural resources have been reported in countries such as Mali, Kenya, Sudan, Chad, Central African Republic, and Ethiopia. A growing trend, especially in the Sahel, is the fusion of natural resource conflicts with terrorism warfare wherein local communities seeking to defend themselves have been labeled as terrorists, especially pastoralists. In the Lake Chad basin, for example, terrorist groups exploit communal conflicts by offering protection as the states are unable to provide security.[36]

Environmental issues have also been tied to civil wars, especially in cases where local communities suffering from environmental degradation resort to armed conflict to secure fair compensation for the exploitation of natural resources in their territories. In Nigeria, minorities in the Niger Delta have waged wars to ensure that they gain access to the huge revenues from oil extracted from their lands.[37] In Somalia, too, degradation of marine sources resulted in piracy, which fused with terrorism and civil war in Somalia.[38] In other cases, most evident in Angola, Sierra Leone, Liberia, and the Democratic Republic of Congo, natural resources have been used to fund insurgencies and civil wars.[39]

All of these forms of environmental issues and conflicts have generated regional and global efforts to exert order in what is truly a glocalized problem. Global and local environmental problems have led to efforts to exert a global environmental regime to reduce greenhouse gases and protect communities and the planet through national and multilateral policy frameworks, with one example of such an effort being the 2015 Paris Agreement on climate changes and its related national policies.[40] In addition, civil wars and communal conflicts connected to natural resources have triggered various forms of interventions through the global war on terror and international peacekeeping missions.[41]

Themes and Scope: National Interest, Terrorism, and Intersectionality

This book connects the domestic and the global dynamics of international security through the notion of glocalized security. A crucial part in that effort is understanding the intersection of domestic matters and interests and external ones. As a multiauthored book, the work provides rich cases that simultaneously address the overarching issue and the nuances of glocalized security based on cases from Asia, Africa, and Europe. Notably absent are cases from the Americas, even though countries there, especially in Latin America, experienced highly glocalized wars during the Cold War. Certainly, global and domestic factors are still shaping the current security situations in Ecuador and Columbia. However, this work is not about examining each country that has experienced a highly glocalized war, nor is it about providing a representative sample of such cases. Given the glocalized nature of Cold War and post–Cold War conflicts from Africa and Asia to the Americas, it may be impossible to cover each case or provide an exhaustive list of cases in a single work. The core contribution of the book is to conceptualize glocalized security through relevant cases. By providing such a conceptual framing of security, the work offers an opportunity for further studies that cover a wide range of historical and contemporary cases of conflicts characterized by glocalized security situations. In that sense, the absence of the Americas in this book is not a denial of the relevance of those countries but simply the result of a more contemporary focus.

Indeed, the Americas would provide insightful cases of glocalized security. During the Cold War, the Americas experienced significant levels of conflicts driven by left-wing and right-wing ideologies.[42] In Nicaragua for example, the Sandinista movement, led by the Sandinista National Liberation Front (FSLN), waged a violent rebellion against the pro-Western government of Anastasio Somoza in what is known as the Nicaraguan revolution (1978 to 1990). The Nicaragua war quickly became a geopolitical battleground between the United States and the Soviet Union as the Contras took up arms against the Sandinista junta. The Cold War provided the external foil through which domestic social, economic, and political problems fused into a war that was driven by capitalist and communist external powers.[43] A similar situation played out in El Salvador (1979 to 1992), where the leftist Farabundo Martí National Liberation Front (FMLN) waged war against the government of General Carlos Romero and the Revolutionary Government Junta as well as the subsequent governments. The United States supported the governments of El Salvador against the FMLN as part of its effort to combat communism in the America.[44] As in Nicaragua, the war in

El Salvador was driven by both domestic problems and the Cold War ideological battle between the United States and the Soviet Union.[45] Notwithstanding the violence in Ecuador and Columbia, the Americas may have graduated from Cold War proxy wars and the kinds of civil wars that currently plague other regions, notably Africa, Asia, and Europe.[46] Yet, the Cold War–era conflicts in the Americas would be useful historical cases to show the extensive roots and forms of glocalized security situations, well beyond the contemporary cases of glocalized security examined in this work.

In essence, this book examines the conceptual issues of glocalized security through deep historical analysis of relatively contemporary wars that have taken on a glocalized character. The case studies weave the domestic aspects of the wars in Afghanistan, Iraq, Nagorno-Karabakh, Somalia, Nigeria, and Nepal with the roles of major global and regional powers that shape the wars, notably: the United States, Russia, Turkey, China, India, Iran, and Kenya. Three themes emerge from the book that cut across the various chapters and contribute to the notion of glocalized security: (a) national interest, (b) terrorism, and (c) intersectionality.

In all the chapters, national interest emerges as a key element in how domestic political issues become entangled in external interests fueling more war. In chapter 2, Abu Bah examines the ways major and emerging powers define national interest and weave it with nationalism to justify militarism and generate domestic support even in the face of steep economic and human costs. Using nationalism as a frame for national security, Bah examines the contestations for military power among major powers and emerging powers on issues such as nuclear weapons, spheres of influence, and terrorism. In chapter 3, Haqmal Daudzai and Farooq Yousaf examine the US war in Afghanistan, which became increasingly regional as other (regional) powers joined the United States' campaign in the country, which the United States had based largely on its national security concerns following the 9/11 terrorist attacks. Notably, Russia, Pakistan, India, China, Iran, and the Gulf countries all found reasons to be involved in the Afghan conflict, which is mostly rooted in local political issues of governance, albeit glocalized into a war of regional and global consequence. Similar issues of national security interest emerge in chapter 5, by Francis Onditi and James Yuko, on Kenya's intervention in Somalia. According to Onditi and Yuko, as Somalia became a failed state it increasingly affected Kenyan security as Al Shaabab and other terrorist groups began to launch attacks, especially against Western targets, in Kenya. Kenyan intervention in Somalia was supposed to stabilize Somalia and prevent terrorist attacks in Kenya. In reality, Kenya got sucked into the global war on terror and became an even more desired target for terrorists as retaliation for its intervention efforts. Kenya found itself in the difficult situation of having to participate in the international military intervention in Somalia to gain recognition as a valuable member of the Western-dominated global order while trying to figure out what the best way to ensure its national security is, which is not necessarily the same as those of Western powers.

In chapter 4, we see how a local conflict in Azerbaijan became international with major national security consideration. As a start, it should be noted that the conflict in Nagorno-Karabakh itself is local in its roots as it centers on issues of marginalization between ethnic Armenians and Azerbaijanis living in Azerbaijan. Yet as soon as Armenia and Azerbaijan seceded from the Soviet Union, Nagorno-Karabakh, which Armenia attempted to annex from Azerbaijan, became an international conflict of major interest to regional powers. Turkey showed a very broad scope of national interest in defending Azerbaijan against the Armenian annexation of Nagorno-Karabakh territory. Turkey's strong support for Azerbaijan points to three national interests: namely, maintaining cultural solidarity with the people of Azerbaijan; showing that Turkey is a formidable regional power in the Caucasus, especially in relation to Russia; and gaining domestic political support for the Turkish government during elections. In this chapter, Ünsal Sığrı and Taha Kalaycı frame the Turkish involvement in the Nagorno-Karabakh war in terms of gaining prestige in the international security arena. Turkish involvement in the war has helped Azerbaijan regain territory while enhancing Turkey's international standing. In a similar way, Nepal also became a place where both India and China became critical factors in how domestic politics and efforts to overthrow the monarchy evolved. As Ches Thurber notes in chapter 8, Nepal became a yam between two boulders. Wedged between two major powers that have contentious relations, Nepalese opposition forces and government always sought support from India and China in their effort to gain or retain power. In the process, Nepal became a space of significant external national interest that neither India nor China could ignore. At various points in Nepal's long struggle for democracy, India and China separately supported the (armed) insurgency, provided the government with critical support, and served as peace mediators. In a way, the trajectories of the struggle for democracy in Nepal became contingent upon what kind of support India and/or China were willing to provide and how those countries defined their interests in Nepal.

In Iraq and Nigeria, the national interests of outsiders took the form of ideology that conditioned the nature of the violence. This is most vivid in Iran's deep involvement in Iraq. Through the notion of ideological vector, Massimo Ramaioli shows in chapter 6 how Iran has been able to deeply insert itself into Iraqi politics and challenge US domination in the region. The chapter shows how national interest is weaved into an ideology that taps into the common religion (i.e., Shiʿa Islam) of the Iranian and Iraqi people. In the process, Iraq became a war theater where US and Iranian interests for domination translated into continuous political violence that took the form of terrorism warfare. Ironically, Iran ended up playing a double-edged role as a stabilizer and a destabilizer in Iraq. For Iran, Iraq became important for ensuring Iranian security given its war with Iraq under Saddam Hussain, guarding Shiʿa Islam, and being a bulwark against American imperialism in the region. In regards to Nigeria, Gbemisola Animasawun examines how radicalization into grievance-fueled violent extremism feeds into terrorism in Nigeria. As he shows in chapter 7, conflicts that are deeply local at root have become of interest to outsiders because of the loops between local conflicts in Southern Kaduna and radicalization into nonjihadi extremist violence that can feed into terrorism in Nigeria and the Sahel region. In these deeply local conflicts, mostly around issues of land and autochthony, the national security interest of the Nigerian state ties into those of Western powers through the global war on terror.

Terrorism also became a core issue in glocalized security in nearly all the cases. Even in cases where the wars were conventional wars between two states as in Nagorno-Karabakh and Ukraine, the wars generated forms of violence that are akin to terrorism warfare. In Afghanistan, Somalia and Iraq, the wars are entirely framed as terrorism. As Daudzai and Yousaf show, the global war on terror was the driver of the renewed external interests and militarism in Afghanistan, even though Afghans were really fighting over local issues. The same seems to be true for Somalia. As Onditi and Yuko note, Kenyan intervention in Somalia failed to fully factor the domestic roots of Somali wars as it uncritically saw Somalia through the global war on terror lens. Though Iran's involvement in Iraq goes beyond terrorism warfare, Iranian involvement in Iraq has been cast as terrorism, especially after the US invasion of Iraq. Ramaioli rightly notes the ideological nature of Iranian involvement, which encompasses more than support for groups that engage in terrorism warfare. The terrorism frame has also been used in Nigeria and Nepal. In Nigeria, local conflicts over land and ethnicity quickly became branded as terrorism. Animasawun's chapter shows how non-Jihadi and grievance-based violent extremism became part of the global war on terror narrative. For Nepal too, Thurber shows in his chapter how the fight for democracy fluctuated between an armed struggle and peaceful resistance. However, the opposition was often branded as a terrorist group by the government, even when its violence was relatively short and limited. In all the cases, terrorism is both a real form of warfare and a frame for intervention in glocalized security situations. This is also evident in Bah's chapter on the intersection of national interest and the quest for military power among major and emerging powers. In defining their national security, countries, most notably the United States, elevated terrorism to a global war against nonstate actors and the countries in which terrorists hide.

Finally, the theme of intersectionality emerges in all the chapters. Intersectionality brings home the phenomenon of glocalized security as multiple factors and actors duke it out in conflict areas. Though not often used in international security studies, intersectionality has a rich history in sociological studies of social inequalities, especially gender.[47] Patricia Collins, for example, uses intersectionality to show how race, class, and gender interact to produce a matrix of domination that places African American women in a unique position of oppression in the white male-dominated social and knowledge systems. For Collins, this matrix of domination produces a dialectical situation of powerless and empowerment in that the multiple factors of oppression breed powerlessness, but oppression itself generates an inner strength for empowerment.[48] Intersectionality goes beyond issues of race, class, and gender in the United States as it points to the dialectical interconnectedness of social forces that breed conflicts and oppression. The fusion of domestic and external issues in glocalized security situations points to a form of intersectionality in international security. This intersectionality shows how diverse conflict drivers and conflicting security interests produce peculiar security situations that are simultaneously domestic and international.

In terms of the intersection of conflict drivers, Bah's chapter draws attention to the quest among major and emerging powers for military power, which breeds an arms race and contention around which countries are allowed to have nuclear weapons. The nuclear energy policy of emerging powers simultaneously becomes a domestic and an international issue. In Afghanistan, as Daudzai and Yousaf point out, the war is driven by the intersection of domestic struggles for power among the various ethnic groups and the global war on terror, which was imposed on Afghanistan by terrorist groups and the US led invasion. In Nagorno-Karabakh, the conflict was driven by the intersection of ethnic political grievances by ethnic Armenians in Azerbaijan and Armenia's desire to unify with ethnic Armenians across the border in Azerbaijan. In Somalia, multiple clan identities intersected with Islamism to produce terrorism warfare that extended into Kenya. This made Somali domestic issues matters of international security. In Iraq, as Ramaioli points out, Iran's sense of an external security threat and its feeling of guardianship over Shi'a Islam intersected with Iraqi politics and American interests in Iraq, which fed into the violence between the Sunni and Shi'a. In Nigeria, conflicts over autochthony and landownership among local communities intersected with violent extremism in the context of jihadism and the global war on terror. In Nepal, domestic political conflicts intersected with the geopolitical interests of India and China. Nepal's conflict was driven by demands for democratic reforms from various antigovernment forces fighting against class and ethnic oppression. However, the nature of the struggle for democratic reforms were shaped by the kinds of support India and China were willing to offer as Indian and Chinese interest intersected in Nepal. In all the countries covered in this work, multiple conflict drivers intersected to produce glocalized security situations.

Intersectionality also emerged out of the conflicting security interests in the conflicts. In the conflicts pitting major powers against emerging powers, nationalistic conceptions of national security produced security interests that were incompatible, especially in the realm of nuclear technology and weapons. Bah captures these contradictory conceptions of national security through the discourses of nationalism. In the case of Iran, national interest took the form of an ideology that was applied to gain leverage in Iraq. In Nigeria too, relatively minor local conflicts quickly became weaved into extremism generating deeper national security interest by the Nigerian state and opportunities for outsiders enmeshed in the global war on terror. In cases such as Afghanistan, Nagorno-Karabakh, Somalia, and Nepal, multiple external interests were fused into domestic political issues. As Daudzai and Yousaf point out, Afghanistan became a terrain where the security interests of the United States, Russia, Pakistan, India, China, Iran, and the Gulf countries must be achieved, mostly at the expense of the Afghan people. In Nagorno-Karabakh, Turkish interests, enacted through its support of Azerbaijan, were superimposed on the Russian claim of regional hegemony and Armenia's interest to unify coethnics. So too was Kenyan interest superimposed on Somalia through a military intervention. In Nepal too, as Thurber shows, Indian and Chinese interests became critical determinants of the nature of the conflict, which gravitated between an armed struggle and a nonviolent social movement.

Conclusion: The Conundrums of Peace in Glocalized Security

The cornerstone of this book is the notion of glocalized security and its connections to peace. The notion of glocalized security is used to examine the intersection of domestic and external grievances and interests in and around war-torn countries. As already noted, glocalized security rests on the argument that the fusion of domestic and external matters produces new war dynamics that require both substantial domestic reforms and realignment of external interests in order to achieve sustainable peace. We have thus formed the critical question in this work to be how to promote peace in glocalized security situations. Glocalized security recognizes the existence of the domestic and the external and the dialectical symbiosis they produce. Under these conditions, efforts to promote peace cannot be based on a one-sided understanding of the causes of conflicts or the interests that must be satisfied. As such, international military interventions not only should be anchored in the interests and political values of the intervening powers and Western-dominated international governance mechanisms but must also make fundamental efforts to address domestic grievances through inclusive and locally owned governance arrangements. Glocalized security suggests that the solution to the conflicts undermining regional and international security will involve disentangling the domestic and the external interests, demilitarizing international interventions, and seeking more domestic solutions to the conflicts. It further recognizes that some of the possible domestic solutions many not fit well into the dominant neoliberal notions of democracy and the rule of law. Yet glocalized security sees peace as a critical step to the potential realization of liberal values of governance and rule of law. From the cases discussed in this work, a number of intersectional issues pose challenges to peace, notably the following: (a) the neoliberal bent on governance, (b) statism and transnational cultural connections, and (c) hegemony. In each of these challenges, domestic interests and values easily contradict with external interests and values, which must be recognized and accounted for in peace efforts.

As already noted, the problem of governance is a key conflict driver. However, there are both internal and external visions of governance. Afghanistan, Iraq, Somalia, and Nepal all present clear cases where peace was premised on neoliberalism. The international interventions in all these countries were geared toward creating conditions for an elected government and holding multiparty elections. However, multiparty elections and the governments that came to power through those elections failed in part because the solution to the problem of governance was largely premised on neoliberal democracy alone. In a way, the neoliberal approach to power seems to be disconnected from core societal values of inclusive power and conceptions of political identity, which are strongly based on group identity (e.g., ethnic, clan, religion). To properly factor domestic factors into the problem of governance would require stepping a bit outside of the neoliberal democracy model anchored in what Duffield referred to as global liberal governance.[49]

Such efforts would require creative (postconflict) institutional design arrangements.[50] Notably, mechanisms of power sharing and inclusivity rooted in local cultures must be explored and given a fair chance along the lines of what Beck refers to as contextual universalism.[51]

The efforts to build peace also suffer from statism and failure to appreciate transnational cultural connections, as is most evident in Nagorno-Karabakh, Iraq, and Nigeria. In each of these cases, conflicts were rooted in identifies that go beyond state boundaries, but international interventions seem to be very fixed on the state. In Nagorno-Karabakh, Azerbaijani insistence on state sovereignty did not align with the Armenian state claim to cultural rights and affinity with coethnics across the border. The state becomes a boundary that defies the real identities of the people and their actual location. Questions of the national state and the multiethnic state need to be factored into potential political solutions on minority rights and society.[52] In Iraq, Iranian cultural affinity with fellow Shi'ites in Iraq was suppressed by a statist approach to security. In Nigeria, the state security and authority superseded deep cultural issues over ancestral places as communal violence get sucked into the global war on terror approach to solving violence. Yet Nigeria has a rich history of creating mechanisms for reducing ethnic marginalization that can be further enhanced.[53]

Hegemony is, perhaps, the biggest challenge to resolving conflicts. Hegemony provokes resistance from locals and other contending powers. Glocalized security situations have been plagued by efforts to grab power and assert expansive national security interests that leave very little room for the interests of other countries and local people. This certainly breeds more militarism and violent resistance. On the issues of nuclear technology, for example, exaggerated rights of established nuclear powers directly contradict the security concerns of emerging powers with contentious relations with the United States and its allies, as is most evident in the cases of North Korea and Iran. In both Iraq and Afghanistan, an expansive notion of US national security interest has led to the United States' effort to assert hegemony in both countries and the surrounding regions. Such efforts have resulted in not only domestic resistance within Afghanistan and Iraq but also the involvement of other military powers, as we see from Russia, Iran, and Turkey. In the Caucasus, Russian hegemony invited a Turkish challenge, as shown in the Nagorno-Karabakh conflict. A key step toward peace in glocalized security situations is the moderation of national security interests, which can open more room for compromise and reduce the perception of threat from other countries. Overall, the global war on terror has become an excessively expanded notion of national security that has morphed from a war against the nonstate actor al-Qaeda to one against several countries that have been branded as belonging to an axis of evil as well as against various insurgencies against domestic injustices. However, a narrower definition of national security can potentially roll back the global war on terror and move it away from a war against nonconformists to a war on terrorists. Perhaps, Ukraine is the clearest case of the diabolical consequences of expansive notions of national interest. NATO's and Russia's expanded view of their own interests and spheres of influence not only have led to a catastrophic war in Ukraine but also have significantly increased the risk of a nuclear war. This hegemonic fight has made Ukraine a huge and catastrophic case of a yam between two boulders, just as Nepal has been between India and China, if on a smaller scale.

Notes

1. Autesserre, *Peaceland*; Bah, "Democracy and Civil War," 597–615; Adebajo, *Building Peace in West Africa*.
2. Bah, *International Security and Peacebuilding*.
3. Horowitz, *Ethnic Groups in Conflict*; Bah, "Changing World Order and the Future of Democracy in Sub-Saharan Africa," 3–12; Collier and Hoeffler, "On Economic Causes of Civil War," 563–73; Bratton and Van de Walle, *Democratic Experiments in Africa*; Bah, "State Decay," 71–89.
4. Oliver and Shapiro, *Black Wealth/White Wealth*; Collins, *Black Feminist Thought*; Bonilla-Silva, *Racism without Racists*.
5. Moore, *Social Origins of Dictatorship and Democracy*; Tilly, *Coercion, Capital, and European States, AD 990–1992*; Skocpol, *States and Social Revolutions*.
6. Sassen, *Global City*; Rumbaut and Portes, *Ethnicities*.
7. Mamdani, *Citizen and Subject*; Mamdani, "Good Muslim, Bad Muslim," 766–775; Said, *Orientalism*; Beck, *What Is Globalization?*
8. Mills, " Promise," 3–24.
9. Friedman, *World Is Flat*.
10. Robertson, "Globality and Modernity," 153–61.
11. Robertson, "Globalisation or Glocalisation?," 33–52; Robertson, "Glocalization," 25–44; Giulianotti and Robertson, "Globalization of Football," 545–68; Giulianotti and Robertson, "Glocalization, Globalization and Migration," 171–98; Robertson and White, "What Is Globalization," 54–66.
12. Beck, *What Is Globalization?*; Beck, Sznaider, and Winter, *Global America?*
13. Sassen, *Global City*; Robertson, "Glocalization," 24–44; Köhler and Wissen, "Glocalizing Protest," 942–51; Kjeldgaard and Askegaard, "Glocalization of Youth Culture," 231–47; Giulianotti and Robertson, "Globalization of Football," 545–68; Beck, *What Is Globalization?*
14. Martin and Woodside, "Dochakuka," 19–32; Roudometof, " Glocal and Global Studies," 774–87.
15. Marfo, Musah, and Arthur, "Beyond Classical Peace Paradigm," 48.
16. Marfo, Musah, and Arthur, "Beyond Classical Peace Paradigm," 48.
17. Waltz, *Man, the State, and War*.
18. McKenna, "Hegelian Dialectics," 155–72; Gadamer, *Hegel's Dialectic*.
19. Buzan, *Regions and Powers*; Waltz, *Theory of International Politics*.

20. Bah, "State Decay," 71–89; Reno, *Corruption and State Politics in Sierra Leone*; Bates, *When Things Fell Apart*; Posen, "Security Dilemma and Ethnic Conflict," 27–47; Lake and Rothchild, "Containing Fear," 41–75; Collier and Hoeffler, "On the Incidence of Civil War in Africa," 13–28; Tilly, *From Mobilization to Revolution*; Horowitz, *Ethnic Groups in Conflict*.

21. Peterson, "President's Dominance in Foreign Policy," 228.

22. Tilly, "War Making and State Making as Organized Crime"; Tilly, *Coercion, Capital, and European States*.

23. McMahon, *Cold War on the Periphery*; Wallerstein, *Present State of the Debate on World Inequality*; Mazrui, *Africa's International Relations*; Fanon, Sartre, and Farrington, *Wretched of the Earth*.

24. Wallerstein, "US Weakness and the Struggle for Hegemony," 23–29; Wallerstein, *Capitalist World-Economy*; Baldwin, *Power and International Relations: A Conceptual Approach*.

25. Marshall, "From Civil War to Proxy War," 183–95.

26. Jervis, "Understanding the Bush Doctrine," 365–88; Glasius and Kaldor, *Human Security Doctrine for Europe*; Bah and Emmanuel, "Migration Cooperation between Africa and Europe."

27. Bah, *International Security and Peacebuilding*.

28. Adebajo, *Building Peace in West Africa*; Bah, *International Security and Peacebuilding*; Bah, " Contours of New Humanitarianism," 3–26; Kaldor, *New and Old Wars*; Crawford, *Argument and Change in World Politics*. Bah, *African Security*; Bah, *African States*.

29. Horowitz, *Ethnic Groups in Conflict*; Collier and Hoeffler, "On Economic Causes of Civil War," 563–73; Bratton and Van de Walle, *Democratic Experiments in Africa*; Bah, Abu, "State Decay," 71–89.

30. Bratton and Van de Walle, *Democratic Experiments in Africa*.

31. Duffield, *Global Governance and the New Wars*.

32. Huang, *Wartime Origins of Democratization*.

33. Blair, *Peacekeeping, Policing, and the Rule of Law after Civil War*.

34. Paris, *At War's End*.

35. Babatunde, "Environmental Insecurity and Poverty in the Niger Delta," 36–59; Varin, "No Opportunity Lost," 141–57; Turner, "Livelihood Transitions," 183–206.

36. Varin, "No Opportunity Lost," 141–57.

37. Osaghae, "Ogoni Uprising," 325–44; Bah, *Breakdown and Reconstitution*; Babatunde, "Environmental Conflict," 33–54.

38. Jeong, "Piracy and Crime Embeddedness," 72–99.

39. Beevers, "Governing Natural Resources for Peace," 227; Bah, *Post-Conflict Institutional Design*; Prunier, *Africa's World War*; Hoekstra, "Conflict Diamonds," 1322–39.

40. Bodansky, *Art and Craft of International Environmental Law*.

41. Bah, "Contours of New Humanitarianism," 3–26; Charbonneau, "Climate of Counterinsurgency," 97–104.

42. Brands, *Latin America's Cold War*; Iber, *Neither Peace nor Freedom*; Castañeda, *Utopia Unarmed*.

43. Ortega, "State, the Peasantry and the Sandinista Revolution," 122–42; Prévost, "'Contra' War in Nicaragua."

44. Ladwig, "Influencing Clients in Counterinsurgency," 99–146.

45. Wood, *Insurgent Collective Action and Civil War in El Salvador*; Stanley, *Protection Racket State*.

46. Castañeda, *Utopia Unarmed*.

47. Shields, "Gender," 301–11; Collins and Bilge, *Intersectionality*; Bose, "Intersectionality and Global Gender Inequality," 67–72; Winker and Degele, "Intersectionality as Multi-Level Analysis," 51–66.

48. Collins, *Black Feminist Thought*.

49. Duffield, *Global Governance and the New Wars*.
50. Bah, *Post-Conflict Institutional Design*.
51. Beck, *What Is Globalization?*
52. Tilly, *Formation of National States in Western Europe*; Evans, Rueschemeyer, and Skocpol, *Bringing the State Back In*.
53. Bah, *Breakdown and Reconstitution*.

References

Adebajo, Adekeye. *Building Peace in West Africa: Liberia, Sierra Leone, and Guinea-Bissau*. Boulder, CO: Lynne Rienner, 2002.

Autesserre, Sverine. *Peaceland: Conflict Resolution and the Everyday Politics of International Intervention*. Cambridge: Cambridge University Press, 2014.

Babatunde, Abosede Omowumi. "Environmental Conflict, Traditional Institutions, and Durable Peace in Niger Delta." *African Conflict & Peacebuilding Review* 9, no. 2 (2019): 33–54.

———. "Environmental Insecurity and Poverty in the Niger Delta: A Case of Ilaje." *African Conflict and Peacebuilding Review* 7, no. 2 (2017): 36–59.

Bah, Abu Bakarr, ed. *African Security: Local Issues and Global Connections*. Athens: Ohio University Press, 2024

———, ed. *African States: Domestic and External Security Challenges*. Albany: SUNY Press, 2025.

———. *Breakdown and Reconstitution: Democracy, the Nation-State, and Ethnicity in Nigeria*. Lanham, MD: Lexington Books, 2005.

———. "Changing World Order and the Future of Democracy in Sub-Saharan Africa." *Proteus* 21, no. 1 (2004): 3–12.

———. "The Contours of New Humanitarianism: War and Peacebuilding in Sierra Leone." *Africa Today* 60, no. 1 (2013): 3–26.

———. "Democracy and Civil War: Citizenship and Peacemaking in Côte d'Ivoire." *African Affairs* 109, no. 437 (October 2010): 597–615.

———, ed. *International Security and Peacebuilding: Africa, the Middle East, and Europe*. Bloomington: Indiana University Press, 2017.

———, ed. *Post-Conflict Institutional Design: Peacebuilding and Democracy in Africa*. London: Bloomsbury Publishing, 2020.

———. "State Decay: A Conceptual Frame of Failing and Failed States in West Africa." *International Journal of Politics, Culture, and Society* 25, no. 1 (2012): 71–89.

Bah, Abu Bakarr, and Nikolas Emmanuel. "Migration Cooperation between Africa and Europe: Understanding the Role of Incentives." *Oxford Research Encyclopedia of International Studies*. September 15, 2022. https://doi.org/10.1093/acrefore/9780190846626.013.735.

Baldwin, David A. *Power and International Relations: A Conceptual Approach*. Princeton, NJ: Princeton University Press, 2016.

Bates, Robert H. *When Things Fell Apart: State Failure in Late-Century Africa*. New York: Cambridge University Press, 2008.

Beck, Ulrich. *What Is Globalization?* New York: John Wiley & Sons, 2018.

Beck, Ulrich, Natan Sznaider, and Rainer Winter, eds. *Global America? The Cultural Consequences of Globalization*. Vol. 8. Liverpool, UK: Liverpool University Press, 2003.

Beevers, Michael D. "Governing Natural Resources for Peace: Lessons from Liberia and Sierra Leone." *Global Governance* 21 (2015): 227.

Blair, Robert. *Peacekeeping, Policing, and the Rule of Law after Civil War*. Cambridge: Cambridge University Press, 2020.

Bodansky, Daniel. *The Art and Craft of International Environmental Law*. Cambridge, MA: Harvard University Press, 2010.

Bonilla-Silva, Eduardo. *Racism without Racists: Color-Blind Racism and the Persistence of Racial Inequality in the United States*. Lanham, MD: Rowman and Littlefield, 2006.

Bose, Christine E. "Intersectionality and Global Gender Inequality." *Gender & Society* 26, no. 1 (2012): 67–72.

Brands, Hal. *Latin America's Cold War*. Cambridge, MA: Harvard University Press, 2012.

Bratton, Michael, and Nicholas Van de Walle. *Democratic Experiments in Africa: Regime Transitions in Comparative Perspective*. Cambridge: Cambridge University Press, 1997.

Buzan, Barry, et al. *Regions and Powers: The Structure of International Security*. Vol. 91. Cambridge: Cambridge University Press, 2003.

Castañeda, Jorge G. *Utopia Unarmed: The Latin American Left after the Cold War*. New York: Vintage, 2012.

Charbonneau, Bruno. "The Climate of Counterinsurgency and the Future of Security in the Sahel." *Environmental Science & Policy* 138 (2022): 97–104.

Collier, Paul, and Anke Hoeffler. "On Economic Causes of Civil War." *Oxford Economic Papers* 50, no. 4 (1998): 563–73.

———. "On the Incidence of Civil War in Africa." *Journal of Conflict Resolution* 46, no. 1 (2002): 13–28.

Collins, Patricia Hill. *Black Feminist Thought: Knowledge, Consciousness, and the Politics of Empowerment*. New York: Routledge, 2002.

Collins, Patricia Hill, and Sirma Bilge. *Intersectionality*. Cambridge: Polity Press, 2020.

Crawford, Neta. *Argument and Change in World Politics: Ethics, Decolonization, and Humanitarian Intervention*. Cambridge: Cambridge University Press, 2002.

Duffield, Mark. *Global Governance and the New Wars: The Merging of Development and Security*. London: Bloomsbury, 2014.

Evans, Peter B., Dietrich Rueschemeyer, and Theda Skocpol, eds. *Bringing the State Back In*. Cambridge: Cambridge University Press, 1985.

Fanon, Frantz, Jean-Paul Sartre, and Constance Farrington. *The Wretched of the Earth*. Vol. 36. New York: Grove Press, 1963.

Friedman, Thomas L. *The World Is Flat: A Brief History of the Twenty-First Century*. Updated and expanded ed. New York: Macmillan, 2006.

Gadamer, Hans-Georg. *Hegel's Dialectic: Five Hermeneutical Studies*. New Haven, CT: Yale University Press, 1976.

Giulianotti, Richard, and Roland Robertson. "The Globalization of Football: A Study in the Glocalization of the 'Serious Life.'" *British Journal of Sociology* 55, no. 4 (2004): 545–68.

———. "Glocalization, Globalization and Migration: The Case of Scottish Football Supporters in North America." *International Sociology* 21, no. 2 (2006): 171–98.

Glasius, Marlies, and Mary Kaldor. *A Human Security Doctrine for Europe*. London: Routledge, 2005.

Hoekstra, Quint. "Conflict Diamonds and the Angolan Civil War (1992–2002)." *Third World Quarterly* 40, no. 7 (2019): 1322–39.

Horowitz, Donald L. *Ethnic Groups in Conflict*. Berkeley: University of California Press, 1985.

Huang, Reyko. *The Wartime Origins of Democratization: Civil War, Rebel Governance, and Political Regimes*. Cambridge: Cambridge University Press, 2016.

Iber, Patrick. *Neither Peace nor Freedom: The Cultural Cold War in Latin America*. Cambridge, MA: Harvard University Press, 2015.

Jeong, Keunsoo. "Piracy and Crime Embeddedness: State Decay and Social Transformation in Somalia." *African Conflict and Peacebuilding Review* 9, no. 1 (2019): 72–99.

Jervis, Robert. "Understanding the Bush Doctrine." *Political Science Quarterly* 118, no. 3 (2003): 365–88.

Kaldor, Mary. *New and Old Wars: Organised Violence in a Global Era*. Chicester, UK: John Wiley & Sons, 2013.

Kjeldgaard, Dannie, and Søren Askegaard. "The Glocalization of Youth Culture: The Global Youth Segment as Structures of Common Difference." *Journal of Consumer Research* 33, no. 2 (2006): 231–47.

Köhler, Bettina, and Markus Wissen. "Glocalizing Protest: Urban Conflicts and the Global Social Movements." *International Journal of Urban and Regional Research* 27, no. 4 (2003): 942–51.

Ladwig, Walter C., III. "Influencing Clients in Counterinsurgency: US Involvement in El Salvador's Civil War, 1979–92." *International Security* 41, no. 1 (2016): 99–146.

Lake, David A., and Donald Rothchild. "Containing Fear: The Origins and Management of Ethnic Conflict." *International Security* 21, no. 2 (1996): 41–75.

Mamdani, Mahmood. *Citizen and Subject: Contemporary Africa and the Legacy of Late Colonialism*. Princeton, NJ: Princeton University Press, 1996.

———. "Good Muslim, Bad Muslim: A Political Perspective on Culture and Terrorism." *American Anthropologist* 104, no. 3 (2002): 766–75.

Martin, Drew, and Arch G. Woodside. "Dochakuka: Melding Global inside Local: Foreign-Domestic Advertising Assimilation in Japan." *Journal of Global Marketing* 21, no. 1 (2008): 19–32.

Marshall, Alex. "From Civil War to Proxy War: Past History and Current Dilemmas." *Small Wars & Insurgencies* 27, no. 2 (2016): 183–95.

Marfo, Samuel, Halidu Musah, and Dominic DeGraft Arthur. "Beyond Classical Peace Paradigm: A Theoretical Argument for a Glocalized Peace and Security." *African Journal of Political Science and International Relations* 10, no. 4 (2016): 47–55.

Mazrui, Ali A. *Africa's International Relations: The Diplomacy of Dependency and Change*. New York: Routledge, 2019.

McKenna, Tony. "Hegelian Dialectics." *Critique* 39, no. 1 (2011): 155–72.

McMahon, Robert J. *The Cold War on the Periphery: The United States, India, and Pakistan*. New York: Columbia University Press, 1994.

Mills, C. Wright. "The Promise." *Sociological Imagination*, 1959: 3–24. http://people.uncw.edu/levyd/soc105/Mills,%20the%20Promise.PDF.

Moore, Barrington. *Social Origins of Dictatorship and Democracy: Lord and Peasant in the Making of the Modern World*. Vol. 268. Boston: Beacon, 1993.

Oliver, Melvin, and Thomas Shapiro. *Black Wealth/White Wealth: A New Perspective on Racial Inequality*. New York: Routledge, 2013.

Ortega, Marvin. "The State, the Peasantry and the Sandinista Revolution." *Journal of Development Studies* 26, no. 4 (1990): 122–42.

Osaghae, Eghosa E. "The Ogoni Uprising: Oil Politics, Minority Agitation and the Future of the Nigerian State." *African Affairs* 94, no. 376 (1995): 325–44.

Paris, Roland. *At War's End: Building Peace after Civil Conflict*. Cambridge: Cambridge University Press, 2004.

Peterson, Paul, E. "The President's Dominance in Foreign Policy." *Political Science Quarterly* 109 (Summer 1994): 228.

Posen, Barry R. "The Security Dilemma and Ethnic Conflict." *Survival* 35, no. 1 (1993): 27–47.

Prévost, Gary. "The 'Contra' War in Nicaragua." *Journal of Conflict Studies* 7, no. 3 (1987): 5–21.

Prunier, Gérard. *Africa's World War: Congo, the Rwandan Genocide, and the Making of a Continental Catastrophe*. Oxford: Oxford University Press, 2008.

Reno, William. *Corruption and State Politics in Sierra Leone*. New York: Cambridge University Press, 2008.

Robertson, Roland. "Globalisation or Glocalisation?" *Journal of International Communication* 1, no. 1 (1994): 33–52.

———. "Globality and Modernity." *Theory, Culture & Society* 9, no. 2 (1992): 153–61.

———. "Glocalization: Time-Space and Homogeneity-Heterogeneity." *Global Modernities* 2, no. 1 (1995): 25–44.

Robertson, Roland, and Kathleen E. White. "What Is Globalization." In *Blackwell Companion to Globalization*, edited by George Ritzer, 54–66. Malden, MA: Blackwell Publishing, 2007.

Roudometof, Victor. "The Glocal and Global Studies." *Globalizations* 12, no. 5 (2015): 774–87.

Rumbaut, Rubén G., and Alejandro Portes, eds. *Ethnicities: Children of Immigrants in America*. Berkeley: University of California Press, 2001.

Said, Edward. *Orientalism: Western Concepts of the Orient*. New York: Pantheon, 1978.

Sassen, Saskia. *The Global City: New York, London, Tokyo*. Princeton, NJ: Princeton University Press, 2013.

Shields, Stephanie A. "Gender: An Intersectionality Perspective." *Sex Roles* 59 no. 5 (2008): 301–11.

Skocpol, Theda. *States and Social Revolutions: A Comparative Analysis of France, Russia and China*. Cambridge: Cambridge University Press, 1979.

Stanley, William. *The Protection Racket State: Elite Politics, Military Extortion, and Civil War in El Salvador*. Philadelphia: Temple University Press, 2010.

Tilly, Charles. *Coercion, Capital, and European States, AD 990–1992*. Oxford: Blackwell, 1992.

———. *The Formation of National States in Western Europe*. Princeton, NJ: Princeton University Press, 1975.

———. *From Mobilization to Revolution*. Reading, MA: Addison-Wesley, 1978.

———. "War Making and State Making as Organized Crime." In *Bringing the State Back In*, edited by Peter Evans, Dietrich Rueschemeyer, and Theda Skocpol, 169–92. Cambridge: Cambridge University Press, 1985.

Turner, Matthew D., et al. "Livelihood Transitions and the Changing Nature Of Farmer-Herder Conflict in Sahelian West Africa." *Journal of Development Studies* 47, no. 2 (2011): 183–206.

Varin, Caroline. "No Opportunity Lost: The ISWAP Insurgency in the Changing Climate of Lake Chad Region." *African Conflict & Peacebuilding Review* 10, no. 2 (2020): 141–57.

Wallerstein, Immanuel. *The Capitalist World-Economy*. Cambridge: Cambridge University Press, 1979.

———. *The Present State of the Debate on World Inequality*. New York: Routledge, 2019.

———. "US Weakness and the Struggle for Hegemony." *Monthly Review, New York* 55, no. 3 (2003): 23–29.

Waltz, Kenneth Neal. *Man, the State, and War: A Theoretical Analysis*. New York: Columbia University Press, 2001.

———. *Theory of International Politics*. Long Grove, IL: Waveland Press, 2010.

Winker, Gabriele, and Nina Degele. "Intersectionality as Multi-Level Analysis: Dealing with Social Inequality." *European Journal of Women's Studies* 18, no. 1 (2011): 51–66.

Wood, Elisabeth Jean. *Insurgent Collective Action and Civil War in El Salvador*. Cambridge: Cambridge University Press, 2003.

ABU BAKARR BAH is Presidential Research Professor of Sociology and Chair of the Department of Sociology at Northern Illinois University. He is Editor in Chief of *African Conflict & Peacebuilding Review*, African Editor for *Critical Sociology*, and Founding Director of the Institute for Research and Policy Integration in Africa (IRPIA). His works include *International Statebuilding in West Africa* (with Nikolas Emmanuel, Bloomington: Indiana University Press, 2024), *African Security* (Athens: Ohio University Press, 2024), *Post-Conflict Institutional Design* (London: Zed Books, 2020), *International Security and Peacebuilding* (Bloomington: Indiana University Press, 2017), and *Breakdown and Reconstitution* (Lanham, MD: Lexington Books, 2005). His articles have been published in top journals such as *African Affairs; Administrative Theory & Praxis; Critical Sociology;*

Journal of International Peacekeeping; *International Journal of Politics, Culture, and Society*; and *Africa Today*. Bah has been an invited speaker at major institutions such as Stanford University, University of Illinois at Urbana Champaign, University of South Florida, Virginia Commonwealth University, Global Center for Pluralism (Canada), Social Science Research Council (New York), US State Department, ETH (Switzerland), University of Nairobi (Kenya), Laikipia University (Kenya), Renmin University (China), and Sant'Anna School of Advanced Studies (Italy).

2

CONTEMPORARY NATIONALISMS AND CONCEPTIONS OF NATIONAL SECURITY

Military Power and the Reshaping of International Security

Abu Bakarr Bah

Introduction

National security concerns are at the center of both the domestic politics within major and emerging powers and international security. Too often, the focus of international security discourses has been on state militarization and warfare. However, a critical issue in international security is the way external threats are framed and promoted within countries through the discourse of national interests, most notably national security interest. National security discourses are shaped by various forms of nationalisms associated with national interests. Conceptions of national interests by major powers have resulted in numerous threats and conflicts around the world. Critically important, issues of national interests often turn into national security issues as they become serious threats to the state or the well-being of its people. While any credible physical threat to the state and the lives of its people automatically becomes a matter of national security, other threats that severely affect the well-being of the people can also be elevated to the level of national security. Thus, the fusion of national security with nationalism points to the glocalized nature of international security, and in a way, international conflicts and wars are driven by domestic considerations and narratives that then lead to the acquisition and application of military power.

Since the end of World War II, there have been varying types of international security challenges. At the end of the Cold War, a new breed of conflicts emerged that have been dubbed new wars. New wars quickly dovetail with terrorism warfare, making violent nonstate actors a key category in the discourse of international security.[1] For example, the 9/11 terrorist attacks on the United States led to a wide-ranging war on terror across the world that dawned a new breed of war in the form of terrorism warfare in the Middle East, central Asia, and Africa.[2] In all of these kinds of wars, the major powers have not engaged in direct war with one another. The conflicts have mostly been between a superpower and what is considered a rogue state or a violent nonstate actor, but sometimes they have been wars within countries destabilized by neoliberalism. In all of the post–World War II conflicts, the major powers, especially the United States and Russia, have been involved either directly or indirectly. Moreover, the wars have mostly been directed at countries without very strong conventional military forces or nuclear weapons. In cases where there are only threats of war, most of those threats tend to be directed at emerging military powers, often regarded as rogue states because of their (alleged) pursuit of nuclear weapons. Three central axes of conflict stand out in international security: (a) tensions among nuclear powers over territorial spheres of influence, (b) tensions between nuclear powers and emerging military powers, and (c) wars between major powers and violent nonstate actors, mostly conducted through terrorism warfare. These axes point to the major actors in contemporary international security issues, which can be categorized as old military powers, emergent military powers, and violent nonstate actors.

The old military powers are essentially Russia, with its huge nuclear arsenal, and the United States (along with its core NATO partners), with a similar stockpile of nuclear weapons. China has also been a nuclear state since 1964, but until recently, its military capacity was far behind that of Russia and United States. However, China has rapidly modernized its military, and it is now a very strong rival to the military capacities of the United States and Russia. The emergent military powers are countries with a small nuclear arsenal (i.e., India, Pakistan, Israel, North Korea) and those countries on the verge of developing a nuclear arsenal (i.e., Iran). These countries also have some significant conventional military capabilities. Violent nonstate actors, in the context of international security, are essentially global terrorist organizations, most notably al-Qaeda and Islamic State in Iraq and Syria (ISIS). Contemporary international security issues mostly revolve around the demands and interests of these sets of actors. Old military powers seek to maintain dominance and exert hegemony in their regions of national interest, while emergent military powers want to thwart the dominance of the old military powers within their subregion.[3] At the same time, global terrorist organizations are challenging old military powers, especially the United States, in the

Middle East, central Asia, and Africa. These actors have conflicting interests and worldviews that put them in open confrontation and asymmetric warfare.

A critical question in unpacking this complex web of international conflicts and actors is understanding how the actors rationalize and justify their quest for military power. In particular, the old and emergent military powers are not only sovereign entities in the international systems, but also countries with huge populations and histories of conflicts with other powers. As such, they not only need to acquire military power, but must also galvanize domestic support to endure the economic, human and political costs of asserting military power. Global terrorist organizations exploit political, economic, and social discontents around the world to challenge Western hegemony, but their method of warfare feeds into the national security narratives of old military powers. Unpacking the narratives of national threats and interests is critical to understanding contemporary security challenges and the way domestic issues are fused into international security issues. As such, this chapter addresses a critical question in relating international security to the narratives of threats and interests: How do contemporary nationalisms shape conceptions of national security and rationalize the pursuit of military power? This question requires a fresh theoretical and historical look into contemporary forms of nationalism, the struggles for military power, and the instrumentalization of terrorism warfare. The intersection of these issues points to the glocalized nature of international security. The chapter focuses on three sets of cases to capture these axes: (a) the global war on terror in Afghanistan and Iraq, (b) the nuclear confrontations between the United States and North Korea, and (c) the Russian invasion of Ukraine.

Glocalized Security: Nationalism and Conceptions of National Security

Nationalism has been a central element of national security. As such, it brings a unique lens into the fusion of domestic factors with geopolitical issues in international security. The intersection of the domestic and the global points to the glocalized nature of international security. Unlike extant notions of international security, glocalized security captures the fusion of domestic and external matters in international security, akin to the way the notions of globalizations and glocalization have been deployed to understand the intricacies of global homogenization and local resistances.[4] Most of the initial critiques of globalization and framings of glocalization were in the realms of business, culture, and social movement, especially as time and space are homogenized.[5] However, glocalization is hardly used in international security discourses. One notable effort in this direction is the study of Samuel Marfo et al. As they argue, a glocalized peace and security architecture "attempts to suggest an approach which can foster a peaceful co-existence among states without necessarily endangering domestic politics in a seemingly chaotic global environment."[6] Contemporary nationalism becomes a useful lens for understanding the fusion of the domestic into international security as evident in the global war on terror and the conflicts over nuclear weapons and spheres of influence.

Nationalism is a concept that captures the ideological and sentimental connections among people of a certain culture and place in relation to other people which generate a sense of shared belonging, history, and destiny.[7] Nationalism evolves and takes different forms across historical contexts.[8] To unpack the notion of nationalism, it is important to examine nationalism through the historical events in which it emerges and the issues that drive its evolution. While the historical events are largely tied to the formation of states, the issues that drive nationalism are fused in narratives of national security. National security then becomes a nationalistic frame for defining a country's interests and reacting to threats, whose meanings are open and contextual.

Nationalism and the Making of Nation-States

Contemporary understandings of nationalism are generally rooted in the wars and struggles to establish states out of the vestiges of empires. In that sense, nationalism is about the genesis of nation-states.[9] The most notorious form of nationalism is the emergence of national socialism in Germany during the Nazi regime. Under this variant of nationalism, conceptions of the nation-state and national interest are tied to cultural purity and solidarity in ways that assert racial superiority. German nationalism quickly moved from an ideology of social and cultural survival within the volatile postempire European political context to a genocidal system based on othering and sense of superiority.[10] In the end Nazism became a catastrophic manifestation of nationalism that posed dangers beyond German land, and its legacies continue to manifest today in Israel and Palestine. Nazism became an ideology and a political system that had to be stopped as diabolical forms of nationalism erupted in places such as Italy and Japan.[11] It is important to note that these forms of nationalism are rooted in specific historical contexts in which European powers sought dominance within Europe and beyond. In other historical contexts, nationalism has taken different meanings and trajectories. In eastern Europe, for example, nationalism took the form of ethnic-cum-national liberation as various groups of people sort their own state to assert ownership of historic lands and revive their culture in their own national state. This effort was mixed with the communist revolution, which promoted nationalism in the developmental sense of modernization.[12] In Russia, nationalism is rooted in the glory of imperial Russia and the communist revolution that resulted in the Soviet Union. In many ways, nationalism in Russia is imperialistic as it rests on military glory and exertion of control over historical lands and absorbing nonethnic Russians into a Pan-Russian nation, especially as it existed during the Soviet Union.[13]

Nationalism has also evolved out of liberation wars. As far back as the American Revolutionary War, nationalism has been weaved into the struggles against colonial rule. Although the notion of nationalism was subtle in the nascent country made of various colonies, patriotism did gain roots and provided a channel for the fermentation of nationalistic sentiments for a new state rooted in freedom, albeit a racialized one.[14] Not surprisingly, the Patriots became the embodiment of the love of freedom and the United States.[15] In Africa the liberation struggle grew through the lens of nationalism. In many parts of Africa, the struggle against colonial rule was called the nationalist movement.[16] Nationalism was tantamount to attaining political independence. In the Middle East, nationalism found its strongest roots in Pan-Arabism.[17] However, that nationalist ideology quickly got entangled in international politics as Israel occupied Palestine and other Arab lands. More recently, Pan-Arabism has morphed into Islamist movements seeking to restore the glory of Muslims in the Middle East.[18]

Nationalism has also evolved out of national development agenda, most notably in Asia. The push for rapid industrialization in China and many Southeast Asian countries rested on doctrines of national development. In countries such as Singapore and Malaysia, developmental nationalism took hold, leading to significant progress in building democratic and economically developed states.[19] In China, developmental nationalism took the form of a state-controlled system that began with Maoism. Chinese nationalism morphed into communism, which has evolved through various political reforms such as the Cultural Revolution, to the controlled opening under Deng Xiaoping, and the extensive economic and social reforms under Xi Jinping.[20] China's rise to economic powerhouse and superpower status is one of the most notable cases of nationalism rooted in economic development. Chinese nationalism became a complex mix of authoritarianism, akin to the Nazi hold on German, and visionary economic and social policies that gravitate between socialism and global capitalism.

National Security: National Interests and Nationalism

The histories of nationalism show that in addition to being rooted in sentiments of belonging to a people and a country, nationalism takes shape around specific issues that are central to the collective survival and well-being of a people. Ultimately, those issues are weaved into national security discourses and policies. Such issues are often framed as interests that transcend any particular group in the country—hence, they are elevated to a core national interest (i.e., national security interest).[21] National interests translate into national security matters in two ways. First are national interests relating to the physical integrity of the state and lives of its citizens. These are issues of national security in the orthodox sense.[22] Second are national interests relating to the well-being and identity of the people, which can be framed in terms of national security when they become acute. Indeed, what constitutes national security interest is open and contextual.[23] However, certain national interests are deemed very critical to the survival of the state and the well-being of its people and so can easily be framed as matters of national security. They are reflected in policies that are consistently pursued domestically and protected in interactions with other states, and they are molded within discourses of patriotism and nationalism. National interests can be grouped into three categories: (a) state and human security, (b) cultural preservation, and (c) economic survival.

A key feature of the modern international system is the sovereignty and territorial integrity of states as enshrined in the UN Charter of 1945. The Westphalian system became entrenched in international relations after World War II; in this system, states see their territories as sacrosanct for their existence.[24] For this system to work, states must have clear and effective control over their territorial borders in order to protect their citizens from mass violence and be able to independently make decisions about internal matters. Sovereignty, which is the quintessential idea of national interest, has recently been framed in terms of state security and human security.[25] The physical survival of the state and its citizens is the strictest and most orthodox sense of national security. The central issue in this orthodox national security interest of states is (credible threat of) mass violence within the country, be it in the form of conventional war against the country or terrorist attacks. The clearest forms of infringement on orthodox national security interest are (a) direct military attack against the territory or (physical) assets of a country by another state or a nonstate actor and (b) the threat of war against a country by another state. A central role of the state is to guard against these kinds of threats and combat them whenever they become credible threats. States galvanize nationalistic sentiments to ensure public support for policies aimed at protecting their national security. Nationalism becomes critical in mobilizing robust reaction and persevering with the costs that the county may suffer in pursuing its national security interest. Countries also appeal to universal humanistic principles and international support when there is a significant human security threat beyond their means. Violation of a country's national security interest is likely to provoke a military response, especially if diplomatic efforts fail.

Cultural preservation is also a core national interest of states. It is often fused with the history of the country and the core values it projects, domestically and internationally. While the notion of culture is loose, cultural preservation generally relates to the systems and historical symbols that shape the identity and way of life of the citizens of a country, especially members of its dominant group. These include language, historical artifacts, and the core values inscribed in everyday life and in the laws of the country.[26] As such, cultural preservation is framed as part of the national interests of countries, which can morph into national security issues if the threat to the culture becomes too acute. Threats to cultural preservation can occur within or outside the territory of a country. Threats within the territory often relate to minorities' efforts to assert their rights or instances of mass migration, which dominant groups can see as detrimental to national identity and cohesion. Threats that occur outside include gross violation of the rights of coethnics in other countries to preserve their culture as a minority group, such as the use of their language or the practice of their religion. Other forms of threat to cultural preservation include the looting and appropriation of historical artifacts that are sacred to the history and cultures of the citizens of a country. Threats that occur outside are typically perpetuated by another state, often in the forms of nationalist policies. Threats to cultural preservation are most often addressed through nonviolent means, including diplomatic negotiation, restrictions of minority rights, and anti-immigration laws. However, when the threats to cultural preservation become acute, they can morph into national security issues. Countries draw on cultural sentiments to promote patriotism and nationalism as they pursue cultural preservation policies, especially when those policies may contradict universal human rights norms.

Economic survival is also a major national interest of states. Notably, preservation of the natural resources of a country and fair access to critical natural resources in other countries and the global trade, transportation, and communication infrastructure are all key elements of the economic survival of countries.[27] As such, the preservation and fair access to those resources and infrastructure systems are part of the national interests of countries. Countries position themselves to safeguard their economic survival by forging bilateral relations with other countries, joining international organizations and agreements on trade, and asserting rights to international navigation spaces. Efforts to illegally appropriate a country's national resources or to deny it fair access to global economic resources and infrastructure are viewed as threats to economic survival and violations of the national interest of the country. If these threats reach a severe enough level, putting a country's economic survival in question, they may become national security concerns. Threats to the economic survival of countries are most often resolved through diplomatic means and punitive measures in the form of economic sanctions and boycotts. Countries further promote patriotism and nationalism when they are subjected to punitive economic measures that cause domestic disruptions. They appeal to higher values, solidarity, and national interests and combine those sentiments with social support measures to soften the effects of policies associated with defending their national interests. Adverse economic conditions often become temporary or medium-term cost that countries pay in pursing their national (security) interests in an adversarial way.

Military Power: Old and Emergent Nuclear States

A critical component of international security is the way states pursue and protect their national interests, most notably when these interests are framed in terms of national security. States typically use nonmilitary means to safeguard their national interests but also develop military capabilities that can be used (preferably as a last resort) in defending their national security. As such, military power has always been at the center of international security. Until recently, military power has been associated with states and regulated through various treaties on the conduct of war and accumulation of weapons, such as the Geneva Convention and Treaty on the Non-Proliferation of Nuclear Weapons (NPT). Since the 9/11 terrorist attacks on the United States, however, nonstate actors have also developed capabilities to engage in asymmetric warfare and infringe on the national security of states.

At the heart of interstate relations is power—the ability to pursue and exert national interests even against the resistance of other states.[28] Power is achieved in a variety of ways, most notably through the accumulation of resources and wealth within the global capitalist economy and through the accumulation of huge and sophisticated stockpiles of weapons and capable military forces.[29] While economic power is mostly used in the form of (dis)incentives and influence in the international system, military power is used as a deterrent against the violation of a country's national security interest and a tool to exert its national interests. Importantly, nuclear weapons have emerged as the ultimate form of military power. Since the United States first tested and used nuclear weapons in 1945, several kinds of states have emerged within the arms race that typifies the international security realm: (a) old military powers with declared nuclear weapons and parties to the NPT, (b) known nuclear states that are not parties to the NPT, and (c) states with nuclear technology that are parties to the NPT, including those that gave them up or abandoned the effort to develop nuclear weapon. Countries that have not tried to develop nuclear weapons and those that either abandoned such efforts or gave up nuclear weapons are not problematic cases. Notably, such countries include Belarus, Kazakhstan, Ukraine, South Africa, Brazil, Libya, and South Korea.

The most contentious cases in terms of the projection of military power and contemporary international security challenges are the countries that either possess nuclear weapons or are actively developing nuclear weapons. These countries see their national security in terms of having a nuclear deterrent, which will give them significant military leverage in the international security system, notably, the United States, France, the United Kingdom, Russia, China, India, Pakistan, Israel, North Korea, and Iran. The United States, France, and the United Kingdom are members of the North Atlantic Treaty Organization (NATO), which makes NATO the central military entity in the international security system. I refer to these countries as old military powers and emergent military powers. The old military powers are those countries whose nuclear weapons are recognized and allowed under the NPT, while emergent powers are those that either have nuclear weapons or are developing them in contravention of the NPT. To understand the interconnections between military power and contemporary international security issues, it is useful to provide a brief profile and contextualization of the routes and level of nuclear capabilities of old and emergent military powers.

Old Military Powers

The old military powers are the five countries with nuclear weapons at the time of the signing of the NPT in 1968 (i.e., the United States, France, the United Kingdom, Russia, and China). These are also the major military powers that came out of World War II, and interestingly, the only ones with a veto power at the United Nations Security Council, which is the world body with decision-making powers on matters of international security. The use of nuclear weapons began with the United States in 1945, followed by the Soviet Union testing nuclear weapons in 1949; the United Kingdom, in 1952; France, in 1960; and China, in 1964. When the Soviet Union fell in 1991, Russia inherited all of its nuclear weapons. In addition to developing nuclear weapons, these are among the biggest and most powerful military powers since World War II—with the United States and Russia being nuclear superpowers. According to current estimates, the United States has 1,389 strategic nuclear warheads that are deployed. The other two NATO members have 515 warheads (France with 290 and United Kingdom with 225). Russia has about 1,458 strategic warheads deployed. China also has around 350 warheads.[30] Another key factor in the nuclear capabilities of countries is the ability to launch the weapons from air, sea, and land, especially across long distance. All of these countries possess delivery means such as bombers, submarines, and ballistic missiles. For example, the United States is believed to have 665 warheads currently deployed on intercontinental ballistic missiles, submarine-launched ballistic missiles, and strategic bombers, while Russia has 527 warheads currently deployed on similar modes of delivery.

The development of the nuclear arsenal of the old military powers is characterized by two key features that continue to impact the international security regime. First is the defeat of Germany and Japan during World War II and their demilitarization. Both countries have largely stayed out of the arms race and have only very recently shifted toward some form of militarization. Japan is shifting toward militarization as a result of rapid expansion of the military powers of China and North Korea and doubts over the weight of US security guarantees, while Germany's shift has been prompted by Russia's brazen invasion of Ukraine. Second is the signing of the NPT in 1968 and the development of an international arms control regime, which now revolves around twenty-eight treaties and the work of the International Atomic Energy Agency (IAEA), established in 1957. The NPT and the arms control regime center on halting the spread of weapons of mass destruction and reducing the existing stockpiles of the old military powers. Nonproliferation of nuclear weapons has become a critical issue in the international security realm as stringent policies and mechanisms have been adopted to prevent countries from developing nuclear weapons. In addition to nonproliferation is the issue of reducing the nuclear stockpiles of the United States and Russia, notably under the Strategic Arms Reduction Treaty, which started with the Strategic Arms Limitation Talks in 1972. While the United States and Russia were technically working toward reducing their stockpiles prior to the Ukraine war, China has been increasing its small arsenal to catch up with Russia and the United States.

Emergent Military Powers

Emergent military powers are countries that are known to have nuclear weapons or are in the process of developing them in contravention of NPT.

The emergent military powers that are known to possess nuclear weapons are India, Pakistan, Israel, and North Korea. India, Pakistan, and Israel never joined the NPT, while North Korea withdrew from NPT in 2003. In 1974, India tested a nuclear device, and did a nuclear weapons test in 1998. At the same time, Pakistan had been developing nuclear weapons, which it tested in 1998, right after India tested its nuclear weapons. India and Pakistan have been locked in a long territorial dispute and an arms race. In addition, India has contentious boarder disputes with China that have resulted in several small border clashes. India has about 156 nuclear warheads while Pakistan has around 165. Both countries have significant missile delivery systems. Israel has at least 90 nuclear warheads but has not publicly done a test or admitted possessing nuclear weapons. Israel's nuclear program is highly tied to the security challenges in the Middle East and ongoing conflicts with neighboring (Arab) countries, particularly Iran, over the occupation of Palestine and the Golan Heights.[31] North Korea has acknowledged possessing nuclear weapons. It has tested nuclear devices and developed ballistic missiles to deliver nuclear weapons. Since 2003, it continuously demonstrates its capabilities to deploy nuclear weapons. It is estimated that the country has nearly 50 nuclear warheads.[32]

Currently, Iran is the emergent powers that is on the verge of developing a nuclear weapon. Iran, which has been a party to the NPT since 1970, has an advanced nuclear program that it officially characterizes as a peaceful nuclear program to produce energy. However, the United States and its allies argue that the program is for military purpose and have vigorously tried to stop the program through tough sanctions and sabotage. Iran's nuclear program has been the subject of intense negotiation and threat of all possible actions to stop Iran from developing nuclear weapons.[33] Progress was made in 2015 leading to the signing of the Joint Comprehensive Plan of Action, but the agreement collapsed as the United States backtracked from the sanction relief part of the agreement during the administration of Donald Trump. The overall assessment is that Iran is at a breakthrough point that will make it able to produce nuclear weapons within a short period. Iran has also developed some missile delivery systems.

Contentious National Security Issues and Deployment of Nationalism

The central issue in this chapter is the intersection of national security and nationalism in the ways countries rationalize and justify the acquisition and application of military power. In that sense, the pursuit of military power and its application to exert national security interests is wrapped in domestic narratives of patriotism and nationalism. This interplay of domestic and geopolitical issues makes international security a glocalized security phenomenon. As already noted, there are various forms of contemporary nationalisms, which are not necessarily totalitarian ideologies. Rather, they are narratives used to justify and solidify support for core national security interests in dealing with states and nonstate actors. Nationalism in this sense is connected not solely to the genesis of the nation-state, but more importantly to policies aimed at ensuring the continued survival of the state and maintaining an advantageous position in the international system. Because the international security system revolves around military power, issues involving the accumulation or application of military power are not only framed in terms of national security but also weaved into narratives of patriotism and nationalism among old and emergent military powers. In particular, terrorism, nuclear weapons, and territorial control and spheres of influence have emerged as key national security issues in international security. Countries pursuing these issues, notably old military powers, galvanize domestic support and thwart domestic opposition by invoking patriotism and nationalistic sentiments—hence the glocalized nature of international security. The chapter focuses on three kinds of cases to show the intersection of international security and contemporary nationalism through the prism of glocalized security. These are (a) the global war on terror, (b) the nuclear weapons control regime, and (c) conflicts over territorial control and spheres of influence.

The Global War on Terror: Afghanistan and Iraq

The war on terror has become a global effort by the United States, along with its allies, to dismantle terrorist networks threatening its national security interests through direct attacks on the US homeland and assets. These networks are able to fester in unstable countries, from which they can grow, disrupt the production and transportation of crude oil, and attack US assets and citizens around the world. The primary targets are al-Qaeda and ISIS, along with their affiliates and related organizations, such as the Taliban. The United States has been most notably involved in fighting terrorist groups in Afghanistan, Iraq, Syria, and Yemen as well as having undertaken low-scale and indirect fights in Africa (e.g., Somalia, Sahel, Libya). The US global war on terror started right after the 9/11 terrorist attacks on the US homeland with the invasion of Afghanistan and soon after Iraq. These two countries have been the epicenters of the global war on terror, and both countries have been subjected to total US occupation and efforts to install friendly governments that can put the countries under the ambit of US liberalism. In the end, military operations in both countries cost far more than what the United States had anticipated as the wars dragged on and the justifications for the wars increasingly became problematic. From the start, the wars in Afghanistan and Iraq were framed in terms of US national security and liberal values that tie into American patriotism and exceptionalism.[34]

Invasion of Afghanistan

US military involvement in Afghanistan goes back to the Soviet invasion of Afghanistan in 1979 and subsequent US support for the mujahideen, which included people like Osama bin Laden, who later masterminded the 9/11 terrorist attacks.[35] Afghanistan experienced continual power struggles after the Soviet invasion, and by 1995 an Islamist militia, the Taliban, had gained power. It was in the midst of the Afghan conflict that al-Qaeda emerged as a significant nonstate military actor and a terrorist organization. In 1998, al-Qaeda bombed the US embassies in Kenya and Tanzania. Al-Qaeda's most notorious act was on September 11, 2001, when it attacked the World Trade Center in New York and the Pentagon in Washington with four hijacked US planes that were used to destroy the targets; the attacks killed around three thousand people. The United States quickly determined that the 9/11 attacks were carried out by al-Qaeda and that its leaders, including Osama bin Laden, were based in Afghanistan near the border with Pakistan.[36] The United States demanded that the Taliban handover the al-Qaeda leaders, which the Taliban did not do. The United States and allied NATO countries invaded Afghanistan in October 2001.

During the first phase of the US invasion of Afghanistan, around 2,500 US troops were deployed that ousted the Taliban from power, paving the way for the instalment of Hamid Karzai as head of the Afghan Transitional Government in July 2002.[37] Afghanistan degenerated into a civil war that pitted the Taliban against the North Alliance along with US and NATO troops. The war became both a civil war and a resistance against US occupation. As the war intensified, the United States dramatically increased its troop levels with the aim of dismantling al-Qaeda and the Taliban and rebuilding Afghanistan into a stable state with a government that would be friendly to the United States under the Bush doctrine.[38] The number of US troops quickly grew to around 10,000 by December 2002 and reached a peak of 100,000 in August 2010.[39] After bin Laden was killed in neighboring Pakistan in May 2011, the United States started to reduce the number of troops in Afghanistan. However, in March 2014 there were still around 36,000 US troops there. Despite the Obama administration's desire to withdraw from Afghanistan, there were still around 8,400 troops in July 2016 due to continued resistance by the

Taliban.⁴⁰ The US mission centered on training Afghan forces to fight the Taliban and defend the US-backed government. However, that effort failed to stabilize Afghanistan, and US troop casualties significantly increased. Under the "Agreement for Bringing Peace to Afghanistan between the Islamic Emirate of Afghanistan which is not recognized by the United States as a state and is known as the Taliban and the United States of America," signed on February 29, 2020, the United States effectively agreed to withdraw from Afghanistan and handover the country to the Taliban. In August 2021, the US swiftly withdrew its remaining troops, allowing the Taliban to immediately capture the country and come back into power.

The twenty-year war resulted in the assassination of Osama bin Laden and other al-Qaeda leaders in Afghanistan and Pakistan. Al-Qaeda was dispersed from its base in Afghanistan and greatly reduced. However, the Taliban simply laid low and eventually recaptured Afghanistan under the same ideology that had welcomed al-Qaeda. Al-Qaeda spread around the world and proliferated into other forms of terrorist groups, such as ISIS and AQIM (al-Qaeda in the Islamic Maghreb). The war became very costly in terms of lives and resources. Notably, 2,448 American service members were killed and more than 20,000 US soldiers wounded in Afghanistan between October 2001 and April 2022. An additional 3,846 US contractors were killed during the same period.⁴¹ Around 241,000 people, including over 71,000 civilians, were killed in the fighting that took place in the Afghan and Pakistani war zone.⁴² The US spent around $2.261 trillion on the war in Afghanistan from 2001 to 2021.⁴³

Certainly, the terrorist attacks on the United States was an unprecedented national security trauma that required a decisive response. However, the issue that often unfolds in warfare is the cost of war—human and financial. Given the nature of the 9/11 terrorist attacks, the American people did not really need much convincing on the need to strike back at al-Qaeda wherever they were and holding the people responsible accountable. The more critical question was how to do that and how far to go with such an effort. President George W. Bush quickly framed the issue as a fight between evil and good and saw the remedy in the total transformation of Afghanistan into a democratic country with a liberal economy free from Islamists. This totalizing approach was framed in terms of justice and humanism. Under the Bush doctrine, the American people were to get justice, while the Afghans get liberation from those using Afghanistan to oppress the people and terrorize the US and the rest of the world. Indeed, this was an appealing message to a lot of people—if successfully implemented. According to a *Washington Post*/ABC News poll released two days after the 9/11 attack, 93 percent of

Americans supported military response and over 80 percent supported waging a war. Public support for sending US troops was still high at 71 percent in November 2001 according to another *Washington Post*/ABC News poll.[44] During this traumatic period very few alternative approaches emerged as the US Congress voted almost unanimously to authorize the war according to the Bush doctrine. In the Senate, 98 senators voted in favor of S.J.Res. 23 ("A joint resolution to authorize the use of United States Armed Forces against those responsible for the recent attacks launched against the United States") and the remaining 2 senators did not vote.[45] In the House of Representative, the resolution passed with 420 votes in favor and only 1 opposed.[46] In hindsight, the few marginal voices that saw the solution to Al-Qaeda largely in some form of police measure and counterinsurgency operations may have had a potentially better approach. The United States not only galvanized the forces of patriotism to support the Bush doctrine but also gained the sympathy and support of many countries, especially its traditional allies. A notable sign of patriotism-cum-nationalism was the rise in voluntary enlistment into the US military. According to one estimate, 72,908 people joined the US military during the first year of the 9/11 attack.[47] Though support for the war was mostly strong, it increasingly became questionable as the cost increased. By the time the United States withdrew in August 2021, 62 percent of the people believed that the war was not worth fighting according to an AP/NORC poll on August 16, 2021. Also, an NPR/PBS NewsHour/Marist poll found that 71 percent of the public considered the war a failure.[48]

The critical issue in terms of maintaining support for the Afghanistan war was how to define and achieve victory and tie it to the US global war on terror in the Middle East, especially in Iraq. This became increasingly difficult as the war in Iraq began to be seen as a mistake. The war in Afghanistan somehow continued to be viewed as the right war as most of the discourse shifted toward military strategy, notably an elaborate democratic state-building approach or a smaller engagement centered on counterinsurgency. Eventually, support for the war waned as it became clear that the Taliban was somehow unbeatable and liberal democracy unattainable, despite President Obama's modification of the Bush approach to a much narrower mission. US policies toward the Afghanistan war became more chaotic as Donald Trump entered the political fray and eventually became president. By the time Trump left office, the American public was very tired of war, and Joe Biden quickly implemented a total withdraw, thereby ending the (largely failed) US war in Afghanistan.

A central feature of US nationalism during the Afghan war was the extremely lofty rhetoric of justice, deterrence, and humanism, which was high during the first half of the war under Bush but quickly started to wane during the Obama presidency and collapsed under Trump. A notable fact is that whenever the US suffered major economic crisis, support for the war generally fell and antiwar voices increased. This was true during the Great Recession inherited by Obama and the COVID-19 crisis under Trump. In fact, major policy shifts toward scaling back the war happened during those economic crises. As the human and financial costs of the war increased with no significant result, patriotism shifted more toward supporting the troops. In fact, calls for ending of the war were often framed as support for the troops and their families, who were bearing the real cost of the war. The Afghanistan war was waged outside the United States but was driven by domestic perceptions of war success and costs through varying frames of patriotism-cum-nationalism and American exceptionalism; in this way, the war points to the glocalized nature of international security issues. Further driving home the glocalized nature of this conflict, similar issues of declining support for the war occurred in other NATO countries that were aiding the United States in Afghanistan. As US policies became erratic and public support declined, other NATO countries also started to withdraw from the war in Afghanistan. In essence, NATO participation in the Afghan war was largely dependent on strong US commitment to the war.[49] A final critical takeaway from the US and NATO withdrawals from Afghanistan is that the risks of international interventions are high in an acutely glocalized war. As Ashraf Ghani and Clare Lockhart show in their work, Afghanistan is one of those cases in which international military interventions wrapped in building neoliberal states fail in glocalized conflicts.[50]

Invasion of Iraq

The second US war against Iraq happened alongside the war in Afghanistan, which was a grave expansion of the Global War on Terror under the Bush doctrine. The two critical issues that drove the US wars against Iraq are oil and the militarization of the Ba'ath regime.[51] These issues have been wrapped in varying forms of liberal, humanistic, and national security agendas since 1990. US interests in the Middle East started with oil probing after World War I. However, in 1972 the Ba'ath Socialist party under Saddam Hussein nationalized Iraqi oil, which created a contentious relation with Western powers.[52]

The first US war against Iraq was triggered by the Iraqi invasion of Kuwait in August 1990 and threats to oil producing Gulf states. Also, Iraq was believed to have developed a biological weapons program in contravention of NPT. In August 1990, George H. W. Bush deployed over 500,000 US troops to Saudi Arabia to prevent Iraqi attacks under Operation Desert Shield.[53] This mission was transformed into Operation Desert Storm in January 1991. By the end of February 1991, Iraq had been defeated and subjected to UN-backed arms control and inspection regime. Iraq was required to eliminate all its weapons of mass destruction program. However, Iraq was often accused of violating the arms control agreement and hindering UN inspections, leading to sanctions against Iraq.[54] In the spring of 1998, UN inspectors confirmed that Iraq had passed inspection. Iraq demanded that the inspections and sanctions against it be ended, but the United States and Britain accused Iraq of continuing its weapons program.[55]

It is within this context of contempt between the United States and Iraq that the 9/11 terrorist attacks occurred. Although it quickly became clear that Iraq was not involved in the 9/11 terrorist attacks, Iraq became a target of the United States as George W. Bush defined the war on terror as a global fight against evil and an effort to root out regimes that might support terrorism or become a place for terrorists. In his January 2002 State of the Union speech, Bush labeled Iraq part of an "axis of evil" along with Iran and North Korea, classifying them as enemies of the United States. In targeting Iraq, Bush stated that "some governments will be timid in the face of terror. And make no mistake about it: If they do not act, America will. Our second goal is to prevent regimes that sponsor terror from threatening America or our friends and allies with weapons of mass destruction. Some of these regimes have been pretty quiet since September 11, but we know their true nature... Iraq continues to flaunt its hostility toward America and to support terror. The Iraqi regime has plotted to develop anthrax and nerve gas and nuclear weapons for over a decade."[56] Bush extended the global war on terror to Iraq with the hope of quickly defeating the regime of Saddam Hussain and transforming Iraq into a friendly liberal state. The United States, with the lone support of Britain, invaded Iraq on March 20, 2003, based on the pretext of ending Iraqi weapons of mass destruction program. Internationally, the war was widely opposed as US imperialism, while progressives in the US saw the war as a distraction from the real war on terror in Afghanistan and a cynical move by the Bush regime to promote neoliberalism and regime change in Iraq. Even worse, the invasion of Iraq has been attributed to corporate financial interests of people connected to the US government.[57] In her critique of the 2003 US invasion of Iraq, Deniz Gökalp notes that "though there were originally conflicting views in Washington regarding what kind of role to play in the reconstruction of the new Iraq after the invasion, the one requiring the most radical agenda, a deeply invasive neoliberal intrusion into the Iraqi state and society, came to dominate the nature of the United States involvement in Iraq starting from the early months of the invasion.[58] This cynical neoliberal approach accentuate the corporate oil interests in the US wars on Iraq, which seems to be a continuation of the historical corporate colonial interest in the Middle East.

The Iraqi regime was quickly deposed, and Bush claimed victory in what became known as the "Mission Accomplished" speech. The US disbanded the Iraqi army, removed all Ba'athists from the Iraqi government, and installed Paul Bremer as the US administrators heading the Coalition Provisional Authority. In December 2003, Saddam Hussein was captured and eventually executed by the Iraqi government. In 2004, the search for weapons of mass destruction was halted as no such weapons were found. The war quickly transformed into terrorism warfare as former regime elements regrouped into a Sunni resistance movement against the US occupation and the subsequent Shi'a government that came to power in 2005. A civil war between Sunni and Shi'a groups flared as Kurds formed their own autonomous region and Al-Qaeda, through Abu Musab al-Zarqawi, joined the war to combat the US occupation.[59] In May 2008, Britain withdrew from the war, leaving the US to fight it alone.

At the start of the 2003 Iraq war, the US deployed 67,700 troops. As the Iraqi resistance and civil war intensified, the US dramatically increased the number of troops. In 2004, the number of US troop was 130,600, which quickly grew to a peak of 157,800 troops in 2008. US troop size was reduced to 135,600 in 2009, and by 2011, it was at 42,800.[60] According to the US Department of Defense, 4,431 US service personnel died in Operation Iraqi Freedom (March 19, 2003, to August 31, 2010), and another 74 died in Operation New Dawn (September 1, 2010, to December 31, 2011).[61] Around 3,588 US contractors also died in the war. Another 31,947 US service personnel were wounded.[62] Over 48,000 Iraqi personnel were killed along with over 34,806 opposition fighters and over 184,382 civilians.[63] The 2003 Iraq war is believed to have cost at least $1.7 trillion.[64] While the human and material costs of the Afghanistan war are always referenced back to the need to mete out justice for the victims of 9/11, the Iraq war tainted the global war on terror as US imperialism and made the US more vulnerable to geopolitical resistance.

As US casualties rose, the financial cost skyrocketed, and the US economy entered the great recession, US public support for the war evaporated. People disassociated Iraq from the 9/11 attacks and redefined patriotism to mean supporting the troops. Hawkish and progressive politicians vied to shape the narrative of the war and how to end it. Withdrawing the troops quickly became a more patriotic position than fighting the war. In August 2010, President Obama announced that the US mission in Iraq is over and withdrew US forces in 2011.[65] By this time, the Global War on Terror had encompassed Syria as ISIS gained strongholds in Iraq and Syria.

Nationalism took two varying forms during the Iraq war. During the initial phase, which was shaped by the Bush doctrine, nationalism was tied to national security and American exceptionalism. Even though the actual security risks posed by Iraq to the United States were very minimal, if any, national security became a rallying point among conservative voters and national security hawks. The 9/11 terrorist attacks resonated with the idea that rogue regimes could harbor terrorists as Bush's doctrine of preemption gained support among people who saw the 9/11 attacks as jihadism. Protecting the homeland, especially when the cost was perceived to be low, became a palpable act of patriotism. In addition to protecting the homeland, American liberalism and America's image as the guardian of freedom and liberal society gained sympathy among conservatives who saw the Iraqi regime as oppressive to its people, especially the Christian minority. Bush's compassionate conservatism campaign promise was weaved into a narrative of freeing the Iraqi people and building democratic and liberal states that would not only ensure stability but also facilitate the production and sale of oil. Optimism about Iraq was carefully crafted by a narrative of military superiority and liberal humanism. National security and American exceptionalism led to significant support for the 2003 Iraq war during the Bush administration, especially among Republicans, who are conservative and tend to be hawkish. Throughout the Bush years, a majority of Republicans supported the Iraq war. From the start of the war to 2005, more than 80 percent of Republicans believed that the war was going well. As the United States began losing ground in the war, Republican support dipped from around 80 percent in 2005 to a low of around 50 percent in 2007 but bounced again to over 80 percent by 2008.[66] While Democrats, who are mostly progressives, generally opposed the war, they too showed some support when the United States was winning. At the start of war, around 80 percent of Democrats believed that the war was going well, but that percentage quickly dropped and stayed mostly under 40 percent throughout the Bush presidency, with a low of 18 percent in 2007.[67]

Toward the end of the Bush administration, when the Iraq war had gone very bad, nationalism was refined largely along the lines of progressive and hypernationalist politics. Both progressives and hypernationalists opposed the continuation of the Iraq war, albeit for different reasons. For progressives, the Iraq war was simply wrong because it was based on a false premise of Iraq possessing weapons of mass destruction. Moreover, it undermined US standing in the international community. Hypernationalists wanted to end the war because they opposed the nation-building aspect of the war, which was draining US resources. They saw the war as an elitist agenda that does very little to benefit the American working class. Withdrawing the troops became a patriotic act because it would save money. The narrative of patriotism in the Iraq war had more to do with pragmatic contextualism as opposed to principled positions, except for the few die-hard progressives and libertarians.[68] Contextual pragmatism shows why support for the war was high when the cost was low and victory seemed within reach and how slogans of "America-first" and "support the troops" became patriotic calls to end the war as the cost increased and victory became illusive. The Iraq war again exemplifies glocalized security. The war was projected to be a global war on terror to be fought outside the United States, but it was driven by domestic issues, most notably politics and economy.

Nuclear Weapons Control Regime: North Korea

The acquisition of nuclear weapons is a highly contentious issue in international security often pitting the United States and its allies against countries that are actively developing nuclear weapons and the means to deliver them, most notably North Korea and Iran.[69] While North Korea has openly shown the military nature of its nuclear program, Iran has not acknowledged developing nuclear weapons—even though all evidence points to a well-advanced nuclear weapons program. Nuclear conflicts essentially center on the ways countries define external threats and aggression. Both North Korea and Iran view their nuclear programs as essential to thwarting external aggression from their neighbors and outside military powers. For North Korea, the United States along with South Korea pose an existential threat. For Iran, the United States along with Israel and Saudi Arabia are threats to the Islamic Republic of Iran. On the other side of the conflicts, the United States along with its allies see both North Korea and Iran as authoritarian regimes that oppress their people and are likely to attack their neighbors. As such, they cannot be trusted with nuclear weapons and must be subjected to the terms of NPT. A critical juncture in such conflicts is the breakthrough moment when a country successfully develops nuclear weapons and effective means of delivering them, especially through long-range missiles. Once a country possesses nuclear weapons and the means to deliver them, military options against that country significantly diminish, as we see with the very limited options to punish Russia after it invaded Ukraine. North Korea is an insightful case precisely for being the latest country to have developed nuclear weapons and the means to deliver them despite international sanctions against it.

Conflicts over the development of nuclear weapons are very tense and costly as they involve the imposition of severe economic sanctions. Sanctions tend to be costly for all countries, especially those directly sanctioned. As such, countries involved in conflict over nuclear weapons have to justify their actions to ensure domestic support, even when the costs are very high. Justifying and building support often involve couching the conflict in terms of patriotic and nationalistic national security sentiments. In a similar way, countries trying to prevent others from developing nuclear weapons have to justify their threat of aggression to maintain domestic support. All of these are very evident in the case of North Korea.

The key driver of North Korea's nuclear program is the Korean War and the stationing of US troops in South Korea, including the deployment of US tactical nuclear weapons in South Korea. The armistice concluded the Korean War with agreements to stop all fighting, withdraw troops, release war prisoners, and establish a demilitarized zone between the north and the south.[70] However, the agreement did not lead to peace. North Korea started its secretive nuclear program in 1959 with the help of the Soviet Union. In 1982, the United States learned of North Korea's first nuclear facility 5-MW(e), which become operational around 1986.[71] North Korea's continued work on its nuclear program has led to tensions and intense efforts, mostly in the form of punitive sanctions, by the United States and South Korea to halt North Korea's nuclear program; however, the results have been minimal, with North Korea refusing to comply with the NPT rules even through bouts of intermittent negotiations.[72] North Korea eventually developed nuclear weapons and missiles to deliver them, and it has demonstrated its capacity through repeated tests, most notably the underground test in 2006.

A significant step in the effort to control the North Korean nuclear program was the establishment of the Joint Nuclear Control Commission (JNCC) between the Democratic People's Republic of Korea (DPRK, or North Korea) and the Republic of Korea (ROK, or South Korea) with the involvement of the IAEA in January 1992. JNCC was to facilitate the inspection regime, but it failed because the DPRK and ROK could not agree on a reciprocal system of inspection.[73] In March 1992, the Joint Declaration of South and North Korea on the Denuclearization of the Korean Peninsula was issued; under this agreement, the two countries consented to refrain from using nuclear energy, including uranium procurement, for any military purpose. They also agreed to conduct inspections of specific nuclear facilities.[74] Between 1993 and 1994, DPRK gave IAEA limited access to its program but rejected complete inspections.[75] In 1998, North Korea tested the Taepo Dong-1 ballistic missile, which drew further concerns about its nuclear program.⁷⁶ Multiple talks were held throughout 1999 during which the United States promised two light-water reactors to meet North Korea's peaceful energy needs.⁷⁷ North Korea agreed to a moratorium on missile testing, but in 2001, the United States imposed aid and trade sanctions on North Korea for proliferating weapons of mass destruction and developing missiles.⁷⁸

Between 2003 and 2005, the confrontation and negotiations intensified as North Korea indicated its possession of nuclear weapons and resumed uranium enrichment. It also threatened to leave the 1953 armistice if the United States did not refrain from bringing more troops into the region. In 2003, a minor armed friction occurred between DPRK and ROK troops in the Demilitarized Zone. In August 2003, the Six Party Talks were initiated and included the DPRK, ROK, China, Japan, Russia, and the United States. By expanding the negotiation, the United States was hoping for China and Russia to pressure North Korea into compliance. However, North Korea insisted on the demilitarization of the Korean peninsula, which would include removing US troops in South Korea. The Six Party Talks failed, as neither North Korea nor the United States could compromise on core demands and China showed minimal interest in pressuring North Korea. In 2005, North Korea officially acknowledged possession of nuclear weapons and withdrew from the Six Party Talks.⁷⁹

Since 2006, North Korea has intensified its display of military power beginning with an underground nuclear weapon test that affirmed its status as a nuclear state despite the objections of the United States and its allies and being in violation of UN sanctions.⁸⁰ A modified Taepo Dong-2 three stage rocket was tested in 2009 in violation of UN Security Council Resolution 1718.⁸¹ North Korea continually tests various types of missiles in varying degrees of frequency often as protests against what it sees as threatening actions from the United States, such as sanctions and military exercises on the Korean peninsula. In March 2014, for example, North Korea launched thirty short-range rockets.⁸² It also fired two medium-range Rodang missiles into the Sea of Japan.⁸³

It is within the context of frequent missile tests and US protest actions that the meetings between North Korean leader Kim Jong-Un and US president Donald Trump occurred in an attempt to resolve the conflict. The start of the Trump presidency coincided with an intensive North Korean display of military capability to which Trump responded with threatening hyperbolic statements. The erratic war of words between Trump and North Korea gave way to messages of affinity with Kim and a willingness to meet for face-to-face talks. Trump's overture to Kim was driven by his eccentric personality rather than US policy, which has been a hard-line approach. Kim and Trump had three meetings, in (a) Singapore (June 12, 2018), in (b) Hanoi (February 28, 2019), and at (c) the Korean Demilitarized Zone (June 30, 2019).[84] Prior to the first meeting, the United States requested that three Americans held captive in North Korea be released, which was granted.[85] Also, South Korean president Moon Jae-In had a meeting with Kim for the first time in April 2018. They agreed to alleviate hostilities and stated a common goal of denuclearizing the peninsula.[86] In September 2018, the Pyongyang Joint Declaration was issued; it called for retreating military fronts, reuniting split families, establishing continuous contact, and joint economic supports.[87] Though highly symbolic, none of the meetings between Trump and Kim achieved any change in US sanctions or North Korean nuclear weapons development policies. In October 2019, US and North Korean officials met in Stockholm, but the talks collapsed without any progress. In early 2021, the Biden administration attempted to reset the relation with North Korean through conventional diplomacy; however, the missile tests and sanctions regime continued, and the conflict remains a stalemate.

A key element in the effort to prevent North Korea from developing nuclear weapons is the sanctions regime that has been imposed by the United States and the United Nations. The United Nations has imposed numerous sanctions against North Korea, notably between 2006 and 2017. The sanctions that come in the form of UN Security resolutions are often passed after North Korea reaches a milestone in its nuclear program or when it withdraws from negotiations. Most of the sanctions are in the form of restrictions on technology and trade, asset freezes, and travel bans. In October 2006, for example, UN Security Council Resolution 1718 prohibited "direct or indirect supply, sale, or transfer" of heavy weapons and their spare parts and material and technologies that could be used to make WMD or ballistic missiles. The resolution also prohibited exporting luxury goods to North Korea and asked countries to freeze the funds and assets of entities supporting North Korea's weapons program. More sanctions were added under Resolution 1874 (June 2009), which prohibited loans to North Korea (except for humanitarian or development purposes). A seven-member expert panel was created to enforce the sanctions. Resolution 2087 (January 2013) added travel bans on certain North Korean officials. Resolution 2094 (March 2013) further restricted North Korean access to the international banking and money transfer systems. Tougher sanctions were added as North Korea continued to show more military capabilities. Under Resolution 2375 (September 2017), for example, a ban was placed on North Korean textile exports and a cap placed on exporting crude oil and natural gas to North Korean. Resolution 2397 (December 2017) expanded the export bans and further reduced the amount of crude oil and gas that can be exported to North Korea. Other countries were empowered to impound ships caught smuggling illicit items, including oil and coal, to North Korea. The United States incorporated and expanded the UN sanctions, making the US the core country seeking to implement the sanction.[88]

The United States and North Korea each has been able to mobilize domestic support, even in the face of adverse effects, especially for North Korea. While the actual security threat to the US homeland is low, the United States has been able to maintain domestic and some international support for its hard-line policies by framing North Korea as an authoritarian state that threatens US allies in and around the Korean peninsula in addition to proliferating weapons of mass destruction, especially to Iran, which further threatens US interests and allies in the Middle East. In reality, the only cost North Korea has been able to inflict is holding US citizens who venture into North Korea as hostages. However, it has gained a nuclear deterrent and greatly boosted the domestic image of the regime. US posture toward North Korea takes two forms: namely, the stationing of US forces and military assets in South Korea and engaging in punitive sanctions against North Korea. Domestic support for the deployment of US troops in South Korea goes back to the US role in World War II and the Korean War, in which the United State was positioned as the guardian of capitalism and freedom around the world. As such, maintaining support for US policies toward North Korea entails reminding the public of US global leadership, which the public generally accepts. Since there is a relatively low human cost of US policies toward North Korea, the public generally does not pay too much attention to them, except in times of heightened crisis. Overall, the public supports the sanctions against North Korea. A 2017 opinion poll shows that 76 percent of Americans support tougher sanctions as fear of North Korea's nuclear program reached 75 percent among respondents.[89] US policies toward North Korea fit into American nationalism through the idea of American exceptionalism. North Korea too shows how international security dovetails with domestic issues. The Korean War and the confrontation with North Korea are glocalized security issues in which the US public has to be periodically reminded of US exceptionalism and its global leadership role.

For North Korea, US presence on the Korean peninsula is an existential threat especially given the history of the Korean War. North Korea sees its weapons program both as a deterrent and source of pride for standing up to a global supper power. North Korea navigates sanctions through a variety of evasion mechanisms and the support of friendly states, especially China, which has an interest in the stability of North Korea and limiting US power in the Korean peninsula.[90] As a communist country that has been ruled by a family dynasty, North Korean is able to forcefully promote nationalism, and it is therefore far more engrained in the state.[91] Even when North Korea suffers severe economic hardship, including famine, it has been able to maintain domestic cohesion through authoritarianism and nationalistic propaganda. For North Korea, there is no line between its domestic security and geopolitics as the very survival of the regime and the state is tied to its resistance against the United States and South Korea, which is a clear case of glocalized security.

Territorial Control and Spheres of Influence: Ukraine

Another highly contentious issue is the effort to control territories and claims of rights and sovereignty. Until the Russian invasion of Ukraine, such conflicts have mostly been in the form of military posture and occasional clashes along border areas, such as on the India-Pakistan border, the Golan Heights, the India-China border, and minor military intrusions of airspaces and national waters. However, the Russian annexation of Crimea and the current invasion/occupation of mainland Ukraine is a seismic shift in conflicts over territory, including the Chinese claim over Taiwan. Efforts to control territories typically emanate from historical and cultural claims over spaces and deep economic and geopolitical interests. While there are numerous unresolved disputes over territories, conflicts that pit major powers against each other are disproportionately consequential for international security because they fuel the arms race among major powers and put them at greater risk of direct armed conflict in case of a miscalculation. Notably, Russian appropriation of Ukrainian territory and China's claim over Taiwan, as well as its controversial creation of artificial islands in the South China Sea, represent the most challenging cases because each of these pits the United States and its allies against another global power. In the case of Ukraine, while the United States has refrained from sending troops to defend Ukraine, it is openly arming Ukraine and funding the Ukrainian resistance. At this point, Russia and the United States are locked in what is more than a proxy war in Ukraine.

The Ukraine war evokes critical questions about conceptions of national security and deployment of nationalism. As the Ukraine war unfolds, three issues are critical for understanding the intersection of national security and nationalism under glocalized security: (a) geopolitics, (b) liberalism, and (c) minority issues and cultural affinity. These three issues have been weaved into various narratives coming from Russia on the one hand and Ukraine along with its NATO supporters on the other.

Perhaps a starting point to the contemporary evolution of the Ukraine war is the fall of the Soviet Union in 1991, when Ukraine and the other Soviet republics became independent. Indeed, Russian interests were very deep in nearly all the former Soviet republics, most notably by way of significant numbers of ethnic Russians living in them, which was especially true of the Baltic states and Ukraine; aerospace assets in Kazakhstan; military access points especially on the Sea of Azov, the Black Sea, and Baltic Sea; and nuclear assets in Belarus, Ukraine, and Kazakhstan. Ukraine stood out as a particularly difficult case for Russia as it dealt with the security implications of the fall of the Soviet Union. This is because of the multiple ways in which Ukraine was critical to Russian national security interests as it had a huge ethnic Russian population, possessed a lot of nuclear weapons, had a common border with Russia, and had significant access to the Sea of Azov, the Black Sea, and the Crimean Peninsula. Given these interests, Ukraine's independence from Russian control became extremely delicate. From the start, Russia insisted that Ukraine and the other former Soviet republics had to handover all nuclear weapons to Russia. As the Arms Control Association notes, "at the time of Ukraine's independence from the Soviet Union in 1991, Ukraine held the third largest nuclear arsenal in the world, including an estimated 1,900 strategic warheads, 176 intercontinental ballistic missiles (ICBMs), and 44 strategic bombers. By 1996, Ukraine had returned all of its nuclear warheads to Russia in exchange for economic aid and security assurances, and in December 1994, Ukraine became a non-nuclear weapon state-party to the 1968 nuclear Nonproliferation Treaty."[92] This arrangement was arrived at through agreements supported by Western powers, most notably the Minsk Agreement on Strategic Forces (1991), the Lisbon Protocol (1992), and the Budapest Memorandum on Security Assurances (1994). Under these agreements, Russia inherited all the nuclear weapons of the Soviet Union and all other former Soviet republics became nonnuclear states and joined the NPT in return for security assurances supported by the United States, the United Kingdom, and Russia. As Ukraine asserted its sovereignty over the years by pursing a more liberal economic and political path that aligned with the West, the Russians' sense of security threat grew, leading to various efforts to control Ukrainian politics by supporting and coopting ethnic Russians in Ukraine, which culminated with the invasion and annexation of Ukrainian territory.

In a way, Russia considered Ukraine its backyard where it could assert influence as well as use Ukraine as a buffer against Western military and political encroachment toward Russia. This approach fits into Russian geopolitics vis-à-vis the West, especially as Russia was the losing party in the Cold

War.[93] Prior to the annexation of Crimea, Russia pursued a policy of political interference to ensure that Ukraine was ruled by pro-Russian governments and its economy controlled by pro-Russian Oligarchs. This worked until the removal of President Viktor Yanukovych in 2014 during the Maidan revolution, which led to a drastic Western bent in Ukraine's political, economic, and security vision. Yanukovych, who is an ethnic Russian, was a strong ally of Russia.

The 2014 Maidan revolution became a critical point in Ukraine's turn toward the West and erosion of Russian influence over the central government in Kyiv. As pro-Western politicians gained power, such as Presidents Petro Poroshenko in 2014 and Volodymyr Zelensky in 2019, Russia embarked on military strategy that included the annexation of Crimea and a proxy war in eastern Ukraine, which is demographically composed of mostly ethnic Russians. In 2014, Russian-backed separatists in eastern Ukraine launched a rebellion in the Donbas region and proclaimed the independence of the Donetsk and Luhansk People's Republics, while Russia annexed Crimea. Ukraine did not militarily resist the Russian annexation of Crimea but did launch a military campaign against the Russian-backed separatists in eastern Ukraine. It is within this separatist quagmire that Ukraine, notably the western part of Ukraine, categorically turned toward the West with the strong desire to join Western military, political, and economic alliances (i.e., NATO and the European Union).

Russian discontent about Ukraine and NATO rapidly grew as Vladimir Putin asserted Russian resistance toward the West and defined Ukraine as a redline in Russia's relations with the West.[94] In particular, Ukraine's desired membership in NATO became very contentious even though NATO has maintained support for Ukraine since 1990. In 1997, the NATO-Ukraine Commission was established under the Charter on a Distinctive Partnership. In September 2020, Ukraine approved a new National Security Strategy, which sought a distinctive partnership with NATO with the aim of Ukraine's becoming a NATO member. Though Ukraine has not been offered a Membership Action Plan, NATO refused to rule out Ukraine's eventual membership.[95] NATO's stance coupled with strong pro-Western political support and control in Kyiv and the decline of Russian influence over Ukraine's central government led Russia to directly invade Ukraine in February 2022 in what Russia described as special operation to presumably topple the government of Ukraine and replace it with a pro-Russian regime. In essence, as Ukraine turned more toward the West, Russia saw it as a major security threat that would lead to the deployment of Western military assets next to the Russian border and undermine its control of the Sea of

Azov. Russia framed its invasion as campaign of "denazification of Ukraine," which is an implicit Russian nationalist frame for supporting ethnic Russians in Ukraine. Russian geopolitical considerations dovetailed with Russian nationalism.

Since the fall of the Soviet Union, Ukraine has found itself in a precarious situation as it sought to fulfil its vision of being a liberal state under the systems of a Western free market economy and democracy. Ukraine became sandwiched between the wave of Western liberalism in Europe and Russian gravitation toward authoritarianism and vision of a Greater Russia that would be a bulwark against Western hegemony. In the tango between Russia and the West, Ukraine took an extra level of importance as Russia saw Ukraine as a place to hold the line against the West, while the West saw Ukraine as a place to cement its Cold War victory. In the process, liberalism became the actualization of geopolitics. Russia saw liberalism as a threat to its geopolitical power, while the West saw liberalism as a weapon against Russia that can be deployed within and around Russia. Ukraine's liberal bent toward the West also necessitated a domestic struggle to defeat pro-Russian popular and political forces and the need for an insurance against Russian anger. Domestically, Ukraine not only has a significant Russian population, but also significant economic and political forces aligned with Russian vision of a Greater Russia and crony capitalism.[96] Ukraine's ideological division tends to overlap with the ethnoregional divide that makes the eastern part mainly Russian, while the western part is tied to Ukrainian nationalism and Western liberalism.

As Ukraine was embracing liberalism, Russia was mostly becoming antiliberal under Putin's firm grip and vision of a stronger and more cohesive Russia. Putin's grasp has grown even stronger with the death of key opposition leader Alexei Navalny and Putin's election to a fifth term as president. Putin's vision of a powerful Russia required defeating liberalism in Russia and in Ukraine. While Russia operates a free-market system and holds periodic multiparty elections, its economic and political system are not necessarily liberal.[97] Rather, Russian democracy and free-market economy are conditioned on the existence of a powerful Russian state that would ensure economic resilience against the Western-dominated capitalist system, be able to militarily challenge NATO, and be able to promote Russian cultural and strategic interests in Eurasia. While Ukraine saw Western liberalism as a path to greater well-being and within its sovereign rights, Russia saw Western liberalism as a threat to Russian cohesion that could lead to military and geopolitical weaknesses. Liberalism became a hook in Ukraine. For the West, supporting Ukraine and opening the door to potential membership in Western alliances, especially NATO and the European Union, not only would expand the reach of the West but also could be a way to further influence Russia and strengthen prodemocracy forces therein. Ultimately, Ukraine became a space to be coopted by the West or controlled by Russia, and now, in a series of events that underscores the glocalized nature of international security, domestic political struggles in Ukraine have led to a major geopolitical war.

The February 2022 Russian invasion of Ukraine was preceded by a tense relationship between Russia and the West while Ukraine downplayed the actual risk of a full-scale invasion. Pressure mounted as Russia increased its military activities near the Russia-Ukraine border. In June 2021, Putin addressed NATO for a negotiation focused on Russia's position and Western involvement in Ukraine, which led to multiple meetings aimed at alleviating tensions and the imminent invasion of Ukraine. In December 2021, for example, Russia put forth the Agreement on Measures to Ensure the Security of the Russian Federation and Member States of the North Atlantic Treaty Organization, which sought written guarantees that Ukraine would not be allowed to join NATO.[98] In addition to seeking a veto on Ukraine's membership of NATO, Russia had other requests that would effectively restrict NATO military activities in the former Soviet geopolitical space. These included a ban on intermediate-range missiles as envisioned in the defunct 2019 Intermediate Nuclear Forces Treaty. Russia also wanted NATO to refrain from military activities within the borders of eastern Europe to central Asia and specifically to cease its involvement in Ukraine. Importantly, Russia wanted a ban on NATO deployment of weapons and reinforcements in all central and eastern European countries that had joined NATO after 1997.[99] Russian demands clearly cast the Ukraine conflict as a geopolitical conflict with NATO and a way to regain the geopolitical space Russia lost with the fall of the Soviet Union, and in response, NATO, ostensibly casting the issue as a matter of Ukrainian sovereignty but also likely sensing an opportunity to expand its region of influence, rejected all of Russia's demands. NATO's standard argument was that the organization's 1949 treaty gives any nation the option to request membership and partake in the process of joining, but fundamentally, NATO saw Russian demands as unacceptable, leaving no room for compromise despite efforts by French president Emmanuel Macron to broker a last-minute deal.

The Russian invasion of Ukraine led to strong NATO support for Ukraine through a direct supply of weapons, training outside of Ukraine, and various forms of financial and humanitarian support. Effectively, the United States and its NATO allies have been providing the resources for Ukrainians to fight Russia. NATO countries quickly sent weapons to Ukraine and have been significantly increasing and improving the supply of weapons. So far, NATO has refused to deploy troops inside Ukraine or declare a no-fly zone over Ukraine for fear of escalation into a nuclear war as Russia continues to assert its nuclear weapons policy. However, further support to Ukraine is becoming shaky as the United States and some European countries are facing domestic opposition to continuously funding the war. In addition to military support, the United States and its Western allies have imposed widespread economic sanctions against Russia designed to destroy the Russian economy.[100] Sanctions have been placed on Russian products and Russia's financial system, and the assets of key Russian figures connected to Putin have been frozen. So far, the Russian economy has proved to be resilient in part due to continued collaboration with non-Western powers, such as China, India, Iran, and Turkey, and in part due to domestic economic resilience emanating from Russia's vast resources, domestic know-how, and domestic investment on the war. Furthermore, Western sanctions on Russia energy exports have been timid because of European dependency on Russian gas and oil.

Owing to strong NATO support, the war, which Putin described as a special operation intended to last just a few months, has dragged on—and it is projected to continue for a long time, even though Russia has been making slow-but-steady gains. Russia tried to capture Ukraine's capital city of Kyiv but retreated in the face of strong resistance. Russia went on to occupy around 15 percent of Ukrainian territory, mostly in the Donbas region.[101] Russia organized referenda in Donetsk, Luhansk, Kherson, and Zaporizhzhia officially annexing them in October 2022.[102] However, with the strong NATO support, Ukraine took back some of the territories occupied by Russia. Unfortunately, Ukraine continues to lose territory as the war drags on. For some time, the war has been in a state of stalemate as Russian advancement has been halted, but Ukraine has not recovered much territory and is at the present writing losing territory as Russian forces have started advancing again. The war has also taken on a form of terrorism warfare, especially after the Kerch Strait Bridge connecting Russia to the Crimea was bombed in October 2022. The Russian response has included devastating destruction of critical energy and water infrastructure across Ukraine, which has destroyed cities and created dire humanitarian conditions, especially during colder-weather months.

The Ukrainian war stalemate has been one that reinforces the divides between the two sides and accentuates the geopolitical, ideological, and humanitarian stakes. By the end of 2022, Russia and Ukraine had each lost over 100,000 people—a number that is still growing.[103] In addition, Ukrainian cities have been devastated and around 8 million Ukrainians are refugees in Europe. By May 2022, the United States alone had spent over $54 billion to support Ukraine, mostly in arms supply.[104] Europe and the United States have also suffered from soaring energy costs, which created adverse economic conditions. So far, no significant progress has been made in resolving the conflict. Negotiations between Russia and Ukraine have halted, and there are no meaningful negotiations between NATO and Russia. The only limited progress in negotiation has been on limited humanitarian issues relating to prisoner release, export of Ukrainian grains, and protecting Ukraine's Zaporizhzhia nuclear power plant.

A question that is becoming critical is how the countries involved will continue to justify the costs and maintain support for the war. Despite the unexpected difficulties of the military engagement, Russian support for the war is still strong. Putin has managed to maintain domestic support through a combination of draconian crackdowns on dissent, hypernationalist rhetoric, policies that insulate Russia proper from the adverse economic and military cost of the war, and building strong ties with non-Western powers, most notably China, Iran, India, Turkey, and North Korea. Russian support for Putin had been very high over the past few decades. Though the support is declining, it still seems strong. Indeed, while opinion polls in authoritarian regimes are highly doubtful, what is clear is that there is no significant mass opposition to the war, despite the fact that Russians were fleeing the military draft.[105] Putin seems to have effectively cast the war to Russians as a fight for Russian geopolitical and cultural survival instead of aggression. This fits into the Russian conception of national security, which is rooted in the idea of the Greater Russian nation in and around Russia and Russian status as a world power. Russia wants the rest of the world to view the Ukraine war as induced by NATO in what should be a Russian "domestic matter" that would deny Ukraine's sovereignty and reinforce Russian cultural nationalism.

For Ukraine, the Russian invasion has become an existential issue. Ukrainians, especially those in the western part of the country, see the war as a rightful resistance against Russian aggression and an opportunity to shed themselves of Russian control and actualize their vision of becoming a liberal Western state. In the process, Ukrainian nationalism dovetails neatly with liberalism and its strategic geopolitical interest. Ukrainian suffering has been met with Western generosity and strategic interests, which have been deployed to dampen Ukrainian suffering by way of military and humanitarian support and generous policies toward Ukrainian refugees. Ukrainian bravery, liberal vision, and sufferings have been embodied by President Volodymyr Zelensky, who was named *Time*'s 2022 Person of the Year.[106] In a way, Zelensky has come to embody Ukraine's liberal vision and resistance against Russian aggression. Media reports and polls tend to show strong approval ratings for Zelensky in Ukraine and in the United States.[107] According to a September 2022 Gallup poll, "A clear majority—70% of all Ukrainians interviewed in early September—say their country should continue fighting until it wins the war with Russia. Just over one in four (26%) favor negotiating to end it as soon as possible."[108] Zelensky has emerged as an effective spokesperson who continues to convince Western powers to support Ukraine and implores Ukrainians to persevere and resist. Zelensky's narrative continues to cast Russia as a terrorist state while insisting on Ukrainian sovereignty. Overall, Ukraine has been able to deploy a humanistic nationalism that taps into international humanitarian morality and the geopolitical confrontation between Russia and the West.

In the United States, the Ukraine war has been cast in both a humanitarian moral frame and a preservation of liberalism one. In the process, the United States emphasizes American exceptionalism as the guardian of free society and casts Russia as a rogue authoritarian state that is a danger to its people and European security. American support for Ukraine is generally strong. According to a November 2022 survey by the Chicago Council, there was still a fairly strong public support for US policy toward the Ukraine war. Roughly, 40 percent of the public wanted the United States to maintain its support for Ukraine indefinitely. Furthermore, 65 percent supported supplying Ukraine with arms, 66 percent supported economic aid, 73 percent supported accepting Ukrainian refugees, and 75 percent supported the sanctions against Russia.[109] Despite critical voices on the right wing of American politics about the cost of the war, the US government has been able to maintain bipartisan support to fund the Ukraine war. American support for the war fits into American conception of national security, which sees illiberal and authoritarian regimes, such as Russia, as a threat to an American vision of the world. Moreover, as Russia shows brute force and willingness to use nuclear weapons, the United States is able to project Russia as a real security danger to US allies in Europe and American geopolitical and economic interests. By the sheer financial cost to the United States and the potential risk of direct war with Russia, the Ukraine war is a domestic issue for the United States. For both historical and strategic reasons, the United States sees Europe as part of its domestic space, which fits into a glocalized security frame of the Ukraine war.

Conclusion: Military Power, Nationalism, and Glocalized Security

Since the end of the Cold War, international security has taken some unexpected turns. The fall of the Soviet Union was supposed to mark the end of history by creating a stable world order based on economic and political liberalism.[110] Instead, the world is faced with an increased risk of nuclear war as Russia and NATO are locked in a war for Ukraine and the new nuclear states are emerging. The Ukraine war follows a long list of terrorism related wars under the global war on terror; devastating civil wars, especially in Middle East, central Asia, Europe, and Africa; and growing ultranationalism in the West. All of these conflicts have propelled new actors into the international security scene, most notably nonstate actors and emergent military powers that are challenging old military powers. A key marker of this new international security landscape is the intersection of domestic and external issues in a way that is transforming international security issues into a glocalized security phenomenon as we see in the wars in Afghanistan, Iraq, and Ukraine and tensions over the nuclear weapons programs of North Korea and Iran.

A critical lens into this glocalized security phenomenon is examining the ways countries rationalize and justify the pursuit and use of military power through nationalism. Nationalism becomes not necessarily a totalizing ideology but a political and social frame for defining the national interests and security concerns of countries. National interests, particularly national security, become domestic drivers of international conflicts and security policies. As this chapter shows, international security issues are increasingly weaved into the domestic affairs of countries. This intertwining generates the need for aggressive national security policies at the global level, which further complicate international conflicts because they end up in multiple domestic manifestations. This entangled glocal space makes narratives of national interests, security risks, and values highly contextual and contentious as patriotism-cum-nationalism becomes an everyday trouble for the masses to endure.

Glocalized security provides a lens into the domestic and external drivers of conflicts and how they shape regional and international security. A key element of glocalized security is the emergence of new war dynamics that cannot be reduced to the local or the external. It is these new war dynamics that are transforming contemporary wars into spaces where major powers are involved along with national governments and violent nonstate actors. Glocalized security situations take different forms, ranging from ones in which major powers and emergent powers are directly involved to ones in which major powers shape how national actors and (violent) nonstate actors address national and regional security issues. So too do the triggers and forms of conflict drivers vary, which can range from environmental to governance and geopolitical issues under expansive conceptions of national security. As this chapter shows, the United States and Russia have been implicated in too many conflicts where domestic issues have taken on an international character, as is most evident in the wars in Iraq, Afghanistan, and Ukraine. The chapter also shows that national security and geopolitics are critical elements of glocalized security. Expansive notions of national security have contradicted with domestic interests in countries such as Iraq, Afghanistan, Iran, North Korea, and Ukraine in ways that have made all of those countries centers of international conflict pitting major powers against emergent powers and, in some cases, against nonstate actors.

Notes

1. Kaldor, *New and Old Wars*; Bah, "Civil Non-State Actors in Peacekeeping and Peacebuilding in West Africa," 313–36.

2. Bah, "Racial Profiling and the War on Terror," 76–100; Bah, *International Security and Peacebuilding*; Buzan, "Will the 'Global War on Terrorism' Be the New Cold War?," 1101–18.

3. Wallerstein and Bhanu, "Major Powers and the Security of Southeast Asia," 315–42.

4. Friedman, *World Is Flat*; Beck, What Is Globalization?; Robertson, "Glocalization," 25–44; Buzan et al., *Regions and Powers*; Waltz, *Theory of International Politics*.

5. Sassen, *Global City*; Robertson, "Glocalization," 25–44; Köhler and Wissen, "Glocalizing Protest," 942–51; Kjeldgaard and Askegaard, "Glocalization of Youth Culture," 231–47.

6. Samuel, Musah, and Arthur, "Beyond Classical Peace Paradigm," 48.

7. Kedourie, *Nationalism*; Znaniecki, *Modern Nationalities*; Anderson, *Imagined Communities*; Hobsbawm and Ranger, *Invention of Tradition*; Herder, *JG Herder on Social and Political Culture*.

8. Arendt, *Origins of Totalitarianism*; Mamdani, "Citizen and Subject"; Anderson, *Imagined Communities*.

9. Tilly and Ardant, *Formation of National States in Western Europe*; Brubaker, *Nationalism Reframed*.

10. Arendt, *Origins of Totalitarianism*; Neumann, *Behemoth*; Mann, *Fascists*.

11. Hofmann, *Fascist Effect*.

12. Zhelev, "Fashizmat [The Fascism]"; Roshwald, *Ethnic Nationalism and the Fall of Empires*.

13. Tuminez, *Russian Nationalism since 1856*; Sakwa, "Greater Russia," 334–62; Plokhy, *Ukraine and Russia*.

14. Tocqueville, *Democracy in America*.

15. Waldstreicher, *In the Midst of Perpetual Fetes*; O'Leary, *To Die For*; Du Bois, "Souls of White Folk."

16. Mamdani, "Citizen and Subject"; Coleman, "Nationalism in Tropical Africa," 404–26; Kohn and Sokolsky, *African Nationalism in the Twentieth Century*; Crowder, *History of West Africa*; Ajayi, "Expectations of Independence," 1–9.

17. Said, *Orientalism*; Farah, *Pan-Arabism and Arab Nationalism*.

18. Frisch, "Pan-Arabism and Its Competitors," 1–17.

19. D'Costa, *Globalization and Economic Nationalism in Asia*; Anderson, *Spectre of Comparisons*; Selden, "Economic Nationalism and Regionalism in Contemporary East Asia," 33–58.

20. Chang, *Return of the Dragon*; Clark, *Chinese Cultural Revolution*; Economy, *Third Revolution*.

21. Weldes, "Constructing National Interests," 275–318; Trubowitz, *Defining the National Interest*.

22. Mathews, "Redefining Security," 162–77; Leffler, "American Conception of National Security and the Beginnings of the Cold War, 1945–48," 346–81.
23. Bah and Emmanuel, "Migration Cooperation between Africa and Europe."
24. The concept of the Westphalian system came from the Treaties of Westphalia in 1648, which ended the Thirty Years War. It is essentially a principle of interstate relations that stresses states' exclusive sovereignty over their territories (see Farr, "Point: The Westphalia Legacy and the Modern Nation-State," 156–59).
25. Makinda, "Sovereignty and Global Security," 281–92; Bah, *International Security and Peacebuilding*.
26. Anderson, *Imagined Communities*; Bah, "Racial Profiling and the War on Terror," 76–100; Brubaker, "Ethnicity, Race, and Nationalism," 21–42; Bélanger, "Redefining Cultural Diplomacy," 677–99.
27. Beeson, "Trade and the National Interest"; Kaempfer and Lowenberg, "Political Economy of Economic Sanction," 867–911.
28. Thompson and Morgenthau, *Politics among Nations*.
29. Wallerstein, *Politics of the World-Economy*; Wallerstein, *Capitalist World-Economy*; Plous, "Perceptual Illusions and Military Realities," 363–89.
30. Arms Control Association, "Nuclear Weapons: Who Has What at a Glance."
31. Arms Control Association, "Nuclear Weapons: Who Has What at a Glance."
32. Arms Control Association, "Nuclear Weapons: Who Has What at a Glance."
33. Arms Control Association, "Nuclear Weapons: Who Has What at a Glance."
34. Hodgson, *Myth of American Exceptionalism*.
35. Pear, *Arming Afghan Guerrillas*; US Senate, "Tora Bora Revisited."
36. Kean and Hamilton, *9/11 Commission Report*.
37. US Senate, "Operation Enduring Freedom."
38. Ghani and Lockhart, *Fixing Failed States*; Monten, "Roots of the Bush Doctrine," 112–56.
39. Associated Press, "Timeline of U.S. Troop Levels in Afghanistan since 2001."
40. Associated Press, "Timeline of U.S. Troop Levels in Afghanistan since 2001."
41. US Department of Defense, Immediate Casualty Status, 10:00 a.m., April 25, 2022; Lock, "How Many U.S. Soldiers Died in Afghanistan?"
42. Brown University, "Afghan Civilians."
43. Crawford and Lutz, *U.S. Costs to Date for the War in Afghanistan, 2001–2021*.
44. Shortridge, "U.S. War in Afghanistan Twenty Years On."
45. US Senate. S.J. Res. 23.
46. Wire, "Road to Vindication for California's Barbara Lee."
47. DeSimone, "Why 9/11 Inspired These Service Members to Join the Military."
48. Shortridge, "U.S. War in Afghanistan Twenty Years On."
49. Shea, "NATO Withdraws from Afghanistan."
50. Ghani and Lockhart. *Fixing Failed States*.
51. Bah, *International Security and Peacebuilding*; Haass, *War of Necessity, War of Choice*.
52. Hahn, "*Century of U.S. Relations with Iraq*."
53. Collins, "Desert Storm."
54. Office of Foreign Assets Control, "Iraq—United States Secretary of the Treasury."
55. Arms Control Association, "Iraq: A Chronology of UN Inspections."
56. eMediaMillWorks, "Text of President Bush's 2002 State of the Union Address."
57. Agathangelou, "Bodies of Desire, Terror and the War in Eurasia," 693–722; Brown, "American Nightmare," 690–714.
58. Gökalp, "Regime Change," 175.
59. Council on Foreign Relations, "2003–2011: The Iraq War"; Pfiffner, "US Blunders in Iraq"; Freedom of Information Act, "FOIA Electronic Reading Room."
60. Belasco, "Troop Levels in the Afghan and Iraq Wars, FY2001–FY2012."

61. US Department of Defense, Immediate Casualty Status, November 7, 2022.
62. Goldberg, "Updated Death and Injury Rates of U.S. Military Personnel during the Conflicts in Iraq and Afghanistan."
63. Crawford and Lutz, "Human Cost of Post–9/11 Wars: Direct War Deaths in Major War Zones."
64. Trotta, "Iraq War Costs U.S. More Than $2 Trillion: Study."
65. Lee, "President Obama's Address on the End of the Combat Mission in Iraq."
66. Pew Research Center, "Reviewing the Bush Years and the Public's Final Verdict Bush and Public Opinion."
67. Pew Research Center, "Reviewing the Bush Years and the Public's Final Verdict Bush and Public Opinion."
68. Pynn, "Pragmatic Contextualism," 26–51.
69. Chubin, *Iran's Nuclear Ambitions*; Cha and Kang. *Nuclear North Korea*.
70. Korean War Armistice Agreement, July 27, 1953.
71. Szalontai and Radchenko, "North Korea's Efforts to Acquire Nuclear Technology and Nuclear Weapons"; Global Security, "Weapons of Mass Destruction (WMD)."
72. Office of Foreign Assets Control, "North Korea Sanctions."
73. UN General Assembly. Forty-seventh session. General and Complete Disarmament: Conventional disarmament on a regional scale Report of the Secretary-General (A/47/316) July 28, 1992. https://documents.un.org/doc/undoc/gen/n92/346/05/pdf/n9234605.pdf.
74. Nuclear Threat Initiative, "Joint Declaration of South and North Korea on the Denuclearization of the Korean Peninsula."
75. International Atomic Energy Agency, "Fact Sheet on DPRK Nuclear Safeguards."
76. Missile Threat: Missile Defense Project, "Taepodong-1."
77. Chung, *Prospects for US-South Korean-Japanese Trilateral Security Cooperation*.
78. Council on Foreign Relations, "Timeline: North Korean Nuclear Negotiations."
79. Arms Control Association, "Six-Party Talks at a Glance"; *Washington Post*, "Full Text: N. Korea's Statement on Its Nuclear Program."
80. BBC News, "North Korea Claims Nuclear Test."
81. Korea News Service, "DPRK Foreign Ministry Vehemently Refutes UNSC's 'Presidential Statement.'"
82. Al Jazeera America, "North Korea Test-Fires Rockets into Sea."
83. US Mission to International Organizations in Geneva, "Fact Sheet: DPRK Resolution 2270."
84. CNN, "READ: Full Text of Trump-Kim Signed Statement"; Lederman and Nichols, "Trump Meets Kim Jong Un."
85. Sang-Hun, "North Korea Frees American Prisoners, Lifting Hurdle to Nuclear Talks."
86. Taylor, "Full Text of North and South Korea's Agreement, Annotated."
87. Jae-in and Jong Un, "Pyongyang Joint Declaration of September 2018."
88. Office of Foreign Assets Control, "North Korea Sanctions."
89. McCarthy, "Poll: Most Americans Support Sanctions to Halt North Korea's Nuclear Program [Infographic]."
90. Wu, "What China Whispers to North Korea," 35–48.
91. Buzo, *Guerilla Dynasty*.
92. Arms Control Association, "Ukraine, Nuclear Weapons, and Security Assurances at a Glance."
93. NATO, "NATO Enlargement & Open Door"; Fukuyama, *End of History and the Last Man*.
94. Bah, "Banality of Oppression, Multipolarity and the Ukraine War"; Sachs, "West's Dangerously Simple-Minded Narrative about Russia and China."
95. NATO, "Relations with Ukraine."

96. Kuzio, *Ukraine*.

97. Guriev and Rachinsky, "Role of Oligarchs in Russian Capitalism," 131–50; Fish, *Democracy Derailed in Russia*.

98. NATO, "NATO-Russia Relations"; NATO, "Brussels Summit Communiqué"; Ministry of Foreign Affairs of the Russian Federation, "Agreement on Measures to Ensure the Security of the Russian Federation and Member States of the North Atlantic Treaty Organization"; Brunnstrom, "Susan Cornwell NATO Promises Ukraine, Georgia Entry One Day."

99. Maynes, "4 Things Russia Wants Right Now"; Sullivan, "How NATO's Expansion Helped Drive Putin to Invade Ukraine."

100. Northam, "NATO Is Threatening Russia with Sanctions to Protect Ukraine, but Do Sanctions Work?"; Office of Foreign Assets Control, "Ukraine-/Russia-Related Sanctions"; Office of Foreign Assets Control, "Ukraine/Russia-Related Sanctions Program."

101. Karklis and Cunningham, "Three Maps That Explain Russia's Annexations and Losses in Ukraine."

102. Reuters, "Russia's Federation Council Ratifies Annexation of Four Ukrainian Regions."

103. Cooper, "Russia and Ukraine Each Have Suffered over 100,000 Casualties, the Top U.S. General Says."

104. Pallaro and Parlapiano, "Four Ways to Understand the $54 Billion in U.S. Spending on Ukraine."

105. Coalson, "What's Behind Russian Support for Putin's War in Ukraine?"

106. Radford, "Volodymyr Zelensky Is Time Magazine's 2022 Person of the Year."

107. Poushter and Connaughton, "Zelenskyy Inspires Widespread Confidence from U.S. Public as Views of Putin Hit New Low."

108. Reinhart, "Ukrainians Support Fighting until Victory."

109. Smeltz, Kafura, and Sullivan, "Growing US Divide on How Long to Support Ukraine."

110. Fukuyama, *End of History and the Last Man*.

References

Agathangelou, Anna M. "Bodies of Desire, Terror and the War in Eurasia: Impolite Disruptions of (Neo)Liberal Internationalism, Neoconservatism and the 'New' Imperium." *Millennium: Journal of International Studies* 38, no. 3 (2010): 693–722.

Ajayi, J. F. Ade. "Expectations of Independence." *Daedalus* (1982): 1–9.

Al Jazeera America. "North Korea Test-Fires Rockets into Sea." March 21, 2014. http://america.aljazeera.com/articles/2014/3/21/north-korea-testfires30missilesintoseasouthsays.html.

Anderson, Benedict. *Imagined Communities: Reflections on the Origin and Spread of Nationalism*. New York: Verso Books, 2006.

———. *The Spectre of Comparisons: Nationalism, Southeast Asia, and the World*. New York: Verso, 1998

Arendt, Hannah. *The Origins of Totalitarianism*. Boston: Houghton Mifflin Harcourt, 1973.

Arms Control Association. "Iraq: A Chronology of UN Inspections." Arms Control Today. Accessed March 20, 2022. https://www.armscontrol.org/act/2002-10/features/iraq-chronology-un-inspections.

———. "Nuclear Weapons: Who Has What at a Glance." Last reviewed January 2024. https://www.armscontrol.org/factsheets/Nuclearweaponswhohaswhat.

———. "The Six-Party Talks at a Glance." Fact Sheets & Briefs, last reviewed February 2023. https://www.armscontrol.org/factsheets/6partytalks.

———. "Ukraine, Nuclear Weapons, and Security Assurances at a Glance." Fact Sheets & Briefs, last reviewed December 2020. https://www.armscontrol.org/factsheets/Ukraine-Nuclear-Weapons.

Associated Press. "A Timeline of U.S. Troop Levels in Afghanistan since 2001." *Military Times*, July 6, 2016. https://www.militarytimes.com/news/your-military/2016/07/06/a-timeline-of-u-s-troop-levels-in-afghanistan-since-2001.

Bah, Abu Bakarr. "The Banality of Oppression, Multipolarity and the Ukraine War." *Elephant*, November 11, 2022. https://www.theelephant.info/features/2022/11/11/the-banality-of-oppression-multipolarity-and-the-ukraine-war.

———. "Civil Non-State Actors in Peacekeeping and Peacebuilding in West Africa." *Journal of International Peacekeeping* 17, no. 3–4 (2013): 313–36.

———, ed. *International Security and Peacebuilding: Africa, the Middle East, and Europe.* Bloomington: Indiana University Press, 2017.

———. "Racial Profiling and the War on Terror: Changing Trends and Perspectives." *Ethnic Studies Review* 29, no. 1 (2006): 76–100.

Bah, Abu Bakarr, and Nikolas Emmanuel. "Migration Cooperation between Africa and Europe: Understanding the Role of International Incentives." In *Oxford Research Encyclopedia of International Studies*. Oxford University Press, published online September 15, 2022. DOI: 10.1093/acrefore/9780190846626.013.735.

BBC News. "North Korea Claims Nuclear Test." Asia-Pacific, October 9, 2006. http://news.bbc.co.uk/2/hi/asia-pacific/6032525.stm.

Beck, Ulrich. *What Is Globalization?* Cambridge: Polity Press, 2000.

Beeson, Mark. "Trade and the National Interest." *An Australian Review of Public Affairs* 28 (2003).

Bélanger, Louis. "Redefining Cultural Diplomacy: Cultural Security and Foreign Policy in Canada." *Political Psychology* 20, no. 4 (1999): 677–99.

Belasco, Amy. "Troop Levels in the Afghan and Iraq Wars, FY2001-FY2012: Cost and Other Potential Issues." Congressional Research Service, July 2, 2009. https://sgp.fas.org/crs/natsec/R40682.pdf.

Brown, Wendy. "American Nightmare: Neoliberalism, Neoconservatism and De-Democratization." *Political Theory* 34, no. 6 (2006): 690–714.

Brown University. "Afghan Civilians." Costs of War, Watson Institute of International and Public Affairs, April 2021. https://watson.brown.edu/costsofwar/costs/human/civilians/afghan.

Brubaker, Rogers. "Ethnicity, Race, and Nationalism." *Annual Review of Sociology* 35 (2009): 21–42.

———. *Nationalism Reframed: Nationhood and the National Question in the New Europe.* Cambridge: Cambridge University Press, 1996.

Brunnstrom, David. "Susan Cornwell NATO Promises Ukraine, Georgia Entry One Day." Reuters. April 2, 2008. https://www.reuters.com/article/us-nato/nato-promises-ukraine-georgia-entry-one-day-idUSL0179714620080403.

Buzan, Barry. "Will the 'Global War on Terrorism' Be the New Cold War?" *International Affairs* 82, no. 6 (2006): 1101–18.

Buzan, Barry, and Ole Wæver. *Regions and Powers: The Structure of International Security.* Cambridge: Cambridge University Press, 2003.

Buzo, Adrian. *The Guerilla Dynasty: Politics and Leadership in North Korea*. New York: Routledge, 2018.

Cha, Victor D., and David C. Kang. *Nuclear North Korea: A Debate on Engagement Strategies*. New York: Columbia University Press, 2018.

Chang, Maria H. *Return of the Dragon: China's Wounded Nationalism.* New York: Routledge, 2018.

Chubin, Shahram. *Iran's Nuclear Ambitions*. Washington, DC: Brookings Institution Press, 2010.

Chung, Min Lee. *Prospects for US-South Korean-Japanese Trilateral Security Cooperation.* Atlantic Council, Scowcroft Center for Strategy and Security, December 2018. https://www

.atlanticcouncil.org/wp-content/uploads/2018/12/Prospects_for_US-South_Korean-Japanese_Trilateral_Security_Cooperation.pdf.

Clark, Paul. *The Chinese Cultural Revolution: A History*. Cambridge: Cambridge University Press, 2008.

CNN. "READ: Full Text of Trump-Kim Signed Statement." Politics, June 12, 2018. https://edition.cnn.com/2018/06/12/politics/read-full-text-of-trump-kim-signed-statement/index.html.

Coalson, Robert. "What's Behind Russian Support for Putin's War in Ukraine?" Radio Free Europe/Radio Liberty, March 12, 2022. https://www.rferl.org/a/russia-war-support-putin-analysis/31749491.html.

Coleman, James S. "Nationalism in Tropical Africa." *American Political Science Review* 48, no. 2 (1954): 404–26.

Collins, S. "Desert Storm: A Look Back." US Department of Defense, January 11, 2019. https://www.defense.gov/News/Feature-Stories/story/Article/1728715/desert-storm-a-look-back.

Cooper, Helene. "Russia and Ukraine Each Have Suffered over 100,000 Casualties, the Top U.S. General Says." *New York Times*, November 10, 2022. https://www.nytimes.com/2022/11/10/world/europe/ukraine-russia-war-casualties-deaths.html.

Council on Foreign Relations. "2003–2011: The Iraq War." Accessed March 20, 2022. https://www.cfr.org/timeline/iraq-war.

———. "Timeline: North Korean Nuclear Negotiations." Accessed March 28, 2022. https://www.cfr.org/timeline/north-korean-nuclear-negotiations.

Crawford, Neta, and Catherine Lutz. "Human Cost of Post–9/11 Wars: Direct War Deaths in Major War Zones." Costs of War, Watson Institute of International and Public Affairs, Brown University, November 13, 2019. https://watson.brown.edu/costsofwar/figures/2019/direct-war-death-toll-2001-801000.

———. "U.S. Costs to Date for the War in Afghanistan, 2001–2021." Human and Budgetary Costs to Date of the U.S. War in Afghanistan, April 15, 2021. Watson Institute of International & Public Affairs, Brown University. https://watson.brown.edu/costsofwar/files/cow/imce/figures/2021/Human%20and%20Budgetary%20Costs%20of%20Afghan%20War%2C%202001-2021.pdf.

Crowder, Michael. *History of West Africa*. New York: Columbia University Press, 1972.

D'Costa, Anthony P., ed. *Globalization and Economic Nationalism in Asia*. Oxford: Oxford University Press, 2012.

DeSimone, Danielle. "Why 9/11 Inspired These Service Members to Join the Military." USO, September 7, 2021. https://www.uso.org/stories/2849-why-9-11-inspired-these-patriots-to-join-the-military#:~:text=In%20response%2C%20181%2C510%20Americans%20enlisted,that%20inspired%20them%20to%20enlist.

Du Bois, W. E. B. "The Souls of White Folk." *Independent*, August 18, 1910.

Economy, Elizabeth. *The Third Revolution: Xi Jinping and the New Chinese State*. Oxford: Oxford University Press, 2018.

eMediaMillWorks. "Text of President Bush's 2002 State of the Union Address." *Washington Post*, January 29, 2002. https://www.washingtonpost.com/wp-srv/onpolitics/transcripts/sou012902.htm.

Farah, Tawfic E. *Pan-Arabism and Arab Nationalism: The Continuing Debate*. New York: Routledge, 2019.

Farr, Jason. "Point: The Westphalia Legacy and the Modern Nation-State." *International Social Science Review* 80, no. 3/4 (2005): 156–59.

Fish, M. Steven. *Democracy Derailed in Russia: The Failure of Open Politics*. Cambridge: Cambridge University Press, 2005.

Freedom of Information Act. "FOIA Electronic Reading Room." Defense Intelligence Agency. 2022. https://www.dia.mil/FOIA/FOIA-Electronic-Reading-Room/FileId/161882.

Friedman, Thomas L. *The World Is Flat: A Brief History of the Twenty-First Century*. Updated and expanded ed. New York: Macmillan, 2006.
Frisch, Hillel. "Pan-Arabism and Its Competitors: Islamic Radicals and the Nation State." *Critical Review* 22, no. 1 (2010): 1–17.
Fukuyama, Francis. *The End of History and the Last Man*. New York: Simon and Schuster, 2006.
Ghani, Ashraf, and Clare Lockhart. *Fixing Failed States: A Framework for Rebuilding a Fractured World*. Oxford: Oxford University Press, 2009.
Global Security. "Weapons of Mass Destruction (WMD): Yongbyon (Nyongbyon)." Last modified September 28, 2019. https://www.globalsecurity.org/wmd/world/dprk/yongbyon-5.htm.
Gökalp, Deniz. "Regime Change: Neoliberal State Building and Its Collapse on Iraqi Society." In *International Security and Peacebuilding*, edited by Abu Bakarr Bah, 148–69. Bloomington: Indiana University Press, 2017.
Goldberg, Matthew. "Updated Death and Injury Rates of U.S. Military Personnel during the Conflicts in Iraq and Afghanistan." Working Paper 2014-08, December 17, 2014. Congressional Budget Office. https://www.cbo.gov/publication/49837.
Guriev, Sergei, and Andrei Rachinsky. "The Role of Oligarchs in Russian Capitalism." *Journal of Economic Perspectives* 19, no. 1 (2005): 131–50.
Haass, Richard N. *War of Necessity, War of Choice: A Memoir of Two Iraq Wars*. New York: Simon and Schuster, 2009.
Hahn, Peter. "A Century of U.S. Relations with Iraq." Origins: Current Events in Historical Perspective, April 2012. Ohio State University. https://origins.osu.edu/article/century-us-relations-iraq?language_content_entity=en.
Herder, Johann Gottfried. *JG Herder on Social and Political Culture*. Cambridge: Cambridge University Press, 1969.
Hobsbawm, Eric, and Terence Ranger, eds. *The Invention of Tradition*. Cambridge: Cambridge University Press, 2012.
Hodgson, Godfrey. *The Myth of American Exceptionalism*. New Haven, CT: Yale University Press, 2009.
Hofmann, Reto. *The Fascist Effect: Japan and Italy, 1915–1952*. Ithaca, NY: Cornell University Press, 2015.
International Atomic Energy Agency. "Fact Sheet on DPRK Nuclear Safeguards." Accessed March 28, 2022. https://www.iaea.org/newscenter/focus/dprk/fact-sheet-on-dprk-nuclear-safeguards.
Iraqi Breach of International Obligations. Joint Resolution. 105th Congress. Public Law 105–235—Aug. 14, 1998.
Jae-in, Moon, and Kim Jong Un. "Pyongyang Joint Declaration of September 2018." National Committee on North Korea, September 19, 2018. https://www.ncnk.org/node/1633.
Kaempfer, William H., and Anton D. Lowenberg. "The Political Economy of Economic Sanction." *Handbook of Defense Economics* 2 (2007): 867–911.
Kaldor, Mary. *New and Old Wars: Organised Violence in a Global Era*. Newark, NJ: Wiley, 2013.
Karklis, Laris, and Erin Cunningham. "Three Maps That Explain Russia's Annexations and Losses in Ukraine." *Washington Post*, September 30, 2022. https://www.washingtonpost.com/world/2022/09/30/map-ukraine-regions-annexation-russia.
Kean, Thomas, and Lee Hamilton. *The 9/11 Commission Report: Final Report of the National Commission on Terrorist Attacks upon the United States*. Washington, DC: Government Printing Office, 2004.
Kedourie, Elie. *Nationalism*. New York: Wiley-Blackwell, 1993.
Kjeldgaard, Dannie, and Søren Askegaard. "The Glocalization of Youth Culture: The Global Youth Segment as Structures of Common Difference." *Journal of Consumer Research* 33, no. 2 (2006): 231–47.

Köhler, Bettina, and Markus Wissen. "Glocalizing Protest: Urban Conflicts and the Global Social Movements." *International Journal of Urban and Regional Research* 27, no. 4 (2003): 942–51.

Kohn, Hans, and Wallace Sokolsky. *African Nationalism in the Twentieth Century.* Vol. 79. Princeton, NJ: Van Nostrand, 1965.

Korea News Service. "DPRK Foreign Ministry Vehemently Refutes UNSC's 'Presidential Statement.'" April 14, 2009. Available on Internet Archive: Wayback Machine. https://web.archive.org/web/20120910123631/http://www.kcna.co.jp/item/2009/200904/news14/20090414-23ee.html.

Korean War Armistice Agreement, July 27, 1953. Treaties and Other International Agreements Series 2782. General Records of the United States Government, Record Group 11, National Archives. Accessed March 28, 2022. https://www.archives.gov/milestone-documents/armistice-agreement-restoration-south-korean-state.

Kuzio, Taras. *Ukraine: Democratization, Corruption, and the New Russian Imperialism: Democratization, Corruption, and the New Russian Imperialism.* Santa Barbara, CA: ABC-CLIO, 2015.

Lee, Jesse. "President Obama's Address on the End of the Combat Mission in Iraq." White House: President Barack Obama, blog, August 31, 2010. National Archives and Records Administration. https://obamawhitehouse.archives.gov/blog/2010/08/31/president-obamas-address-end-combat-mission-iraq.

Lederman, Josh, and Hans Nichols. "Trump Meets Kim Jong Un, Becomes First Sitting U.S. President to Step into North Korea." NBC News, June 30, 2019. https://www.nbcnews.com/politics/donald-trump/trump-kim-jong-un-meet-dmz-n1025041.

Leffler, Melvyn. "The American Conception of National Security and the Beginnings of the Cold War, 1945–48." *American Historical Review* 89, no. 2 (1984): 346–81.

Lock, Samantha. "How Many U.S. Soldiers Died in Afghanistan?" Newsweek, August 16, 2021. https://www.newsweek.com/number-us-soldiers-who-died-afghanistan-war-1619685.

Luleva, Ana. "The Concept of Totalitarianism in the Bulgarian Public Discourses." *Balkanistic Forum* 2 (2020): 231–42.

Makinda, Samuel M. "Sovereignty and Global Security." *Security Dialogue* 29, no. 3 (1998): 281–92.

Mamdani, Mahmood. *Citizen and Subject: Contemporary Africa and the Legacy of Late Colonialism.* Princeton, NJ: Princeton University Press, 2018.

Mann, Michael. *Fascists.* Cambridge: Cambridge University Press, 2004.

Marfo, Samuel, Halidu Musah, and Dominic DeGraft Arthur. "Beyond Classical Peace Paradigm: A Theoretical Argument for a Glocalized Peace and Security." *African Journal of Political Science and International Relations* 10, no. 4 (2016): 47–55.

Mathews, Jessica Tuchman. "Redefining Security." *Foreign Affairs* 68, no. 2 (1989): 162–77.

Maynes, Charles. "4 Things Russia Wants Right Now." NPR, January 24, 2022. https://www.npr.org/2022/01/12/1072413634/russia-nato-ukraine.

McCarthy, Niall. "Poll: Most Americans Support Sanctions to Halt North Korea's Nuclear Program [Infographic]." Forbes, August 8, 2017. https://www.forbes.com/sites/niallmccarthy/2017/08/08/poll-most-americans-support-sanctions-to-halt-north-koreas-nuclear-program-infographic/?sh=59eb2fd35986.

Ministry of Foreign Affairs of the Russian Federation. "Agreement on Measures to Ensure the Security of the Russian Federation and Member States of the North Atlantic Treaty Organization." December 17, 2021. https://mid.ru/ru/foreign_policy/rso/nato/1790803/?lang=en.

MissileThreat: Missile Defense Project. "Taepodong-1." Center for Strategic and International Studies. Last updated April 23, 2024. https://missilethreat.csis.org/missile/taepodong-1.

Monten, Jonathan. "The Roots of the Bush Doctrine: Power, Nationalism, and Democracy Promotion in US Strategy." *International Security* 29, no. 4 (2005): 112–56.

NATO. "Brussels Summit Communiqué." Newsroom. Issued June 14, 2021. Last updated July 1, 2022. https://www.nato.int/cps/en/natohq/news_185000.htm?selectedLocale=en.
———. "NATO Enlargement & Open Door." NATO Fact Sheet, July 2016. https://www.nato.int/nato_static_fl2014/assets/pdf/pdf_2016_07/20160627_1607-factsheet-enlargement-eng.pdf.
———. "NATO-Russia Relations." NATO Fact Sheet, February 2022. https://www.nato.int/nato_static_fl2014/assets/pdf/2022/2/pdf/220214-factsheet_NATO-Russia_Relations_e.pdf.
———. "Relations with Ukraine." What We Do. Last updated July 19, 2024. https://www.nato.int/cps/en/natohq/topics_37750.htm.
Neumann, Franz Leopold. *Behemoth: The Structure and Practice of National Socialism, 1933–1944*. Lanham, MD: Rowman and Littlefield, 2009.
Northam, Jackie. "NATO Is Threatening Russia with Sanctions to Protect Ukraine, but Do Sanctions Work?" Weekend Edition Saturday, January 22, 2022. NPR. https://www.npr.org/2022/01/22/1075049567/nato-is-threatening-russia-with-sanctions-to-protect-ukraine-but-do-sanctions-wo.
Nuclear Threat Initiative. "Joint Declaration of South and North Korea on the Denuclearization of the Korean Peninsula." Signed January 20, 1992. Entered into force February 19, 1992. https://www.nti.org/education-center/treaties-and-regimes/joint-declaration-south-and-north-korea-denuclearization-korean-peninsula.
Office of Foreign Assets Control. "North Korea Sanctions." US Department of the Treasury. Accessed August 26, 2024. https://ofac.treasury.gov/sanctions-programs-and-country-information/north-korea-sanctions.
———. "Ukraine-/Russia-Related Sanctions." US Department of the Treasury. Accessed August 26, 2024. https://home.treasury.gov/policy-issues/financial-sanctions/sanctions-programs-and-country-information/ukraine-russia-related-sanctions.
———. "Ukraine/Russia-Related Sanctions Program." US Department of the Treasury, June 16, 2016. https://ofac.treasury.gov/media/8741/download?inline.
O'Leary, Cecilia Elizabeth. *To Die For: The Paradox of American Patriotism*. Princeton, NJ: Princeton University Press, 2000.
Pallaro, Bianca, and Alicia Parlapiano. "Four Ways to Understand the $54 Billion in U.S. Spending on Ukraine." *New York Times*, May 20, 2022. https://www.nytimes.com/interactive/2022/05/20/upshot/ukraine-us-aid-size.html.
Pear, Robert. "Arming Afghan Guerrillas: A Huge Effort Led by U.S." *New York Times*, April 18, 1988. https://www.nytimes.com/1988/04/18/world/arming-afghan-guerrillas-a-huge-effort-led-by-us.html.
Pew Research Center, "Reviewing the Bush Years and the Public's Final Verdict Bush and Public Opinion." December 18, 2008. https://www.pewresearch.org/politics/2008/12/18/bush-and-public-opinion.
Pfiffner, James P. "US Blunders in Iraq: De-Baathification and Disbanding the Army." *Intelligence and National Security* 25, no. 1 (February 2010): 76–85. http://pfiffner.gmu.edu/files/pdfs/Articles/CPA%20Orders%2C%20Iraq%20PDF.pdf.
Plokhy, Serhii. *Ukraine and Russia: Representations of the Past*. Toronto: University of Toronto Press, 2008.
Plous, Scott. "Perceptual Illusions and Military Realities: The Nuclear Arms Race." *Journal of Conflict Resolution* 29, no. 3 (1985): 363–89.
Poushter, Jacob, and Aidan Connaughton. "Zelenskyy Inspires Widespread Confidence from U.S. Public as Views of Putin Hit New Low." Pew Research Center, March 30, 2022. https://www.pewresearch.org/short-reads/2022/03/30/zelenskyy-inspires-widespread-confidence-from-u-s-public-as-views-of-putin-hit-new-low/.
Pynn, Geoff. "Pragmatic Contextualism." *Metaphilosophy* 46, no. 1 (2015): 26–51.
Radford, Antoinette. "Volodymyr Zelensky Is *Time* Magazine's 2022 Person of the Year." BBC News, December 7, 2022. https://www.bbc.com/news/world-63890775.

Reinhart, RJ. "Ukrainians Support Fighting until Victory." Gallup, October 18, 2022. https://news.gallup.com/poll/403133/ukrainians-support-fighting-until-victory.aspx.

Reuters. "Russia's Federation Council Ratifies Annexation of Four Ukrainian Regions." October 4, 2022, https://www.reuters.com/world/europe/russias-federation-council-ratifies-annexation-four-ukrainian-regions-2022-10-04.

Robertson, Roland. "Glocalization: Time-Space and Homogeneity-Heterogeneity." *Global Modernities* 2, no. 1 (1995): 25–44.

Roshwald, Aviel. *Ethnic Nationalism and the Fall of Empires: Central Europe, the Middle East and Russia, 1914–23.* New York: Routledge, 2002.

Sachs, Jeffrey. "The West's Dangerously Simple-Minded Narrative about Russia and China." Common Dreams, August 23, 2022. https://www.commondreams.org/views/2022/08/23/wests-dangerously-simple-minded-narrative-about-russia-and-china.

Said, Edward. *Orientalism: Western Concepts of the Orient.* New York: Pantheon, 1978.

Sakwa, Richard. "Greater Russia: Is Moscow Out to Subvert the West?" *International Politics* 58, no. 3 (2021): 334–62.

Sang-Hun, Choe. "North Korea Frees American Prisoners, Lifting Hurdle to Nuclear Talks." *New York Times*, May 9, 2018. https://www.nytimes.com/2018/05/09/world/asia/north-korea-americans-detainees-released.html.

Sassen, Saskia. *The Global City: New York, London, Tokyo.* Princeton, NJ: Princeton University Press, 2013.

Selden, Mark. "Economic Nationalism and Regionalism in Contemporary East Asia." In *Globalization and Economic Nationalism in Asia*, edited by Anthony P. D'Costa, 33–58. Oxford: Oxford University Press, 2012.

Shea, Jamie. "NATO Withdraws from Afghanistan: Short-Term and Long-Term Consequences for the Western Alliance." Friends of Europe, September 3, 2021. https://www.friendsofeurope.org/insights/nato-withdraws-from-afghanistan-short-term-and-long-term-consequences-for-the-western-alliance/.

Shortridge, Anna. "The U.S. War in Afghanistan Twenty Years On: Public Opinion Then and Now." *Water's Edge* (blog), October 7, 2021. Council on Foreign Relations. https://www.cfr.org/blog/us-war-afghanistan-twenty-years-public-opinion-then-and-now.

Singh, Singh, and Udai Bhanu. "Major Powers and the Security of Southeast Asia." *Strategic Analysis* 24, no. 2 (2000): 315–42.

Smeltz, Dina, Craig Kafura, and Emily Sullivan. "Growing US Divide on How Long to Support Ukraine." Chicago Council on Foreign Affairs, December 5, 2022. https://globalaffairs.org/research/public-opinion-survey/growing-us-divide-how-long-support-ukraine?utm_source=media&utm_campaign=rpt&utm_medium=email&utm_term=fall-Ukraine-data.

Sullivan, Becky. "How NATO's Expansion Helped Drive Putin to Invade Ukraine." NPR, February 24, 2022. https://www.npr.org/2022/01/29/1076193616/ukraine-russia-nato-explainer.

Szalontai, Balazs, and Sergey Radchenko. "North Korea's Efforts to Acquire Nuclear Technology and Nuclear Weapons: Evidence from Russian and Hungarian Archives." Cold War International History Project Working Paper no. 53, August 2006. Woodrow Wilson International Center for Scholars. https://www.wilsoncenter.org/sites/default/files/media/documents/publication/WP53_web_final1.pdf.

Taylor, Adam. "The Full Text of North and South Korea's Agreement, Annotated." *Washington Post*, April 27, 2018. https://www.washingtonpost.com/news/worldviews/wp/2018/04/27/the-panmmunjom-declaration-full-text-of-agreement-between-north-korea-and-south-korea.

Thompson, Kenneth, and Hans Morgenthau. *Politics among Nations: The Struggle for Power and Peace.* New York: Alfred A. Knopf, 1985.

Tilly, Charles, and Gabriel Ardant. *The Formation of National States in Western Europe.* Princeton, NJ: Princeton University Press, 1975.

Tocqueville, Alexis de. *Democracy in America*. New York: Penguin, 1956.
Trotta, Daniel. "Iraq War Costs U.S. More Than $2 Trillion: Study." Reuters, March 14, 2013. https://www.reuters.com/article/us-iraq-war-anniversary/iraq-war-costs-u-s-more-than-2-trillion-study-idUSBRE92D0PG20130314.
Trubowitz, Peter. *Defining the National Interest: Conflict and Change in American Foreign Policy*. Chicago: University of Chicago Press, 1998.
Tuminez, Astrid S. *Russian Nationalism since 1856: Ideology and the Making of Foreign Policy*. Lanham, MD: Rowman and Littlefield, 2000.
UN General Assembly. Forty-seventh session. General and Complete Disarmament: Conventional disarmament on a regional scale Report of the Secretary-General (A/47/316) July 28, 1992. https://documents.un.org/doc/undoc/gen/n92/346/05/pdf/n9234605.pdf.
US Department of Defense. "Immediate Casualty Status." November 7, 2022. https://www.defense.gov/casualty.pdf.
US Mission to International Organizations in Geneva. "Fact Sheet: DPRK Resolution 2270." March 3, 2016. https://geneva.usmission.gov/2016/03/03/fact-sheet-dprk-resolution-2270/#:~:text=The%20UN%20Security%20Council%20unanimously%20adopted%20Resolution%202270,using%20ballistic%20missile%20technology%2C%20on%20February%207%2C%202016.
US Senate. "Operation Enduring Freedom." S. Hrg. 107-801. 107th Cong., 2nd sess. Washington DC: US Government Printing Office, 2002. https://www.govinfo.gov/content/pkg/CHRG-107shrg83471/html/CHRG-107shrg83471.htm.
US Senate. S.J. Res. 23. Roll call vote, 107th Cong., 1st sess. https://www.senate.gov/legislative/LIS/roll_call_votes/vote1071/vote_107_1_00281.htm.
US Senate. "Tora Bora Revisited: How We Failed to Get bin Laden and Why It Matters Today." S. Prt. 111-35. 111th Cong., 1st sess. Washington, DC: US Government Publishing Office, 2009. https://www.govinfo.gov/content/pkg/CPRT-111SPRT53709/html/CPRT-111SPRT53709.htm.
Waldstreicher, David. *In the Midst of Perpetual Fetes: The Making of American Nationalism, 1776–1820*. Chapel Hill: University of North Carolina Press, 2012.
Wallerstein, Immanuel. *The Capitalist World-Economy*. Cambridge: Cambridge University Press, 1979.
——. *The Politics of the World-Economy: The States, the Movements and the Civilizations*. Cambridge: Cambridge University Press, 1984.
Waltz, Kenneth N. *Theory of International Politics*. Long Grove, IL: Waveland Press, 2010.
Washington Post. "Full Text: N. Korea's Statement on Its Nuclear Program." February 10, 2005. https://www.washingtonpost.com/wp-dyn/articles/A13987-2005Feb10.html.
Weldes, Jutta. "Constructing National Interests." *European Journal of International Relations* 2, no. 3 (1996): 275–318.
Wire, Sarah D. "Road to Vindication for California's Barbara Lee, the Only Member of Congress to Vote against Afghanistan War." *Los Angeles Times*, August 20, 2021. https://www.latimes.com/politics/story/2021-08-20/road-to-vindication-for-barbara-lee-the-only-member-of-congress-to-vote-against-afghanistan-war.
Wu, Anne. "What China Whispers to North Korea." *Washington Quarterly* 28, no. 2 (2005): 35–48.
Znaniecki, Florian. *Modern Nationalities: A Sociological Study*. Westport, CT: Greenwood Press, 1973.

ABU BAKARR BAH is Presidential Research Professor of Sociology and Chair of the Department of Sociology at Northern Illinois University. He is Editor in Chief of *African Conflict & Peacebuilding Review*, African Editor for *Critical Sociology*, and Founding Director of the Institute for Research and Policy Integration in Africa (IRPIA). His works include *International Statebuilding in West Africa* (with Nikolas Emmanuel, Bloomington: Indiana University Press, 2024), *African Security* (Athens: Ohio University Press, 2024), *Post-Conflict Institutional Design* (London: Zed Books, 2020), *International Security and Peacebuilding* (Bloomington: Indiana University Press, 2017), and *Breakdown and Reconstitution* (Lanham, MD: Lexington Books, 2005). His articles have been published in top journals such as *African Affairs; Administrative Theory & Praxis; Critical Sociology; Journal of International Peacekeeping; International Journal of Politics, Culture, and Society;* and *Africa Today.* Bah has been an invited speaker at major institutions such as Stanford University, the University of Illinois at Urbana Champaign, the University of South Florida, Virginia Commonwealth University, the Global Center for Pluralism (Canada), the Social Science Research Council (New York), the US State Department, ETH (Switzerland), the University of Nairobi (Kenya), Laikipia University (Kenya), Renmin University (China), and Sant'Anna School of Advanced Studies (Italy).

3

THE TALIBAN'S RETURN, TERRORISM, AND REGIONAL SECURITY POLICY CONVERGENCE ON AFGHANISTAN

Haqmal Daudzai and Farooq Yousaf

INTRODUCTION

Since the US-led coalition's withdrawal from Afghanistan and the Taliban's subsequent takeover in August 2021, the regional security landscape in South and central Asia has been constantly evolving.[1] Regional stakeholders like Pakistan, China, Russia, Iran, and India are looking toward the Taliban (a group formerly designated a terrorist outfit) to fill the security gaps that arise from local and transnational terrorist groups like the Tehrik e Taliban Pakistan (TTP), the Islamic State–Khorasan (ISKP), the East Turkestan Islamic Movement (ETIM), and al-Qaeda. The changing landscape indicates a lack of trust in the Western bloc's security alliances—such as NATO—in the Global South while also underscoring the creation of "eastward" partnerships and security alliances, as witnessed with China and Russia's support for the US-Taliban Doha "Peace" Deal in February 2020. With the Taliban back in power, Afghanistan's neighbors and regional powers have expressed concerns over the presence of local and transnational terrorist groups in the country, posing the threat that violence might spill over into the region. Even Russia, which may traditionally be considered a foe of the Taliban due to the mujahideen's (holy warriors) role in the Soviet Union's defeat in Afghanistan, has taken the front seat in engaging with the Taliban as Moscow fears any potential instability could negatively impact Russian security along the border with central Asia. Against this backdrop, this chapter, incorporating regional security complex theory (RSCT), highlights how regional states, with different motivations and foreign policies, have, in some form, united over the potential threat of terrorism emanating from Afghanistan. The theoretical perspective also takes inspiration from Robertson's theorization of glocalization,[2] where militant groups and security risks can be understood to act and think locally as well as globally.[3] In doing so, the chapter argues that incorporating a glocalized security prism becomes important for Western interventions (often enshrined in the political objectives of the intervening powers). As seen in Afghanistan's case, the failure to incorporate a glocalized security prism resulted in failed interventions; as posited by the glocalized security theory, the inability to properly address local and domestic grievances makes establishing sustainable (or positive) peace impossible.

RSCT is a theoretical perspective developed by Barry Buzan, Ole Wæver, and Jaap de Wilde in their book *Security: A New Framework for Analysis*. "Security complexes" are security features of interstate systems and comprise states "whose major security perceptions and concerns are so interlinked that their national security problems cannot reasonably be analyzed or resolved apart from one another."[4] Therefore, the theoretical perspective also fits well with the glocalization focus of this edited volume, as we observe and discuss in detail throughout this chapter how Afghanistan's domestic security issues and concerns impact the securitization and desecuritization thinking of major regional powers. Even before the US withdrawal from Afghanistan in August 2021, scholars had argued that the security situation within Afghanistan impacts the security thinking of major regional powers, particularly Russia and China, in how political transformation in Afghanistan took place.[5] The RSCT also argues that "security dynamics have a strong territoriality, and on this basis, it can accommodate non-state actors without too much difficulty," which indicates why regional actors and their governments were willing to engage with the Taliban (a nonstate actor) before their takeover.[6] Similarly, in contemporary conflicts, regional security complexes take an important role as a lack of understanding of such complexes and the interplay of proxy warfare ultimately led to the failure of the United States in Vietnam and Afghanistan and the Soviet Union in Afghanistan.[7] Therefore, the security situation in Afghanistan can be better explained through the lens of RSCT and glocalization, as various neighboring and regional states have escalated their efforts to engage with the de facto regime to protect their security interests.

In terms of structure, in its second section, the chapter briefly discusses the pre-and post-2001 situation in Afghanistan, discussing how since the 1970s, Afghanistan has witnessed protracted conflict imposed on it by external forces and states. Following this discussion, the chapter briefly discusses the terrorism landscape in the third section of the chapter concerning the presence of local and transnational terrorist groups including the TTP, ETIM, al-Qaeda, and the Islamic State. In its fourth section, and incorporating the RSCT and glocalization, the chapter argues how major neighboring and regional states—including Pakistan, China, Russia, Iran, and India—are formulating their security policies vis-à-vis Afghanistan, keeping an eye on the potential threat of terrorism emanating from the country. In its final section, the chapter, while concluding the overall discussion, paints a picture of regional security in South Asia with the Taliban's takeover of Afghanistan. Due to the nature and scope of the topic, and the presence of a plethora of literature on pre-2001 Afghanistan, the discussion in this chapter predominantly focuses on the post-2001 situation. Moreover, even though some states have initiated economic engagement with the de facto regime, the discussion in this chapter predominantly revolves around the security landscape of both Afghanistan and the region. In doing so, the chapter seeks to address the major questions this volume attempts to answer, the most important of which is *How does the fusion of domestic issues and interests with external ones undermine international security?* More specifically in our case, we aim to understand how the fusion of domestic security fault lines and regional security interests contributed to the US coalition failure in Afghanistan and how this failure impacted domestic, regional, and international security.

ISLAM, STATE, AND FOREIGN INVASIONS IN AFGHANISTAN

Islam has remained the dominant religion, culture, political ideology, and state legitimacy throughout modern Afghan history. In Afghanistan, with local traditional customs, particularly with the Pashtun cultural code of Pashtunwali (literally translated as the "way of the Pashtuns"), Islam comes second only to local customs when dealing with matters concerning daily life. According to Olivier Roy, historically the Islamic religion has evolved from traditional fundamentalism in the eighteenth and nineteenth centuries to the political Islam of jihadism in the mid-twentieth century and what he also calls the popular religions in the Afghan political context.[8] The emergence of first the mujahideen and then the Taliban in the late twentieth century was the rebirth of the traditional fundamentalism of the Afghan ulema (religious scholars).[9] The traditional Afghan ulema are predominantly followers of the Deobandi school of Islam, who until the mid-nineteenth century, regularly traveled to the Indian subcontinent to gain Islamic education in Deoband Madrasa,[10] with some of those in northern Afghanistan attending the Diwan Begi Madrasa in Bukhara.[11]

Following the partition of India and the creation of Pakistan in 1947, Peshawar—the capital of North-West Frontier Province and the home of various chains of madrassas (religious seminaries), including the Deobandi school of Islam—became the center for Islamic education for the Afghan ulema.[12] The creation of Deoband aimed at consolidating the fundamental teaching of Islam through the strict interpretation of the holy book, Quran, and the sayings and tradition (hadith) of Prophet Mohammad for the sake of the fate of the Muslim *ummah* (community) in British India.[13] Upon the completion of their studies at Deoband, the Afghan ulema were to open their local "private" madrassas throughout the country, particularly in the rural regions of Afghanistan. Hence, the opening of madrassas provided both the legalistic and mystic religious elites with a significant legitimacy and influence on their communities and, in some instances, a role superior even to that of the tribal elders in matters concerning the state and society. Although the Afghan ulema did not form their political parties until the 1960s, they have long played an active legitimacy role in Afghan politics. For example, Abdul Rahman Khan (1880–1901) urged the Afghan ulema to preach jihad against the British infidels and proclaimed himself emir (commander or leader in the religious context). Likewise, the overthrow of King Amanullah by Habibullah Bach-e-Saqau in 1929 was directly supported by the traditional Afghan ulema (both the legalistic and mystics) in accordance with their tribal alliances.[14] When Bach-e-Saqau took over Kabul, "he was crowned king with the title of Habibullah" (friend or beloved of God) by the *pir* of Tagab and in return, he exclusively served the religious elites with whatever means and treasury he had at his disposal.[15]

During the Cold War, when the Soviet communist regime invaded Afghanistan, a majority of the Afghan ulema fled to neighboring Pakistan and Iran, where they established several mujahideen resistance movements.[16] Nevertheless, some of the leading members of the mujahideen were inspired by the political Islam of the Muslim Brotherhood in Cairo and also by the teachings of Indian subcontinent–based Sayyid Abul Ala Maududi. Maududi's ideology starkly confronted nationalism, capitalism, and socialism and sought a Pan-Islamism, but he also distanced his teachings from traditional Islam by redefining the relation of faith to state and society.[17] This was also the reason why thousands of soldiers within the Muslim world joined the Afghan Jihad against the Soviet invasion, among them Osama bin Laden of al-Qaeda. The Maududi Jamiat-e-Islami (JI) political party was among the main fundraisers and recruiters in helping the Afghan mujahideen at local madrassas in Khyber Pakhtunkhwa and Balochistan Provinces of Pakistan. The US Central Intelligence Agency (CIA) and Saudis assigned the Pakistani Inter-Services Intelligence (ISI) to fund the Sunni madrassas in Pakistan, whereas the Islamic regime of Khomeini in Iran, as the major neighbor to the west of Afghanistan, funded the Shi'a Afghans to fight the Russian Red Army and its "puppet" regime on the frontline.[18]

Following the failed attempt of the political Islam of the mujahideen in building an Islamic state in Kabul, subsequent warlordism facilitated the rebirth of traditional fundamental Islam under the name of the Taliban, yet this time in its extreme form. Although the exact root of the Taliban's fundamental extremism remains unclear, nevertheless the movement's ideological thread goes back to the Pakistani-based Jamiat Ulama-e-Islam (JUI-F, meaning the Islamic Society of Ulema) of Maulana Fazul-ur-Rahman, from which the Taliban received substantial political and technical support during its time in power between 1994 and 2001.[19] Following the US invasion, most of the Taliban leaders found havens at various religious seminaries in Pakistan from where they remobilized their guerrilla warfare against US/NATO forces until their apparent victory on August 15, 2021. In the current Taliban emirate, a majority of the ministers are graduates of the JUI-F-affiliated madrassas in Pakistan. The Jamiat Ulama-e-Islam is one of the largest mainstream Islamic political parties in Pakistan. Its members follow the Deoband strict traditional school of thought, and its leaders have distinguished the party considerably from that of Maududi's moderate JI that supported the mujahideen resistance in the 1980s. The JUI-F leadership and members are predominantly graduates of the traditional madrassas, and the party receives its political support from the lower social class, while the JI leadership structure is composed of university intellectuals and is mainly backed by the middle-class Pakistanis. Moreover, although both parties follow the Hanafi jurisprudence, unlike the JI of Maududi, the JUI-F has a strict stance vis-à-vis the Shi'a Muslims, minority sects such as the Ahmadiyya and the role of women in society.

The 9/11 Attack and the US Intervention of Afghanistan

It was the Taliban Emirate's refusal in late 2001 to hand over Osama bin Laden, the al-Qaeda leader held responsible for the 9/11 attacks, that led the United States to embark on the war on terror against al-Qaeda and the Taliban in Afghanistan. Nevertheless, the exclusion of the Taliban initially from the Bonn Conference, the empowerment of warlords and military groups, and the underestimation of the regional countries and their interests in Afghanistan were some of the factors that led to the US failure in Afghanistan.[20] Today, the Taliban have returned to power stronger than they were in the late 1990s. The Taliban not only won the battlefield but also played well with their strict diplomacy at the negotiation table in Doha by not agreeing to any major guarantees demanded by the United States. In 2001, there was not only a regional and international consensus on the US invasion of Afghanistan but even countries like Iran, Tajikistan, Pakistan, and Uzbekistan provided direct and indirect military support on the ground. This consensus could be attributed to the concepts of both glocalized security concerns (from the states aiming to counter terrorism and groups like al-Qaeda) and the regional security complex, where terrorism in Afghanistan and strengthening of groups like al-Qaeda had regional and global security implications. It was due to al-Qaeda's high-profile attacks outside South Asia that there remained concerns among security experts in the West that groups like al-Qaeda were not monolithic and were instead tightly knit coalitions of "local" splinter groups in various countries, including Algeria, Nigeria, Syria, Iraq, Yemen, Somalia, Afghanistan, and Pakistan.[21] Therefore, the US-led coalition's initially short-term invasion of Afghanistan gained traction and support from other states as terrorism, in a post-9/11 world, was seen as a glocalized threat. Nevertheless, as the United States showed its intention for a longer mission in the region, countries like Pakistan, Iran, Russia, and China reversed their policies by directly and indirectly supporting the Taliban. Due to the presence of several international terrorist organizations—including the ISKP, or Daesh—in Afghanistan and the conflict in Ukraine, the Taliban today enjoy either close economic and diplomatic ties or a working relationship with regional stakeholders, particularly Russia and China.

The unconditional withdrawal of the coalition forces from Afghanistan left a regional power vacuum for the United States' archrivals Russia, China, and Iran to fill. Even before the US intervention, Afghanistan was prone to regional powers' proxy wars and interests and still is today. Dependent on foreign aid even for its basic needs, the country has never managed to gain its long-dreamed-of sovereign and modern statehood. Among other influences, Islam and strict traditional local customs have played a fundamental role in shaping the Afghan political ideology for statehood throughout Afghanistan's modern history. Any state modernization attempts that presumably contradicted the local cultural and religious norms have been met with bitter resistance that resulted in overthrowing Afghan rulers (Amanullah Khan 1923) and regimes (Communists PDPA 1977–91). Moreover, Islam was the driving force behind the bitter withdrawal of invaders from Afghan soil, including in three Afghan-Anglo wars during the mid-nineteenth and early twentieth centuries, the Soviet Union invasion between 1979 and 1989, and the US/NATO occupation between 2001 and 2021. However, the same driving force has created a dilemma for the country, inviting religious fundamentalist terrorist groups to seek refuge and establish their bases in Afghanistan. This process, especially in the case of al-Qaeda in the initial years after 9/11, resulted in the glocalization of al-Qaeda and its brand name, with local terrorist groups pledging allegiance to both al-Qaeda and its leader Osama bin Laden. As a result, the fusion of global and local jihadism coupled with the overlapping of different alliances between terrorists and criminals in a so-called ungovernable Afghanistan created more complications for counterterrorism experts and efforts.[22] However, a cursory analysis of the reasons behind the Taliban's return to power also warrants some attention.

The Return of Taliban to Kabul 2.0 (2001–Present)

Multiple factors led to the return of the Taliban back to power in Kabul. Among other powers, the United States, instead of making peace between the main conflicting parties—namely, the Taliban and the Northern Alliances (the frontline enemy of the Taliban in the North)—directly engaged in the state-building process in Afghanistan resulting from the Bonn Conference in late 2001. Additionally, the United States armed and financed the Northern Alliance's warlords to act against the Taliban on the ground. Stakeholders, especially those supporting the Taliban, who showed interest in peace talks were either arrested or brought to Guantanamo Bay—the United States military detention camp in Cuba. At that time, the George W. Bush administration was in the euphoria of winning the Afghan war and purposely excluded the Taliban from the peace talks. This overconfidence from Washington also played a major role in underestimating the return of the Taliban to the battlefield. Moreover, a legitimate government in Afghanistan required ethnically broad representation, which the Bonn Conference failed to fulfill. Instead, political power was distributed between the predominantly non-Pashtun warlord mujahideen and a few exiled Pashtun elites who had little support from the masses in Afghanistan.[23] Finally, the United States' initial aim was to hunt down al-Qaeda leader Osama bin Laden, not the Taliban regime. Eleven years later, Osama bin Laden was killed in Abbottabad, Pakistan, whereas Pakistan was then a major non-NATO ally in the war on terror in Afghanistan. When the Taliban regime collapsed, many of its fighters surrendered to the Uzbek militias of General Abdul Rashid Dostum of the Northern Alliance; however, these fighters were either arrested or allegedly killed.[24] Irish filmmaker Jamie Doran collected the video footage of the atrocities in a documentary entitled *Afghan Massacre: Convoy of Death* in which it was revealed that around three thousand Taliban prisoners were suffocated or shot dead in shipping containers by General Dostum's militiamen in 2001.[25] However, as Dostum was allegedly on the US government's payroll, it became difficult to try him for his human rights violations.[26]

Other than the aforementioned rights violations, the collateral damage resulting from the US and NATO combat forces significantly helped the Taliban win back local Afghan support in the early days of the occupation, especially in the rural and remote centers.[27] The US forces' night raids and air strikes aimed at capturing and killing the al-Qaeda and Taliban leaders also resulted in massive civilian causalities. Home searches by armed male US soldiers in a traditional Afghan society—particularly in southern Pashtun communities, where female family members are perceived as the *nang* or *namus* (pride) of family and clan, and where even their appearance in the presence of male strangers is forbidden—resulted in anti-American and pro-Taliban sentiments among the local population.[28] Often local civilians were detained and mistreated by the coalition forces on suspicion of their affiliation with the Taliban or al-Qaeda. A 2004 Human Rights Watch report notes, "It appears that faulty and inadequate intelligence has resulted in targeting civilians who had not taken part in the hostilities, in unnecessary civilian deaths and inquiry during arrest operations, and in the needless destruction of civilian homes and property."[29] As a result, the US and coalition's refusal to negotiate an amnesty forced the Taliban fighters to seek refuge in neighboring Pakistan.[30] The Pakistani military and its intelligence agency (i.e., ISI) allegedly evacuated a large number of leading Taliban commanders from the Kunduz and Kandahar Provinces to safety in Pakistan. For Pakistan—which played the role of both friend and foe in the US war on terror—the Taliban remained a strategic proxy against archrival India and its expansion in Afghanistan. Moreover, the United States' extended war in Afghanistan also meant extended financial and military support to Pakistan while it remained a non-NATO major ally.

By mid-2002, soon after resettling in Pakistan, Taliban leaders began reorganizing their remaining fighters to wage another *Jihad* against the US occupation and the puppet Afghan government.[31] The Pakistani Islamic political parties generously helped the Afghan Taliban in fundraising and recruiting new fighters.[32] In the spring of 2003, the Taliban launched their first assault by assassinating an international aid worker in Kandahar and by mid-2004 killing dozens of Afghans and foreign military and aid personnel and seizing areas in Zabul and Helmand provinces. By early 2009, the Taliban's guerrilla warfare, suicide bombings, and kidnappings had destabilized over 60 percent of the Afghan territory.[33] Nearly one year after the International Security Assistance Force mission termination and the withdrawal of the US combat forces, on September 28, 2015, the Taliban managed to seize the northern Kunduz Province capital and kept control of it for about two weeks.[34] It was their first major success since their removal from power in

2001. Notwithstanding their limited personnel and military equipment, the Taliban's success lay in their ideological war of fighting "the occupation" and the "infidels" and "defending Islam," coupled with wider local support in rural and remote parts of the country. Thus, the international troops' presence in Afghanistan significantly undermined the ideological aspect of the global war on terror among the poorly educated Afghan army, which often came under more major attacks from the Taliban. Similarly, the widespread corruption within the Afghan government and security forces was another factor that strengthened the support for the Taliban.[35]

The lack of a clear peace strategy vis-à-vis the Taliban was another major flaw in which the United States/NATO lost on the diplomatic front. Since the first initiation of the peace talk with the Taliban by the Obama administration in 2009, the United States had loosened the thread of its conditions and redlines for the Taliban. The unconditional withdrawal of the coalition forces also led the regional countries, including Pakistan, China, Russia, Iran, and Turkey, to intensify their tacit support for the Taliban, hedging their bets on the group to counter the threat of the Islamic State in the region. However, the Taliban are not a united group as they were in the late 1990s. The power in the present emirate is unevenly divided into three major groups. There is a Doha group that consists of members who are moderate Muslim and Afghan nationalists. Then there is the Haqqani group, allegedly backed by the Pakistani military establishment and more pragmatic in its politics. And lastly, there is the Quetta group, led by Hebatullah Akhunzada, the Taliban current supreme leader, a traditional Islamist with an extreme ideology. All three groups have different understandings, interpretations, and practices of the Sharia government under the area of their control. However, at the time of writing this chapter, Hebatullah's group holds the ultimate decision-making power. Due to this divide, we can predict that even though the external conflict in Afghanistan has ceased, the internal conflict will remain in the coming years. The internal conflict also means that until the de facto regime becomes a unified front, with mass public support, the security fault lines will remain visible in the country, forcing regional and neighboring states to engage with the regime to counter terrorist threats emanating from the country. Finally, the diverging nature of the Taliban's splinters and the different regional affiliations of top leadership indicate why the security threats in Afghanistan under the de facto Taliban regime are glocal in nature and require a holistic approach to counter such threats. Therefore, it is also important to briefly analyze the threat of current terrorism, post–US withdrawal, in Afghanistan and how this threat impacts Afghanistan locally and regional stakeholders globally.

Understandably, since the Taliban's takeover, regional states have expressed concerns over the terrorism threat emanating from Afghanistan. This is because terrorist groups, including the Afghan Taliban, have often adopted a glocalized approach (forming local alliances) to become more resilient.[36] A major contributing factor that made al-Qaeda, the Afghan Taliban (including the Haqqani Network), and the Pakistani militant groups more resilient to coalition and the Pakistani military operations and attacks was their intergroup alliances and support for each other in the Afghanistan-Pakistan region.[37] Even the recently evolved threat of the Islamic State in the region has, in some ways, benefited from local support and alliances.[38] The three major terrorist groups based in the country include TTP, ISKP, and al-Qaeda. Moreover, the Uyghur Muslim–focused ETIM also has a limited presence in the country. When it comes to Pakistan, the TTP has remained the biggest terror and security threat in the country in the past fifteen years. After successful military operations in the erstwhile Federally Administered Tribal Areas (FATA), which are located next to the Afghan border, the TTP militants and leadership fled to Afghanistan and operated from the country. With the Taliban constantly praising the TTP's role in a successful insurgency against the coalition forces in Afghanistan, Pakistan feared that the de facto regime would choose to side with the TTP over Pakistan. With the Taliban in power, Pakistan feared that the group would embolden and escalate attacks in the country. However, it was recently reported that with the mediation of the Taliban leadership, especially de facto interior minister Sirajuddin Haqqani (commonly known as Siraj), the TTP and the Pakistani military have initiated talks on a possible ceasefire from the TTP and Pakistan granting amnesty for TTP's fighters.[39] The talks are ongoing, but experts believe that with the Taliban's mediation, both sides may agree to a long-term ceasefire (further details on Pakistan, TTP, and the Taliban's nexus in regional security can be found in the next section). On August 7, 2022, it was reported that TTP's spokesperson and senior leader Omar Khalid Khorasani was killed in an improvised explosive device (IED) attack in Afghanistan. Although it is not yet clear who was behind the attack, it will likely dent the progress in the TTP-Pakistan talks as it is probable that the TTP will blame Pakistan and its intelligence agency for carrying out this attack.

When it comes to transnational groups such as al-Qaeda and ISKP, the Taliban regime has reassured the global community that it will prevent terrorist groups from committing terrorist acts in other countries. In terms of ground capacity and influence, al-Qaeda is neither as strong nor as influential as it was before 2010. The group's leader Ayman al-Zawahiri, who succeeded bin Laden after his assassination in Pakistan, remained the subject of uncorroborated news stories that claimed his death in both Pakistan and Afghanistan. However, because the Taliban defended al-Qaeda founder Osama bin Laden, many feared al-Qaeda's revival under the Taliban regime.[40] The constant defense of bin Laden and al-Qaeda also indicates a soft spot the Taliban had for both the group and its founder. Soon after the Taliban's Afghanistan takeover, al-Qaeda issued a statement congratulating the Islamic emirate (read: Taliban) for its victory in Afghanistan. An excerpt from the statement noted, "On this historic occasion, we would like to offer our congratulations to the leadership of the Islamic Emirate, specifically Hebatullah Akhundzada."[41] Ayman al-Zawahiri has also, in the past, given *bay'ah* (or pledge of allegiance) to all Taliban heads, including Mullah Omar, Mullah Akhtar Mansour, and Hebatullah Akhundzada.[42] Al-Qaeda's pledge to the Taliban also meant that the de facto regime may not go against al-Qaeda and also may allow the group to carry out some limited activity (recruitment and propaganda on social media) from Afghanistan. It is also worth mentioning that Afghanistan's de facto interior minister Siraj is still wanted by the US Federal Bureau of Investigation and has a bounty of up to $10 million on his head for his close ties with al-Qaeda.[43] Until 2022, with Siraj in charge of the country's internal security, any action against al-Qaeda seemed improbable. However, on July 30 of that year, a CIA drone unleashed two hellfire missiles in Kabul, targeting and reportedly killing Ayman al-Zawahiri. His death came almost one year after the US/NATO withdrawal from Afghanistan and the return of the Taliban. The attack raised several questions within Afghanistan on whether the Taliban provided intelligence on al-Zawahiri's location, but the de facto regime both condemned the attack and claimed ignorance of the al-Qaeda chief's presence in the country. Similarly, the attack also coincided with Pakistan's military chief increased communication with the United States, with many suspecting that the United States may have used Pakistan's intelligence and airspace for the strike. Pakistan's cooperation (if it did happen) would have come in the wake of the country's ailing economy and in return for economic support, such as the releasing of funds by the International Monetary Fund through its loan program for Pakistan. Pakistan, however, denied such collaboration with the United States on the strike.

As for the ISKP, the group remains a point of contention for the de facto regime. The Kabul airport attack on August 26, 2021, which claimed nearly two hundred lives (mostly those of Afghans), brought into perspective the seriousness of the ISKP's threat in the country. While the attack certainly created panic within Afghanistan, regional states also expressed concerns about the threat. China called on the Taliban to take stern action against the ISKP after the attack, with Zhao Lijian, deputy director of China's Foreign Office, claiming that the Taliban had assured Beijing of not allowing any forces or groups to harm China.[44] Moreover, Russia also fears that a strong ISKP would mean the spread of terrorism in Russia via central Asia, which is why Moscow opted to diplomatically engage with the Taliban even before the group's return to power in Kabul. Just like Russia, Iran also sees the ISKP as a threat and has advocated engagement with the Taliban to counter terrorist threats. On paper, even though it seems that the Taliban regime is concerned about the group and will try to act against the group when it comes to action, the practicalities of such actions are both vague and complex. In their local media talks, Taliban spokespersons have hoped that the US withdrawal from Afghanistan, which marks an end of a foreign occupation, will encourage ISKP fighters to stop conducting terrorist attacks. However, constant attacks from the ISKP suggest that the group remains the biggest security threat not only for the de facto regime but also for regional stakeholders. Also, due to the Taliban's internal ideological divisions and the presence of hard-line members, military operations against the ISKP, which also consists of Muslims, may be difficult to sell. That is why, since their takeover of Afghanistan, the Taliban have found it difficult to formulate a clear and coherent policy against the ISKP. Additionally, the presence of the Uyghur separatist group ETIM, even though on a limited scale, has generated concerns in Beijing and resulted in China's engagement with the Taliban. The Chinese government hopes that in return for diplomatic and economic support, the de facto regime will take decisive actions against the ETIM.

Regional States and Security in Afghanistan

Even though the Taliban now claim nearly absolute control over Afghanistan, attacks from both the TTP and ISKP within and outside Afghanistan indicate that security fault lines still exist in the country. Moreover, al-Zawahiri's presence and targeting in Kabul in July 2022 also suggests that a weakened al-Qaeda is still getting protection and support from the de facto Taliban regime. Hence, in order to counter these glocal security threats, regional and neighboring states, including Pakistan, China, Russia, Iran, and India, have started their security-focused engagement with the de facto regime on various defense concerns. Moreover, even though these states have occasionally announced humanitarian assistance for Afghanistan, the primary agenda, apart from India, so far is focused on security. The role of regional states has often been acknowledged by US policymakers, however, coalition forces' intensive engagement within Afghanistan meant that little was done to address external factors in Afghanistan's security. General David Petraeus, who at the time, in 2009, was serving as the commander of United States Central Command, remarked, "It's not possible to solve the challenges internal to Afghanistan without addressing the challenges, especially in terms of security, with Afghanistan's neighbours. A regional approach is required."[45] Therefore, even after the Taliban's takeover, regional states and powers such as Russia, China, Pakistan, and Iran have all called for a continuous engagement with the de facto regime for sustainable peace in Afghanistan and the region.[46] Keeping in context the importance of such a regional approach, the forthcoming discussion, therefore, focuses on these states separately and delineates their engagement vis-à-vis Afghanistan, along with arguing how, even with different orientations of Afghanistan's bilateral ties with these states, the goal of all states is ensuring durable peace and security in both the country and the region.

Pakistan

Pakistan shares a love-hate relationship with Afghanistan. Whenever a democratic/civilian government was in power in Kabul, relations remained sour as Afghan authorities blamed Pakistan for its active and tacit support for anti-Afghanistan militant groups, such as the Taliban. These allegations are grounded in Pakistan's history of supporting the anti-Soviet mujahideen (with US and Saudi support) back in the 1980s, recognizing the first Taliban regime (1996–2001), and providing sanctuaries to the Taliban and the Haqqani Network post-2001. Pakistan's agenda of supporting proxy groups in Afghanistan is enshrined in its (often inaccurate) threat perception on the border (the Durand Line), which Afghanistan has not accepted since it was demarcated by the British raj in the 1890s. Afghanistan, even today, lays claim to Pakistan's Pashtun parts in Khyber Pakhtunkhwa and Balochistan Provinces; however, Pakistan maintains the border is now an internationally accepted boundary. For many years, and even today, critics of the Taliban call the group a proxy of Pakistan. This is because soon after the US invasion of Afghanistan, the Afghan Taliban escaped into Pakistan's erstwhile FATA on the Afghan border. Even though Pakistan, under the then military dictator General Pervez Musharraf, entered an alliance with the United States on the global war on terror, the Pakistani military under Musharraf was consistently accused of playing a double game for tacitly providing active support and refuge to Afghan Taliban and Haqqani Network fighters.

These fighters, using Pakistani territory as an operational base, were waging an insurgency against the coalition forces and the Afghan National Army in Afghanistan. Therefore, it is argued that Musharraf, during this time, was taking the United States for a ride by both pretending to be on the

US side and tacitly supporting the Taliban as well.[47] As a result, today, Pakistan enjoys close relations with most, if not all, of the Taliban officials. More importantly, India has been sidelined from Afghanistan, which is also one of the major reasons for Pakistan's support of the Taliban regime. Nevertheless, the Taliban's apparent victory over the coalition forces in Afghanistan has given the TTP significant ideological and military morale to intensify their fight against the so-called un-Islamic regime in Pakistan. Since the Afghan Taliban takeover of Kabul, the TTP has increased its guerrilla warfare against Pakistani on the border areas. The TTP freely move between both countries' borders, which is why the Pakistani military establishment is putting political pressure on the Afghan Taliban to bring their friends (i.e., TTP) to the negotiating table. The Afghan Taliban are in a complicated position, mediating between a former ally and a former tacit supporter. If the TTP continue its assaults against the Pakistani establishment, it will have a significant impact on the relations with the Taliban government in Kabul, as most of the local commanders of the Afghan Taliban are also sympathizers of the TTP fighters. It was the TTP support and alleged hospitality in Pakistan that helped the Afghan Taliban win their war in Afghanistan. That is why the Taliban has played a major role in mediating talks between the TTP and the Pakistani government.

In May 2022, it was announced that both Pakistan and the TTP had agreed to a ceasefire, laying the ground for peace talks (mediated by the Afghan Taliban) between both parties.[48] Since then, multiple rounds of talks have taken place between the TTP and the Pakistani state, with the latter being represented by military officials, tribal elders, and religious leaders. However, the talks took a major blow on August 7, 2022, when it was reported that a senior leader and spokesperson, Abdul Wali also known as Omar Khalid Khorasani, of the TTP, was killed in a targeted IED attack in the Paktika Province of Afghanistan.[49] The TTP suspects that the Pakistan army may have had a role in this assassination, however, Pakistan has denied such accusations. It is also worth noting that during the talks, one of the major points of contention from the TTP was the reversal of the merger of the erstwhile FATA (tribal areas on the Afghan border) with the Khyber Pakhtunkhwa Province. Pakistan merged the FATA region, formerly governed under colonial laws as a semiautonomous region, with the Khyber Pakhtunkhwa Province in 2018 after more than fifteen years of counterterrorism and peace operations. Reversing the merger, therefore, was unacceptable for the Pakistani side, which led to an impasse in the talks. However, the peace talks and their mediation from the de facto Taliban regime suggest that engagement with both Afghanistan and the de facto regime remains important for Pakistan, especially for its all-powerful military establishment. In recent months, both Pakistan and Afghanistan, through high-level delegations, have engaged in bilateral talks, with cross-border terrorism remaining a major concern for Islamabad. Pakistan believes that the Taliban regime is not doing enough when it comes to curbing cross-border TTP attacks on Pakistan. At the time of writing, the situation on the border remains tense, with the TTP increasing its attacks on both the Pakistani security forces and civilians.

China

China's recent focus on Afghanistan stems from its security interests and the possibility that a terrorist threat emerges from the country. It was for these concerns that China remained one of the major backers of the US-Taliban peace talks, which were intended to cease conflict in Afghanistan. China feared that ETIM, a separatist group seeking the independence of Xinjiang Province and the Uyghur people from the Chinese government, would grow in power and influence if terrorism keeps escalating in Afghanistan.[50] Therefore, stability in Afghanistan is of prime importance to Chinese foreign policy, as Beijing seeks to prevent violent extremism from spreading to its western part. Historically, China has been criticized for its treatment of and human rights violations against Uyghur Muslims. Therefore, China's engagement with the Taliban (a Muslim entity) and the latter's positive reception of Beijing during the dialogue process indicate an interesting ideological paradox. During various high-level meetings, the Taliban delegates have assured China that no terrorist or militant outfits will be allowed to conduct activities against Chinese interests.[51] In one instance, in July 2021, shortly before the Taliban takeover, the then head of the Afghan Taliban Political Commission, Abdul Ghani Baradar visited China and the following statement was released: "The Afghan Taliban has the utmost sincerity to work toward and realise peace. The Afghan Taliban will never allow any force to use the Afghan territory to engage in acts detrimental to China. The Afghan Taliban believes that Afghanistan should develop friendly relations with neighbouring countries and the international community."[52]

Therefore, even when China was engaging with both the Taliban and the Ghani government, statements from Beijing suggested that it was betting on the Taliban, not the civilian government, to counter terrorist groups, mainly the ETIM and the Islamic State.[53] That is why, since the Taliban's takeover, China has maintained a positive diplomatic and economic engagement with the de facto regime. Moreover, recent meetings between Chinese and Afghan Taliban officials have also indicated that security concerns, primarily from China, have brought both countries together. As a result, the growing ties and the current isolation of the de facto Taliban regime in the global arena have provided Beijing with an opportunity to become a key stakeholder in Afghanistan. Through this role, China has joined the international community in asking the de facto regime to implement reforms, such as "forming an inclusive government with representation for all Afghan ethnicities and respect for women's rights, particularly when it comes to education and work."[54] On the bilateral and economic front, the Chinese government allowed the de facto regime to reopen the Afghan embassy in Beijing, whereas Chinese officials have also met with the Taliban representatives to discuss Chinese investments in Afghanistan.[55] However, even with the Chinese government providing economic and diplomatic assistance to Kabul, indications and statements suggest that like other regional states and powers, China's interest in Afghanistan is primarily security-focused.

Russia

During the 1990s, Russia actively supported the anti-Taliban militant Northern Alliances against the Taliban. Due to their strict Islamic ideology and support for the international jihad, the Taliban were seen as a potential supporter of the central Asian Islamic movements and Chechen separatists. Thus, Russia did not oppose the US military invasion of Afghanistan in late 2001. However, as the coalition intended to stay longer than expected, Russia was forced to shift its policy regarding the Taliban. This is because Russia sought to protect the border with Afghanistan's central Asian neighbors, namely Tajikistan, Uzbekistan, and Turkmenistan. Moscow fears that the escalation of Islamic State activity in Afghanistan can have negative repercussions, where terrorism can spread into Russia through central Asia.[56] Just like China, the Taliban have also given certain assurances to Moscow. During a Taliban delegation's visit to Moscow in July 2021, Russia's envoy Zamir Kabulov emphasized the importance of tensions not "spreading beyond the country's borders."[57] Kabulov also claimed he had received assurances from the Taliban that Afghanistan's territory would not be used for activities against Russia. Afghanistan's importance for Russia and its foreign policy can be gauged from the fact that Foreign Minister Sergei Lavrov, who hadn't left Russia since its invasion of Ukraine, arrived in Tunxi (China) in March 2022 to hold talks on Afghanistan.[58] As Russia is currently preoccupied with its invasion of Ukraine, its engagement with the de facto regime is so far limited. However, whatever engagement that has taken place between Moscow and the Taliban indicates Afghanistan's security importance to Russia and the glocalized nature of Afghanistan's securitization and conflict landscape.

Iran

As the major Shiʻa Muslim regime in the region, Iran has been never in favor of Saudi Arabia's presence and its Sunni influence in the region. To counter the predominantly Sunni jihadists during the Soviet invasion of Afghanistan, Iran had to support the Shiʻa sect of mujahideen freedom fighters who were mainly Hazaras from central Afghanistan. Inspired and backed by the Iranian Islamic Revolution of Khomeini, the Hazaras for the first time formed several political parties based on Shiʻa-Islamic ideology, including An-Nasr (the victory) and Sipah-e Pasdaran (Islamic Revolutionary Guard Corps) in Iran and the Hazarajat region in 1979.[59] In 1989, when the Soviets were forced to withdraw, the Khomeini regime mediated an agreement among all Hazara parties to consolidate under one armed and political movement of Hezb-e Wahdat-e Islami (Islamic Unity Party) led by Ali Mazari.[60] The Taliban's anti- Shiʻa sentiments extended Iranian support for the Shiʻa-led militant groups of Karim Khalili and Mohamad Mohaqiq in Afghanistan. In 1998, Iran had to announce a state of emergency by bringing its heavily armed army to its eastern border with Afghanistan, after its diplomats were kept hostage and killed in Mazar-e-Sharif city by the Taliban. Following the fall of the Taliban regime, Iran had to lobby for both Khalili and Muhaqiq for high-ranking positions in the Afghan interim government at the Bonn conference in early 2002. Khalili moved from Bamyan to Kabul and twice became second vice president under President Karzai between 2004 and 2014. Muhaqiq, who was by then deputy leader of the Wahdat Party, initially became minister of planning, however, he soon switched to the opposition party against Karzai. Nevertheless, both Khalili and Wahdat remained loyal when it came to Iran's interests in Afghanistan. According to various reports, nearly eighteen thousand Afghan Shiʻas were trained and sent to the war against the Islamic State in Syria by the Islamic Revolution Guard Corps of Iran in late 2016. Known as the Lashkar-e-Fatemiyoun (Fatemiyoun troops), the Wahdat Party played a significant role in recruiting these soldiers in Afghanistan.[61] While Iran continued to keep its friendly relation through its Shiʻa interlocutors with the Afghan democratic government in Kabul, its secret affairs with the Taliban were revealed after a US drone killed Mullah Akhtar Mansur—the supreme leader and successor of Mullah Mohammad Omar in 2015—while he was crossing the border from Iran into Pakistan. In response to President Donald Trump's aggressive approach toward Iran and the withdrawal from the Joint Comprehensive Action Plan in 2018, Iran went public in its close ties with the Taliban militant group in Afghanistan. In the last few years, before the Taliban's takeover, Iran saw the Taliban as an important actor to not only counter the threat of the Islamic State in

Afghanistan but also as a disrupting force for other stakeholders, including the US-led coalition forces, based in the country.[62] Today, even though several anti-Taliban political leaders are hosted by Iran and Tehran facilitated dialogue between the Taliban and the National Resistance Front (NRF), Taliban-Iran engagement has remained consistent even after the coalition's withdrawal. Moreover, the Taliban's apparent policy shift toward Iran can also be witnessed from the de facto regime's interim setup (announced in September 2021) where six Taliban commanders, amenable to Tehran, were added in the setup. These commanders include Mullah Abdul Qayyum Zakir, Mullah Sadr Ibrahim, Haji Nooruddin Azizi, Haji Mohammad Bashir, Haji Mohammad Azim Sultanzada, and Dr. Mohammad Hassan Ghiasi.[63] Iran understands that fragility in Afghanistan and a possible collapse of the regime can lead not only to another civil war but also to the spread of radical and terrorist groups in both the country and the region. The recent attacks in both Iran and Afghanistan show that the ISKP is a common enemy to the Taliban and Iran. As a result, Iran's pragmatic policy of engagement with the de facto regime, like other states, is enshrined in a security-centric approach.

India

Soon after the withdrawal of the Soviet troops from Afghanistan in 1989, the CIA had lost its interest in the region, meaning that the fate of the mujahideen was left to Saudi Arabia and Pakistan. Hence, with the jihad ending in Afghanistan, a large number of well-trained international mujahideen, including Pakistanis, moved to fight in the Indian-controlled Kashmir. This, again, highlighted the glocalized nature of conflict and militancy in South Asia, where fighters who were part of a somewhat global war (US-Soviet Cold War) in one country (Afghanistan), after their victory, were now fighting a local war in another (India). To secure its long-term interests in Afghanistan, Pakistan provided the Hezb-e-Islami (Islamic Party) of Gulbuddin Hekmatyar—a predominantly Pashtun ethnic party—financial and military support to take control of the government in Kabul. As a counterstrategy, India supported the Tajik militants' parties Jamiat-e-Islami (Islamic Group) of Burhanuddin Rabbani and the Shura-e-Nazar (Supervisory Council) of Ahmad Shah Massoud—later, both joined the Northern Alliances to fight Hekmatyar and then the Taliban in Afghanistan. Following the ouster of the Taliban by the United States and the installment of a predominantly Northern Alliances' republic, India enjoyed the closest relationship with the government in Kabul, which never sat well with Pakistan. India not only invested in major infrastructure projects across the country but also trained the Afghan army and police in New Delhi. Pakistan repeatedly shared its concern with both President Karzai and President Ghani and asked for limited influence from India in Afghanistan in return for bringing the Taliban to the negotiating table. However, the government in Kabul chose to side with India instead of Pakistan. Therefore, the Indian embassy and nationals were targeted in Kabul and around the country, whereas such attacks were claimed by the Haqqani Network—a tacit ally of the Pakistani military establishment.[64] Following the takeover of Kabul by the Taliban, India shut down its embassy and consulates in the country. With Pakistan's presence in the country, India could not afford to "sit and watch." In June 2022, India reopened its diplomatic mission in Kabul, ostensibly for better channeling of humanitarian services to Afghanistan. India may have perceived that both the Doha group led by Mullah Baradar and the Quetta Shura council led by Mullah Yaqub within the Taliban are not happy with the stronger influence of the Haqqani Network and Pakistan in Afghanistan's governance. Therefore, the resumption of diplomatic ties from New Delhi may be seen as an opportunity to preserve gains by India in Afghanistan during the coalition's presence in the country. However, even though India has publicly declared that it would not recognize the Taliban's emirate, it will navigate to see if it could win one or the other group to secure its interests in Afghanistan. After the Taliban's return to Kabul, India expressed its concerns that the Taliban victory would embolden Kashmiri militants. Hence, the resumption of diplomatic engagement suggests that India is keeping a close watch on Afghanistan and any potential threat of militancy rising from the country in Indian Kashmir.

Conclusion: Afghanistan and the Future of Regional Security

Afghanistan, since the Taliban's return, is going through another phase of negative peace (absence of violence), similar to the Taliban's first regime (1996–2001). Many argue that the main responsible parties for this situation are the United States (for the hasty Doha peace deal and the August 2021 withdrawal) and the Taliban (who survived two decades of the US coalition presence in the country). However, as discussed at length in this chapter, the situation was catalyzed by the glocal nature of the Afghan conflict and the regional security complex, where states united on the common agenda of regional security and keeping the threat of terrorism in check in each country. Therefore, the chapter aimed at answering these questions: How does the fusion of domestic issues and interests with external ones undermine international security? How did the fusion of domestic security fault lines and regional security interests contribute to the US coalition failure in

Afghanistan, and how did this failure impact domestic, regional, and international security?

By employing RSCT and the concept of glocalization, this chapter discusses the changing dynamics of regional security and argues how Afghanistan's neighbors, even with different motivations and policies, found policy convergence vis-à-vis the Taliban regime in Afghanistan. For all regional stakeholders discussed in this chapter, durable and sustainable peace in Afghanistan remained, and still remains, a primary security concern. The US–Taliban Doha Peace talks were, on paper, local in nature as they focused on Afghanistan and the future of the coalition forces and the civilian government in the country. However, the participation of regional stakeholders in addition to the mediation efforts by Qatar to initiate the process suggest the talks were both global and local, or glocal, in their outlook. Different regional powers who participated in the dialogue process pursued different foreign policy agendas; however, the future of securitization in Afghanistan post–US withdrawal proved to be uniting factor for them. Similarly, the glocal threat of the Islamic State and al-Qaeda and local threats of TTP (against Pakistan) and ETIM (against China) also created a policy convergence among different states on Afghanistan and its long-term security.

It is due to the glocalized nature of Afghanistan's security that abandoning the country at this critical juncture can present global and regional security complications. Therefore, a glocalized security approach is required to address and prevent security risks for regional and global stakeholders. An abandoned Afghanistan, as discussed in detail here, will mean vacuum and space for radical and terrorist groups. However, Afghanistan, at the moment, remains isolated on the global level when it comes to the Western bloc, especially with a former terrorist group in power. However, engagement from regional powers and stakeholders suggests that the security landscape within the country, directly and indirectly, impacts security in other parts of the region and hence projects glocal characteristics. Similarly, even though the Taliban's takeover ceased active conflict and achieved negative peace to some degree, constant attacks from the Islamic State on Afghan civilians, on the Taliban fighters, and on minority religious and ethnic groups suggest that positive peace in the country remains a distant dream. Therefore, engagement from both regional and international stakeholders, through a glocalized approach, remains important to achieve the broader security goals laid out in the Doha Peace Agreement between the United States and the Taliban. Finally, even though having a security-centric policy on Afghanistan is a rational approach on behalf of regional and neighboring states, engagement with the de facto regime from these states should not come at the cost of violation of human and gender rights in the country.

Notes

1. Yousaf and Jabarkhail, "Afghanistan's Future under the Taliban Regime," 17.
2. See for example, Robertson, "Globalisation or Glocalisation?"; Robertson, *Globalization: Social Theory and Global Culture*.
3. Turner, "Glocalisation," 123.
4. Buzan, Wæver, and Jaap De Wilde, *Security*, 12.
5. Rytövuori-Apunen, introduction, 1.
6. Buzan and Wæver, *Regions and Powers*, 91:29.
7. Ibid., vol. 61.
8. Roy, *Islam and Resistance in Afghanistan*, 8:31.
9. Maley, "Interpreting the Taliban."
10. *Madrassa* literally means a school or educational institution in Arabic and Farsi; however, in the Afghan context, it connotes primarily a religious school.
11. Roy, *Islam and Resistance in Afghanistan*, vol. 8.
12. Ibid.
13. Metcalf, *Islamic Revival in British India*.
14. Saikal, Farhadi, and Nourzhanov, *Modern Afghanistan*; Roy, *Islam and Resistance in Afghanistan*, vol. 8.
15. *Pir* is a religious leader in the Sufi tradition of Islam. Tagab is a district of northern Kapisa Province in Afghanistan.
16. Daudzai, *State-Building Dilemma in Afghanistan*.
17. Nasr, *Vanguard of the Islamic Revolution*, 8.
18. Saikal, Farhadi, and Nourzhanov, *Modern Afghanistan*.
19. Maley, "Interpreting the Taliban."
20. Daudzai, *State-Building Dilemma in Afghanistan*; Zulfia Abawe et al., "Afghanistan and the Way Forward."
21. Mahadevan, "Glocalisation of Al Qaedaism," 93.
22. Ibid., 6.
23. Rubin, "Crafting a Constitution for Afghanistan."
24. Rashid, *Descent into Chaos*; Mashal, "Once Jailed in Guantánamo, 5 Taliban Now Face U.S. at Peace Talks."
25. Democracy Now, "'Afghan Massacre: The Convoy of Death,' Part 2."
26. Sorkin, "Close Read: New Crimes for Old."
27. Peters, "How Opium Profits the Taliban."
28. An ex-Taliban member and continuing sympathizer told the following to one of the authors in an off-the-record interview: "The Americans are mercilessly bombing our villages, disgracing, and raping our women and children in their night rides, whereas the United Nations and Human Rights Watch watches it all. The United Nations and Human Rights is only a drama against the Muslim and Mujahideen."
29. Daudzai, *State-Building Dilemma in Afghanistan*, 138.
30. Rubin, "Open Letter to the Taliban."
31. Rashid, *Descent into Chaos*, 242–43.
32. At that time, both authors were based in Peshawar and witnessed the Pakistani Islamic parties and movements, including the Jamiat Ulama-e-Islam, Jaish-e-Mohammad, and the Lashkar-e-Taiba campaign for Afghan Taliban through collecting charities in Masques

but also recruiting volunteer fighters to fight against US troops in Afghanistan. They regularly erect charity tents in Friday prayers at mosques and call on local people to contribute with whatever they can to support the holy cause of jihad in Afghanistan.

33. Masadykov, Giustozzi, and Page, "Negotiating with the Taliban," 3.
34. LandInfo, "Report Afghanistan: Recruitment to Taliban," 6.
35. The US government's special inspector general for Afghanistan reconstruction (SIGAR) has periodically published reports highlighting the rampant corruption in Afghanistan during the coalition presence in the country. See Special Inspector General for Afghanistan Reconstruction, "All Reports."
36. Mahadevan, "Glocalisation of Al Qaedaism," 86.
37. See, for example, Shahzad, *Inside Al-Qaeda and the Taliban.*
38. Jadoon and Mines, "Broken, But Not Defeated."
39. Mir, "Five Things to Watch in the Islamabad-Pakistani Taliban Talks."
40. Pannett, "Taliban Spokesman Says 'No Proof' bin Laden Was Responsible for 9/11 Attacks."
41. Mehsud, "Dear Ummah."
42. El-Bay, "Afghanistan."
43. FBI, "Sirajuddin Haqqani."
44. Xin, Yunyi, and Wenwen, "China Urges Terrorist Crackdown by Taliban."
45. Motwani and Bose, "Afghanistan," 268.
46. Reuters, "China, U.S., Russia, Pakistan to Hold Talks on Afghanistan—China, U.S. say."
47. Yousaf, *Pakistan, Regional Security and Conflict Resolution*, 66.
48. Gul, "Pakistan, Militants Pause Afghan-Hosted Peace Talks for Internal Discourse Amid Cautious Optimism."
49. Saifi and Mehsud, "Senior Leader of Pakistani Taliban Killed in IED Attack, Sources Say."
50. Murtazashvili, "China's Activities and Influence in South and Central Asia."
51. Carlson, "Taliban Takeover and China-Russia Relations."
52. Kynge, Astrasheuskaya, and Yu, "China and Russia Poised to Step into the Afghanistan Gap."
53. Kofman, Stein, and Sun, "After Withdrawal."
54. Rehman, "Security Concerns Bring China Closer to Taliban."
55. Ibid.
56. Carlson, "Taliban Takeover and China-Russia Relations."
57. Kofman, Stein, and Sun, "After Withdrawal."
58. Reuters, "China, U.S., Russia, Pakistan to Hold Talks on Afghanistan—China, U.S. Say."
59. Amstutz, *Afghanistan*, 116–18.
60. Griffin, *Reaping the Whirlwind*, 23.
61. Majidyar, "Iran Recruits and Trains Large Numbers of Afghan and Pakistani Shiites."
62. Akbarzadeh and Ibrahimi, "Taliban."
63. Bolourchi, "Iran's Strategy in Afghanistan."
64. A chronological account of all such attacks can be found on South Asia Terrorism Portal, "Terrorist Attacks and Threats on Indians in Afghanistan since 2003."

References

Abawe, Zulfia, Bilquees Daud, Haqmal Daudzai, Moheb Jabarkhail, and Farooq Yousaf. "Afghanistan and the Way Forward: Incorporating Indigenous Knowledge into Policymaking." *Global Policy* 14, no. 1 (February 2023): 192–98.
Akbarzadeh, Shahram, and Niamatullah Ibrahimi. "The Taliban: A New Proxy for Iran in Afghanistan?" *Third World Quarterly* 41, no. 5 (2020): 764–82.

Amstutz, J Bruce. *Afghanistan: The First Five Years of Soviet Occupation*. Collingdale, PA: Diane Publishing, 1994.

Bolourchi, Neda. "Iran's Strategy in Afghanistan: Pragmatic Engagement with the Taliban." Newlines Institute, September 23, 2021. https://newlinesinstitute.org/afghanistan/irans-strategy-in-afghanistan-pragmatic-engagement-with-the-taliban/.

Buzan, Barry, and Ole Wæver. *Regions and Powers: The Structure of International Security*. Vol. 91. Cambridge: Cambridge University Press, 2003.

Buzan, Barry, Ole Wæver, and Jaap De Wilde. *Security: A New Framework for Analysis*. Boulder: Lynne Rienner, 1998.

Carlson, Brian G. "The Taliban Takeover and China-Russia Relations." Center for Security Studies (CSS) Analyses in Security Policy, No. 294, November 2021. CSS ETH Zurich. https://css.ethz.ch/content/dam/ethz/special-interest/gess/cis/center-for-securities-studies/pdfs/CSSAnalyse294-EN.pdf.

Daudzai, Haqmal. *The State-Building Dilemma in Afghanistan: The State Governmental Design at the National Level and the Role of Democratic Provincial Councils in Decentralization at the Sub-National Level*. Opladen, Germany: Barbara Budrich, 2021.

Democracy Now. "'Afghan Massacre: The Convoy of Death,' Part 2: Award Winnign Director/Producer Jamie Doran Alleges a Media Cover-Up of US Complicity in the Massacre of Up to 3,000 Taliban Prisoners." May 25, 2003. https://www.democracynow.org/2003/5/26/afghan_massacre_the_convoy_of_death.

El-Bay, Driss. "Afghanistan: The Pledge Binding Al-Qaeda to the Taliban." BBC, September 7, 2021. https://www.bbc.com/news/world-asia-58473574.

FBI. "Sirajuddin Haqqani." Most Wanted. Accessed August 26, 2024. https://www.fbi.gov/wanted/terrorinfo/sirajuddin-haqqani.

Griffin, M. *Reaping the Whirlwind: The Taliban Movement in Afghanistan*. London: Pluto Press, 2001.

Gul, Ayaz. "Pakistan, Militants Pause Afghan-Hosted Peace Talks for Internal Discourse amid Cautious Optimism." Voice of America, May 30, 2022. https://www.voanews.com/a/pakistan-militants-pause-afghan-hosted-peace-talks-for-internal-discourse-amid-cautious-optimism-/6595633.html.

Jadoon, Amira, and Andrew Mines. *Broken, but Not Defeated: An Examination of State-Led Operations against Islamic State Khorasan in Afghanistan and Pakistan (2015–2018)*. West Point, NY: Combating Terrorism Center at West Point, 2020. Ebook.

Kofman, Michael, Aaron Stein, and Yun Sun. "After Withdrawal: How China, Turkey, and Russia Will Respond to the Taliban." War on the Rocks, August 31, 2021. https://warontherocks.com/2021/08/after-withdrawal-how-china-turkey-and-russia-will-respond-to-the-taliban/.

Kynge, James, Nastassia Astrasheuskaya, and Sun Yu. "China and Russia Poised to Step into the Afghanistan Gap." *Financial Times*, August 17, 2021. https://www.ft.com/content/7ceb9e3b-bd6e-43fe-bb86-80353249e6ac.

LandInfo. "Afghanistan: Recruitment to Taliban." Report, June 29, 2017. Norwegian Country of Origin Information Centre. https://landinfo.no/wp-content/uploads/2018/03/Afghanistan-Recruitment-to-Taliban-29062017.pdf.

Mahadevan, Prem. "The Glocalisation of Al Qaedaism." In *Strategic Trends 2013: Key Developments in Global Affairs* edited by Oliver Thränert, 83–101. Zurich: CSS, ETH Zurich, 2013.

Majidyar, Ahmad. "Iran Recruits and Trains Large Numbers of Afghan and Pakistani Shiites." Middle East Institute, January 18, 2017. https://www.mei.edu/publications/iran-recruits-and-trains-large-numbers-afghan-and-pakistani-shiites.

Maley, William. "Interpreting the Taliban." In *Fundamentalism Reborn? Afghanistan and the Taliban*, edited by William Maley, 1–28. New York: New York University Press, 1998.

Masadykov, Talatbek, Antonio Giustozzi, and James Michael Page. "Negotiating with the Taliban: Toward a Solution for the Afghan Conflict." Working Paper no. 66, London School of Economics and Political Science, Crisis States Programme. Crisis States Research Centre, London, 2010.

Mashal, Mujib. "Once Jailed in Guantánamo, 5 Taliban Now Face U.S. At Peace Talks." *New York Times*, March 26, 2019. https://www.nytimes.com/2019/03/26/world/asia/taliban-guantanamo-afghanistan-peace-talks.html.

Mehsud, Ihsanullah Tipu (@IhsanTipu). "'Dear Ummah, it's time for you to prepare for next stage for the struggle. This historic victory will open way for Muslim masses to achieve liberation from despotic rule of tyrants who have been imposed by the West on Islamic World,' AlQaeda statement congratulating Taliban says." Twitter, August 31, 2021. https://twitter.com/IhsanTipu/status/1432751036612108297.

Metcalf, Barbara D. *Islamic Revival in British India: Deoband, 1860–1900*. Vol. 778. Princeton, NJ: Princeton University Press, 2014.

Mir, Asfandyar. "Five Things to Watch in the Islamabad-Pakistani Taliban Talks." United States Institute of Peace, June 21, 2022. https://www.usip.org/publications/2022/06/five-things-watch-islamabad-pakistani-taliban-talks.

Motwani, Nishank, and Srinjoy Bose. "Afghanistan: 'Spoilers' in the Regional Security Context." *Australian Journal of International Affairs* 69, no. 3 (2015): 266–84.

Murtazashvili, Jennifer B. "China's Activities and Influence in South and Central Asia." United States–China Economic and Security Review Commission, May 1, 2022. Carnegie Endowment for International Peace. https://carnegieendowment.org/2022/05/17/china-s-activities-and-influence-in-south-and-central-asia-pub-87146.

Nasr, Seyyed Vali Reza. *The Vanguard of the Islamic Revolution: The Jama'at-I Islami of Pakistan*. Berkeley: University of California Press, 1994.

Pannett, Rachel. "Taliban Spokesman Says 'No Proof' Bin Laden Was Responsible for 9/11 Attacks." *Washington Post*, August 26, 2012. https://www.washingtonpost.com/world/2021/08/26/taliban-bin-laden/.

Peters, Gretchen. "How Opium Profits the Taliban." United States Institute of Peace Washington, DC, August 2, 2009. https://www.usip.org/publications/2009/08/how-opium-profits-taliban.

Rashid, Ahmed. *Descent into Chaos: The US and the Disaster in Pakistan, Afghanistan, and Central Asia*. New York: Penguin, 2008.

Rehman, Zia ur. "Security Concerns Bring China Closer to Taliban." Voice of America, August 11, 2022. https://www.voanews.com/a/security-concerns-bring-china-closer-to-taliban-/6697339.html.

Reuters. "China, U.S., Russia, Pakistan to Hold Talks on Afghanistan—China, U.S. Say." March 29, 2022. https://www.reuters.com/world/china-says-us-representative-will-attend-afghanistan-meeting-china-2022-03-29/.

Robertson, R. "Globalisation or Glocalisation?" *Journal of International Communication* 1, no. 1 (1994): 33–52.

———. *Globalization: Social Theory and Global Culture*. London: Sage, 1992.

Roy, Olivier. *Islam and Resistance in Afghanistan*. Vol. 8. Cambridge: Cambridge University Press, 1990.

Rubin, Barnett R. "Crafting a Constitution for Afghanistan." *Journal of Democracy* 15, no. 3 (2004): 5–19.

———. "An Open Letter to the Taliban." *New Yorker*, February 27, 2018. https://www.newyorker.com/news/news-desk/an-open-letter-to-the-taliban.

Rytövuori-Apunen, Helena. Introduction to *The Regional Security Puzzle around Afghanistan: Bordering Practices in Central Asia and Beyond*, edited by Helena Rytövuori-Apunen, 1–28. Opladen, Germany: Barbara Budrich, 2016.

Saifi, Sophia, and Saleem Mehsud. "Senior Leader of Pakistani Taliban Killed in Ied Attack, Sources Say." CNN, August 8, 2022. https://edition.cnn.com/2022/08/08/asia/pakistan-taliban-leader-killed-intl/index.html.

Saikal, Amin, A. G. Ravan Farhadi, and K. Nourzhanov. *Modern Afghanistan: A History of Struggle and Survival*. London: Bloomsbury Academic, 2006.

Shahzad, S. S. *Inside Al-Qaeda and the Taliban: Beyond bin Laden and 9/11*. London: Pluto Press, 2011.

Sorkin, Amy Davidson. "Close Read: New Crimes for Old." *New Yorker*, July 13, 2009. https://www.newyorker.com/news/news-desk/close-read-new-crimes-for-old.

South Asia Terrorism Portal. "Terrorist Attacks and Threats on Indians in Afghanistan since 2003." Institute for Conflict Management. Accessed August 30, 2024. https://www.satp.org/satporgtp/countries/india/database/afganistanindianattack.htm.

Special Inspector General for Afghanistan Reconstruction. "All Reports." Accessed August 30, 2024. https://www.sigar.mil/allreports.

Turner, John A. "Glocalisation: Al-Qaeda and Its Constituents." In *Religious Ideology and the Roots of the Global Jihad*, 123–39. Basingstoke, Hampshire, Palgrave Macmillan, 2014.

Xin, Liu, Bai Yunyi, and Wang Wenwen. "China Urges Terrorist Crackdown by Taliban, as Kabul Deadly Blasts Exemplify Us Failure." *Global Times*, August 27, 2021. https://www.globaltimes.cn/page/202108/1232641.shtml.

Yousaf, Farooq. *Pakistan, Regional Security and Conflict Resolution: The Pashtun 'Tribal' areas*. New York: Routledge, 2020.

Yousaf, Farooq, and Moheb Jabarkhail. "Afghanistan's Future under the Taliban Regime: Engagement or Isolation?" *Journal of Policing, Intelligence and Counter Terrorism* 17, no. 1 (2022): 117–34.

HAQMAL DAUDZAI is an Afghan German citizen who works as a researcher at the Institute for War, Holocaust, and Genocide Studies (NIOD) in Amsterdam. He is currently a research member of the "Netherlands and Afghanistan 2001–2021" program, commissioned by the Dutch parliament to investigate the Netherlands' military and diplomatic involvement in Afghanistan between 2001 and 2021. His book, *The State-Building Dilemma in Afghanistan*, critically examines the US/NATO peace and state-building intervention in Afghanistan since 2001.

FAROOQ YOUSAF holds a PhD in Politics from University of Newcastle, Australia. He is currently based in Australia and is former Senior Researcher at SwissPeace (Basel). He is author of *Pakistan, Regional Security and Conflict Resolution: The Pashtun "Tribal" Areas*. His research focuses on gender, peace, and security in South Asia.

4

PRESTIGE SEEKING AND INTERNATIONAL COMMITMENTS
Turkey's Involvement in the Nagorno-Karabakh Conflict

Ünsal Sığrı and Taha Kalaycı

Introduction: Conflict Resolution and Prestige Seeking

Third-party involvement in both inter- and intrastate conflicts is not a new phenomenon and, in fact, has been the subject of numerous studies. Many of these studies deal with the mediation activities of foreign actors.[1] Although the motivations behind the interventions of third parties in conflicts vary, William Zartman and Saadia Touval emphasize how power politics play a key role in states' decisions to partake in conflict resolution. The main driver of a state's decision to become involved in a conflict often comes down to a cost-benefit analysis. Being involved in an international conflict brings with it some challenges, so foreign policy executives weigh whether the consequences of a possible conflict involvement will be more or less beneficial for their states. According to Zartman and Touval, two main interests affect this analysis. First, if the existing conflict jeopardizes the interests of a state, that state tends to end or at least control the conflict via mediation. Second, a state may aim to increase its influence in the eyes of the belligerents by helping end the conflict or becoming a guarantor.[2] Mediating actions may increase the influence of third-party mediators in the conflict countries and improve these countries' perceptions of the mediator, ensuring that intervening countries have a stronger hand in their future relations with the belligerents.

The involvement of third parties in conflicts is not always for mediation purposes, however. In their cost-benefit analysis, foreign policymakers may find that supporting one side is more profitable in some instances. In this case, third parties are involved in the conflict to help a certain side win. NATO's intervention in Kosovo can be considered in this context. NATO, in particular the United States, aimed to extend its influence in the Balkans in the post-Soviet period as well as to prevent the oppression of the Milosevic administration. Considering the dissolution of the Soviet Union, the active involvement of the United States would increase its influence in the Balkans. Therefore, American foreign policy executives decided the intervention was in line with the interests of the country. Involvement in conflicts can be direct, as in this example of American involvement, or indirect, through weapons assistance and diplomatic means, as the United States is doing in the Ukraine-Russia war. Although Western countries are not fighting directly, they have been involved in the war by supplying arms to Ukraine and imposing economic sanctions against Russia. The main reason for the Ukraine-Russia war stems from Russia's desire not to lose its influence in the post-Soviet geographical space of their region. The possibility of Russia taking control of Ukraine and reestablishing its influence in the country does not comply with the interests of NATO and the EU. As shown in these examples, power politics has an important place in the participation of third parties in conflicts. So why should international prestige matter in a system where states make decisions in line with their material and other national interests?

The foreign policy agenda of a state is determined by its foreign policy executives. Although the scope and breadth of foreign policy executives vary according to the political system of the country, policy decisions are always made by leaders. Therefore, leader perceptions play an important role in the policymaking process. They interpret the signals coming from the international system by filtering them and transforming them into foreign policy options.[3] On the other hand, foreign policy executives are aware that they also send signals to the international system with the foreign policy preferences they follow. The international prestige of a country emerges as a result of these signals sent to the international system.

In this chapter, we argue that international prestige is one of the main components of power politics, which we demonstrate by examining Turkey's involvement in the Nagorno-Karabakh War and the conflict more broadly. Foreign policymakers consider prestige as a tool to strengthen their hand in foreign policy negotiations. Along with material gains, international prestige is one of the benefits that states obtain as a result of their engagement with the conflicts. Moreover, political leaders can deploy the acquired prestige in domestic politics to enhance their political advantage. Robert Gilpin argued that prestige enables states to resolve conflicts without using their military power. He defines prestige as the reputation of military power. While the power of a state can be determined through tangible components such as military capacity or economy, prestige is also essential in the perceptions of other countries.[4] Realist scholars claim that states act in line with their positions in the international system.[5]

In this context, prestige is an indicator that shows that a state can use its military power when it deems it necessary. Military capacity can be observed from the outside. However, the main question is whether this capacity can be used effectively or not. International prestige and involvement in conflicts intersect at this point. Factors such as military performance in conflicts, the consequences of economic sanctions, or the efficient use of military technology may provide information about the state's military capacity, create deterrence, or increase bargaining power in future conflicts. However, how accurate would it be to explain the governments' pursuit of international prestige only with external factors? Domestic dynamics affect the foreign policy preferences of foreign policymakers. Similarly, governments can use the policy choices they make in the international arena to strengthen their position at home. Global security choices made by states affect the local, and local choices affect the global issues.

Undoubtedly, the 1990s witnessed a radical transformation in the world socially, politically, and economically. Factors such as the facilitation of transportation between countries, the development of communication technologies, and the increase in foreign investments of developed countries brought about "global world" discussions. The cooperation of the Russian Federation with international economic institutions such as the International Monetary Fund and the integration of China, under the Communist Party, into the world economy, indeed strengthened the idea of a globalizing world. The claim that the world is increasingly uniform started a homogeneity-heterogeneity debate, as Roland Robertson has stated. However, according to Robertson, the tendency in the literature to examine these two concepts as a dichotomy is wrong. These two concepts actually complement each other. Robertson uses the concept of glocalization to describe this association. Glocalization explains the meeting of the local with the global, and its proponents claim that local dynamics cannot be separated from the global.[6] The theory of glocalization argues that the local does not contrast with the global; on the contrary, it is included within it.[7] Glocalization extends into security studies. While it is discussed that the world has turned into a more global structure, security issues such as international terrorism, the Iraq War, the Arab Spring, and Russia's annexation of Crimea and other parts of Ukraine show that the world's security agenda is parallel to the globalization tendency of world politics. Governments changed by force and rebellions; newly established countries such as Kosovo; and conflicts in eastern Europe, the Middle East, and Africa have affected not only the surrounding regions but also the agenda of the whole world. The local motivations of the conflicts have gained a universal status due to the results of the conflicts and the involvement of international actors. The third parties involved in the conflicts not only aim to protect their interests but also want to build international prestige for their countries by showing their military capabilities to the world.

This chapter argues that one of the main drivers of Turkey's tendency to be involved in conflicts in its neighboring regions is to extend Turkey's international prestige. The study is based on the analysis of Turkey's involvement in the 2020 Nagorno-Karabakh War between Azerbaijan and Armenia. Turkey's open support of Azerbaijan is closely related to Turkey's active foreign policy, especially since 2016. After the Recep Tayyip Erdoğan administration came to power in 2002, Turkey aimed to play a problem-solver role in the Middle East. In this sense, the new Turkish government desired to take part in the conflicts as a mediator thanks to its positive stance toward almost all the countries in the region. Mediation efforts between Syria and Iraq, which started secretly in 2005 and were officially announced in 2008, are an example of this policy.[8]

Over the past decade, Turkish foreign policy has evolved into a more active phase. Uprisings in the Middle East and North Africa deeply changed the political dynamics in the entire region. Mustafa Kutlay and Ziya Öniş argue that Turkish foreign policy has become more assertive, and Turkey has begun to use its military capacity to solve its external problems since the uprisings.[9] Indeed, Turkey has been overtly involved in several conflicts in its region in recent years. The development of Turkish combat drone technology has enabled Turkey to intervene in conflicts by using small military units or by providing drone support to the warring parties. Perceiving the power vacuum that emerged in Syria as a security threat, the Turkish government launched cross-border military operations against ISIS and the People's Defense Units (PYD/YPG), which is considered by Turkey to be the Syrian branch of the Kurdistan Workers' Party (PKK), between 2016 and 2019. With these military interventions, Turkey has placed itself among the other players in the civil war, such as Russia, the United States, and Iran, and as part of this group of interested parties, the Erdoğan administration has established an interesting structure of relations, resulting in a risky security partnership, with Russia.[10] Another conflict in which Turkey is involved in this direction is the ongoing Libyan civil war. Changing security dynamics of the region compelled Turkey to use its military capabilities. Libya's geographical proximity to Europe caused major powers such as Germany and France to actively monitor the civil war.[11] However, Turkey's military support of the UN-recognized Government of National Accord (GNA) against the embattled Libyan National Army (LNA), supported by European countries such as France and Greece, changed the course of the civil war in Turkey's own interests.[12] The roots of both military interventions (i.e., Syria and Libya) can be traced to Turkish efforts to keep the changing geopolitical balances in the region in its favor.

The geopolitical concerns behind the Turkish government's resort to hard power as a foreign policy tool are evident in all the aforementioned cases.[13] Preserving existing economic and political profits is as important as gaining new ones. In Syria, geographical proximity and eliminating the security threat posed by terrorist organizations played important roles in instigating Turkish involvement. In Libya, LNA's gaining strength against the Turkish-backed GNA pushed Turkey to intervene in the country's internal conflict. However, the signal sent by both interventions to the international system was that Turkey was ready to use military force to protect its interests, and those signals have translated into international prestige for Turkey. Furthermore, for the Turkish government, this prestige acquired from involvement in conflicts abroad has allowed the Justice and Development Party (JDP) to gain power in domestic politics. Interests obtained or protected in the international arena strengthen the military reputation of Turkey and creates opportunities for the Erdoğan government to consolidate support domestically.

An illuminating case of the intersection of external intervention and state prestige is Turkey's involvement in the Nagorno-Karabakh War between Azerbaijan and Armenia. As a region that has grappled with a neverending conflict since the dissolution of the Soviet Union, Nagorno-Karabagh is a significant factor in Turkey's policy on the Caucasus region. Considering their historical and cultural ties, Turkey is among Azerbaijan's most important international partners. Azerbaijan's geopolitical location and its important place in the energy market promise great potential for the country and its international partners. Apart from Azerbaijan's economic and geopolitical potential, supporting the country in its conflict with Armenia is also a symbol of both domestic and international prestige for the Erdoğan administration. Turkish foreign policy executives consider involvement in international conflicts as an indicator of international prestige. Moreover, political leaders use international commitments and prestige as a tool to increase domestic popularity and political support. In this study, we argue that prestige seeking at the international level is interconnected with domestic politics. Turkey desires to increase its international prestige by getting a seat as a conflict-resolution party in the regional crisis and helping Azerbaijan take back its UN-recognized lands.[14] By so doing, the government also garners domestic support. Notably, this chapter analyzes Turkey's role in Azerbaijan's conflict with Armenia by examining Turkey's military and diplomatic efforts on the issue. In doing so, the study shows that prestige seeking is a major factor behind international security commitments.

Background of the Nagorno-Karabakh Conflict

When the Soviet Union was dissolved in 1991, fifteen new republics briskly appeared in the international scene. The end of the Cold War changed the dynamics of international politics dramatically. Although decades have passed since the collapse of the Soviet Union, the remaining problems of the union could not be completely resolved, even though one might argue that the Cold War ended peacefully. In the Caucasus the situation has not been a bed of roses. Border disputes over the status of the Nagorno-Karabakh region have led to a long conflict between Azerbaijan and Armenia. Since the conflict began in 1988, thousands of people have died on both sides.[15] Not surprisingly, the most significant foreign actor in the conflict has been Russia. Russia, which was the ruling power in the region for more than a century, had to intervene in the conflict in the Caucasus as a third party. With the dissolution of the Soviet Union, Russia lost official political control of the region which it annexed in the early nineteenth century.[16] However, this did not end Russian influence in the region. Despite the emergence of the new sovereign republics, Russian strategic policy has kept seeing the post-Soviet space as its backyard. Consequently, Russia remained the main actor in the economic, political, and security issues of the Caucasus.

The Nagorno-Karabakh conflict was the first ethnic conflict in the Soviet Union. Nagorno-Karabakh was a predominantly Armenian-populated autonomous region within the Azerbaijan Socialist Soviet Republic. However, when Armenia and the Nagorno-Karabakh region explicitly expressed their desire for unification in 1988, Azerbaijan strongly opposed the unification idea. As the support for joining Armenia grew in the autonomous region, Azerbaijan dissolved the autonomous status of Nagorno-Karabakh.[17] Although the Supreme Soviet of the Soviet Union stated that the demands of Armenia violated the Constitution of the Soviet Union, the Armenian Supreme Soviet passed a resolution to unite with Nagorno-Karabakh in order to annex Azerbaijan's territory.[18] At the time, the conflict between Azerbaijan and Armenia was not a priority for the Soviet Union, which was in its last days. As such, Moscow made no significant effort to end the conflict when the dispute first erupted. Armenia declared independence from the Soviet Union on September 21, 1991, and Azerbaijan too declared its independence on October 18, 1991. Both countries became officially independent on December 26, 1991, when the Soviet Union was dissolved.

By not being involved in the ethno-territorial dispute, Moscow essentially allowed the dispute to turn into a major conflict. Arguably, the inadequacy of the Soviet system prevented the establishment of a successful conflict resolution mechanism. Armenia and Azerbaijan began to form paramilitary armed groups and constantly increased their numbers.[19] In January 1992, Nagorno-Karabakh declared independence from Azerbaijan, which led to war.[20] Armenia tried to annex the mostly Armenian-populated region on its borders as Azerbaijan fought to protect its state borders. On February 26, 1992, Armenian forces killed more than six hundred Azerbaijani civilians in the town of Khojaly. Around thirty thousand people died on both sides during the war and up to one million people had to leave their homes before a ceasefire was agreed in 1994.[21] Via resolutions in 1993, the UN Security Council called on both sides to end the conflict and for Armenia to leave the occupied regions of Azerbaijan, but Armenia did not comply with the Security Council resolutions.[22] Armenia occupied not only the region of Nagorno-Karabakh but also a number of settlements located between the Karabakh region and the Armenian border. The Armenian controlled Azerbaijani territory amounted to almost 20 percent of Azerbaijan. Armenia was able to achieve this because its forces were in a better position in terms of military organization and equipment.[23] Although Russia seemed to be out of the conflict, it was aware of the military capabilities of the two countries, and Russian soldiers serving in the Soviet army provided military support to the Armenian forces.[24] By not intervening in the conflict, Russia was essentially aiding Armenia. Azerbaijan lost around 20 percent of its territory to Armenia. According to the United Nations High Commissioner for Refugees, nearly 13 percent of people in Azerbaijan were forced to leave their hometowns as a result of the conflict.[25] Azerbaijan did not receive international support, even though its land was occupied. Notably, the United States did not provide financial aid to Azerbaijan, even though it gave financial aid to all countries that gained their independence with the dissolution of the Soviet Union, including the Russian Federation.[26]

Despite the ceasefire, the conflict between Azerbaijan and Armenia has not ended. In 1992, Conference on Security and Co-operation in Europe (renamed Organization for Security and Co-operation in Europe after 1994) established the Minsk Group to resolve the conflict between Armenia and Azerbaijan. The Minsk Group was cochaired by the United States, France, and Russia. The mediation attempts of the OSCE Minsk Group did not achieve significant success, and the conflict still continues. Keeping Nagorno-Karabakh under its control, Armenia aimed for the official right of self-determination for the Armenians living there. Conversely, the main objective of Azerbaijan was to expel the Armenian troops from its territory and to ensure the territorial integrity of the country.[27] In addition, Azerbaijan wanted to reestablish control of the region and resettle back in their cities and towns the people displaced by the Armenian occupation. The stalemate continues as neither side has agreed to compromise on its demands. Between 2009 and 2010, up to forty-four soldiers were killed in the region. The region suffered further destabilization as a result of the 2008 Russia-Georgia war.

Despite the geopolitical challenges, Azerbaijan has not abandoned its desire to retake the territories occupied by Armenia. During the funeral of two Azerbaijani soldiers who died in Nagorno-Karabakh line of contact in November 2010, President Ilham Aliyev reiterated that Azerbaijan would use military force to restore its territorial integrity.[28] One notable advantage for Azerbaijan is its economic growth. When the Soviet Union dissolved, Armenia had a much better economic situation as compared to Azerbaijan. However, Azerbaijan has now outperformed Armenia. In 2013, for example, Azerbaijan's GDP was seven times higher than that of Armenia. Similarly, Azerbaijan's GDP/per capita was twice that of Armenia in 2013.[29] Although Azerbaijan's GDP decreased a bit, its GDP was four times larger than Armenia's GDP in 2021.[30] Azerbaijan's successful economic performance has been boosted by oil and natural gas exports.[31] Not surprisingly, Azerbaijan has significantly increased its military expenditures and modernized its armed forces. The main military supplier of both countries has been Russia. However, Azerbaijan has taken important steps to diversify its military technology by buying more arms from other countries, notably Israel and Turkey.[32]

Turkey and Early Stages of the Conflict

Turkey, a country with a long history in the Caucasus, was one of the countries that followed the developments in the region closely. Turkey was the first country to recognize the independence of Azerbaijan.[33] The conflict with Azerbaijan naturally concerned Turkey because of the strong historical and cultural ties. The Turkish government was unhappy with the one-sided attitude of the Russian Federation. However, Russia did not want other states to get involved in the conflict. For Russia, the Caucasus was still an area of influence. Therefore, Moscow wanted to preserve its position to be the country that has the final say regarding political and security issues in the region. After Turkish president Turgut Özal stated that Turkey would send military support to Azerbaijan in 1993, the Russian defense minister visited Ankara and conveyed Moscow's dissatisfaction with the decision.[34] Turkey explicitly supported Azerbaijan but did not take concrete action to militarily help Azerbaijan as it did not want to risk its relations with Russia. At the time, Turkey was unable to provide adequate support to Azerbaijan due to domestic problems and lack of capacity. During the short presidency of Ebulfez Elçibey in Azerbaijan, Turkey became the most important country in Azerbaijan's foreign policy, which made Russia concerned. Elçibey refused to join the Commonwealth of Independent States (CIS), which Russia created to ensure control over the former Soviet republics.[35] Another country that was concerned about the developing Turkey-Azerbaijan relation was Iran. With a population of almost twenty million Iranian Azerbaijanis, Iran has been closely following the developments in the region since Azerbaijan became independent. Iran actually has a strong desire to strengthen its influence in the region due to the fact that Azerbaijani Muslims mostly follow Shi'a Islam.

After President Heydar Aliyev came to power in 1993, a transformation took place in Azerbaijan's foreign policy. Aliyev was aware of the role of Russia in the region and pursued good relations with Russia, including joining the CIS. However, Azerbaijan's rapprochement toward Russia did not make a big difference in the conflict with Armenia. Russian foreign policy objectives for Azerbaijan were only based on benefiting from the country's natural resources and resisting the military involvement of any other country in the conflict.[36] However, as the rapprochement toward Russia failed to yield tangible support in the conflict, Azerbaijan moved to further strengthen ties with Turkey. On January 24, 1992, Turkey and Azerbaijan signed the Friendship, Cooperation, and Good Neighborhood Agreement, aimed at developing wide ranging relations between the two countries, including consular relations and press cooperation. In addition, the Military Training Cooperation Agreement was signed between Turkey and Azerbaijan in 1992, which paved the way for the training of Azerbaijani military personnel by the Turkish army. The agreement was followed by the Cooperation and Mutual Assistance Protocol signed on February 9, 1994, which included elements of strategic consideration in the ongoing conflict between Azerbaijan and Armenia. According to the protocol, the countries agreed to provide assistance to one another if attacked by a third country. Azerbaijan and Turkey strengthened their cooperation by establishing new bilateral bodies and personnel training programs. Moreover, Turkey essentially agreed to assist in the establishment of new facilities to contribute to Azerbaijan's sovereignty and security. Three months after the February 9, 1994, protocol, a ceasefire agreement was signed in Bishkek by Azerbaijan, Armenia, and Russia. The ceasefire stopped the conflict for a while but did not solve it. Almost 20 percent of Azerbaijan's UN-recognized border territories were still under Armenian occupation. Even though there were clashes from time to time, they did not turn into a war.

However, the ceasefire gave the Armenian army the chance to deploy in and around Nagorno-Karabakh and strengthen its positions. Azerbaijan continued to suffer diplomatic and military disadvantages until 2020 when it was able to make a counterattack. Azerbaijan had been plagued by inadequate military technology and lack of well-trained strategic cadres to command an all-out war. Under the agreements with Azerbaijan, Turkey undertook important steps to strengthen Azerbaijan's military capacity by modernizing the Azerbaijani army. According to Haldun Yalçınkaya, Turkey's most important role in the Karabakh war was the army-building process that took almost thirty years.[37] Indeed, Turkey's contribution to the Azerbaijani army is more than a simple weapon aid. In line with the military agreements made between the two countries, cadets from Azerbaijan have been trained in Turkish military schools, including military high schools, military academies, air force academies, naval academies, military medical schools, and war institutes. In addition, the Turkish Armed Forces have assisted in restructuring military schools in Azerbaijan. In addition to the Military Training Cooperation Agreement signed in 1992, the Military Training, Technical, and Scientific Cooperation Agreement was signed in 1996 between two governments. For example, in 2008 the Turkish General Staff and the Ministry of Defense of Azerbaijan signed a protocol on restructuring the education and training system of the Military Aviation School of Azerbaijan along the lines of the Turkish Air Force Academy. Additionally, Turkey's NATO membership has accelerated Azerbaijan's integration into the transatlantic military system and brought the Azerbaijani army to a level that can contribute to NATO missions such as Afghanistan and Kosovo.[38]

An important milestone in the relations between Azerbaijan and Turkey is the Strategic Partnership and Mutual Assistance Agreement signed in 2010. According to the agreement, which emphasized the inviolability of internationally recognized borders, protecting their national security is one of the priorities of the two countries. Both countries agree to enhance their cooperation in the fields of military readiness and military technology. The agreements recommitted to mutual support in case of aggression against one of them, including the use of military capacity, if necessary, within the rights given by article 51 of the UN charter. According to article 9 of the agreement on military-technical cooperation, assistance was to be rendered in matters related to

1. supply of defense products and material-technical means for the defense needs and security of the parties
2. design and production of defense products
3. providing defensive services
4. carrying out joint military exercises and activities related to defense readiness
5. training specialists for armed forces
6. providing logistic support to the armed forces
7. military medicine and medical service[39]

The importance of the ongoing Nagorno-Karabakh conflict is evident in the articles of the 2010 agreement. Unlike previous agreements, the 2010 agreement specifically detailed the military cooperation between the two countries and strengthened the international dimension of the issue. In 1995, Russia established a military base in the territory of Armenia and signed a defense agreement with Armenia. Another security agreement was signed between Russia and Armenia on August 20, 2010, under which Russia would continue to use its military base in Armenia with Mig29 fighter jets and an S-300 air defense system until 2044.[40] The timings of the Strategic Partnership and Mutual Assistance Agreement signed by Turkey and Azerbaijan and the defense pact between Russia and Armenia can be read as messages sent by the parties to each other. By referring to the importance of the internationally recognized borders in the Strategic Partnership and Mutual Assistance Agreement, Turkey and Azerbaijan sent a signal to the international system, particularly Armenia and Russia, that Turkey openly backs Azerbaijan in the border issues between Azerbaijan and Armenia.

Although Turkish foreign policy executives openly supported Azerbaijan, they did not want to provoke Russia, which has been asserting its power in the region. Indeed, the Russia-Georgia war, notably Russian support for the breakaway regions of Abkhazia and South Ossetia, and more recently the annexation of Crimea and invasion of Ukraine show that Russia would use military means to defend its interests in the region. Indeed, Luhansk People's Republic and Donetsk People's Republic in Ukraine and Abkhazia and South Ossetia in Georgia all declared independence with the military support of Russia. Given Russian objections, Turkey and Azerbaijan conducted their relations while being cognizant that Russia may decide to militarily intervene on the side of the Armenian-controlled Nagorno-Karabakh region. As such, Turkey has continued to provide technical and strategic support to Azerbaijan, including conducting joint military exercises, but has not deployed

Turkish Armed Forces in the conflict, despite holding thirteen military exercises in 2019 alone.[41]

The War in 2020 and the Building of Turkish Prestige

The ceasefire signed in 1994 determined a line between Armenia and Azerbaijan but did not end the conflict. Periodic deadly clashes continue to occur, and in 2020, the war erupted again. In July 2020, dozens of soldiers from both sides were killed in clashes on the Azerbaijan-Armenia border as each side accused the other of violating the ceasefire agreement.[42] On July 12, 2020, the first day of the war, the Turkish Ministry of Foreign Affairs made a statement accusing Armenia of aggressive nationalism and occupation.[43] Armenia accused Turkey of provoking the conflict and destabilizing the region by siding with Azerbaijan.[44] Although the Armenian Foreign Ministry did not openly name the Libyan and Syrian civil wars, Turkey's interventions in those wars has shown that Turkey could solve international problems through military means, which strengthened Turkey's international military prestige. Accusations continued as Turkey's role in the conflict became more pronounced. On July 17, 2020, Armenian ambassador Andranik Hovhannisyan stated at the UN Human Rights Council that Azerbaijan started the assault right after it announced that they could solve the crisis by force. Armenia asserted that Nagorno-Karabakh was never under the sovereignty of an independent Azerbaijan and that the region was independent under international law.[45] Azerbaijan, on the other hand, rejected the claims of Armenia by citing the four Security Council resolutions on Nagorno-Karabakh in 1993 and the relevant OSCE documents that recognized the region as Azerbaijani territory.[46] On July 30, 2020, Armenian ambassador Armen Papikyan stated at the OSCE Permanent Council that Turkey was involved in the Nagorno-Karabakh conflict. Papikyan highlighted the military exercises between Turkey and Azerbaijan, accusing the Erdoğan administration of having regional aims in the South Caucasus.[47]

Turkey's interest in the region was not new. Based on a more assertive foreign policy, the Erdoğan government wanted to show Turkey's influence in the crises and the surrounding regions. During his visit to Baku in February 2020, Erdoğan took six ministers, including Foreign Minister Mevlüt Çavuşoğlu, Minister of National Defense Hulusi Akar, Communications Director Fahrettin Altun, and Director of Turkish National Intelligence Agency Hakan Fidan with him.[48] Besides being very close countries in terms of culture and ethnicity, the security of Azerbaijan is of great geopolitical importance to Turkey. For example, Turkey is a major consumer of Azerbaijani petroleum and natural gas, and ensuring stability in the region is important for the security of the Baku-Tbilisi-Ceyhan and Baku-Tbilisi-Erzurum energy pipelines. In addition, involvement in the conflict also helps construct the international image that the Erdoğan government has been trying to promote. Solving the Azerbaijan-Armenia conflict that has been going on for almost thirty years would make a significant contribution to Turkey's prestige in foreign policy.

After a week of border clashes in mid-July, the armed forces of Turkey and Azerbaijan conducted a joint military drill in Azerbaijan. The military exercises began on July 29, 2020, and lasted until August 10, 2020. Both land and air forces took part in the military exercise held in the Azerbaijani regions of Baku, Nakhchivan, Ganja, Kurdemir, and Yevlah.[49] This exercise was followed by another one held in Nakhchivan. About 2,600 soldiers, 200 tanks and armored vehicles, 18 helicopters and aircraft, and more than 30 air defense systems participated in the joint military exercise held on September 5, 2020.[50] The exercises aimed to show the interoperability of the Turkish and Azerbaijani armed forces as well as contribute to the operational capabilities of the Azerbaijani army. One of Turkey's foremost contributions to the operational capabilities of the Azerbaijani army was unmanned aerial vehicles (UAVs). Recently, Azerbaijan has been using armed and unarmed Turkish drones against Armenian targets.[51] In addition to unmanned aerial vehicles, Turkish defense exports to Azerbaijan cover armored vehicles, rocket artillery, and missiles. Turkey, along with Russia and Israel, is among the major arms suppliers to Azerbaijan.[52] But it was the drones that would change the trajectory of the Nagorno-Karabakh War. Just before the beginning of the Second Nagorno-Karabakh War, Turkey delivered at least five Bayraktar TB-2 armed drones to Azerbaijan.[53] Turkish drones had previously been used in operations against the PKK in Syria and in Libya. The use of Bayraktar TB-2 in Nagorno-Karabakh demonstrated Turkish military capabilities. Since then, Bayraktar TB-2 has gained significant international recognition

On September 27, 2020, the ceasefire in the Nagorno-Karabakh region was broken again. The clashes that started on that day ignited the longest and harshest fighting in the conflict since 1992. As always, both sides accused the other of starting the conflict. The Azerbaijan Ministry of Defense stated that Armenian forces started intensive shelling using large-caliber weapons, and mortars around 6:00 a.m. on September 27. According to Azerbaijan, Armenia shelling wounded and killed civilians in the Gapanly village of Terter region, the Chiragli and Orta Gervend villages of Aghdam region, the Alkhanli and Shukurbeyli villages of Fizuli region, and the Jojug Marjanli village of Jabrayil region.[54] The Armenian Ministry of Foreign Affairs, on the other side, claimed that Azerbaijan first launched the missile attacks and defined the situation as aggression against the Republic of Artsakh (i.e., the breakaway Nagorno-Karabakh region).[55] OSCE and the European Union urged both sides to return to the ceasefire situation.[56] Like Azerbaijan, Turkey unconditionally recognizes Nagorno-Karabakh as Azerbaijani territory. For Azerbaijan and Turkey, a ceasefire simply meant accepting Armenian control over the area. The Turkish Ministry of Foreign Affairs made a statement that the Armenian side initiated the attack and affirmed that Azerbaijan has the right to protect its lands.[57] In another statement, Turkey reiterated that it would not support any solution that Azerbaijan did not accept.[58] Speaking on television on the first day of the war, Turkish defense industry president İsmail Demir said that the Turkish defense industry will always be at the disposal of Azerbaijan with all of its capacities.[59] As fighting intensified, the Azerbaijan Ministry of Defense stated that Azerbaijani army had launched a counteroffensive operation along the entire front line by using mechanized troops, rocket and artillery systems, and UAVs.[60] During this round of the war, Azerbaijan's armed forces performed well. They quickly retook the Fizuli-Jabrayil line and six villages in the Fizuli region.[61]

The war continued until November 10, 2020, during which the Azerbaijani army outmaneuvered the Armenian army and took back a significant amount of its land from Armenia. The Azerbaijani army destroyed a significant number of military equipment, air defense systems, and armored vehicles of the Armenian forces by using armed drones.[62] For the first time since 1992, Azerbaijan regained control of the occupied areas around Nagorno-Karabakh. On November 8, 2020, Azerbaijani armed forces captured the city of Shusha, which is very close to Stepanakert/Khankendi, the capital of the Nagorno-Karabakh region. On the same day, Turkish Foreign Minister Mevlüt Çavuşoğlu and Minister of National Defense Hulusi Akar visited President Ilham Aliyev in Baku. Aliyev stated that the political and moral support of Turkey was very important in resolving the conflict.[63] However, Azerbaijan's control of Shusha pushed Russia to take a tangible step. Russian president Vladimir Putin met with President Aliyev and Armenian prime minister Nikol Pashinyan and persuaded them to sign a ceasefire agreement.

According to the ceasefire agreement, the parties would suspend the conflict as of November 10, 2020, and maintain their current positions. Armenia agreed to return the Kalbajar region to Azerbaijan within five days, the Agdam region within ten days, and Lachin by December 1, 2020. Notably,

Lachin was the main connection between Nagorno-Karabakh and Armenia. For Azerbaijan, retaking Lachin was a critical step in regaining its territory. The parties decided to open a five-kilometer-wide corridor in Lachin to provide transportation between Nagorno-Karabakh and Armenia According to the agreement, Russian peacekeeping forces would be deployed in the places where the Armenian forces were withdrawing, including the Lachin corridor.[64] Russia did not want any third party other than itself involved in the ceasefire process, and therefore, neither the OSCE Minsk group nor any other international actor was involved in the signed agreement, including Turkey, despite its support of Azerbaijan. Nevertheless, being involved in the ceasefire process was an important goal for Turkish foreign policy executives, who wanted to increase Turkey's international prestige. On the day the agreement was revealed by the Russian, Armenian, and Azerbaijani authorities, Foreign Minister Çavuşoğlu and director of Turkish Intelligence Fidan again visited President Aliyev, who stated that Azerbaijan's victory was a joint victory with Turkey and that he would like Turkey and Russia to play a joint role in resolving the crisis.[65] Thereafter, Turkey and Russia decided to establish a joint ceasefire monitoring center, consisting of sixty Russian and Turkish military personnel, was opened in the Agdam region on January 30, 2021.[66] Thus, despite Russian reservations, Turkey managed to become involved in the postconflict process and achieve its international prestige goal.

Turkey's role in the recent conflict goes beyond its diplomatic and moral support. The effective use of Turkish-made UAVs by the Azerbaijani army was one of the most distinctive features of the war. The armed Turkish drones acutely changed the power balance in the conflict. Experts claim that the 2020 Nagorno-Karabakh War proved the significance of armed drones in conventional wars.[67] Since Nagorno-Karabakh is a mountainous area, it limits the mobility of military operations. Geographical conditions of the region also prevent efficient air strikes due to the reduced maneuverability of combat planes. The drones used in the conflict provided a significant firepower advantage to the Azerbaijani army. The defense lines, which the Armenian army had successfully defended for years, were hit hard by the firepower provided by the drones. The drone attacks prevented the Armenian side from responding to the attacks launched by the Azerbaijani army.[68] The success of Turkish UAVs in the 2020 Nagorno-Karabakh War, as in the civil wars in Libya and Syria, has increased international interests in the Turkish defense industry, especially in the Bayraktar drone manufacturer Baykar.[69] Turkey's ability to produce armed drones and the successful performance of the drones in conflicts has increased the international reputation of Turkey. In an interview with France24 after the ceasefire, Ilham Aliyev stated that they destroyed $1 billion worth of Armenian military equipment with Turkish drones alone. When the reporter asked, "How many drones do you have?" Aliyev laughed and said "enough."[70] Since then, the arms trade between the two countries has increased significantly. In 2021, Azerbaijan was the second-largest importer of Turkish aerospace products.[71]

The dominant view of Turkish decision-makers is that the international community was covertly supporting Armenia. This is because it would be in the interests of Armenia to declare a ceasefire at a time when Azerbaijan was starting to take back its lands. Therefore, by supporting Azerbaijani operation, Turkey positioned itself against countries that support Armenia, such as France and the United States. The Turkish Presidency, Ministry of Foreign Affairs, and Ministry of National Defense reiterated Turkish support at every opportunity and stated that Turkey was ready to help Azerbaijan. In essence, this was a message sent by Turkey to the international system to show that it is capable of facing major powers on the Azerbaijan issue. At the same time, a similar message was being sent to Turkish citizens. The government aimed to assure the Turkish public that it could take the necessary steps to support Azerbaijan as it increased Turkish prestige. As the conflict raged in 2020, Russian foreign ministry spokeswoman Maria Zakharova acknowledge that Russia was in contact with the Minsk Group and the Turkish authorities, and called for peace.[72] On October 5, 2020, Recep Tayyip Erdoğan accused the Minsk Group, which consists of France, the United States, and Russia, of not being able to solve the problem and stated that Turkey is ready to give all kinds of support to Azerbaijan.[73] Turkey and Russia had different preferences for the solution to the problem. Turkey supported the idea that Azerbaijan could fight for its territory due to the inability of international actors to solve the problem. Russian foreign minister Sergey Lavrov, on the other hand, argued that military solutions should not be supported.[74] Also, Russia did not want an outside actor to be involved in the conflict. However, the dynamics between Turkey and Azerbaijan were preventing Turkey from keeping itself out of the war. Also, domestic political dynamics in Turkey meant that Turkey could not be indifferent to the security problem that Azerbaijan was experiencing. Both the international and domestic dynamics were strong enough for Turkey to confront Russia and even risk damaging Turkish-Russian relations, which has been good in recent years. Deterioration of relations with Russia, which is an important balancing point in Turkey's relations with the West, would seriously affect Turkish foreign policy. Nevertheless, Turkey was able to navigate the situation and came out as a significant player, thereby gaining international prestige.

The Glocal Nature of Turkish Involvement: From External Prestige to Domestic Support

The cultural and historical ties between Azerbaijan and Turkey are often used to explain the good relations between them. In fact, since the collapse of the Soviet Union, political leaders often refer to the two countries as "One Nation, Two States." In many ways, what happens in Azerbaijan has domestic and regional significance for Turkey. Turkey was not really involved during the first Nagorno-Karabakh War as Turkish security forces were focused on fighting the PKK. Although capacity problems prevented Turkey from being directly involved in the conflict, Turkey has always been providing indirect and systematic support to Azerbaijan, which kept growing as Turkey increased its capacity. In fact, Turkey has always signaled its willingness to directly intervene in the conflict if necessary. Under the Erdoğan government, Turkey has become more assertive in its foreign policy, which has enhanced the country's military reputation. Overall, Turkish foreign policymakers aim to increase Turkey's influence in the surrounding regions and position Turkey as an international peace broker.

Political leaders make foreign policy decisions based on signals from the international system and domestic consideration. For this reason, domestic factors such as the worldview of the leaders, strategic culture, and state-society relations have an impact on foreign policy.[75] The most remarkable domestic factor in the transformation of Turkish foreign policy is the nationalist orientation of the Erdoğan government. This nationalist orientation is most evident in the alliance between the JDP and the Nationalist Movement Party (NMP), which started in 2016.[76] Due to its party ideology, the NMP attaches great importance to Turkey's relationship with the Turkic republics that gained independence from the Soviet Union. Turkey's Azerbaijan policy is important to the NMP for both the international factors and the historical and cultural ties between the two countries. In a statement made in October 2020, NMP leader Devlet Bahçeli stated that Nagorno-Karabakh is Turkish and belongs to Azerbaijan. Bahçeli not only backs Turkish military operation in support of Azerbaijan but actually sees Azerbaijan and Turkey as constituting the Turkish nation as a whole.[77] This nationalist narrative made Turkey's involvement in the Nagorno-Karabakh conflict popular in Turkey, which generated domestic political support for the NMP.

The signals received from the international system play an effective role in the foreign policy decisions taken by foreign policy executives. However, these decisions are not independent of internal developments: the desire to stay in power affects the foreign policy decisions taken by political leaders. This intertwining of internal and external factors shows the glocalized nature of Turkey's foreign policy. While the Turkish government wants to strengthen its international prestige with the foreign policy it follows, it also aimed to cement the domestic political alliance it had established. In this context, domestic policy and foreign policy are not two opposite behaviors but two complementary elements as claimed by the glocalization theory. The Erdoğan administration popularized its assertive foreign policy with the nationalist rhetoric in domestic politics, which was aimed at consolidating their voters. The military operations launched in Syria after 2016, the intervention in the Libyan civil war, and, finally, the involvement in the Nagorno-Karabakh War in 2020 were all in line with the nationalist orientation of Turkish domestic politics.

In order to influence voters, Erdoğan frequently refers to his foreign policy during political rallies. In a public meeting in 2019, for example, Erdoğan noted that Turkey has become stronger and more independent in its foreign policy as compared to the previous government. He touted the fact that Turkey can now conduct international military operations without obtaining permission from any country.[78] In a meeting with JDP grass-roots leaders in September 2020, Erdoğan urged them to tell the public about what his government has done in improving Turkey's reputation, power, and capabilities in the international arena.[79] According to research on public perceptions of Turkish foreign policy conducted by Kadir Has University in 2022, Turkish people see Azerbaijan as the friendliest country in foreign policy as Armenia was ranked as third among the countries that pose a threat to Turkey.[80] Similar public views of Azerbaijan and Armenia are evident in prior opinion polls.[81] Clearly, Turkish decision-makers, especially Erdoğan, are aware that being involved in the Nagorno-Karabakh War would bring benefits in domestic politics. Erdoğan often mentions Turkish UAVs in his foreign policy messages to voters. During the delivery ceremony of the new UAVs to the Turkish Armed Forces on August 29, 2021, Erdoğan stated that Turkey prevented human tragedies in Syria, Libya, and Azerbaijan, and attributed those achievements to the Turkish defense industry.[82] During the 2024 general elections, the poor performance of the Turkish economy led Erdoğan to turn to more advantageous areas in his election campaign, most notably foreign policy.

Conclusion

Obtaining material benefits is often one of the main motivations in the foreign policy of states. However, there are also nonmaterial benefits that states can gain. Why is international prestige important for states? Although it may seem that there is no financial benefit at first glance, international prestige is important in terms of preventing possible conflicts in the future. First of all, increasing military reputation provides deterrence. Moreover, prestige gives countries bargaining power in international negotiations and strengthens the hand of political leaders in domestic politics. The intersection of internal and external dynamics shows the glocal nature of the pursuit of international prestige in foreign policy, which is evident in Turkey's involvement in the conflict between Azerbaijan and Armenia.

The Nagorno-Karabakh War in 2020 certainly marked a new turning point in military relations between Turkey and Azerbaijan. Although Turkey did not directly participate in the war, it was the biggest supporter of Azerbaijan and publicly stated its support of Azerbaijan. Hence, the success of Azerbaijan became critical to Turkey's international prestige. Turkey's involvement in the Nagorno-Karabakh conflict was seen as a foreign policy success by the Turkish government. By playing a major role in the restructuring of the Azerbaijani army, which performed well in the 2020 war, Turkey has strengthened its military reputation within the region and beyond.

Turkey has also increased the reputation of its defense industry. Notably, the development of armed UAV technology coincided with the Erdoğan administration's effort to increase the prestige of the country by asserting a military dimension into its foreign policy. Bayraktar TB-2 armed drones destroyed a significant number of Armenian military equipment which mainly consists of Russian-made weapons and missile systems. The fact that Turkish armed drones proved their effectiveness in a real war gave the Turkish drone industry significant visibility. The Turkish defense industry has become reputable for a variety of air, land, and sea vehicles; military communication equipment; and rocket and missile systems. The Erdoğan administration wanted to enhance Turkish prestige by getting involved in international conflicts and gaining the status of a regional power.

Domestically, the nationalist transformation in domestic politics and the desire to consolidate electoral votes also tied into the foreign policy of the Erdoğan government. For the JDP administration led by Erdoğan, successes in foreign policy were vital in ensuring electoral victory given the administration's poor economic performance. Gains made in the international arena, especially the Nagorno-Karabakh War, were used to influence public opinion and win votes. Prestige became useful in both the international and domestic arenas. Notably, prestige went well with the nationalist orientation of the JDP and its alliance with the NMP.

Notes

1. Ott, "Mediation as a Method of Conflict Resolution," 595–618; Kriesberg, "Mediation and the Transformation of the Israeli-Palestinian Conflict," 373–92.
2. Zartman and Touval, "International Mediation," 32–33.
3. Rose, "Neoclassical Realism and Theories of Foreign Policy," 148.
4. Gilpin, *War and Change in World Politics*, 31.
5. Lobell, Ripsman, and Taliaferro, *Neoclassical Realism, the State, and Foreign Policy*, 28.
6. Robertson, "Time-Space and Homogeneity-Heterogeneity," 29.
7. Robertson, "Globalisation or Glocalisation?," 191–208.
8. Tür, "Turkey's Role in Middle East and Gulf Security," 592–603; Davutoğlu, "Turkey's Mediation," 85.
9. Kutlay and Öniş, "Understanding Oscillations in Turkish Foreign Policy," 3052.
10. Köstem, "Russian-Turkish Cooperation in Syria," 806–10.
11. Kardaş, "Turkey's Libya Policy," 328–30.
12. Megerisi, "It's Turkey's Libya Now."
13. Kardaş, "Turkey's Libya Policy," 325–36; Köstem, "Russian-Turkish Cooperation in Syria," 806–10.
14. United Nations Security Council, Resolution 874.
15. BBC News, "Nagorno-Karabakh Conflict Killed 5,000 Soldiers"; Rehimov, "Azerbaycan Ordusu, Karabağ'daki Savaşta 2 Bin 908 Şehit Verdi."
16. Yamskov, "Ethnic Conflict in the Transcausasus," 651.
17. Babayev, "Nagorno-Karabakh," 21.
18. Resolution of the Presidium of the USSR Supreme Soviet regarding the Decisions of the Supreme Soviets of Azerbaijan and Armenia on Nagorny Karabakh.
19. Cornell, "Turkey and the Conflict in Nagorno Karabakh," 54–55.
20. Babayev, "Nagorno-Karabakh," 21.
21. McGuinness, "Nagorno-Karabakh."
22. United Nations Security Council, Resolution 874; Resolution 884; Resolution 853.
23. Babayevl, "Nagorno-Karabakh," 23.
24. Cornell, "Turkey and the Conflict in Nagorno Karabakh," 56.
25. United Nations High Commissioner for Refugees, "UNHCR Publication for CIS Conference."
26. Cornell, "Turkey and the Conflict in Nagorno Karabakh," 57.
27. Ayunts, Zolyan, and Zakaryan, "Nagorny Karabakh Conflict," 1–3.
28. German, "Nagorno-Karabakh Conflict between Azerbaijan and Armenia," 217; Radio Free Europe/Radio Liberty, "More Armenian, Azeri Bodies Exchanged."
29. Broers, "From 'Frozen Conflict' to Enduring Rivalry," 565.
30. World Bank Group, "Azerbaijan"; "Armenia."
31. Broers, "From 'Frozen Conflict' to Enduring Rivalry," 565.
32. Mehdiyev, "Azerbaijan, Israel Expand Defense Cooperation with New Joint Venture"; TRT Haber, "Türkiye Ile Azerbaycan Arasındaki Askeri İş Birliği Artıyor."
33. Rehimov, "Aliyev."
34. Cornell, "Turkey and the Conflict in Nagorno Karabakh," 65.
35. Sarıahmetoğlu, "Karabağ Sorununun Çözüm Sürecinde Türkiye Ve Rusya," 97.
36. Sarıahmetoğlu, "Karabağ Sorununun Çözüm Sürecinde Türkiye Ve Rusya," 97.
37. Yalçınkaya, "Turkey's Overlooked Role in the Second Nagorno-Karabakh War."
38. Yalçınkaya, "Turkey's Overlooked Role in the Second Nagorno-Karabakh War."
39. "Türkiye Cumhuriyeti ve Azerbaycan Cumhuriyeti Arasında Stratejik Ortaklık ve Karşılıklı Yardım Anlaşması," *Resmi Gazete*.

40. O'Rourke, "Russia, Armenia to Sign Defense Pact."
41. Göksedef, "Dağlık Karabağ."
42. BBC News World, "Armenia and Azerbaijan Fight over Disputed Nagorno-Karabakh"; Ministry of Foreign Affairs of the Republic of Azerbaijan, "No:158/20, Statement by the Ministry of Foreign Affairs of the Republic of Azerbaijan."
43. Ministry of Foreign Affairs of the Republic of Turkey, "No: 149, 12 July 2020, Press Release Regarding the Armenian Attack on Azerbaijan."
44. Ministry of Foreign Affairs of the Republic of Turkey, "Statement by the Foreign Ministry of Armenia on the Statement of the Turkish Foreign Ministry."
45. Ministry of Foreign Affairs of the Republic of Turkey, "Permanent Representative of Armenia in Geneva Made a Statement at the UN Human Rights Council on the Offensive Unleashed by Azerbaijan against Armenia."
46. Ministry of Foreign Affairs of the Republic of Turkey, "Conflict Settlement Process (1991–2020)."
47. Ministry of Foreign Affairs of the Republic of Armenia, "Ambassador Papikyan Presented Turkey's Policy in the South Caucasus at the Session of the OSCE Permanent Council."
48. Beyaz and Rehimov, "Erdoğan Azerbaycan Cumhurbaşkanı Aliyev Tarafından Resmi Törenle Karşılandı."
49. TRT Haber, "Türkiye Ve Azerbaycan Ortak Tatbikatı Başladı."
50. Rehimov, "Türkiye Ve Azerbaycan'dan Savaş Sahnelerini Aratmayan Tatbikat."
51. BBC Monitoring, "Explainer: What Is behind Turkey's Ramped up Support for Azerbaijan?"
52. Stockholm International Peace Research Institute, "Arms Transfers to Conflict Zones: The Case of Nagorno-Karabakh."
53. Stockholm International Peace Research Institute, "Arms Transfers to Conflict Zones: The Case of Nagorno-Karabakh."
54. "Armenian Armed Forces Committed Large-Scale Provocations along the Entire Length of the Front," Ministry of Defense of the Republic of Azerbaijan, September 27, 2020.
55. Ministry of Foreign Affairs of the Republic of Armenia, "Statement by the MFA of Armenia."
56. OSCE Chairpersonship, "OSCE Chairperson-in-Office Calls for Return to Ceasefire around Nagorno-Karabakh and Resumption of Substantive Negotiations."
57. Ministry of Foreign Affairs of the Republic of Turkey, "Dışişleri Bakanlığı Sözcüsü Hami Aksoy'Un Ermenistan'In Bu Sabah Azerbaycan'a Karşı Başlattığı Saldırı Hakkındaki Soruya Cevabı."
58. Ministry of Foreign Affairs of the Republic of Turkey, "Azerbaycan Ile Ermenistan Arasında İlan Edilen Ateşkes Hk."
59. SSB (@SavunmaSanayii), "Başkan @Ismaildemirssb'den Azerbaycan Açıklaması: 'Türkiye'nin Savunma Sanayii Alanında Her Ne Imkanı Varsa Kardeş Ülke Azerbaycan'ın Emrindedir."
60. Ministry of Defense of the Republic of Azerbaijan, "Azerbaijan Army's Troops Launched a Counter-Offensive Operation along the Entire Front."
61. Ministry of Foreign Affairs of the Republic of Azerbaijan, "Azerbaijan Army Has Liberated a Number of Occupied Villages and Important High Grounds."
62. Ministry of Defense of the Republic of Azerbaijan, "List of the Enemy's Destroyed Military Equipment"; Ministry of Defense of the Republic of Azerbaijan, "Enemy Supply and Combat Equipment Destroyed."
63. Ministry of Foreign Affairs of the Republic of Azerbaijan, "President Ilham Aliyev Received from Turkish Foreign Minister and Minister of National Defense."
64. President of Russia, "Statement by President of the Republic of Azerbaijan, Prime Minister of the Republic of Armenia and President of the Russian Federation."

65. Ministry of Foreign Affairs of the Republic of Azerbaijan. "President Ilham Aliyev Received Turkish Foreign Minister, Minister of National Defense and Director of National Intelligence Organization."
66. Reuters, "Russia and Turkey Open Monitoring Centre for Nagorno-Karabakh."
67. Köker, "Dağlık Karabağ: İha ve si'ha'ların Rolü Ne Oldu, Azerbaycan'a Nasıl Avantaj Sağladı?"
68. Ibid.
69. Witt, "Turkish Drone That Changed the Nature of Warfare."
70. France 24 English, "Azerbaijani President Ilham Aliyev: 'We Never Deliberately Attacked Civilians.'"
71. BBC News Türkçe, "Dağlık Karabağ: Azerbaycan, Ermenistan'la Yeni Bir Savaşa Mı Hazırlanıyor?"
72. Ministry of Foreign Affairs of the Russian Federation, "Briefing by Foreign Ministry Spokeswoman Maria Zakharova, Moscow, October 1, 2020."
73. Sözcü Gazetesi, "Erdoğan'dan Azerbaycan'a Destek: Türkiye Bütün Imkanları Kullanmaya Kararlıdır."
74. Ministry of Foreign Affairs of the Russian Federation, "Briefing by Foreign Ministry Spokeswoman Maria Zakharova, Moscow, October 5, 2020."
75. Ripsman, Taliaferro, and Lobell, *Neoclassical Realist Theory of International Politics*, 58.
76. Euronews, "Cumhur i'ttifakı Bir Yaşında: Nasıl Başladı, Bir Yılda Neler Oldu?"
77. Beyaz, "MHP Genel Başkanı Bahçeli: 'Nahçıvan Özerk Cumhuriyeti'nin Azerbaycan Cumhuriyeti'ne Katılması Şarttır.'"
78. Aktaş et al., "Cumhurbaşkanı Erdoğan: Bugün Dış Politikası Bağımsız Bir Türkiye Var."
79. Türkiye Cumhuriyeti Cumhurbaşkanlığı, "Türkiye'nin Uluslararası Alandaki Itibarını, Gücünü, Kabiliyetlerini Geliştirdik," September 17, 2020.
80. Kadir Has Üniversitesi, "Türk Dış Politikası Kamuoyu Algıları Araştırması 2022 Sonuçları Açıklandı," September 8, 2022.
81. Kadir Has Üniversitesi "Türk Dış Politikası Kamuoyu Algıları Araştırması 2022 Sonuçları Açıklandı."
82. TRT Haber, "Cumhurbaşkanı Erdoğan: Milli Si'ha'larımız İçin Pek Çok Ülke Sırada Bekliyor."

References

Abbasov, Shahin. "Azerbaijan-Turkey Military Pact Signals Impatience with Minsk Talks—Analysts." Eurasianet, January 18, 2011. https://eurasianet.org/azerbaijan-turkey-military-pact-signals-impatience-with-minsk-talks-analysts.

Aktaş, Yıldız, Ahmet Sertan Usul, Ferdi Türkten, Enes Kaplan, and Tayfun Salcı. "Cumhurbaşkanı Erdoğan: Bugün Dış Politikası Bağımsız Bir Türkiye Var." Anadolu Ajansı, December 4, 2019. https://www.aa.com.tr/tr/politika/cumhurbaskani-erdogan-bugun-dis-politikasi-bagimsiz-bir-turkiye-var/1664159.

Ayunts, Artak, Mikayel Zolyan, and Tigran Zakaryan. "Nagorny Karabakh Conflict: Prospects for Conflict Transformation." *Nationalities Papers* 44, no. 4 (2016): 543–59.

Babayev, Azer. "Nagorno-Karabakh: The Genesis and Dynamics of the Conflict." In *The Nagorno-Karabakh Deadlock: Insights from Successful Conflict Settlements*, edited by Bruno Schoch, Hans-Joachim Spanger, and Azer Babayev, 17–38. Wiesbaden, Germany: Springer, 2020.

BBC. "Nagorno-Karabakh Conflict Killed 5,000 Soldiers." December 3, 2020. https://www.bbc.com/news/world-europe-55174211.

BBC Monitoring. "Explainer: What Is behind Turkey's Ramped up Support for Azerbaijan?" September 29, 2020. https://monitoring.bbc.co.uk/product/c2022b3j.

BBC News Türkçe. "Dağlık Karabağ: Azerbaycan, Ermenistan'la Yeni Bir Savaşa Mı Hazırlanıyor?" March 3, 2021. https://www.bbc.com/turkce/haberler-dunya-56256463#:~:text =Azerbaycan%20ile%20Ermenistan%20aras%C4%B1nda%2044,da%20bir%20k%C4 %B1sm%C4%B1n%C4%B1%20geri%20ald%C4%B1.

BBC News World. "Armenia and Azerbaijan Fight over Disputed Nagorno-Karabakh." September 27, 2020. https://www.bbc.com/news/world-europe-54314341.

Beyaz, Zafer Fatih. "MHP Genel Başkanı Bahçeli: 'Nahçıvan Özerk Cumhuriyeti'nin Azerbaycan Cumhuriyeti'ne Katılması Şarttır.'" Anadolu Ajansı, October 4, 2020. https://www .aa.com.tr/tr/politika/mhp-genel-baskani-bahceli-nahcivan-ozerk-cumhuriyetinin -azerbaycan-cumhuriyetine-katilmasi-sarttir/1995205.

Beyaz, Zafer Fatih, and Ruslan Rehimov. "Erdoğan Azerbaycan Cumhurbaşkanı Aliyev Tarafından Resmi Törenle Karşılandı." Anadolu Ajansı, February 25, 2020. https://www .aa.com.tr/tr/dunya/-erdogan-azerbaycan-cumhurbaskani-aliyev-tarafindan-resmi -torenle-karsilandi-/1744240.

Broers, Laurence. "From 'Frozen Conflict' to Enduring Rivalry: Reassessing the Nagorny Karabakh Conflict." *Nationalities Papers* 43, no. 4 (2015): 556–76.

The Conflict of Nagorno Karabakh. "Resolution of the Presidium of the USSR Supreme Soviet regarding the Decisions of the Supreme Soviets of Azerbaijan and Armenia on Nagorny Karabakh, Moscow, July 18, 1988." Armenica.org and the Union of Armenian Associations in Sweden. Accessed August 29, 2024. https://www.legal-tools.org/doc/5ed6e6/pdf/.

Cornell, Svante E. "Turkey and the Conflict in Nagorno Karabakh: A Delicate Balance." *Middle Eastern Studies* 34, no. 1 (1998): 51–72.

Davutoğlu, Ahmet. "Turkey's Mediation: Critical Reflections from the Field." *Middle East Policy* 20, no. 1 (2013): 83–90.

Euronews. "Cumhur i̇ttifakı Bir Yaşında: Nasıl Başladı, Bir Yılda Neler Oldu?" February 21, 2019. https://tr.euronews.com/2019/02/21/cumhur-ittifaki-bir-yasinda-nasil-basladi-bir -yilda-neler-oldu.

European Union External Action Service. "Nagorno Karabakh: Statement by the High Representative/Vice-President Josep Borrell." September 27, 2020. https://www.eeas.europa.eu /eeas/nagorno-karabakh-statement-high-representativevice-president-josep-borrell_en.

France 24 English. "Azerbaijani President Ilham Aliyev: 'We Never Deliberately Attacked Civilians.'" Posted on YouTube, October 14, 2020. https://www.youtube.com/watch?v =vUhXEJoRLu4.

German, Tracey. "The Nagorno-Karabakh Conflict between Azerbaijan and Armenia: Security Issues in the Caucasus." *Journal of Muslim Minority Affairs* 32, no. 2 (2012): 216–29.

Gilpin, Robert. *War and Change in World Politics*. Cambridge University Press, 1981.

Göksedef, Ece. "Dağlık Karabağ: Türkiye, Azerbaycan'ın Askeri Kapasitesini Geliştirmesinde Nasıl Rol Oynadı?" BBC News Türkçe, October 2, 2020. https://www.bbc.com/turkce /haberler-turkiye-54379105.

Isachenko, Daria. "Turkey–Russia Partnership in the War over Nagorno-Karabakh." Stiftung Wissenschaft und Politik (SWP), November 19, 2020. https://www.swp-berlin.org/en /publication/turkey-russia-partnership-in-the-war-over-nagorno-karabakh.

Kadir Has Üniversitesi. "Khas Kurumsal Araştırmalar." Khas Institutional Research, September 8, 2022. https://www.khas.edu.tr/khas-kurumsal-arastirmalar/.

———. "Türk Dış Politikası Kamuoyu Algıları Araştırması 2022 Sonuçları Açıklandı." News, September 8, 2022. https://www.khas.edu.tr/turk-dis-politikasi-kamuoyu-algilari -arastirmasi-2022-sonuclari-aciklandi/.

Kardaş, Şaban. "Turkey's Libya Policy: Militarization of Regional Policies and Escalation Dominance." *China International Strategy Review* 2, no. 2 (2020): 325–36.

Köker, İrem. "Dağlık Karabağ: İha Ve Si'ha'ların Rolü Ne Oldu, Azerbaycan'a Nasıl Avantaj Sağladı?" BBC News Türkçe, November 12, 2020. https://www.bbc.com/turkce/haberler-dunya-54917938.

Köstem, Seçkin. "Russian-Turkish Cooperation in Syria: Geopolitical Alignment with Limits." *Cambridge Review of International Affairs* 34, no. 6 (2020): 795–817.

Kriesberg, Louis. "Mediation and the Transformation of the Israeli-Palestinian Conflict." *Journal of Peace Research* 38, no. 3 (2001): 373–92.

Kutlay, Mustafa, and Ziya Öniş. "Understanding Oscillations in Turkish Foreign Policy: Pathways to Unusual Middle Power Activism." *Third World Quarterly* 42, no. 12 (2021): 3051–69.

Lobell, Steven E., Norrin M. Ripsman, and Jeffrey W. Taliaferro. *Neoclassical Realism, the State, and Foreign Policy*. Cambridge: Cambridge University Press, 2009.

McGuinness, Damien. "Nagorno-Karabakh: Remembering the Victims of Khojaly." BBC News, February 27, 2012. https://www.bbc.com/news/world-europe-17179904.

Megerisi, Tarek. "It's Turkey's Libya Now." European Council on Foreign Relations, May 20, 2020. https://ecfr.eu/article/commentary_its_turkeys_libya_now/.

Mehdiyev, Mushvig. "Azerbaijan, Israel Expand Defense Cooperation with New Joint Venture." Caspian News, March 27, 2021. https://caspiannews.com/news-detail/azerbaijan-israel-expand-defense-cooperation-with-new-joint-venture-2021-3-26-48/.

Ministry of Defense of the Republic of Azerbaijan. "Armenian Armed Forces Committed Large-Scale Provocations along the Entire Length of the Front." September 27, 2020. https://mod.gov.az/en/news/armenian-armed-forces-committed-large-scale-provocations-along-the-entire-length-of-the-front-32311.html.

———. "Azerbaijan Army's Troops Launched a Counter-Offensive Operation along the Entire Front." September 27, 2020. https://mod.gov.az/en/news/azerbaijan-army-s-troops-launched-a-counter-offensive-operation-along-the-entire-front-32318.html.

———. "Enemy Supply and Combat Equipment Destroyed." October 2, 2020. https://mod.gov.az/en/news/enemy-supply-and-combat-equipment-destroyed-video-32537.html.

———. "List of the Enemy's Destroyed Military Equipment." October 1, 2020. https://mod.gov.az/en/news/list-of-the-enemy-s-destroyed-military-equipment-video-32469.html.

Ministry of Foreign Affairs of the Republic of Armenia. "Ambassador Papikyan Presented Turkey's Policy in the South Caucasus at the Session of the OSCE Permanent Council." Press release, July 31, 2020. https://www.mfa.am/en/press-releases/2020/07/31/ocse-turkey-armrep/10405.

———. "The Permanent Representative of Armenia in Geneva Made a Statement at the UN Human Rights Council on the Offensive Unleashed by Azerbaijan against Armenia." July 17, 2020. https://www.mfa.am/en/press-releases/2020/07/17/arm-rep-geneva/10384.

———. "Statement by the MFA of Armenia." September 27, 2020. https://www.mfa.am/en/interviews-articles-and-comments/2020/09/27/mfa_st_nk/10462.

Ministry of Foreign Affairs of the Republic of Azerbaijan. "The Azerbaijan Army Has Liberated a number of Occupied Villages and Important High Grounds." September 27, 2020. https://mod.gov.az/en/news/the-azerbaijan-army-has-liberated-a-number-of-occupied-villages-and-important-high-grounds-32351.html.

———. "Conflict Settlement Process (1991–2020)." Accessed July 17, 2022. https://mfa.gov.az/en/category/conflict-settlement-process-1991-2020.

———. "No:158/20, Statement by the Ministry of Foreign Affairs of the Republic of Azerbaijan." July 14, 2020. https://mfa.gov.az/en/news/no15820nbspstatement-by-the-ministry-of-foreign-affairs-of-the-republic-of-azerbaijan-enru.

———. "President Ilham Aliyev Received from Turkish Foreign Minister and Minister of National Defense." November 8, 2020. https://mod.gov.az/en/news/president-ilham-aliyev-received-turkish-foreign-minister-and-minister-of-national-defense-33745.html.

———. "President Ilham Aliyev Received Turkish Foreign Minister, Minister of National Defense and Director of National Intelligence Organization." November 10, 2020. https://mod.gov.az/en/news/president-ilham-aliyev-received-turkish-foreign-minister-minister-of-national-defense-and-director-of-national-intellige-33799.html.

Ministry of Foreign Affairs of the Republic of Turkey. "Azerbaycan Ile Ermenistan Arasında İlan Edilen Ateşkes Hk." October 10, 2020. https://www.mfa.gov.tr/no_-239_-azerbaycan-ile-ermenistan-arasinda-ilan-edilen-ateskes-hk.tr.mfa.

———. "Dışişleri Bakanlığı Sözcüsü Hami Aksoy'un Ermenistan'In Bu Sabah Azerbaycan'a Karşı Başlattığı Saldırı Hakkındaki Soruya Cevabı." September 27, 2020. https://www.mfa.gov.tr/sc_-94_-ermenistan-in-azerbaycan-a-karsi-baslattigi-saldiri-hk-sc.tr.mfa.

———. "No: 149, 12 July 2020, Press Release Regarding the Armenian Attack on Azerbaijan." July 12, 2020. https://www.mfa.gov.tr/no_-149_-azerbaycan-a-yonelik-ermeni-saldirisi-hk.en.mfa.

Ministry of Foreign Affairs of the Russian Federation. "Briefing by Foreign Ministry Spokeswoman Maria Zakharova, Moscow, October 1, 2020." Press service briefings, October 1, 2020. https://mid.ru/en/press_service/spokesman/briefings/1443363/#7.

———. "Briefing by Foreign Ministry Spokeswoman Maria Zakharova, Moscow, October 5, 2020." Press service briefings, October 15, 2020, https://mid.ru/en/press_service/spokesman/briefings/1444355/#20.

O'Rourke, Breffni. "Russia, Armenia to Sign Defense Pact." Radio Free Europe/Radio Liberty, August 20, 2010. https://www.rferl.org/a/Russian_President_Medvedev_To_Visit_Armenia/2131915.html.

OSCE Chairpersonship. "OSCE Chairperson-in-Office Calls for Return to Ceasefire around Nagorno-Karabakh and Resumption of Substantive Negotiations." Newsroom, press statement, September 27, 2020. Organization for Security and Co-operation in Europe. https://www.osce.org/chairmanship/465021.

Ott, Marvin C. "Mediation as a Method of Conflict Resolution: Two Cases." *International Organization* 26, no. 4 (1972): 595–618.

President of Russia. "Statement by President of the Republic of Azerbaijan, Prime Minister of the Republic of Armenia and President of the Russian Federation." Kremlin, November 10, 2020. http://en.kremlin.ru/events/president/news/64384.

Radio Free Europe/Radio Liberty. "More Armenian, Azeri Bodies Exchanged." November 9, 2010. https://www.rferl.org/a/More_Armenian_Azerbaijani_Bodies_Exchanged_/2214686.html.

Rehimov, Ruslan. "Aliyev: Azerbaycan'ı Ilk Tanıyan Ülkenin Türkiye Olması Milli Hafızamıza Ebediyen Kazınmıştır." Anadolu Ajansı, January 14, 2022. https://www.aa.com.tr/tr/dunya/aliyev-azerbaycani-ilk-taniyan-ulkenin-turkiye-olmasi-milli-hafizamiza-ebediyen-kazinmistir/2473659.

——— "Azerbaycan Ordusu, Karabağ'daki Savaşta 2 Bin 908 Şehit Verdi." Anadolu Ajansı, October 21, 2021. https://www.aa.com.tr/tr/dunya/azerbaycan-ordusu-karabagdaki-savasta-2-bin-908-sehit-verdi/2399072.

———. "Türkiye Ve Azerbaycan'dan Savaş Sahnelerini Aratmayan Tatbikat." Anadolu Ajansı, September 5, 2020. https://www.aa.com.tr/tr/dunya/turkiye-ve-azerbaycandan-savas-sahnelerini-aratmayan-tatbikat/1964206.

Resmî Gazete. "Türkiye Cumhuriyeti ve Azerbaycan Cumhuriyeti Arasında Stratejik Ortaklık ve Karşılıklı Yardım Anlaşması." August 16, 2010. https://www.resmigazete.gov.tr/eskiler/2011/05/20110528M1-30.htm.

Reuters. "*Russia* and Turkey Open Monitoring Centre for Nagorno-Karabakh." January 30, 2021. https://www.reuters.com/article/uk-armenia-azerbaijan-monitoring-centre-idUSKBN29Z0FL.

Ripsman, Norrin M., Jeffrey W. Taliaferro, and Steven E. Lobell. *Neoclassical Realist Theory of International Politics*. New York: Oxford University Press, 2016.
Robertson, Roland. "Globalisation or Glocalisation?" *Journal of International Communication* 18, no. 2 (2012): 191–208.
———. "Time-Space and Homogeneity-Heterogeneity." In *Global Modernities*, edited by Mike Featherstone, Scott Lash, and Roland Robertson, 25–44. London: Sage, 1997.
Rose, Gideon. "Neoclassical Realism and Theories of Foreign Policy." *World Politics* 51, no. 1 (1998): 144–72.
Sarıahmetoğlu, Nesrin. "Karabağ Sorununun Çözüm Sürecinde Türkiye Ve Rusya." *Marmara Türkiyat Araştırmaları Dergis* 3, no. 2 (2016): 93–119.
Sözcü Gazetesi. "Erdoğan'dan Azerbaycan'a Destek: Türkiye Bütün Imkanları Kullanmaya Kararlıdır." October 5, 2020. https://www.sozcu.com.tr/2020/gundem/erdogandan-azerbaycana-destek-turkiye-butun-imkanlari-kullanmaya-kararlidir-6067981/.
SSB (@SavunmaSanayii). "Başkan @Ismaildemirssb'den Azerbaycan Açıklaması: 'Türkiye'nin Savunma Sanayii Alanında Her Ne Imkanı Varsa Kardeş Ülke Azerbaycan'ın Emrindedir.'" Twitter, 5:39 a.m., September 27, 2020. https://twitter.com/SavunmaSanayii/status/1310152152136822784.
Stockholm International Peace Research Institute. "Arms Transfers to Conflict Zones: The Case of Nagorno-Karabakh." April 30, 2021. https://www.sipri.org/commentary/topical-backgrounder/2021/arms-transfers-conflict-zones-case-nagorno-karabakh.
TRT Haber. "Cumhurbaşkanı Erdoğan: Milli Si'ha'larımız İçin Pek Çok Ülke Sırada Bekliyor." August 29, 2021. https://www.trthaber.com/haber/gundem/cumhurbaskani-erdogan-milli-sihalarimiz-icin-pek-cok-ulke-sirada-bekliyor-604969.html.
TRT Haber. "Türkiye Ile Azerbaycan Arasındaki Askeri Iş Birliği Artıyor." September 27, 2020. https://www.trthaber.com/haber/gundem/turkiye-ile-azerbaycan-arasindaki-askeri-is-birligi-artiyor-519043.html.
TRT Haber. "Türkiye Ve Azerbaycan Ortak Tatbikatı Başladı." July 29, 2020. https://www.trthaber.com/haber/gundem/turkiye-ve-azerbaycan-ortak-tatbikati-basladi-505585.html.
Tür, Özlem. "Turkey's Role in the Middle East and Gulf Security." *Asian Journal of Middle Eastern and Islamic Studies* 13, no. 4 (2019): 592–603.
Türkiye Cumhuriyeti Cumhurbaşkanlığı. "Türkiye'nin Uluslararası Alandaki Itibarını, Gücünü, Kabiliyetlerini Geliştirdik." September 17, 2020. https://www.tccb.gov.tr/haberler/410/122109/-turkiye-nin-uluslararasi-alandaki-itibarini-gucunu-kabiliyetlerini-gelistirdik-.
United Nations High Commissioner for Refugees. "UNHCR Publication for CIS Conference (Displacement in the CIS)—Conflicts in the Caucasus." Accessed July 9, 2022. https://www.unhcr.org/publications/refugeemag/3b5583fd4/unhcr-publication-cis-conference-displacement-cis-conflicts caucasus.html#:~:text=One%20in%20eight%20people%20in,of%20the%20Nagorno%2DKarabakh%20dispute.
United Nations Security Council. Resolution 853, April 30, 1993. S/RES/822 (1993). https://www.un.org/securitycouncil/content/resolutions-adopted-security-council-1993.
United Nations Security Council. Resolution 874, October 14, 1993. S/RES/874 (1993). https://www.un.org/securitycouncil/content/resolutions-adopted-security-council-1993.
United Nations Security Council. Resolution 884, November 12, 1993. S/RES/884 (1993). https://www.un.org/securitycouncil/content/resolutions-adopted-security-council-1993.
Witt, Stephen. "The Turkish Drone That Changed the Nature of Warfare." *New Yorker*, May 5, 2022. https://www.newyorker.com/magazine/2022/05/16/the-turkish-drone-that-changed-the-nature-of-warfare.
World Bank Group. "Armenia." World Bank Open Data. Accessed August 9, 2022. https://data.worldbank.org/country/AM.

World Bank Group. "Azerbaijan." World Bank Open Data. Accessed August 9, 2022. https://data.worldbank.org/indicator/NY.GDP.MKTP.CD?locations=AZ.

Yalçınkaya, Haldun. "Turkey's Overlooked Role in the Second Nagorno-Karabakh War." German Marshall Fund US, January 21, 2021. https://www.gmfus.org/news/turkeys-overlooked-role-second-nagorno-karabakh-war.

Yamskov, Anatoly N. "Ethnic Conflict in the Transcausasus." *Theory and Society* 20, no. 5 (1991): 631–60.

Zartman, I. William, and Saadia Touval. "International Mediation: Conflict Resolution and Power Politics." *Journal of Social Issues* 41, no. 2 (1985): 32–33.

TAHA KALAYCI is a PhD candidate and research assistant in the Department of International Relations at Middle East Technical University (METU). He holds a bachelor of sicence degree in political science and public administration from METU. Kalaycı received a master of arts degree in political science and international relations from TOBB University of Economics and Technology. He worked as a project assistant for "Enhancing Turkish Counter-Terrorism Capacity: Youth Dimension," which aims to contribute to the fight against radicalization among young people in Turkey. His research interests include international security, Russian foreign policy, and terrorism.

ÜNSAL SIĞRI is Professor of Management and Vice-Rector of Business Management OSTİM Technical University. His teaching and research interests include organizational behavior, leadership, strategic management, organizational development, conflict management, negotiation, mediation, and cross-cultural management. He has worked on several international academic projects within Research Committee 01 "Armed Forces and Conflict Resolution" of the International Sociological Association and ERGOMAS (European Research Group on Military Studies).

5

KENYA'S COLLECTIVE SECURITY APPROACH IN A GLOCALIZED SECURITY ENVIRONMENT IN SOMALIA

Francis Onditi and James Yuko

Introduction: Somali State Failures and Kenyan Security Vulnerabilities

In a collective security system, the enemy is a threat not only to the aggrieved state but also to the regional and sometimes global peace and security architecture. Global peace and security architecture does not exist in a vacuum. It largely operates within a binary global-local relationship. Furthermore, the effects of global-local international interventions (i.e., glocalization), or the lack of such interventions, are accentuating peace and security threats facing people within this glocalized context characterized by increasing interconnectedness.[1] In this chapter, the global and the local are framed as reciprocal. In other words, national security interests are intertwined with global responses against peace and security threats such as terrorism. On the question of interconnectedness, Ronald Robertson's conception of glocalization—as it relates to politics, security, culture, and social daily life—puts more emphasis on the role of local spaces in shaping global processes.[2] For instance, the international collective security system, which is discussed in the core of this chapter, does not exist in vacuum; rather, it is anchored by local dynamics and interests. But also, local security cannot be considered in absolute terms or outside the global context. Victor Roudometof makes an attempt to theorize global-local relationships.[3] Within this purview, local security, popularly known as national security, is an articulation of the global dynamics, constructed through global responses by various players.

In this sense of things, as the effects of peace and security glocalization become more pronounced, the impact on Kenya's local-cum-national security has been the focus of scholarly and policy discourses. Notably, Kenya is a country existing within a complex peace and security architecture based within the Horn of Africa, which is heavily impacted by terrorism. With regard to this peace and security environment, D. Smith Ray's idea of social structuralism seems to reinforce the view that glocalization can be achieved through structures of power within the processes of globalization as a process shaped by various forms of homogenization and differentiation—a process that brings into play the question of the collective security system (CSS).[4] Kenya's deployment of CSS to fight against Al-Shabaab in Somalia is particularly an interesting security (mis)adventure, bringing to the fore the need to untangle the question whether collective security within the broader framework of glocalization is an effective approach for tackling global terror.

The Kenyan intervention has constrained the diplomatic relations between Kenya and Somalia and has potentially made Kenya more vulnerable to further attacks by Al-Shabaab. Kenya's constrained relationship with Somalia is an outcome of its entanglement in the Somali civil war. Although the concept of entanglement has a home in natural sciences, social scientists have adopted it to mean the interdependence between human beings and the things that make up the universe, including processes and decisions.[5] In this application, it is plausible to argue that Kenya's decision to deploy soldiers in Somalia—a decision based on both national and global security concerns—produced an entangled relationship. The two states were caught in the double tragedy of having to balance their national security interests and those of the global order. However, back home, the Kenyan government has remained under intense pressure from citizens and other interest groups to withdraw its military from Somalia.[6] As other sections of this chapter demonstrate, the (blind) collective responsibility approach taken (under the aegis of CSS) by Kenya—most notably through the African Union Mission in Somalia (AMISOM)—seems to have left the country more vulnerable to terror attacks.

Notwithstanding the point that CSS serves some geopolitical interests, it is apparent that asymmetric conflict is quite different from interstate conflict. As it becomes clearer in this chapter, asymmetric conflict challenges the methods of warfare in interstate conflict. This chapter interrogates the extent to which the CSS approach secures Kenyan territory or increases terror threats against the country. Within the system of collective security, member states are dissuaded from behaviors that threaten extranational peace and stability. However, a basic security dilemma remains: How can a state entangled in fighting a nonstate actor in a foreign land effectively apply the principles of CSS in neutralizing such threats (of this kind) to its national security?

The Evolution of Insurgency Intervention in Somalia

Over the years, Somalia has experienced civil conflict culminating in state collapse and terrorism.[7] Prior to the collapse of the state, Somalia has had episodes of fragility under the authoritarian regime of Mohamed Siad Barre (1969–1991) and the Islamic Courts Union (ICU) government in Mogadishu (1991–2007) as well as during the breakaway of Somaliland (1991–present).[8] Collectively, these episodes led to the evolution of Al-Shabaab into a terrorist organization. Al-Shabaab's spread beyond Somali territory demonstrates how a *localized* conflict transformed into a global phenomenon requiring a collective security approach. In this regard, Kenya and other state actors (including the United States) have been at the forefront of enforcing the global collective security approach against Al-Shabaab. The evolution of Al-Shabaab and its regional and global influence has occurred in four phases.

Phase 1: The Era of President Mohamed Siad Barre

The contextual and historical dynamics of Somalia are crucial in understanding the glocalization of the security threats from Somalia and Kenya's entanglement in the Somali civil war. Since the administration of President Mohamed Siad Barre (1969–1991), Somalia has remained a failing state in institutional discordance with minimal authority.[9] The effect of state failure is that various armed groups in Somalia could function by establishing an economic base by which to connect with the outside world through the country's porous seaports.[10] The dictatorial regime of Siad Barre not only failed to promote development but also antagonized the powerful clans—leading them to resume the enforcement of strict clan territorial boundaries.[11] Increasingly, political power has been vested in the clan territories and warlords. In this sense, the Somalian state operated without a unifying factor, which created ungoverned spaces.[12] The ungoverned space created fertile ground for Al-Shabaab to thrive and grow into the most powerful insurgency group holding significant control of the country and posing a significant threat to regional and global security.[13]

Phase 2: The Emergence of Al-Shabaab

Al-Ittihad Al Islamiyah (AIAI) is believed to be the predecessor of Al-Shabaab.[14] However, other scholars have traced the formation of AIAI to the toppling of the Siad Barre regime in 1983.[15] The main motivation was to craft an Islamic state that united all the Somali-speaking people in the Horn of Africa (i.e., Kenya, Djibouti, and Ethiopia).[16] It is therefore plausible to argue that extremist organizations preceded state collapse in Somalia. However, the militarization of Somalia is not a recent phenomenon. As early as the 1960s, the radical Salafi and Wahhabi Islamists were already causing havoc in Somali clan villages as the moderate Sufis became marginalized. During the Soviet invasion of Afghanistan in the 1980s, Somali Wahhabi and Salafi adherents joined the fight against the Soviets. On returning back to Somalia, they aligned with the radical views of Abdulla Azam, who plotted the formation of a fundamentalist organization. Together with Abdulla Azam, a Pan-Islamist, they eventually became the leaders of Al-Shabaab. In 2000, the group transformed into a youth militia, namely, Al-Shabaab. The group continued to receive financial support from the ICU, and its leader held a position in the Shura Council of the ICU government. The group intensified its activities, leading to the capture of the Port of Kismayu in September 2006, giving it a solid financial base.[17]

The collapse of the Somalian state in 1991 increased the influence of AIAI in the country's political order under sharia law. Interestingly, sharia law ushered in relative peace in most of the country (albeit a short-lived one). The Somali youth who participated in the Afghanistan liberation war became influential in the AIAI. Some of the youth, such as Aden Ayro and Mukhtar Robow, maintained their networks with the remnants of the Afghan mujahideen, eventually becoming the face of Al-Shabaab's network in the Horn of Africa.[18]

Phase 3: The Era of International Intervention

The international effort to establish peace and stability in Somalia took place from 1992 to 1995 but was largely unsuccessful. The dominant interventions were the United Nations Operations in Somalia I (UNOSOM I), the United Taskforce, and UNOSOM II.[19] The kinetic diplomacy of the United States received mixed reactions from regional leaders. The question of whose interests prevailed remained prominent among critiques of the US intervention. The US intervention triggered the subsequent military offensive launched from the Khartoum-based al-Qaeda. Osama bin Laden established networks in Kenya to facilitate resistance against US forces in the region.[20]

Phase 4: The Era of Internal Political Wrangles

Between 1996 and 2000, Somalia experienced unprecedented internal political dynamics leading to the formation of several Al-Shabaab cells, which was triggered by several developments. Notably, AIAI was weakened by Ethiopian incursions into Somalia after decrying the involvement of AIAI with the Ogaden rebels in Ethiopia. Also, there were feuds among Islamic fundamentalists within Somalia.[21] The collapse of the warlord coalitions further degraded the capacity of AIAI to control territories and created a power vacuum. In 2006, the radical ICU forcefully took over Mogadishu, which made Somalia a key target of the global war on terror and the application of collective security measures by regional and external powers.[22]

Kenya-Somalia Relations in a Glocalised Security Environment

Kenya's collective security system approach is an integral part of the seemingly glocalized peace and security architecture, most notably represented by AMISOM.[23] AMISOM, in which Kenya is very involved, was created by the African Union's Peace and Security Council on January 19, 2007. The regional formation was approved by the United Nations Security Council (UNSC) with an initial six-month mandate to support the Somali transitional government.[24] The Kenya Defense Force (KDF) joined AMISOM in 2011, initially to create a buffer zone to prevent further kidnappings and cross-border attacks conducted by the Al-Shabaab AMISOM, including Kenyan troops, made significant gains in liberating towns and cities in various parts of Somalia and cutting off Al-Shabaab's access to economic bases in Kismayo. However, the increasing cases of terror attacks by Al-Shabaab in the Horn of Africa, particularly in Kenya, raises a fundamental question: whether the collectivist approach to security is applicable when states respond to nonstate actors from or in a foreign land. For more than a decade, AMISOM has been coalescing states from across the African continent in efforts to neutralize the Al-Shabaab militant group in Somalia. However, the Somali society presents a plethora of contradictions. Some have described it as a social disorder without a state.[25] Yet others view it as a state without a nation.[26] These societal intricacies present Somalia as being a unique country. In other words, the existence of Al-Shabaab is a reflection of Somali society. In the Horn of Africa, Somalia is viewed as being a failed state due to its unstable authority and the lack of the basic rule of law.[27] Clan system is a strong social fabric in Somalia. In fact, some schools of thought have elucidated that Somali clans were acephalous during the precolonial period.[28] However, Mahmood Mamdani refutes this claim—arguing that it is, in fact, a highly centralized and bifurcated society.[29] This unique presumption and tendency to operate in a closed social system among the Somali people could explain their distinctive orientation toward fierce resistance against any external influence—whether through norms or militancy. Militant groups, such as Al-Shabaab, sprawl through the clan social organism. But how did Al-Shabaab emerge in Somalia?

There are varied views and accounts of how the Al-Shabaab group emerged in Somalia. Religious fundamentalist groups thrived on the bedrock of the collapsed state of Somalia in 1991. For instance, Al-Shabaab and a few other Islamic extremists in Somalia, including the ICU, have their roots in the former AIAI, which also evolved from Somalia's religious organization, the Al-Salafiya Al-jadiid in the early 1970s.[30] The fundamentalists drew extremist aspirations from jihadi fighters in Afghanistan.[31] Efforts by the international community to tackle the extremist group in Somalia began in 1992 through UNOSOM I.[32] However, this effort did not bear fruits for various reasons, including the fragility of the state of Somalia, which could not provide effective governance to the population. The most recent account of the group's evolution is based on the youth movement theory advanced by Seth G. Jones, Andrew M. Liepman, and Nathan Chandler.[33] The youth movement theory locates the origin of Al-Shabaab in 2005 as the youth took a step to unify all Islamic radicals and create an Islamic state in the Horn of Africa. In September 2006, Al-Shabaab and the ICU seized the economic hub of Somalia, namely, the Port of Kismayu. The Port of Kismayu is a crucial geo-economic space linking Somali society to the rest of the world through the Indian Ocean. In 2011, President Mwai Kibaki ordered deployment of the KDF, as a response to the Al-Shabaab attacks on Kenyan soil. Despite the incisive offensive put forward by the KDF, Al-Shabaab continues to orchestrate violent attacks in Kenya.

Kenya has had a long history of Somali irredentist behavior dating back to the Shifta conflict of the 1960s. The Shifta conflict, which was mainly driven by militant Somali nationalists and groups of dissident frontier communities, remains a very memorable conflict after Kenya's independence.[34] Scholars have enumerated several socioeconomic and political factors that drove the Shifta conflict—all of which culminated in the need to secede from the rest of Kenya by the Northern Frontier District (NFD) communities (i.e., Somali, Gabra, Borana, and Rendile), an area with a lack of exploitable resources, poor infrastructure (hence, closing off the districts from the rest of the country), and porous borders with the Republic of Somalia. The border porosity and marginalization straddled the communities' drift toward a peripheral ideology. Unlike the post–Cold War discourses that link the extremist group (Al-Shabaab) to Islamic fundamentalism,[35] the Shifta resistance was primarily secular. However, David M. Anderson and Jacob McKnight have vehemently claimed that the targets of most of the attacks in northern Kenya and inside Somalia have been on non-Muslims and Muslims considered as betrayers or Christian sympathizers.[36]

The shift in focus from the NFD secession to Al-Shabaab terrorism highlights the view that the international threats to peace and security, specifically to Kenya, are changing. When several Europeans were kidnapped in Lamu in September and October 2011, hotel reservations plummeted, staff were laid off, and hotel operators demanded increased security.[37] Kenya advanced the argument of its right to self-defense as embodied in Article 51 of the 1945 UN Charter, which clearly recognizes the inherent right of individual and collective self-defense in the wake of an armed attack against a member of the United Nations. While Kenya relied on Article 51 to globalize its military intervention in Somalia, local/domestic security reasons and other interests were utilized to whip up support from the population for the military onslaught in Somalia. Specifically, the increased militant activities by Al-Shabaab within the borders of Kenya were effectively highlighted to mobilize the citizens to support the deployment of the KDF inside Somalia in 2011 to root out the terrorist elements and create a buffer zone in Jubaland.

Despite the self-defense response by Kenya, Al-Shabaab's attacks have escalated since the 2011 KDF incursion into Somalia. The failure of the KDF to secure Kenyans from terror attacks has raised a series of moral and political questions, one of which is whether the Kenyan military intervention in Somalia has been necessitated by self-interest or by collective responsibility within the international order. Could it be that Kenya is simply playing to the gallery of Western interests in the Horn of Africa, putting the interests of the West over that of Kenyans? Yet others view the intervention as being based on a Kenyan quest to secure its borders from the terror group.[38]

Collective Security System and Glocalized Security

The CSS principle is a potent norm in the contemporary world order. Its approach to international peace and security order, as defined in classic international security discourses, is a process of establishing normative, military, and political assets and capabilities for preventing threats and acts of aggression against a cooperating member state.[39] The classic theory of international security broadly classifies the CSS principle into two major typologies: first, a primitive collective security operating under the logic of self-help and, second, a higher-order degree in which the central organ of the community (for example, NATO or AMISOM) takes charge of the actions being taken for collective security.[40] The principle of CSS has a home in the UN Charter (Chapter 7, Article 51). Legal scholars have framed the notion of CSS into a set of principles under general international law. Contrary to the principle of self-help, the principle of collective security states that countries not directly violated in their rights are obliged to assist the violated state. Apart from the legal view of the notion, political scientists treat CSS as a conceptual body of knowledge rather than a full-fledged principle.[41]

From a glocalization standpoint, the CSS principle is simply a global idea made to fit local security concerns. It also entails the adaptation of global and international security interests into the local context and needs. The term *glocal* and the process noun *glocalization* are formed by neologistically telescoping the words *global* and *local* to create a blend of the two.[42] The idea has been modeled on the Japanese concept of *dochakuka* (derived from *dochaku*, meaning "living on one's own land"). This term originally referred to the agricultural principle of adapting one's farming techniques to local conditions but also went on to become adopted in Japanese business circles for the purpose of referring to global localization—that is, a global outlook adapted to local conditions. More specifically, the terms *glocal* and *glocalization* became aspects of business jargon in the 1980s, but their major locus of origin was, in fact, Japan—a country that has strongly cultivated considerations of its spatio-cultural significance and where the general issue of the relationship between the particular and the universal has historically received almost obsessive attention.[43]

Within the security sphere, the concept of glocalization draws on the failures to resolve conflicts in countries where external interests have deeply been fused with domestic issues such as in Somalia, Mali, Nigeria, Libya, Palestine, Yemen, Syria, Iraq, Afghanistan, and Ukraine.[44] Glocalized security hinges on the argument that the fusion of domestic and external matters generates new war dynamics that require both substantial domestic reforms and the realignment of external interests in order to achieve a sustainable peace. As such, international military interventions should not only be anchored in the interests and political values of the intervening powers and Western-dominated international governance mechanisms but also must be made to address domestic grievances through inclusive governance arrangements.[45] Arguably, therefore, conflicts that undermine regional and international peace can only be solved by disentangling the domestic interests from the external ones, demilitarizing international interventions, and seeking more domestic solutions to the same.

As a concept, CSS is fairly recent. It was nonexistent in the World War I era. The "Big Four" movement in the spring of 1919—also known as the Council of Four, led by David Lloyd George (Britain), Georges Clemenceau (France), Vittorio Emanuele (Italy), and Woodrow Wilson (USA)—put more emphasis on the arbitration of disputes and establishment of international institutions rather than on security collectivism.[46] Earlier on, although the three major peace conferences—the Hague Conventions (1899, 1907) and the Paris Conference (1919)—that led to the Treaty of Versailles and the formation of the League of Nations,[47] emboldened collectivist ideals, the real conceptual frame of a modern CSS is mainly associated with the post–World War II era, notably with the formation of NATO in 1948 and the Warsaw Pact in 1955.[48] This is after the new dispensation brought about by World War II ushered in new political realities; problems bedeviling the community of nations can no longer simply be resolved by individual states or by their immediate neighbors. Rather, problems such as armed aggression, climate change, and underdevelopment require a collective responsibility by integrating states into strong and cohesive formations that could look to each other to protect their interests. In the contemporary international system, the rush by Sweden and Finland to join NATO after Russia invaded Ukraine in 2022 is an illustration of the potency of a growing family of collective security alliances, shaped not only by the geography but also by fear of the irredentist behavior of some states. States with irredentist behavior have an appetite for expansionism as they seek to annex neighboring territories on the basis of ethnic, cultural, historical, and territorial ties.[49]

Unlike the individualistic approach, CSS treats an enemy to a member state as being an enemy to the regional or international peace and security regime. In the CSS regime, a coalition member state counts on the support of others in exchange for unequivocal loyalty to such regional or international arrangements. It is usually a long-term formal arrangement among the collaborating states with the aim of protecting the security interests of individual member states within their spheres of interest. Although in the individualistic security system (ISS) approach states look after themselves, they may temporarily sacrifice their national interests for a group on the condition of a reward system. It is therefore conceivable that punishment or reward mechanisms can motivate individual states to abandon their national interests in favor of those of the group. This thinking has been reinforced by social psychologists, who have constructed a collectivist-individual continuum in which collectivist traits among individualists have a tendency to expect either positive or negative outcomes of interaction with others.[50] It is this group-help attitude among the collectivist individuals that guards against the illegal use of force by an aggressive state or group per the logic of "all against one." As one of the principles of the United Nations and its predecessor, the League of Nations, CSS is anchored on three main yardsticks: liberal democracy, strong economic cooperation, and the rule of law.[51] These three norms and values are considered prerequisites for resolving conflicts, whether interstate clashes or those that are driven by nonstate actors.

Resolving the security dilemma emanating from violent nonstate actors through the CSS approach and other models of cooperation remains a challenge. Most of the frameworks and mechanisms operationalized under the CSS are applicable to interstate conflict and wars. Article 51 of the UN Charter puts more emphasis on states involved in self-defense. The essence and limitations of Article 51 in its application to fighting a nonstate actor aggressor is well articulated by Hans Kelsen: "According to Article 51, it is the states involved in the process of self-defense which are competent to interpret Article 51. These states may or may not understand . . . that a state has resorted to war against another state, using its own armed force. They may or may not understand . . . that a state [has] interfered in a civil war taking place within another state by arming or otherwise assisting the revolutionary group in its fight against the legitimate government."[52] Article 51 limits the right of self-defense to interstate conflict or warfare. It is therefore not explicit on how a state could apply CSS principles in responding to a nonstate actor in a foreign land—especially in an asymmetric glocalized environment. This type of environment betrays a certain measure of collective responsibility that is a peculiar prepossession of the collectivism of CSS. Rather, it invites security dilemmas in the international community's efforts to reduce security threats or the risk of war through security cooperation. Security cooperation mechanisms operating under the broader framework of CSS have been deployed by different military formations in order to address threats to peace and security—threats including terrorism. Counterterrorism approaches exhibit some common features of glocalization. Notably, the involvement of Kenya in the global war on terror in Somalia under the umbrella of AMISOM presents two schools of thought on Kenyan security that are crucial in evaluating the merits of a CSS approach for Kenya.

Global-Local Schools of Thought on Kenyan Intervention in Somalia

Throughout the world, there are various strategies and approaches deployed in fighting terror groups, including Al-Shabaab in the Horn of Africa. Given the focus of Article 51 of the UN Charter on interstate conflict, for instance, in the case concerning armed activities on the territory of the Congo, some scholars[53] question whether the global fight against terrorism fits into the CSS arrangement. Their view is that an armed attack must be attributable to a state. Indeed, there has been a loosening commitment of Western countries to intervene in terrorist activities in Africa.[54] This geostrategic vacuum is being filled by regional powers like South Africa, Nigeria, and Kenya to assume a dominant role in fighting terrorism.[55] Across Africa, there have been individual interventions in response to terrorist threats.[56] Kenya is one of the regional powers that has been at the forefront of fighting terrorism in the Horn of Africa.[57] In 2011, the Kenyan government resolved to intervene militarily in Somalia due to continuous terror attacks on Kenyan soil. Somalia is considered the heartland of Al-Shabaab. However, the incursion of KDF into Somalia came with an incisive cost to Kenya's national security and domestic politics. Since September 2013, Kenya has been on the receiving end of Al-Shabaab's attacks in various forms.[58] Clearly, the intervention has taken a glocalized character in Kenya—generating debates over the Kenyan government's decision to deploy KDF in Somalia. The enduring debate in Kenya's decision to adopt the CSS framework has been about why Kenya intervened militarily in Somalia and whose war is being fought there.[59] This debate can be classified into two main views: (a) the narrow localized view and (b) the extranational security view.

Supporters of the CSS approach see the deployment of KDF in Somalia as being driven by national security concerns. They see Kenya's participation in CSS arrangements as being based on the narrowly local security interests of Kenya, instead of simply following a global agenda. As they often point out, the intervention followed considerable developments of security instability in the country as a result of the anarchic nature of Somalia and the growing threats of Al-Shabaab in the Horn of Africa, which directly affected Kenyan domestic security. This narrow localized security view argues that the Kenyan government decided to join AMISOM in order to extricate itself from the external threat posed by Somalia. Moreover, the nature of asymmetric warfare exemplified by Al-Shabaab dictates that the KDF must fight the threat of terrorism from within Somalia. Anderson and McKnight, for example, assert that Kenya's security against terrorist attacks needs to be extended beyond the nation's borders directly into Somalia—which is where Al-Shabaab is centered.[60]

The narrow localized security view has amplified the need for Kenya to engage in the global war on terror by arguing that Al-Shabaab has infiltrated the refugee camps in Kenya. It was on the basis of this security threat that the Kenyan government decided to undertake a military intervention in Somalia. This narrow localized security view has been simplified in slogans such as "Fight Al-Shabaab from within Somalia to safeguard Kenya's national security." In fact, the KDF's doctrinal motto in Somalia is dubbed "Operation Linda Inchi" (Operation Safeguard the Country).

The extranational view sees the Kenyan intervention through the global war on terror. It argues that the KDF intervention in Somalia largely serves the interests of the regional and international communities. They see little authenticity in Kenya's national security claim, especially as Kenya's intervention makes it a prime target for terrorist retribution. For the extranational view, the situation looks like the chicken-egg scenario, as they critically ask: What would be the gain of maintaining international security order at the expense of more Kenyan civilian deaths from further Al-Shabaab attacks? They see the intervention as essentially negating Kenya's national security. Advocates of this school of thought have maintained that the series of terror attacks in Kenya is Al Shabab's way of striking back at Kenya for KDF activities in Somalia. Nongovernmental organizations have become key proponents of this view, arguing that the KDF involvement in Somalia does not proffer national security for the Kenyans.[61] Despite the countersecurity risks, Kenya continued its deployment in Somalia as part of AMISOM and in line with the CSS approach. As part of its security strategy, Kenya is using KDF to boost the widely reported but publicly undeclared plan to establish a semiautonomous region in southern Somalia. KDF has been involved in creating a buffer zone known as Jubaland/Azania (with Kismayu as its capital) that comprises the Gedo, Lower, and Middle Juba regions.[62] The rationale behind establishing the buffer zone is to regulate the influx of Somali refugees in Kenya. However, the Kenyan quest for power in the Horn of Africa, and the repatriation of Somalian refugees, negate the prospects of a CSS approach. The United Nations Agency for Refugees estimates that Kenya is a host to over half a million of Somali refugees who live in Dadaab Refugee Camp.[63] KDF's incursion into Somalia has been based purely on extranational interests' risks alienating Kenyan Somalis from other Kenyans.[64]

Frederic Pearson observes that any military intervention is an attempt by a given state to change the internal structures of a target state through coercive methods.[65] These coercive methods are meant to affect the modus operandi of the political, military, and socioeconomic structures of the target state. Advocates of the extranational school of thought have highlighted two reasons that may drive a state to militarily intervene beyond their borders: (1) when the intervening state sets aside the existing relations with the target state and puts all its efforts toward changing the political structure and authority of that target state, and (2) when the intervening state seeks to preserve the existing political structure and authority of the target state. However, this principle may not apply to the asymmetric war environment where Kenya's target is not the state but rather a nonstate actor—namely, Al-Shabaab.[66]

One way of evaluating the recurring threats of Kenya's military intervention in the Horn of Africa is by evaluating the merits and demerits of collectivist and individualist approaches to peace and security interventions.

The procollectivist approach, which is the narrow localized view of Kenyan security, suggests that KDF should continue with its operation in Somalia.[67] It can be argued that collectivists seem not to take cognizance of the fact that military intervention without complementary domestic political efforts and the rule of law in Somalia will not guarantee Kenya's national security. On the other hand, the individualist approach takes the extranational security view, arguing that Kenya should use a political route to find a solution to the Somali crisis. However, it has been observed that individualists fail to realize that the need for political solutions in Somalia cannot be realized without sending the military to the source of the problem. As such, the Kenyan government is obliged to deploy KDF in Somalia in order to prevent the spread of Al-Shabaab across the porous borders between Kenya and Somalia.[68]

The procollectivist approach criticizes the antimilitary intervention view for lacking consideration of the level of armed threat that Kenya as a country has been encountering. On the other hand, the individualist approach criticizes the procollectivist view for its failure to understand that the Kenyan government did not have sufficient knowledge about the realpolitik of Somalia as a failed state before it committed troops. On this, Peter Haldén, observes that since 1991, the Somali civil war has destroyed the judiciary system, plunging the country into anarchy and creating a scenario where essential human needs such as human security are lacking. This has led to the formation of organized criminal groups who endeavor to protect themselves using all means—including terrorism.[69] State-failure theorists argue that a failed state is likely to attract terrorist organization beyond its borders.[70] This is because failed states are vulnerable to poor governance and therefore are unable to provide certain public goods. Indeed, a fragile and failed state like Somalia suits this terrorist organization in that the inward manifestation of weak governance attracts external intervention. This glocalized environment, where domestic and external matters are fused, generates new war dynamics that require both substantial domestic reforms and realignment of external interests in order to achieve sustainable peace. As such, international military interventions should not only be anchored in the interests and political values of the intervening powers and Western-dominated international governance mechanisms, but fundamental efforts must also be made to address domestic grievances through inclusive governance arrangements.

Kenya in Somalia: Collective Security or Unnecessary Entanglement?

The question whether Kenya's approach to the fight against Al-Shabaab is a legitimate response to domestic security concerns (i.e., *necessary evil*) or merely an international military intervention anchored in the interests and political values of Western-dominated international governance mechanism (i.e., *unnecessary entanglement*) is connected to the operationalization of Article 51 of the UN Charter. Article 51 puts more emphasis on applying the CSS principle in interstate conflict than in the case of asymmetric warfare. Kenya's intervention against a nonstate actor in Somalia has drawn internal criticism. Kenya's support for the global war on terror in the region may have had negative effects on the country's counterterrorism strategy. Indeed, Kenya's close ties with Israel and the United States makes it susceptible to terrorist attacks. This came to light when Kenya's former minister of foreign affairs visited Israel. The leader of the Council of Imams and Preachers of Kenya, Sheikh Ali Shee, warned against the government's policy of supporting the US's fight against terrorism. Several contentious issues have emerged—issues centered on that same question of the true driver of Kenyan intervention.

First, the use of Article 51 as the legal justification for Kenya's incursion into Somalia raises legal questions regarding what constituted an "armed attack" against the state and whether such actions necessitated a large-scale invasion. Provisions of Article 51 demand that Kenya ought to have pursued the right to self-defense procedurally by seeking approval of the UNSC. However, some have argued that Kenya did not follow the right procedure required in pursuit of the right to self-defense, as the country did not report its intended actions to the UNSC, even though UN secretary general Ban Ki-moon later commended Kenya on its efforts to stabilize Somalia.[71] One notable factor in the Kenyan intervention was that France mounted pressure on Kenya to intervene in Somalia due to the frequent kidnappings of French and other European tourists in Kenya.[72]

Secondly, in the CSS approach, states are likely to join members in resisting an aggressor because they have a national interest in preserving peace. Kenya's potential gains from launching the intervention in Somalia have come to the fore following the dispute over the maritime border between the two states. Specifically, oil (among other natural resources) is emerging as a key resource of interest in the Horn of Africa. Kenya is one of the countries in the region that have discovered oil deposits in their territory. Oil explorations are ongoing along the country's coast. Given that Somalia won the case against Kenya at the International Court of Justice over the disputed maritime border, some of the areas where Kenya is exploring for oil are within Somali maritime space. It is therefore conceivable that Kenya's incursion into Somalia might also have been motivated by its exploration for oil deposits.

Third, collectivism envisions international interventions occurring within some form of an international military body. As the *Guardian* noted, "the Kenyan intervention plan was discussed and decided in 2010, then finalized with input from Western partners, including the US and to a lesser extent France." Before then, Kenya had not "actively engaged" in the conflict in Somalia.[73] However, the invasion of Somalia came at a huge cost. Estimates put the cost of the invasion at KES 210 million (US$2.8 million) per month in personnel costs alone, in a year when Kenya recorded a KES 236 billion (US$3.1 billion) total budget deficit.[74] The cost of supporting personnel, doing maintenance, and procuring military equipment and hardware became unbearable for Kenya alone to sustain. Hence, the country turned to the international community, particularly the UNSC and regional organizations like the Intergovernmental Authority on Development and the African Union (AU) for support, in the hope that this support would ease the financial burden of the invasion. The response was positive—on February 22, 2012, the UNSC authorized an increase in the number of AMISOM forces, bringing the total number to 17,731 troops. An increase in funding from US$300 million per annum to around US$500 million was also awarded.[75] The 4,000-strong KDF detachment in southern Somalia was also formally incorporated into the AU mission—making it the AU's largest single military intervention to date. The entanglement of Kenya into the global web of counterterrorism was evident when the AU Peace and Security director El-Ghassim Wane emphasized the need for the wider international support in order to capitalize on the gains made by the Kenyan offensive. In his show of support for Kenya's lone offensive before it was reconfigured under AMISOM, the director reiterated: "We believe the Kenyan operation is further contributing to weakening Al-Shabab and creating space for the political process to take hold and lead to the conclusion of the transition next August. . . . It's a challenging task, and we are fully aware of it, and that's why we are calling for further and enhanced support from the United Nations and the larger international community."[76] With the same measure of authority from the AU, on November 12, 2011, the Kenyan government released a statement announcing that it had approved the redeployment of KDF in Somalia under AMISOM. Under the global war on terror, the CSS approach goes beyond regional formations. It is for this reason that the US army has been sharing with the Kenyan military surveillance data it gathers through air capabilities (e.g., unarmed MQ-9 Reapers and unmanned aerial vehicles). While Israeli and US support of Kenya through military multipliers (drones, tanks, ammunition, and electronic surveillance equipment) paints a positive image of a collective approach to the global war on terror,[77] this same support has further exacerbated the conflict with Al-Shabaab, which views the Kenya-Israel relationship as a threat to its survival, to the point that Kenya's involvement has become more unnecessary entanglement than national security defense. With the involvement of Israel and the United States, Al-Shabaab has been able to cast the Kenyan invasion as fundamentalism, and the group has vowed to help build what it called a "coalition against fundamentalism"—a coalition targeting countries in the Horn of Africa, including Kenya, Ethiopia, South Sudan, and Tanzania.

Fourth, in CSS, individual states may temporarily sacrifice their national interests for a group so long as they can expect rewards for cooperation in the long run. This is what this chapter determines as "a *necessary evil*." In any case, whenever a state decides to join a military alliance against an aggressor, it expects either positive or negative outcomes as it interacts with the rest of the members in the balancing act. One major achievement of KDF in Somalia is the political stabilization of the country. However, the idea that CSS fosters an environment in which aggression is less likely to take place remains controversial in the Kenya-Somalia case. Although the initial purpose of the KDF intervention was to prevent Al-Shabaab from spreading to Kenya, this goal has not always been achieved. Kenya has experienced dozens of attacks along its northeastern border and the coastal region. The attacks target both security forces and civilians, claiming dozens of lives. Al-Shabaab's kinetic military action since 2011 are asymmetric tactics aimed at stirring Kenyan citizens' emotions against the government's decision to retain KDF in Somalia. This has made the glocalized peace and security architecture—a comprehensive peace and security design that is both domestically and externally looking—relevant to Kenyan national interests. However, one major unnecessary political entanglement that Kenya finds itself in is the political dynamics in Jubaland. Kenya treats Jubaland as if it were an independent state. This is confusing and is against the wishes of the Republic of Somalia. Further entanglements have been observed in diplomatic spheres. The Somalia Transitional Federal Government under the then president Sharif Sheikh Ahmed objected to Kenya's intervention, citing it as a unilateral action. Consequently, the relationship between the two countries remains tense. Kenya's military involvement in Jubaland, its support for Jubaland regional leader Ahmed Madobe, and the outstanding maritime dispute between the two countries on which the International Court of Justice pronounced a ruling in favor of Somalia in October 2021 all point to Kenya's *unnecessary entanglement* in what would ordinarily be considered a Somali internal security affair.

Finally, CSS is a function of the underlying interests and intentions of individual states and not necessarily of their participation in a collective resolution of conflict. The principle of CSS assumes that a state will focus more on absolute gains in a security cooperation arrangement when it believes that the relative gains of others will not come back to haunt it. This seems to not be the case with Kenya's CSS approach in Somalia. The Gedo crisis of 2020–21 is an illustration of Kenya's entanglement in clan politics in Jubaland. When Jubaland forces and Somali federal government troops clashed in the Gedo town of Bula Hawo, Kenya allegedly supported and gave refuge to dissident Abdirashid Janan, providing him with a base in Mandera, inside Kenyan territory. The dissident leader used this base on Kenyan soil to recruit militias to carry out attacks on Mogadishu-backed troops stationed in Bula Hawo. The hostility faced by Kenya in Gedo, for instance, is linked to competition for political power inside Jubaland and to competition for resources, especially control of the lucrative port in Kismayu. Although Kenya liberated the city of Kismayu in 2012, changing the community's economic fortunes, the repercussions of the *unnecessary entanglement* to Kenya's national security are far reaching.

Did Kenya Suffer as a Result of the Unnecessary Entanglement?

Charles Kupchan and Clifford Kupchan's *The Promise of Collective Security* (1995) articulated the essence of CSS in promoting a more benign international order in which states can devote less attention and fewer resources to ensuring their survival and more to improving their collective welfare.[78] The Kenyan government decision to deploy KDF in Somalia was in line with Kupchan and Kupchan's dictum. However, given the increasing threats associated with the presence of KDF in Somalia, it is debatable whether the country has lived up to the Kupchan and Kupchan vision. With the deployment of KDF in Somalia in 2011, the number of attacks and deaths increased in Kenya (fig. 5.1). The 2016 El Adde attack on Kenyan soldiers by Al-Shabaab was perhaps the most devastating price Kenya has had to pay for its CSS approach in Somalia.[79] In what Paul Williams has termed a "poor relationship" between the KDF forces and the local population at El Adde, Kenyan soldiers encountered severe attacks from Al-Shabaab.

The number of attacks by Al-Shabaab increased steadily until 2012. On March 10, 2012, the organization killed six people and wounded sixty more after four grenades were detonated at the Machakos bus station in Nairobi. On November 18, 2012, seven passengers were killed and thirty-three others injured following a bomb blast in a city matatu (a passenger minibus). From 2012 through to 2014, Al-Shabaab carried out intermittent attacks but attained major fatalities. This started with an attack on September 21, 2013, when they brought the Westgate Shopping Mall under siege, killing 68 people and injuring over 150 people more.[80] In the subsequent month, suspected Al-Shabaab militants killed at least twenty-eight people on a bus in Arabiya

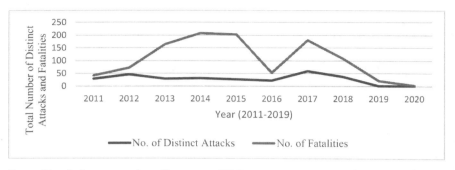

Fig. 5.1 Trend of terror attacks in Kenya since KDF intervention into Somalia, 2011–20. *Source:* Meta-analysis data compiled from the National Intelligence Service (Kenya), NIS. Government of Kenya Print (2021).

area, Mandera County. On this occasion, Al-Shabaab took responsibility for the killings and described it as being a retaliation for raids by Kenyan security forces in the coastal city of Mombasa against Muslim youth and clerics. As part of Kenya's fight against terrorism, the government closed two mosques on suspicion of their hosting radicalized Muslim youth. The government also recovered a cache of firearms and hand grenades.

It is important to emphasize that civilian targets are more of a means than an end in Al-Shabaab's attacks on Kenya. In July 2014, twenty-one people were killed in a Hindi village located in Lamu County, an attack for which Al-Shabaab claimed responsibility. On November 21, 2014, twenty-eight people were killed after suspected Al-Shabaab militants attacked a Nairobi-bound bus in Omar Jilo in Mandera County.[81] Al-Shabaab claimed responsibility for the killing of thirty-six nonlocal Kenyans at a quarry in the Koromei area near Mandera on the night of December 1, 2014, making the announcement through a pro-Al-Shabaab website. The group claimed that the attack on Koromei was part of series of attacks executed by the mujahideen to serve as a response to Kenya's occupation of Somalia. Al-Shabaab escalated its militant activities in Kenya between 2016 and 2017 and slowed down toward 2020. For instance, gunmen attacked the Bhosari Guest House during the early morning hours of October 2016, killing twelve people. This was followed by a series of intermittent attacks, including one on November 6, 2017, when Al-Shabab ambushed and burned two police Land Cruisers in an attack in Daba City, Mandera County. On January 15, 2019, the group attacked the DusitD2 hotel in the suburbs of Nairobi, killing twenty-one people.[82]

With the Kenyan government reacting to offset attacks on civilians and other noncombatant installations, the asymmetric fighters tend to gather enough courage to face off against the military and police—even in their own facilities. On August 13, 2017, Al-Shabaab destroyed a Kenyan police vehicle that was driving through Yadi, Damase, and El Wak towns in Mandera with an improvised explosive device. On September 25, 2018, Al-Shabaab militants claimed to have overrun a Kenyan military base in the Taksile area (north of Pandaguo, Lamu County), killing ten soldiers. The last major attack took place on January 5, 2020, when about twenty Al-Shabaab personnel attacked Camp Simba, leading to the death of a US Army specialist and two other civilian contractors. However, with the confirmation of the first case of COVID-19 in Nairobi on March 12, 2020, Kenya introduced a number of security measures to slow down the spread of the virus, including the suspension of all international flights, the restriction of people's interstate movement, a partial lockdown in all counties, and a daily curfew of 7:00 p.m. to 5:00 a.m.[83] A reduction in the number of Al-Shabaab attacks and fatalities was witnessed in Kenya beginning in the first quarter of 2020 but could be considered an unintended consequence of the COVID-19 security measures put in place. Nevertheless, it is still evident that Kenya's *unnecessary entanglement* in the global war on terror has had far-reaching adverse implications for its national security.

Conclusion

In Kelsenian thought, the collective security system is the product of institutional evolution. If we acknowledge this school of thought, it becomes evident that wars and peacebuilding are not exclusively domestic or international matters, even though scholars sometimes "treat individual nation-states as sovereign systems whose internal politics can be safely ignored."[84] However, international politics and external intervention play crucial roles in domestic politics, just as intrastate politics may affect the international community. Hence, glocalized security is a useful lens into international security issues. It should also be understood that within the system of collective security, the commitment among groups of states endeavors to protect the security interests of the individual members. In other words, collectivism cannot exist in the absence of individual interest. However, in the same context, the term *individual security system* has not existed at all times in the history of international relations but began with the League of Nations and has continued to be used with the transition to the United Nations.[85] At the same time, there have been states that have had nothing to do with the new world order of collective responsibility, cooperative security, or collective self-defense. Despite the conceptual-historical variations in the contemporary world order, there are states that reinforce interdependence (collectivism) and those that look after themselves (individualism). Therefore, the final question to be asked concerns the prospects for a security framework that exhibits features of both individualism and collectivism.

From the analysis in this chapter, it seems that the application of CSS in an asymmetric war environment is problematic. The argument in this chapter is that by developing a framework of intervention that has both features (collectivism and individualism), we might contribute to a better understanding of counterterror interventions in complex environments where states fight nonstate actors in a foreign land. This is the case in Kenya's involvement in the global war on terror in Somalia. Whereas Kenya is bound by the international principles of CSS as encapsulated in Article 51, Chapter 7, of the UN Charter, the Al-Shabaab group is an outlawed terror group that is not bound by the UN Charter. Could the reason for the continued attack on Kenyan soil by Al-Shabaab be the lack of a coherent doctrine on how to apply CSS in an asymmetric war environment? CSS was narrowly designed to respond to interstate conflict during the Cold War era; what about individual or collective states exercising self-defense against a nonstate actor in a foreign land? What is an effective framework of intervention that could enable Kenya to balance its national security interests with its need to sustain its obligation to regional and global order?

This set of questions is a reminder that the glocalized warfare in Somalia and by extension the Horn of Africa cannot be won by simply focusing on the collective approach to security. As part of its efforts to tackle the Al-Shabaab terrorist group, Kenya's national security architecture and the global efforts against terrorism must be cognizant of the pitfalls of the collectivist approach. Given that CSS is a product of international security cooperative engagements at a certain stage of development characterized by the presence of necessary evils and an unnecessary entanglement of individual states, this model therefore cannot operate on the absence of individualism. For instance, the threat of Al-Shabaab to Kenyan society is a result of the CSS approach that Kenya deployed in 2011. It is an individual state problem because deep socioeconomic and political factors have divided Kenyans to the extent that a section of the population seeks external help from groups such as Al-Shabaab. The aggrieved population looks for revenge against the state—a state that they claim is responsible for its plight. On this account, the future model of intervention within the broader framework of globalized security in a complex insurgency setting such as that in Somalia must consider (among other factors) effective sovereignty, territorial integrity, and nation building. Ungoverned space is particularly important in fragile or failed states—but must this always lead to ripple effects within neighboring states?

To sum up, the Kelsenian analysis of CSS is an integral part of a legalistic interpretation of terrorism and counterterrorism. The interstate problems of the Cold War era, when the Kelsenian ideas were developed in the 1940s, seem to have profoundly influenced the approach to international peace and security interventions. The evolution of asymmetric warfare, one-sided violence, and the rapid growth of nonstate actors—and the consequences of this in terms of strategies, tactics, and methods of warfare—fiercely challenge Kelsenian thoughts on collective security approaches. However, states are experiencing asymmetric conflict. States are also experiencing irredentism, causing other states to join regional formations such as NATO and the Collective Security Treaty Organization, an intergovernmental military alliance in Eurasia that consists of six post-Soviet states. That means collective responsibility against aggressors is becoming a political reality like never before. However, Article 51 of the UN Charter remains limited in tackling such complex operations. Rethinking Article 51 in line with the ongoing asymmetric activities across the globe just might be the cure for states such as Kenya that are experiencing an unnecessary entanglement.

Notes

1. Dessi and Sedda, "Glocalisation and Everyday Life."
2. Robertson, "Globalisation or Glocalization?" 33–52.
3. Roudometof, "Theorising Globalization," 391–408.
4. Ray, "Social Structures and Chaos Theory."
5. Hodder, "Entanglement of Humans and Things," 19–36.
6. Olsen, "October 2011 Kenyan Invasion of Somalia," 39–53.
7. Massoud, "Rule of Law in Fragile States," 111–25; Ingirillis, "Profiting from the Failed State of Somalia," 437–58; Ramadane, "Somalia State Failure, Poverty and Terrorism," 13–16; Menkhaus, "State Failure, State-Building and Prospects for a Functional Failed State in Somalia," 154–72.
8. Elliot and Holzer, "Invention of Terrorism in Somalia," 215–44.
9. Fund for Peace, *Measuring Fragility*; Bah, "State Decay," 71–89.
10. Englebert, *Africa*; Menkhaus, "State Failure, State-Building and Prospects for a Functional Failed State in Somalia," 154–72.
11. Ingirillis, "Profiting from the Failed State of Somalia," 437–58.
12. Bryden, "State-within-a-Failed-State."
13. Menkhaus, "No Access," 29–35.
14. Kruber and Stephenies, "Insurgent group cohesion and the malleability of Foreignness."
15. Gartenstein-Ross, "Strategic Challenge of Somalia's Al-Shabaab: Dimensions of Jihad," 25–36.
16. Gartenstein-Ross, "Strategic Challenge of Somalia's Al-Shabaab: Dimensions of Jihad," 28.
17. Hansen, "Kapitel 12 Harakat al-Shabaab and Somali's Current State of Affairs," 279–94.
18. Hansen, *Al-Shabaab in Somalia*.

19. Hansen, "Kapitel 12 Harakat al-Shabaab and Somali's Current State of Affairs," 279–294.
20. Jones et al., *Counterterrorism and Counter-Insurgency in Somalia*.
21. Hansen, "Kapitel 12 Harakat al-Shabaab and Somali's Current State of Affairs," 279–294.
22. Hansen, "Kapitel 12 Harakat al-Shabaab and Somali's Current State of Affairs," 279–294.
23. This comprises the various actors. These include the local military formation of the Transitional Federal Government of Somalia, troops from neighboring countries (including Kenya, Ethiopia, Burundi, Uganda, and other international military forces), and financial support from the United States and its allies.
24. African Union Mission in Somalia (AMISOM).
25. Afrax, "Mirror of Culture."
26. Fahy, "Post-Governance Somalia beyond 2000," 81–104.
27. Fund for Peace, *Measuring Fragility*.
28. Menkhaus, "State Failure, State-Building and Prospects for a Functional Failed State in Somalia," 154–72.
29. Mamdani, *Citizen and Subject*.
30. Ali, "The Al-Shabaab Al-Mujahidiin."
31. Hansen, *Al-Shabaab in Somalia*.
32. United Nations, *Collective Security Systems*.
33. Jones, Liepman, and Chandler, *Counterterrorism and Counterinsurgency in Somalia*.
34. Whittaker, "Socio-Economic Dynamics of the Shifta Conflict in Kenya, c. 1963-8," 391–408.
35. Jackson, "Constructing Enemies," 394–426.
36. BBC, "Kenya Troops 'Pull Out of Somali el-Ade and Badhadhe Bases'"; Anderson and McKnight, "Kenya at War," 1–27.
37. Malkhadir, "Tourists Kidnappings Ravage Kenyan Tourist Area."
38. Cameron, "Kenya's War against Al-Shabab."
39. Kupchan and Kupchan, "Promise of Collective Security," 52–61.
40. Kelsen, "Collective Security and Collective Self-Defense under the Charter of the United Nations," 783–96.
41. Rappard, "Evolution of the League of Nations," 792–826.
42. Tulloch, *Oxford Dictionary of New Words*.
43. Robertson, "Glocalization."
44. Bah, *International Security and Peacebuilding*.
45. Ibid.
46. Desai and Desai, "On the Century of Peace-Making at the 1919 Treaty of Versailles," 201–22.
47. Marks, "Mistakes and Myths," 632–59.
48. Yilmaz, "New World Order," 44–58.
49. Siroky and Hale, "Inside Irredentism," 117–28; Also see Kim, "Irredentism in Disputed Territories and Its Influence on the Border Conflicts and Wars," 87–101.
50. Voronov and Singer, "Myth of Individualism-Collectivism," 461–80.
51. Aleksovski, Bakreski, and Avraovski, "Collective Security."
52. Kelsen, "Collective Security and Collective Self-Defense under the Charter of the United Nations," 791–92.
53. Cassese, *The International Community's Legal Response to Terrorism*.
54. Mentan, *Dilemmas of Weak States*.
55. Ogunnubi, "Recalibrating Africa's Geo-Political Calculus," 387–406.
56. Solomon, *Terrorism and Counter-Terrorism in Africa*.

57. Cannon, "Terrorists, Geopolitics and Kenya's Proposed Border Wall with Somalia," 23–37.
58. Davis, "Kenya and the Global War on Terrorism," 51–68.
59. Regens et al., "Effect of Foreign Military Intervention and Controlled Territory on the Operational Tempo of al-Shabaab Attacks," 95–107; Cannon and Pkalya, "Why al-Shabaab Attacks Kenya," 1–17.
60. Anderson and McKnight, "Understanding al-Shabaab," 536–57.
61. De Guevara, "Studying the International Crisis Group," 545–62.
62. Klobucista, Masters, and Sergio, "Al-Shabaab."
63. Burns, "Preventing the World's Next Refugee Crisis."
64. Walker and Arif, "Al-Shabaab Separates Non-Muslims from Muslims, Kills 36 in Quarry Attack."
65. Pearson, "Geographic Proximity and Foreign Military Intervention," 432–60.
66. Holsti and Rosenau, "The Structure of Foreign Policy Attitudes among American Leaders," 94–125.
67. Kelsen, "Collective Security and Collective Self-Defense under the Charter of the United Nations," 783–96; Haldén, "Somalia."
68. Olsen, "October 2011 Kenyan Invasion of Somalia," 39–53.
69. Hammond, "Somalia Rising," 183–93.
70. Piazza, "Incubators of Terror," 469–88; Takeyh and Gvosdev, "Do Terrorist Networks Need a Home?" 97–108.
71. Tams, "Use of Force against Terrorists," 359–97.
72. Throup, "Kenya's Intervention in Somalia."
73. Straziuso, "Kidnappings: Kenya to Pursue Militants into Somalia."
74. International Crisis Group, "Kenyan Military Intervention in Somalia."
75. United Nations, "United Nations Security Council Resolution 2036 Adopted Unanimously."
76. Rémy, "Kenya Develops Plan for Satellite Region of Jubaland on Somali Border."
77. Perez, "Israel's Big Return to East and Horn of Africa."
78. Kupchan and Kupchan, "Promise of Collective Security," 52–61.
79. Williams, "After Westgate," 907–23.
80. *Guardian*, "Terror in Westgate Mall."
81. *Nation*, "Gunmen Kill 28 in Morning of Terror."
82. *Nation*, "Anatomy of Terrorist Attack on DusitD2 Hotel."
83. Quaife et al., "Impact of COVID-19 Control Measures on Social Contacts and Transmission in Kenyan Informal Settlements."
84. Peterson, "President's Dominance in Foreign Policy," 228.
85. Isagourias, "League of Nations and Visions of World Order," 291–309.

References

Afrax, Maxamed D. "The Mirror of Culture: Somali Dissolution Seen through Oral Expression." *The Somali Challenge: From Catastrophe to Renewal*. Boulder, CO: Lynne Rienner, 1994.

African Union Mission in Somalia. AMISOM. Available at https://amisom-au.org/amisom-background/.

Aleksovski, Stefan, Oliver Bakreski, and Bijana Avraovski. "Collective Security—The Role of International Organizations—Implications in International Security Order." *Mediterranean Journal of Social Sciences* 5, no. 27 (2014): 274–82.

Ali, Abdisaid M. "The Al-Shabaab Al-Mujahidiin—a Profile of the First Somali Terrorist Organisation." April 28, 2008. https://www.files.ethz.ch/isn/55851/AlShabaab.pdf.

Anderson, David M., and Jacob McKnight. "Kenya at War: Al-Shabaab and Its Enemies in Eastern Africa." *African Affairs* 114, no. 454 (2014): 1–27.

———. "Understanding Al-Shabaab: Clan, Islam, and Insurgency in Kenya." *Journal of Eastern African Studies* 9, no. 3 (2015): 536–57.

Bah, Abu Bakarr, ed. *International Security and Peacebuilding: Africa, the Middle East, and Europe.* Bloomington: Indiana University Press, 2017.

———. "State Decay: A Conceptual Frame of Failing and Failed States in West Africa." *International Journal of Politics, Culture, and Society* 25 (2012): 71–89.

BBC. "Kenya Troops 'Pull Out of Somali el-Ade and Badhadhe Bases.'" January 26, 2016. https://www.bbc.com/news/world-africa-35408463.

Bryden, Matt. "State-within-a-Failed-State: Somaliland and the Challenge of International Recognition." In *States-Within-States: Incipient Political Entities in the Post-Cold War Era*, edited by Paul Kingston and Ian S. Spears, 167–88. Basingstoke, UK: Palgrave Macmillan, 2004.

Burns, J. Jordan. "Preventing the World's Next Refugee Crisis: Famine, Conflict, and Climate Change in Nigeria, South Sudan, Somalia and Yemen." American Security Project, May 2017. https://www.jstor.org/stable/resrep06035#metadata_info_tab_contents.

Cameron, Evers. "Kenya's War against Al-Shabab: An Internal/External Affair." 12 March 2014. Accessed August 22, 2022. http://www.consultancyafrica.com/index.php?option=com. https://www.polity.org.za/article/kenyas-war-against-al-shabab-an-internalexternal-affair-2014-03-12.

Cannon, Brendon J. "Terrorists, Geopolitics and Kenya's Proposed Border Wall with Somalia." *Journal of Terrorism Research* 7, no. 2 (2016): 23–37.

Cannon, Brendon J., and Dominic Pkalya. "Why Al-Shabaab Attacks Kenya: Questioning the Narrative Paradigm," *Terrorism and Political Violence* 31, no. 4 (2017): 1–17.

Cassese, Antonio. "The International Community's Legal Response to Terrorism" 38 (1989): ICLQ 589, 5967.

Davis, John. "Kenya and the Global War on Terrorism: Searching for a New Role in a New War." In *Africa and the War on Terrorism*, edited by John Davis, 51–68. London: Routledge, 2016.

De Guevara, Berit Blieseman. "Studying the International Crisis Group." *Third World Quarterly* 35, no. 4 (2014): 545–62.

Desai, Bharat H., and Jay B. Desai. "On the Century of Peace-Making at the 1919 Treaty of Versailles: Looking Back to Look Ahead." *International Studies* 57, no. 3 (2020): 201–22.

Dessi, Ugo, and Franciscu Sedda. "Glocalisation and Everyday Life." *Globalism: Journal of Culture, Politics and Innovation* 3 (2020). https://glocalismjournal.org/issue-2020-3-glocalization-and-everyday-life/. Available at DOI: 10.12893/gjcpi.2020.3.14.

Englebert, Pierre. *Africa: Unity, Sovereignty, and Sorrow.* Boulder, CO: Lynne Rienner, 2009.

Elliot, Ashley, and Georg-Sebastian Holzer, "The Invention of Terrorism in Somalia: Paradigms and Policy in US Foreign Relations." *South African Journal of International Affairs* 16, no. 2 (2009): 215–44.

Fahy, Kathleen. "Post-governance Somalia beyond 2000: Prospects for a Nation without a State?" *Trócairc Development Review,* Dublin (1999): 81–104.

Fund for Peace. *Measuring Fragility: Risk and Vulnerability in 179 Countries, August 2022.* Fragile States Index. https://fragilestatesindex.org/wp-content/uploads/2022/07/22-FSI-Report-Final.pdf.

Gartenstein-Ross, Daveed. "The Strategic Challenge of Somalia's Al-Shabaab: Dimensions of Jihad." *Middle East Quarterly* 16, no. 4 (2009): 25–36.

Guardian. "Terror in Westgate Mall: The Full Story of the Attacks That Devastated Kenya." October 4, 2013. https://www.theguardian.com/world/2013/oct/04/westgate-mall-attacks-kenya.

Haldén, Peter. "Somalia: Failed State or Nascent States-System?" *FOI Somalia Papers: Report 1* (2008): 1–64.
Hammond, Laura. "Somalia Rising: Things Are Starting to Change for the World's Longest Failed State." *Journal of Eastern African Studies* 7, no. 1 (2013): 183–93.
Hansen, J. Stig. *Al-Shabaab in Somalia: The History and Ideology of a Militant Islamist Group, 2005–2012.* London: C. Hurst, 2013.
———. "Kapitel 12 Harakat Al-Shabaab and Somali's Current State of Affairs." *Jahrbuch Terrorism* 5 (2012): 279–294.
Hodder, Ian. "The Entanglement of Human and Things: A Long-Term View." *New Literary History* 45, no. 1 (2014): 19–36.
Holsti, Ole R., and James N. Rosenau. "The Structure of Foreign Policy Attitudes among American Leaders." *Journal of Politics* 52, no. 1 (1990): 94–125.
Ingirillis H. Mohamed. "Profiting from the Failed State of Somalia: The Violent Political Marketplace and Insecurity in Contemporary Mogadishu." *Journal of Contemporary African Studies* 38, no. 3 (2020): 437–58.
International Crisis Group. "The Kenyan Military Intervention in Somalia." Report no. 184, Africa, February 15, 2012.
Isagourias, Nicholas. "The League of Nations and Visions of World Order." *International Community Law Review* 22, no. 3–4 (2020): 291–309.
Jackson, Richard. "Constructing Enemies: Islamic Terrorism in Political and Academic Discourse." *Government and Opposition* 42, no. 3 (2007): 394–426.
Jones, Seth G., Andrew M. Liepman, and Nathan Chandler. *Counterterrorism and Counterinsurgency in Somalia: Assessing the Campaign against Al-Shabaab.* Research report, RAND Corporation, 2016. https://www.rand.org/pubs/research_reports/RR1539.html.
Kelsen, Hans. "Collective Security and Collective Self-Defense under the Charter of the United Nations." *American Journal of International Law* 42, no. 4 (1948): 783–96.
Kim, German. "Irredentism in Disputed Territories and Its Influence on the Border Conflicts and Wars." *Journal of Territorial and Maritime Studies* 3, no. 1 (2016): 87–101.
Klobucista, Claire, Jonathan Masters, and Mohammed A. Sergio. "Al-Shabaab." Council on Foreign Relations. Last updated December 6, 2022. https://www.cfr.org/backgrounder/al-shabaab.
Kruber, Samantha, and Stephenies Carver. "Insurgent Group Cohesion and the Malleability of Foreignness: Al-Shabaab's Relationship with Foreign Fighters." *Studies in Conflict* 46, no. 10 (2023): 1894–911. https://www.tandfonline.com/doi/full/10.1080/1057610X.2021.1889091.
Kupchan, A. Charles, and Clifford A. Kupchan. "The Promise of Collective Security." *International Security* 20, no. 1 (1995): 52–61.
Malkhadir, Muhumed. "Tourists Kidnappings Ravage Kenyan Tourist Area." NBC News, Octobrer 5, 2011. https://www.nbcnews.com/id/wbna44788475.
Mamdani, Mahmood. *Citizen and Subject: Contemporary Africa and the Legacy of Late Colonialism.* Princeton, NJ: Princeton University, 1996.
Marks, Sally. "Mistakes and Myths: The Allies. Germany and the Versailles Treaty, 1918–1921." *Journal of Modern History* 85, no. 3 (2013): 632–59.
Massoud F. Mark. "The Rule of Law in Fragile States: Dictatorship, Collapse and the Politics of Religion in Post-Colonial Somalia." *Journal of Law & Society* 47, no. 1 (2020): 111–25.
Menkhaus, Ken. "No Access: Critical Bottlenecks in the 2011 Somali Famine." *Global Food Security* 1, no. 1 (2012): 29–35.
———. "State Failure, State-Building and Prospects for a Functional Failed State in Somalia." *Annals of the American Academy of Political and Social Science* 656 (2014): 154–72.
Mentan, Tatah. *Dilemmas of Weak States: Africa and Transnational Terrorism in the Twenty-First Century.* London: Routledge, 2017.

Nation. "Anatomy of Terrorist Attack on DusitD2 Hotel." January 16, 2019. https://nation.africa/kenya/news/anatomy-of-terrorist-attack-on-dusitd2-hotel-128584.

———. "Gunmen Kill 28 in Morning of Terror." November 22, 2014. Updated July 2, 2020. https://nation.africa/kenya/news/gunmen-kill-28-in-morning-of-terror-1045770.

Ogunnubi, Olusola. "Recalibrating Africa's Geo-Political Calculus: A Critique of South Africa's Hegemonic Status." *Politikon* 42, no. 3 (2015): 387–406.

Olsen, R. Gorm. "The October 2011 Kenyan Invasion of Somalia: Fighting Al-Shabaab or Defending Institutional Interests?" *Journal of Contemporary African Studies* 36, no. 1 (2018): 39–53.

Pearson, Frederick. "Geographic Proximity and Foreign Military Intervention." *Journal of Conflict Resolution* 18, no. 3 (1974): 432–60.

Perez, Maxime. "Israel's Big Return to East and Horn of Africa." *Africa Report*, December 2011. https://www.theafricareport.com/7917/israels-big-return-to-east-and-horn-of-africa/.

Piazza, James. "Incubators of Terror: Do Failed and Failing States Promote Transnational Terrorism?" *International Studies Quarterly* 52, no. 3 (2008): 469–88.

Peterson, Paul E. "The President's Dominance in Foreign Policy." *Political Science Quarterly* 109 (Summer 1994): 228.

Quaife, Matthew, Kevin van Zandvoort, Amy Gimma, Kashvi Shah, Nicky MacCreesh, Kiesha Prem, Edwine Barasa et al. "The Impact of COVID-19 Control Measures on Social Contacts and Transmission in Kenyan Informal Settlements." *BMC Medicine*, 18, no. 316 (2020). https://doi.org/10.1186/s12916-020-01779-4.

Smith, R. D. "Social Structures and Chaos Theory." *Sociological Research Online* 3, no. 1 (1998). https://doi.org/10.5153/sro.113.

Ramadane, O. Zakaria. "Somalia State Failure, Poverty and Terrorism." *Counterterrorism Trends and Analysis* 6, no. 7 (2014): 13–16.

Rappard, William E. "The Evolution of the League of Nations." *American Political Science Review* 21, no. 4 (1927): 792–826.

Regens, James, Nick Mould, Christopher Sartorious, and Jonathan O'Dell. "Effect of Foreign Military Intervention and Controlled Territory on the Operational Tempo of Al-Shabaab Attacks." *Dynamics of Asymmetric Conflict* 9, no. 1–3 (2016): 95–107.

Rémy, Jean-Philippe. "Kenya Develops Plan for Satellite Region of Jubaland on Somali Border." *Guardian*, November 8, 2011.

Robertson, Roland. "Globalisation or Glocalization?" *Journal of International Communication* 1, no. 1 (1994): 33–52.

———. "Glocalization: Time-Space and Homogeneity-Heterogeneity." In *Global Modernities*, edited by Mike Featherstone, Scott Lash, and Roland Robertson, 24–44. London: SAGE Publications, 1995.

Roudometof, Victor. "Theorising Globalization: Three Interpretations." *European Journal of Social Theory* 19, no. 3 (2015): 391–408.

Siroky, S. David, and Christopher W. Hale, "Inside Irredentism: A Global Empirical Analysis." *American Journal of Political Science* 61, no. 1 (2017): 117–28.

Solomon, Hussein. *Terrorism and Counter-Terrorism in Africa: Fighting Insurgency from Al-Shabaab, Ansar Dine and Boko Haram*. London: Palgrave Macmillan, 2015. Doi: https://doi.org/10.1057/9781137489890

Straziuso, Jason. "Kidnappings: Kenya to Pursue Militants into Somalia." *Arab News*, 15 October, 2011. https://www.arabnews.com/node/394837.

Takeyh, Ray, and Nikolas Gvosdev. "Do Terrorist Networks Need a Home?" *Washington Quarterly* 25, no. 3 (2002): 97–108.

Tams, C. J. "The Use of Force against Terrorists." *European Journal of International Law* 20, no. 2 (2009): 359–97.

Throup, W. David. "Kenya's Intervention in Somalia." Center for Strategic and International Studies, February 16, 2012. https://www.csis.org/analysis/kenya%E2%80%99s-intervention-somalia.

Tulloch, Sara, comp. *Oxford Dictionary of New Words*. Oxford: Oxford University Press, 1991.

United Nations. *Collective Security Systems*. July 2022. https://media.un.org/en/asset/k1y/k1yjz47uf4.

———. "United Nations Security Council Resolution 2036 Adopted Unanimously." February 22, 2012. http://www.un.org/News/Press/docs/2012/sc10550.doc.htm.https://documents.un.org/doc/undoc/gen/n12/238/47/pdf/n1223847.pdf.

United Nations Security Council. *Report of the Monitoring Group on Somalia and Eritrea pursuant to Security Council Resolution 2182*. October 24, 2014. https://documents.un.org/doc/undoc/gen/n14/588/09/pdf/n1458809.pdf.

Voronov, Maxim, and Jefferson A. Singer. "The Myth of Individualism-Collectivism: A Critical Review." *Journal of Social Psychology* 142, no. 4 (2002): 461–80.

Walker, Brian, and Merieme Arif. *Al-Shabaab Separates Non-Muslims from Muslims, Kills 36 in Quarry Attack*. CNN, December 2, 2014. http://edition.cnn.com/2014/12/02/world/africa/kenya-attack.

Whittaker, Hannah A. "The Socioeconomic Dynamics of the Shifta Conflict in Kenya, c. 1963–8." *Journal of African History* 53, no. 3 (2012): 391–408.

Williams, Paul D. "After Westgate: Opportunities and Challenges in the War against Al-Shabaab." *International Affairs* 90, no. 4 (2014): 907–23.

Yilmaz, Muzaffer E. "The New World Order: An Outline of the Post-Cold-War Era." *Alternatives: Turkish Journal of International Relations* 7, no. 4 (2008): 44–58.

FRANCIS ONDITI is Associate Professor of Conflictology and Head of Department at the School of International Relations and Diplomacy, Riara University. He is enlisted as a distinguished research author and professor of research at the Institute for Intelligent Systems (IIS), University of Johannesburg. As author and editor of seven major volumes and over one hundred articles and book chapters, he was awarded in 2023 the Erasmus Mundus Global Teaching Fellowship at Leipzig University.

JAMES YUKO is Adjunct Lecturer at the School of International Relations and Diplomacy, Riara University. He is a PhD candidate in political science at the University of Nairobi. He has been published in issue 12 of the journal *Political Science Applied* (PSCA).

6

SHIʿISM AS IDEOLOGICAL VECTOR

International and Domestic Security in
Iranian Foreign Policy in Iraq

Massimo Ramaioli

Introduction

On June 13, 2014, Najaf-based Grand Ayatollah Ali al-Sistani issued a fatwa calling for the defense of Iraqi cities.[1] Only three days earlier, on June 10, Mosul, the second-largest city in the country, had fallen under the control of the Islamic State of Iraq and Syria (ISIS). On June 15, Iraqis, mostly belonging to the Shiʿa community, formed the Popular Mobilization Units (PMU; also referred to as Al-Hashd al-Shaʿbiyah, or Hashd) to heed Sistani's call.[2] A motley galaxy comprising some fifty formations,[3] the PMU were the last iteration of a trend that had emerged since the fall of Saddam Hussein's regime: the proliferation of nonstate actors in the context of fledgling public security. Furthermore, the mostly Shiʿa character of these formations entailed that "the most powerful groups in the Hashd—indeed, the de facto leadership—are those more closely affiliated with Ayatollah Khamenei."[4] The supreme leader of Iran can command vast allegiance in Iraq: Why is Iran bent on meddling in the politics of its neighbor? More importantly, how can Iran exert such influence and control? And what are the consequences in terms of security for both countries? A critical factor to understanding Iran's role in Iraqi politics and security is its ideological posturing as the leader of the Shiʿa Muslim world, and the attendant framing of Iraq in relation to this claim.

Historically, and more forcefully after the fall of Saddam Hussein in 2003, Iran has sought to expand its influence over Iraq. In its bid to establish itself as the dominant power in the region, Iran considers its control over its neighbor to the west fundamental. From Tehran's vantage point, Iraq represents a key bridgehead leading into the Middle East. The Iraqi territory would increase Iran's strategic reach in the region, fending off rival players (such as Saudi Arabia and the United States) resolved on curbing its ambitions. Relatedly, a strong Iraq has represented an ominous threat not only to Iran's capacity to project power but also to its very survival, as the bloody eight-year Iran-Iraq War reminds us.[5] Iran perceives its security as inextricably linked to Iraqi domestic arrangements and its attendant disposition toward Tehran.

To secure its position, Iran has leveraged sectarian bonds across the border, sponsoring in particular the establishment of Shi'a militias with political parties connected to them. Iranian policies in Iraq lay on the creation of a political space that transcends nation-state borders, resting instead on shared sectarian affiliation. In this sense, Iranian strategy in Iraq represents an instance of glocalization.[6] Tehran's ambitions in the international arena entail imbrication with and molding of a specific Iraqi locale. Conversely, the dynamics unfolding in this locale reinforce Iranian posturing on the world stage qua the eminent Shi'a power.[7]

To analyze the Iranian strategy in Iraq, I propose the concept of ideological vector. I examine its effects, from a security perspective, on both Iran's regional standing and Iraq's domestic landscape. Specifically, I look at how Iranian ambitions insist on and impact the neighbor's security landscape in the context of Iraqi religious-political fabric. The concept of ideological vector explains how Iran manages to exploit the texture of such (local) fabric in order to further its (international) foreign policy agenda. Ultimately, I argue, this operation tends to serve Iran's plans quite effectively. Iran has managed to assert itself as one of the most powerful player in the region, shoring up its security by extending influence on neighboring Iraq. At the same time, Iran's maneuvering substantially compromises Iraq's chances to (re)emerge as a functioning and independent country. In particular, Iranian sponsorship of largely autonomous Shi'a militias—the main manifestation of Iran's foray in Iraq—affects Iraqi domestic order and security. This dynamic illustrates the impossibility of confining security issues strictly to either the domestic or the international arenas. In fact, they are not siloed domains.[8] This study affirms this contention, highlighting specific ways in which they interact and represent an instance of glocalized security.

I proceed as follows. First, I present the concept of ideological vector. It straddles soft and hard power, and it connects global and local domains through the notion of glocalization. Then, I introduce specific traits of the Iranian and Iraqi polities to help contextualize and explain their relationship. In particular, I focus on the politicization of Shi'ism after the 1979 revolution as the lynchpin for the localization in Iraq of Iran's project—a process enabled by Iraq's national fabric and the role of sectarianism within it. At that juncture, I explore how the ideological vector plays out as I make reference to the role of the militias and the attendant consequences for both Iranian and Iraqi security through the prism of glocalized security. I then conclude with additional remarks.

Ideological Vector and Glocalized Security: Straddling International and Domestic Security

Iran's involvement in Iraq exemplifies a glocalized security situation which dovetails with the concept of ideological vector. In this sense, we may account for the deep impact of Iranian foreign policy on Iraq and for its ambition in the region writ large. The term ideological vector indicates a tool at the disposal of a sovereign state in the conduct of its foreign policy.[9] It serves to spread influence, ultimately seeking to establish domination and even hegemony, over other countries and regions. In this sense, it is a tool to shore up and enhance a country's security position in the international domain: the ideological vector steers other states to support or align with the interests and desiderata of the country which deploys it. It acquires allies, or at least favorably disposed regimes, reducing potential security threats; conversely, it enhances the country's status and reach. Iran's actions in Iraq answer to this logic.

The ideological vector consists of a political narrative featuring historical, cultural or identitarian overtones. Such a narrative crafts and promotes a certain worldview and attendant sense of national identity. It singles out locales that may be susceptible to such a narrative: it seeks to tie local/domestic conditions to global/international pretensions. Finally, the ideological vector conjures up a congruent set of foreign policies. The term vector indicates a carrier, a bearer of a project that may be launched across, and regardless of, states' borders—hence its glocalized nature. The "ideological" connotation captures its political bent. It underlines the political undertones trying to connect a given worldview, others' locations within it, and related foreign policies.[10] The ideological vector illustrates how glocalized security may be articulated along efforts to tie the international and the domestic: this dynamic would entail the connection to locales suitable for foreign political interventions. These ideological undertones need not be grounded in an accurate or objective assessment of one's own history, capabilities, or place in the world. Rather, they ought to be functional to the country's political project. The ideological vector must provide rationalization and justification for the country's foreign policy plans and actions.

The core narrative of an ideological vector—and the political project inscribed within it—ought to be made intelligible to and resonate with the foreign audience(s) the regime seeks to engage: foreign leaders and elites, state institutions and agencies, and populations at large (or specific sectors of it). The ideological vector may stand as the version addressing foreign audiences of domestic state discourse and propaganda. To achieve the sympathy of the intended foreign audience, who deploys the ideological vector must build a connection with such a public. Such a connection is all the easier to construct if some cultural elements are perceived to be (already) present and shared across the communities the ideological vector straddles. Alternatively, the ideological vector may be presented as truly global or universal, thus bypassing the need of any specific cultural bond.[11] The American neoconservative agenda promoting liberal democracy worldwide is an example of the latter, as was Soviet communism spurring an international proletarian revolution. Appeals to Pan-Arabism by the Nasser regime in the 1950s to the rest of the Arab world were an example of the former; the same is true for the present study, the promotion of Shi'a Islamic identity in Iraq on the part of Iran.

The ideological vector is a tool that in principle may be at the disposal of any state. However, states must spend time and energy to craft it: framing a certain worldview, developing a specific sense of nationhood, imbuing that with a political project, and devising consonant policies. An ideological vector is, therefore, both the product of a country's capacity to engineer a powerful narrative for foreign projection; and one of the causes enhancing state position and security in the international domain.

Ideological vector may then be regarded as an example of both soft and hard power.[12] In this study, Iran's insistence on the Shi'a bond with Iraq (including the promotion of a specific institutional setting, based on the doctrine of the *velayat-e faqih* [guardianship of the jurists]) exemplifies deployment of glocalized soft power. It is predicated on the construction of a local space underpinned by shared sectarian affiliation, effacing state boundaries. In this way, Iran seeks to secure its (global and regional) standing by posing as the patron of (local Iraqi) Shi'ites. It does so without relying on coercion but rather on the power of seduction and persuasion of a specific narrative. At the same time, the ideological vector is an instance of hard power as it is a means to attract, mobilize, and support actors that do make use of force and coercion. Iran's support for local Iraqi militias well illustrates this side of the ideological vector. It is important to remark that the ideological vector is not a purely accessory element to foreign policy. Neither is it merely epiphenomenal to coercive power. It is constitutive instead of how power works across and over state borders.[13]

Any sovereign state must equip itself with an ideological vector capable of projecting power abroad if it wishes to do so. Short of that, well-crafted narratives may seduce but never quite make others comply; brute material capabilities might do that for a time but fail to sustain long-term and effective projection abroad.

In this sense, it may be useful to make a passing reference to the concepts of domination and hegemony as articulated in the Gramscian vocabulary. Domination relies more on coercion than consent, achieving only begrudging acceptance of the incumbent power relations. It does not entail any internalization on the part of the dominated of the imposed rules, values, and institutions. Hegemony establishes instead a dialectic between coercion and consent, successfully integrating the two. The worldviews, horizons, and goals of the ruling become the ones of the ruled, too.[14] The ideological vector is a tool deployed to achieve hegemony. Needless to say, results do not always match with intentions. Mere domination—if that—may be the end result. This study illustrates how Iran faces limits in its capacity to exert power in Iraq. However, that is its fundamental thrust. The ideological component explicitly tries to lay the ground for the unity of consent with coercion. Effective foreign policymaking requires a careful balance of the two necessary, and separately not sufficient, ingredients.

Therefore, the ideological vector is part of a strategy to enhance the country's international standing and security. When a country uses it in a bid for power, it tends to disregard (possibly entirely) the desires, preferences, and ambitions of the people who are intended to be the audience of the ideology. It is then possible, but not given, that the deployment of an ideological vector exacerbates indigenous rifts, heightening conflicts, making for a violent allogenic (dis)order. Yet specific implications for domestic security can only be assessed in a case-by-case fashion.[15] When it comes to Iranian policies toward Iraq, analysts concur in the detrimental effects for the latter's security in the context of the former's enhanced regional position.[16] To this relation and attendant security dynamics I now turn my attention.

Iran: Empire, Shi'ism, and Seeking Hegemony in Iraq

As an empire nation,[17] the Iranian Persian core has extended its domination over other communities inhabiting the Iranic plateau—its geographic center—and its immediate borderlands. Arabs, Turkmens, Kurds, Loris, Azeris, Baluchis, and Armenians, just to name a few, have become parts of the Iranian nation despite their non-Persian character. All have been assimilated, to a greater or lesser degree, under the same political project. Incarnations of this imperial principle have been visible under various dynasties that routinely attributed to the ruling monarch the title Kings of Kings (*Shah-en Shah*). From 1501, the Safavids added the element of Shi'ism to the Iranian imperial tradition.[18] This formula was adopted too by the subsequent dynasties—Zands, Qajars, and, last, Pahlavis: "the state-sponsored Shi'i creed with a Persian rendering . . . proved to be remarkably enduring."[19] They all represented different embodiments of the same political principles: Iranian monarchical continuity, imperial rule, and (Shi'a) Islam.

This sense of Iranian distinctiveness built on and added to other national indigenous elements, namely, its distinct language and the rich literary tradition in Farsi.[20] This historical continuity is evident in Iranian officials' public discourse. Supreme Leader Ali Khamenei, in addressing Iran's foreign policy tools, "points out that the Islamic Republic's strengths are more than its Islamic ideology; Iran's 'strategic depth' (*'umq-i rāhburdī*) also encompasses the country's language, and by extension culture, along with its specific sect, Shi'ism."[21]

If Shi'ism became the dominant marker within the imperial borders, it could then also sustain Iranian ambitions without. For roughly four centuries, that implied a contest with the Sunni powers to the west, whether Arabs or Turks; the Iranians could confront them with their Shi'a identity. An oppositional discourse of othering thus reinforced the sense of Iranian national identity.[22] The proximity of the Arab-Sunnis made them the nemesis to the Iranian-Shi'ites: a bulwark against Iranian expansion and a threat to Iranian security.[23] Iraq's location has it right at the juncture of this dichotomy, and at the same time, Iran may look at Iraq as the possibility of upending it. Iran can construct the space of neighboring Iraq, with its Arab-Shi'a majority,[24] as the local instantiation of its regional and global drive. Iraq's indigenous historical-cultural fabric is the ideal gateway for Iran to actualize the project of dominating the (Arab, non-Persian) Middle East region.

In this sense, we can argue that the revolution of 1978–79 represented no abrupt severance with the past (if any). Rather, it stood as the latest incarnation of imperial Iran: an empire under not a monarchical but a republican regime. Iran's own understanding of its place in the world, and how to produce a congruent foreign policy, showed remarkable continuity.[25] However, the advent of the Islamic Republic of Iran (IRI) represented a seismic event due to its idiosyncratic ideological features. They allowed for a new construction of the Iraqi locale in relation to (global) Iranian power. The politicization of Shi'ism made it possible to configure an ideological vector capable of deeper and more radical interventions in regional politics.[26]

The Politicization of Shi'ism

The consequences of the Islamic Revolution for Iran were unlike previous dynastic changes. The IRI has since framed Shi'ism in an overtly political fashion, a foundational and guiding principle of its actions.[27] This contention is true not only for Iran's domestic political vicissitudes but also for Iran's behavior in the Middle East and beyond. The entire Islamic world felt the ripple effects of the first self-declared Islamic state, born out of a popular revolution where Shi'ism—articulated along distinctive national sentiments—seemingly played a key role.[28] During the monarchical era, the Shi'a clergy (*marja'iyya*) sanctioned the role of the monarch as protector of Iran qua a Shi'a land. The monarch in turn granted social prestige and economic autonomy to the *hawza*, the network of seminaries, madrasas, and mosques that is a fixture of the Shi'a space in the Middle East.[29] However, in this context, Shi'ism did not stand for any specific political-ideological project.

The Islamic Revolution transformed the way the Iranian regime conceptualized and made use of Shi'ism. Khomeinism was not just a Shi'a based political doctrine. It was also, crucially, an Islamist revolutionary project. The theory of *velayat-e faqih*[30] added to Iranian Shi'ism clear political directives and purposes, conjuring up a novel set of principles to wield power.[31] Under the velayat-e faqih, the Islamic jurists, by virtue of their knowledge of sharia and Islamic affairs, were tasked to rule the state. They did not support the regime anymore: they became the regime. The other state institutions (presidency, cabinet, parliament, judiciary, etc.) were subordinated to that principle. New ones, like the Council of Guardians and the Assembly of Experts, were created—and remain to this day idiosyncratic to postrevolutionary Iran. This framework sought to erase the distinction between the religious and the political, a hallmark of modern-day Islamism, and it found in Khomeini's formulation its first institutional implementation.

Khomeini's attempt to combine revolutionary republicanism,[32] Shi'a gnosticism, and Islamic political theory had two momentous consequences. First, it established an Islamic theocracy, an often unwieldy and confounding hybrid of democratic principles and religiously guided dictatorship.[33] Second, and on the basis of that, it recast the role and pretensions of Iran outside its borders in ways typical of revolutionary regimes worldwide.[34] The combination of these two elements radically changed Iran's stature and perception globally. The combination of Shi'a identity, Islamist political theory, and revolutionary dispositions granted the ruling elites in Tehran renewed interventionist inclinations when it came to foreign policy. Iran's imperial ambitions are inscribed in its capacities, aspirations, and potential. Khomeinism as a political principle would be deployed to further such ambitions: Shi'ites worldwide could now look at the rule of clergy in Tehran and draw inspiration from it. The IRI offered them a template, or at least guidance and support, to which they could readily turn. The Iranian experience with political Shi'ism thus went glocal: it constructed a Shi'a global space projecting a new permutation of Iranian power onto Shi'a locales amenable or willing to be galvanized by it.

The IRI started building its own narrative melding revolutionary Islamism with anti-imperialism (chiefly as anti-Western and anti-US sentiments).[35] Revolutionary Shi'a Islamism came to represent Iran's ideological vector to enhance the regime's ultimate twin aims: domination—and even hegemony—of the region it inhabits and propagation of the revolution. These goals ought not to be seen as merely complementary but rather as mutually constitutive, dovetailing into one another. The space of Iraq lent itself as the terrain to launch both: geographical proximity and shared sectarian affiliation made it possible to conjure up such a vision, as I go on to explain.

This is not tantamount to attributing coherence to specific plans and policies;[36] but it does indicate that the question whether Iran's foreign policy is driven by revolutionary fervor or pragmatic considerations is a rather moot point. These are basically tactical musings. Iran has never steered away from a strategy that mirrors its geography, capacities, and—crucially—sense of national mission. As remarked by former foreign minister Mohammad Javad Zarif, "although Iran's civilization and cultural heritage have remained intact, its political and economic fortunes have fluctuated." Ultimately, he concludes, "it is imperative for other states to accept the reality of Iran's prominent role in the Middle East and beyond and to recognize and respect Iran's legitimate national rights, interests, and security concerns."[37] While we may disagree with Zarif's contention and implications, no one can deny that "no country in the Middle East has Iran's combination of geographic size, human capital, ancient history, and vast natural resources."[38] Iran intends to translate such assets into effective power in the region. The ideological vector may enable it to do just so. Iraq is the locale where the vector has been more readily deployed.

Why Iraq? The Iran-Iraq Entanglement

The IRI sees its neighbor to the west as a key strategic space to control. First, as mentioned, Iran's own security has been historically threatened by rival powers to the west. The apex of this dynamic was the ferocious war with Saddam Hussein's Iraq. Control of this space is thus crucial to prevent other similar occurrences. Second, this space is geographically nestled at the head of the Middle East. Iran's geography largely protects the country from foreign land invasion (deserts and mountains surround the Iranic plateau on all sides). But it also limits Iran's capacity to project power. The Zagros Mountains in particular overlook the fertile Mesopotamian valley: any ambition to project power in the region must therefore cross over this mountain range and land in the Iraqi plains. In this sense, Iranian power is glocalized in its attempt to carve out a space for itself in Iraq. As a consequence, Iran cannot contemplate dominating the Middle East without controlling Iraq.

Therefore, in the post-2003 era, "Iran's primary interest in Iraq is to prevent the country from either breaking up . . . or becoming strong enough to once again pose a military threat."[39] Preventing Iraq's fragmentation would ensure a Shi'a-dominated Iraq emerges as a large and reliable client state. Yet a strong Iraq could threaten Iran. Tehran thus works to maintain a friendly and at the same time weak regime in Baghdad, supporting actors and forces that may deliver that outcome. It is readily apparent how this project rests on a tight and unstable balance whose effects reverberate security wise on both countries.

Iran exploits two sets of elements in its effort to dominate the Iraqi space. First, structural factors: geographical proximity and shared sectarian affiliation—Shi'ism being the dominant faith in both countries.[40] Second, specific historical developments: the post-1979 history between the two countries, with the pivotal events of the Islamic revolution and the Iran-Iraq War, and the US invasion of Iraq in 2003.

The first set represents conditions that make any Iranian foray into Iraq easier than it would be in any other country—if such a venture would be possible in another country at all. The disputes and conflicts Iran has been involved in when it comes to the Arab lands to its immediate western periphery attest to this.[41] The revolution has instead revived and rearticulated Iranian plans. Not only did the revolutionary ideology give impetus to a self-ascribed mission to spread its values, ideas, and perhaps even institutions, but also, it fed into the paranoia of Saddam Hussein, who feared a fate for his rule similar to the shah's. The Iraqi attack in September 1980 only further fueled revolutionary fervor in Iran. It galvanized an otherwise fledgling regime and redoubled its effort to subdue its Arab neighbor.

The removal of archrival Saddam Hussein finally opened up the possibility of Iran's penetrating and influencing the politics of the neighbor in unprecedented ways. Iran no longer faced a strong and aggressive regime: it could now plan to refashion Iraq as a still unitary but also innocuous and disposable space. Laboring for a sectarian and therefore Shi'a-dominated Iraq was part and parcel of this project. Few failed to notice the irony of the American invasion ripple effects: "the US set up post 2003 brought to the fore sectarianism way more than it used to be the case under Saddam.... They handed over a wonderful opportunity for Iran to exploit a card it would have not otherwise had."[42] The US blunder in Iraq allowed Iran to disarticulate American neoconservative plans for the region, removing a competing hegemonic project.

Indeed, the deployment of an ideological vector was enabled by the aggregate of these two sets of elements. It was not a singular, episodic tactic merely engendered by post-2003 dissolution of the Ba'athist regime. Tehran was in a position to make inroads in the country: the most effective tool to do so was represented by the politicization of the Shi'a community across the border, making local Iranian regional ambitions. The stipulations of the Khomeinist ideology, as well as the example set by the IRI itself, injected specific political content into the vector, amplifying its reach and importance.

The Iraqi Locale: Shi'ism, Sectarianism, and Post-2003 Nation Building

Iraq became a Shi'a majority country during the late nineteenth century as result of Ottoman reforms.[43] As nomadic tribesmen settled in and around the holy Shi'a centers of Najaf and Karbala, they started adopting the creed of the clerics who dominated the religious and cultural environment. From a Sunni majority country, Iraq became at the turn of the twentieth century mostly Shi'a, especially from Baghdad down to the Gulf. With the exception of little Bahrein, no other Arab country features more Shi'ites as percentage of its own population as Iraq does.[44]

The progressive mass conversion to Shi'ism of course did not entail an immediate or automatic opening to Iran. Not only did Iran have to willfully deploy a specific brand of Shi'ism to make inroads into Iraqi politics, but also the nature of this divide had to become politically salient for Iraqis themselves. It is a contingent rather than necessary process.[45] The number of publications dedicated to the origins and relations of the different ethnoreligious communities of Iraq has burgeoned after the US invasion of 2003.[46] It seemed the three major groups inhabiting the country—Shi'a Arabs, Sunni Arab, and Kurds[47]—perceived themselves along ethnosectarian lines, with other identity affiliations (be they class, nation, region, or tribe) not as salient. The internecine conflict within the Arab community, that is to say between Sunnis and Shi'ites, attracted particular attention. In terms of security, various militias, armed groups, paramilitary units, and terrorist cells emerged from both Arab communities: they attacked foreign coalition forces as well as engaged in violent infightings, which led to the dramatic civil war of 2006–8. Similarly, the emergence of ISIS in 2014 and the response to it were colored with deep sectarian hues: a particularly violent reenactment of Sunni insurgency and a resolute Shi'a front, embodied in the PMU, that resisted it.

Confronted by sectarian violence of unprecedented scale, scholars and policymakers alike explained the emergence and identity formation of the Sunni and Shi'a communities either via a primordialist-essentialist perspective or via an instrumental-constructivist one. Primordialism would insist on Sunni or Shi'a identity as the result of long-term processes of group formation, by now deeply and inescapably embedded in the individual and collective psyche of Iraqis. The outburst of sectarianism is the (almost necessary) consequence of such primordial affiliations, especially in its most violent forms. In this sense, Iran's vector would leverage sectarian identity as its consonant, immediate ideological reflection. A primordialist perspective would expect the efficacy of the vector as a matter of course.

Instrumentalist-constructivist perspectives maintained, instead, the epiphenomenal nature of sectarianism—in Iraq as elsewhere. Never a prominent feature of the political history of the country until 1991, the Sunni-Shi'a divide came to the fore during the so-called Shi'a Uprising.[48] Sectarianism, in short, emerged as a political phenomenon to express grievances that lay elsewhere (sociopolitical oppression, marginalization, and so on). Albeit a coalescing element in specific circumstances, it was not deeply rooted in people's imagination and identity. Nor did it activate inescapable conflictual mechanisms between the two communities. In this sense, Iran's vector is the cunning construction of an otherwise absent motive for conflict. As the artificial nature of its ideological component is highlighted, it postulates the possibility of defusing the impact of sectarianism in spurring conflicts.

As both perspectives have merits and limits, it is wise to move beyond too dichotomous an analysis.[49] First, sectarianism cannot be dismissed as an epiphenomenon, pace the instrumentalist-constructivist view. Sectarian identities are not necessarily the primary, let alone the only, identity marker of Iraqis. But they are present, they are resilient, and they have the potential to become (very) politically salient in their own right. Second, there is no automatic, much less deterministic, linkage between identity formation and political mobilization—let alone intercommunal conflict. Primordialism may fail to recognize this. Iraq's modern political history presents too long stretches of intercommunal coexistence, where sectarian identity was not politically charged, to claim conflict is woven in the national fabric. Third and consequently, we need to account for the fact that intersectarian relations may change, also relatively quickly, while sectarian identities may do so only limitedly.[50] Hence, we must examine carefully contextual, and oftentimes exogenous, factors. The ideological vector, one of such exogenous factors, operates precisely on this fault line, the constant tension between contextual sectarian relations and rooted sectarian identities. It tries to make sectarian identity politically salient, and to orient one such identity toward the patron across the border.

State and Nation Building Project in Post-2003 Iraq

Since the formation of the modern Iraq in 1921 all the way to 2003 Iraq has been ruled by Sunni leaders, despite its Shiʿa majority. This is true whether we talk of the Hashemite monarchy (1921–58), the first republican regime (1958–68), or the Baʾathist era (1968–2003).[51] Were these regimes and their leaders also perceived primarily as Sunni regimes by the majority of the Iraqis? There is little evidence of that.[52] Certainly, the regime of Saddam Hussein (1979–2003) did repress public displays of Shiʿa faith such as the ʿAshura and Muharram;[53] persecuted Shiʿa movements like Ad-Daʿwa; and imprisoned, tortured, and executed prominent Shiʿa clerics.[54] Most of all, it launched a war of aggression against the IRI in September 1980, with war effort accompanied by virulent anti-Persian cum anti-Shiʿa propaganda,[55] and ordered the brutal repression of the March 1991 Shiʿa Uprising.[56] However, Saddam Hussein did not behave differently with any group or movement he regarded as a threat to his power, regardless, that is, of sectarian coloring.[57] Be that as it may, many Shiʿites did come to occupy most important positions within the regime.

The trajectory of Saddam Hussein's regime dramatically highlights how "throughout its existence, the modern Iraqi nation-state has struggled to manage communal pluralism adequately. This relationship is the product of a history of exclusionary nation-building that was based on problematic conceptions of unity and pluralism."[58] Under Saddam Hussein, nation building was predicated on exclusionary ideological grounds (the Baʾathist version of pan-Arabism). Non-Arab Kurds could hardly fit the project, for instance. Shiʿites were suspected to harbor sympathies for their coreligionists in Iran. In the eyes of Iraq's non-Sunni Arab citizens, the Baʾathist rule over time acquired the trappings of a Sunni regime out of this exclusionary posturing. Conversely, Sunni Arabs, as the group favored by official discourse, never perceived such a posturing. A dynamic that would make all the more incomprehensible (and in cases intolerable) to them the victimhood rhetoric of post-2003 Shiʿites.[59]

The removal of Saddam Hussein in 2003 allowed communal grievances and recriminations to surface in a context of collapsing order and security. The choice of the US Coalition Provisional Authority (CPA) to establish a sectarian system[60]—apportioning key elective positions according to communal affiliation to mirror demographic features—betrayed a primordialist understanding of communal relations. At the same time, Shiʻa leaders retrofitted a narrative of marginalization and oppression that did find evidence in specific readings of Iraqi history. The consequences were to be momentous. The Shiʻites felt emboldened. Demography and the CPA-imposed institutions poised to properly represent the people meant it was their time to craft a new Iraq: the political project was predicated on the assumptions that "Iraqi Shia are the Iraqi *staatsvolk*—Iraq's constitutive people."[61]

Shiʻites in Iraq have ended up claiming to represent Iraq qua a Shiʻa country while stressing—somewhat contradictorily—Iraq's pluralism and diversity. As we have seen, this is not to say that Shiʻites in Iraq look at their faith or sectarian affiliation necessarily as a primary political or identity marker, much less that they compose a homogenous bloc standing in contrast to Sunnis and Kurds.[62] But it does mean that it is possible to craft a narrative of national unity of Iraq along the lines of a Shiʻa unity. This (local) framing then plays squarely into the hands of Iran's own (regional) narrative. Articulated in the ideological vector, it stresses the shared, cross-border religious-sectarian affiliation and then calls for political allegiance on the basis of such affiliation. Iran can pose as the historical center of gravity of the Shiʻa world; moreover, it can offer a related political project by virtue of the (Shiʻa) Islamic revolution. Iraq is the primary locale where this is actualized.

Sunnis could not understand Shiʻa resentment. Even less could they countenance Shiʻites' desire to engrave in the institutional system sectarian affiliation, whereby Sunnis were cast as a permanent minority. The presence of Iran, looming large all over the country, was poised to elicit similar sentiments: furthermore, the narrative inscribed in the ideological vector could not possibly resonate with Arab Sunnis. For them, post-2003 Iraq was equated with the rise of sectarian politics, associated with Shiʻism and Iranian influence.[63]

Yet Iraq is unlike other theaters of sectarian strife.[64] Neither of the two communities sought to break modern Iraq apart. The conflict did not pertain to the existence of unified modern Iraq.[65] It pertained to state and nation building: "political violence between 2003 and 2014 and the ongoing instability in Arab Iraq have been chiefly driven by the dynamic between Shia-centric state-building and Sunni rejection of this state-building project."[66] Tehran cunningly exploited this context to deploy its ideological vector. It heightened the historically contingent sectarian conflict in Iraq by glocalizing its regional aspiration into the domestic politics of its neighbor.

The Ideological Vector, Militias, and Glocalized Security

At this juncture, in order to realize its project of domination over Iraq, Iran sought to translate the soft power inscribed within the ideological vector into hard power sustained by it. Iran has done so primarily by sponsoring a host of different militias. According to current estimates, "the total Shiite militiamen in Iraq number about 110,000–120,000, of which about two-thirds are members of Iran-backed militias. Collectively, all of the Shiite militias are known as Popular Mobilization Units. . . . The PMU reportedly receive funds from Iran and from various parastatal organizations in Iran."[67] Tehran has trained, financed, sheltered, and overseen, to different degrees, armed formations such as the Hizbullah Brigades and the Asa'ib Ahl al-Haq. The sectarian-ideological bond spearheaded by the ideological vector has been crucial in this regard. Yet it does not mean that Iran does not face limits in its attempt at steering militias (and consequently Iraqi politics) according to its preferences: at times, Shi'a militias may play as most reliable proxy agents for Iran; at times, they may be more restive and reluctant to toe the line dictated by Tehran. To illustrate these points, let us consider two cases.

First, we may look at the Supreme Council for Islamic Revolution in Iraq (SCIRI) as an example of successful integration of an Iraqi militia within Iranian strategy.[68] The SCIRI was founded in 1982 in Iran by prominent Iraqi clerics belonging to the Hakim family, who had fled to Iran because of the war Saddam Hussein launched two years before. It intended to fight the Ba'athist regime and establish in Iraq a theocracy based on the principles of Khomeini's velayat-e faqih. For this purpose, the SCIRI was soon flanked by the Badr Brigades, its armed wing. Their training and discipline have been overseen by the Iranian Revolutionary Guards (IRGC), the praetorians of the regime. After the end of Saddam's regime, the Badr Brigades made a fateful comeback to Iraq, making the most of their close relation with the IRGC. They immediately became one of the most powerful armed groups in the evolving postinvasion environment.[69] The SCIRI rebranded itself as the Islamic Supreme Council of Iraq (ISCI) in 2007, thus signaling its acceptance of the new order where it was poised to play a key role as a full-fledged political party. Its allegiance to Iran, at the same time, never wavered, and the rebranding did not affect the Badr Brigades, which were not dismantled.

Second, we may examine the Sadrist movement, which offers a different case in regard to the relation with Iran.[70] Just like those of the SCIRI/ISCI and its Badr Brigades, its leadership hailed from a prominent family of the Hawza. By 2003, Muqtada, then only twenty-nine years old, had taken the helm of the Sadr family. Yet unlike the SCIRI, the Sadrist movement was not born in Iran. It emerged indigenously in Iraq after the fall of Saddam Hussein by capitalizing on the Sadr's family popular prestige. However, this did not deter Tehran from contacting and ultimately working with and through Muqtada's movement. Its Jaysh al-Mahdi (Army of the Savior) developed soon into a large and efficient (and ruthless) militia, fighting in particular coalition troops in the early years of the occupation.[71] What could hurt the upward trajectory of the Sadrist movement was the lack of religious credentials of Muqtada himself, then a low-ranking cleric who could not command much authority in the ways reputed marja'iyya can. At the height of the Sunni-Shi'a civil war, between 2007 and 2011, Muqtada went to Iran to boost his religious credentials, shed the garb of the extreme firebrand, and be groomed as a leader capable of working also within the official Iraqi institutions. The Sadrist movement progressively developed a political wing.[72] The Jaysh al-Mahdi, at the same time, never dismantled either—rather breaking off in a number of factions. Given the staunch nationalist posturing of the Sadrists, in fact among the most forceful proponents of a Shi'a based national rhetoric, the relation between the Sadrists and Iran has known many ebbs and flows. Muqtada and his followers were often at odds with too deep an interference in national affairs of what remains a foreign country; furthermore, the logic of domestic Iraqi politics has pitched the Sadrist movements against other Shi'a movements like the steadfast pro-Iranian ISCI.[73]

The ISCI and the Sadrist movement are two remarkable examples that vividly illustrate the nature of Iraqi militias and the degree of Iranian influence. First, "both the Sadrists and SCIRI go beyond the traditional conceptualizations of the militia in terms of the extent of their legitimacy with the population, their pursuit of social and political agendas, and their participation in the institutions of the state."[74] Second, they may be more (as the ISCI) or less (as the Sadrist) tied to Iran. It is certainly true that, "Iranian policy was to offer aid in the shape of financial support, modern weapons, and a good communication system. Once lured into accepting them, the recipient cannot do without them."[75] However, the Sadrists have shown how the Iraqi nationalist rhetoric they have increasingly championed may sit very uneasily in relation to Tehran's desiderata. Iran's ideological vector is a powerful tool; it also has clear limitations when confronting alternative and popular political projects (i.e., local Arab Shi'a nationalism).

Sunni Insurgency and the PMU: Implications for Iran's Glocalized Security

Shi'a formations like the Badr Brigades, the Jaysh al-Mahdi and the Hizbullah Brigades translate on the ground the main drives of Iranian security policy in Iraq. These drives are centered on three main goals aligned with the logic of glocalized security: (a) to prevent the collapse of Iraq as a unitary state; (b) to ensure it does not reemerge as a threatening actor vis-à-vis Iran itself; and (c) to make the Iraqi space a springboard for regional domination.

In relation to the first goal, Iran sponsored militias fight those movements bent on splintering Iraq. The two main instances of such movements have been the early (2003–8) Sunni insurgency, headed by the local Al-Qaeda franchise, and then, between 2014 and 2017, its metastasis, the Islamic State. Iran could not contemplate the presence of these jihadi formations at its borders, all the more so if—as it happened with ISIS—they were to capture large swaths of Iraqi territory. In fact, insofar as a unified Iraq is dominated by the Shi'ites, then Tehran can find ways to direct its political inclinations. This contention does not mean Shi'ites are a homogenous group within Iraq (the proliferation of Shi'a militias and parties attests to that) or that Shi'ites unfailingly acquiesce to Iran's indications (as the Sadrist case illustrates). But it does mean that Iran enjoys possibilities to work with a plethora of Shi'a actors at any given moment.[76]

Indeed, maintaining a unified and Shi'a-dominated Iraq plays well into the nationalist rhetoric of the indigenous Shi'a community itself, of which the militias are an expression. And it helps Iran securing Iraq as a nonthreatening regional actor, Tehran's second objective. Shi'a militias—way more than Sunni ones—have manifested their military cum political clout by forming political parties vying for elections. Iranian grip on the militias means grip on Iraqi party politics. It entails the capacity to prevent the formation of hostile majorities in the parliament or restive, anti-Iranian governments.

Iran is thus only all too willing to act as the patron of a Shi'a-dominated Iraq, especially in the context of the tremendous challenge posed by ISIS. The rabid anti-Shi'a discourse and practices of ISIS made Sistani's call for a popular mobilization all the more resounding. Fellow religious (and political) leader Khamenei only seconded the popular swell that gave birth to the PMU. This dynamic served well Iran's interests: "the importance of Iran's role in Iraq's fight against ISIS can scarcely be exaggerated, a fact that has naturally raised concerns about expanding Iranian influence. Yet for those who accepted the legitimacy of the Iraqi state and viewed the prevention of its collapse as a strategic objective, there simply was no readily available alternative to the Hashd phenomenon in the summer of 2014."[77]

Finally, the support for the PMU has also soothed Iran's geostrategic anxieties and sustained Iran's strategic plans in the region: "Iran views the Hashd as an insurance policy against the return of a strong, antagonistic Iraqi state on its border, supported by the US and Saudi Arabia, or one controlled by an enemy such as ISIS."[78] Iran's efficacious deployment of the ideological vector has meant the Shi'a militias have become instruments to fight US presence in the region. The inimical relation between Tehran and Washington since 1979 has witnessed the former oppose the influence of the latter in the region, with the ultimate goal of evicting the Americans from it. Making sure the US does not enjoy a firm foothold in the Gulf is paramount in this sense for Iran. Militias fighting US forces in Iraq answered precisely to this logic.

The Persistence of Militias and Iraq's Security Predicament

Shi'a militias may have been instrumental in preventing Iraq from breaking apart. Yet in a most basic Weberian sense, they are also responsible for the security predicament the country has been mired in since 2003. Because of the militias, Baghdad does not enjoy a monopoly of violence over the territory it claims to control. Somewhat paradoxically, the unity of Iraq has come at the cost of its own viability as a functioning state.

In this situation, the PMU display a contradictory position vis-à-vis the state: "they aspire to become a state-recognized actor, but they also wish to retain their own chain of command autonomous from the government."[79] A dedicated provision in the Iraqi legal code allows them to do so, as it declares the Hashd as "an independent military formation as part of the Iraqi armed forces and linked to the Commander-in-Chief [the Prime Minister]."[80] This technicality placed the PMU under the National Security Council: they became de jure a state institution, but de facto kept their autonomy. To maintain and expand this autonomy, members of the Hashd have tried to enter institutional politics, too—yet the constitution does not allow security personnel to "interfere in political affairs."[81] In other words, the PMU as well as their individual members remain in a legal and political gray area.

The PMU mobilization illustrates this issue. On the one hand, the Hashd fought bravely against ISIS in 2014–17 on behalf of the Iraqi state. Their efforts were crucial to destroying the self-styled caliphate, thus providing "a potent rallying point for a reinvigorated sense of Iraqi nationalism, albeit one with distinctly Shi'i overtones."[82] On the other hand, just like the Badr Brigades and the Sadrist militias, they have refused to be fully absorbed into the fold of official Iraqi security forces after defeating ISIS. In this situation, given the PMU's military, organizational, and financial prowess, Baghdad would need to ensure that "the state and its security forces do not end up [as] junior partners to elements of the Hashd." In this regard, Haddad offers a sobering remark: "it may already be too late to accomplish even that."[83] In fact, not only the coercive capacities of the militias must be taken into account but their broader social role as well.[84] Given their state-like welfare service provision,[85] their direct connection with formal political organizations and consequent penetration within the state institutions,[86] and the ineffective attempts on the part of the government to integrate the militias in the regular army, it is already difficult to discriminate between state apparatus and Hashd: they "have assumed quasi-state dimensions in several areas formerly under the jihadists' rule and inserted themselves into national politics as well. No unit has disarmed. In 2016, the government formally integrated the Hashd into the security forces, but it has yet to assert effective control over more than a few of them."[87]

Instead of integration, entire sectors of state security have been taken over—dare we say colonized—by militias and used to pursue their goals. In doing so, they tend to be violent. Militias often behave like organized crime, with racketing, extortions and kidnapping among some of the sources of financing. Sectarian violence may be present, too, targeting non-Shi'ites.[88] However, Shi'a militias never manifested violence of the paroxysmic kind of ISIS, or the same animosity vis-à-vis other sects. They have fought alongside Kurdish, Sunni, and regular forces. This different disposition may depend on the fact that Shi'a militias are bent on "seeking strategic advantage within the regional order," not to upend it via ruthless violence like jihadi groups.[89] Be as it may, militias are at best partners of the Iraqi government; and only very limitedly, if at all, under government control: their coercive and financial capacities depend foremost on Iran's support and their rootedness in Iraqi society. They have therefore few incentives to join the fold of regular forces. And the government has little capacity (either via persuasion or coercion) to have them do so. The Iraqi security landscape thus remains a fragmented one: structurally unstable, routinely violent.

Conclusion

The concept of ideological vector can help us understand how a country influences and steers the politics of other states in order to enhance its international security, which is too often glocalized. Iran is a case in point. Tehran needs a pliant and subdued Iraq to shore up its security and project power in the region. It does so by deploying an ideological vector that offers a narrative predicated on a shared sectarian bond with the majority of the Iraqi population. This operation features aspects of both soft and hard power. By leveraging the common Shi'a belief, and by offering a specific political reading of it, Iran capitalizes on specific features of the Iraqi national religious-political fabric: namely, the Shi'a state building project in the post Saddam era and the threat to state disintegration posed by the Sunni insurgency. The mobilization of local Iraqi militias and their relations with Tehran then shows how the ideological vector manages to become an instrument of hard power. These militias further Iran's goals in Iraq, keeping Iraq unified as a large, Shi'a dominated country, favorably disposed toward Tehran.

This imbrication of the international and the domestic speaks of a glocalized dynamic. Iran has framed Iraq as a most suitable locale for the propagation, via the ideological vector, of its idiosyncratic version of political Shi'ism. Iranian ambitions must pass through the Iraqi theater: control over Iraq would sustain and enhance Tehran's bid for regional hegemony. The domestic/local and international/regional are intimately intertwined in what is a truly glocalized security situation for both Iran and Iraq. Iran's rise as a regional power has hinged on the savvy deployment of the ideological vector in many a theater: Iraq, as examined here, but also Lebanon, Yemen, Syria, Bahrein, and even eastern Saudi Arabia. This strategy has created a swath of land under Iranian political influence, famously given the moniker the Shi'a Crescent by King Abdullah of Jordan as early as 2004. Of course, Iran's project may face setbacks, as the August 2022 rift with the Sadrist movement demonstrates.

For Iraq, the deployment of the ideological vector carries nefarious implications for its security, which has been glocalized as evident in both Iranian and US involvements in the country. Iraq has witnessed a heightened politicization of sectarian issues, which have compromised national unity (sectarianism is now probably heightened throughout the region, too).[90] Indeed, militias "push weak states along the process toward becoming failed states, creating greater regional and global instability."[91] Iran deemed that management of Iraqi (dis)order via the ideological vector may boost its hegemonic project in the Middle East. However, in compromising Iraq's viability as a functioning state, Iran may have forgone long-term security for short term gains. Security can hardly ever be contained by borders.

Notes

1. The fatwa can be found on Sistani's official website.
2. Throughout the text, I will be using Shi'a as the adjective; Shi'ism as the noun; Shi'ites as the believers. Different spellings may in fact be found in the literature.
3. International Crisis Group "Iraq's Paramilitary Groups," i.
4. Ibid., 3.
5. The conflict was one of the most violent during the cold war era, with an estimate 1 million casualties. See Chubin and Tripp, *Iran and Iraq at War*.
6. Robertson, "Globalisation or Glocalisation?"
7. For the co-constitution of global and local, national and international in the context of glocalization see Swyngedouw and Cox, "Neither Global nor Local."
8. Buzan, Wæver, and de Wilde, *Security*.

9. In principle, it is possible to see how an ideological vector may be deployed also by nonstate actors, such as intergovernmental organizations, nongovernmental organizations, corporations, individuals, and so on. However, for the present study, I will confine it to the domain of state foreign policy.

10. "Ideology serves political actors to internally enable . . . certain foreign policy actions" (Glombitza, "Islamic Revolutionary Ideology and Its Narratives," 1157).

11. Robertson, in "Globalisation or Glocalisation?," insists on connecting in a co-constitutive, dialectical fashion otherwise dichotomously opposed terms such as *global/local* and *universal/particular*.

12. The concept of soft power was introduced by Joseph Nye in "Soft Power and American Foreign Policy": "Soft power arises from the attractiveness of a country's culture, political ideals, and policies" (256). Nye further elaborates on the difference between hard and soft power in "Get Smart: Combining Hard and Soft Power." See also Haynes, "Religion and Foreign Policy Making in the USA, India and Iran."

13. Again Nye introduces a new term to clarify its stance: "Smart power is a term I developed . . . to counter the misperception that soft power alone can produce effective foreign policy" ("Get Smart: Combining Hard and Soft Power," 160). I believe the concept of ideological vector captures an instance of what Nye defines as 'smart power.'

14. For an introduction to Gramsci's concepts of hegemony and domination, see Simon, *Gramsci's Political Thought*, especially 24–33.

15. While imperial plans like the ones projected via an ideological vector tend to do so, this instability is not an automatic outcome. Imposition of Pax Americana, for example, resulted in the pacification and prosperity of Western Europe after World War II.

16. Mousavian and Chitsazian, "Iran's Foreign Policy in the Middle East," 100; see also Nasr, "All Against All"; Sadjapour, "Iran's Hollow Victory."

17. Matin-Asgari, "Academic Debate On Iranian Identity," 185.

18. Amanat, "Iranian Identity Boundaries," 13. Shi'ism is the second-largest sect within Islam. It comprises between 10 and 15 percent of the world's Muslim population. Sunnis, the largest sect, represent up to 90 percent of Muslims worldwide. The largest Shi'a branch, which recognizes twelve imams and is therefore known as Twelver Shi'ism, is the dominant Shi'a sect in both Iran and Iraq.

19. Ibid.

20. Ibid., 20.

21. Akbarzadeh and Barry, "State Identity in Iranian Foreign Policy," 614.

22. Amanat, "Iranian Identity Boundaries," 21. See also Matin-Asgari, "Academic Debate On Iranian Identity," 186.

23. Amanat, "Iranian Identity Boundaries," 21.

24. See note 48.

25. Katzman, "Iran's Foreign and Defense Policies," 2.

26. One may even argue that the Iranian regime crafted a narrative with universal undertones, insofar as it appeals to the worldwide ummah and, although foregoing some of the specific Islamic elements, to Third World anti-imperialist tradition. For reasons of space, I will not delve much into these frames.

27. Katzman, "Iran's Foreign and Defense Policies," 1.

28. The literature on the Iranian revolution is vast. See Arjomand, *Turban for the Crown*.

29. Amanat, "Iranian Identity Boundaries," 13.

30. Khomeini elaborated his view in a series of lectures in the Iraqi city of Najaf in 1970. They are collected in Khomeini, *Islamic Government*.

31. Martin, *Creating an Islamic State*.

32. Abrahamian, *Khomeinism*.

33. See Martin, *Creating an Islamic State*.

34. See Walt, *Revolution and War*.
35. Glombitza, "Islamic Revolutionary Ideology and Its Narratives." This was largely due to the close relation of the shah with the United States.
36. Katzman, "Iran's Foreign and Defense Policies," 1.
37. Zarif, "What Iran Really Wants," 52–53 and 59.
38. Sadjapour, "Iran's Hollow Victory."
39. International Crisis Group. "Iraq's Paramilitary Groups," 9.
40. Chehabi, "Iran and Iraq."
41. In particular, we should mention Khuzestan, the southwestern province of Iran at the head of the Gulf. This part of the country is mostly inhabited by Arabs and borders flat plains with the region of Basra. Rich in oil and gas, it saw some of the most important battles during the Iraq-Iran War. The Algiers Accords of 1975 between Ba'athist Iraq and Reza Shah's Iran had sought to demarcate the border along the Shatt al-'Arab, the waterway separating the two countries as the Tigris and Euphrates Rivers flow into the Gulf.
42. Haddad, "Sectarian Relations and Sunni Identity in Post-Civil War Iraq," 82.
43. Nakash, *Shi'is of Iraq*.
44. See note 48 for more details.
45. For an overall discussion on sectarianism in the Gulf, see Potter, *Sectarian Politics in the Persian Gulf*.
46. See in particular Nasr, *Shia Revival*; and Haddad, *Sectarianism in Iraq*.
47. Conventional ethnosectarian classifications of the country speak of (Arab) Shi'is, (Arab) Sunnis, and Kurds. This classification actually lumps together both ethnicity (Arabs versus non-Arab Kurds) and religious affiliation (Shi'is versus Sunnis). Kurds, for instance, can be Sunnis and Shi'is. In this study, I make reference to the split within the Arab community, which comprises between 75 and 80 percent of Iraq's population (as of 2022, slightly over 40 million). Figures regarding this split are notoriously difficult to ascertain, but usually Arab Shi'is are believed to be around 55–60 percent of nationals and Arab Sunnis around 15–20 percent. The Kurds, the second-largest ethnic group in the country (between 15 and 20 percent of the population), have enjoyed a different status in post-2003 Iraq, with considerable autonomy and a degree of insularity from the dynamics I deal with here. Other smaller groups (Turkmen, Yazidis, Assyrians, and so on) do exist in the country (making up to 5 percent of the population). See World CIA Factbook for these estimates.
48. Numerous regiments of the defeated Iraqi army retreating from Kuwait gave way to a full-fledged revolt against the regime in Baghdad. As they were composed mostly of Shi'a soldiers, the sectarian composition of the rebels gave birth to the narrative of a Shi'a uprising.
49. See in particular Haddad, *Sectarianism in Iraq*.
50. Haddad, "Sectarian Relations and Sunni Identity in Post-Civil War Iraq."
51. For a history of Iraq up until the turn of the century, see Tripp, *History of Iraq*.
52. Haddad, *Sectarianism in Iraq*.
53. These are public displays of devotion, where Shi'is commemorate and remember the martyrdom of Husayn, the third imam of Shi'ism.
54. Jabar, *Shi'ite Movement in Iraq*.
55. Chubin and Tripp, *Iran and Iraq at War*.
56. See note 48.
57. Notorious are, for example, Saddam's brutal repression of Kurds in the mid-1970s and late 1980s as well as the brutal suppression of the Communist Party of Iraq. See Ismael, *Rise and Fall of the Communist Party of Iraq*.
58. Haddad, *Shia-Centric State-Building and Sunni Rejection in Post 2003 Iraq*, 121.
59. Ibid., 116–18.
60. In Arabic, *muhasasah'*.

61. Haddad, *Shia-Centric State-Building and Sunni Rejection in Post 2003 Iraq*, 118.
62. Some crude representations of the country did point in that direction. For useful corrections, see Visser, "Other People's Maps."
63. Kotinsly, "Brave New World Order," 50.
64. For instance, Yugoslavia.
65. Haddad, "Sectarian Relations and Sunni Identity in Post-Civil War Iraq," 68.
66. Haddad, *Shia-Centric State-Building and Sunni Rejection in Post 2003 Iraq*, 116.
67. Katzman, "Iran's Foreign and Defense Policies," 34.
68. See Nasr, *Shia Revival*, 142–45. For a detailed report of SCIRI activities and dynamics in the early years after 2003, see International Crisis Group, "Shiite Politics in Iraq."
69. Katzman, "Iran's Foreign and Defense Policies," 33.
70. For an account of the early days of the Sadrist movement in Iraq post 2003, see Cockburn, *Muqtada al-Sadr and the Fall of Iraq*.
71. Cockburn, *Muqtada al-Sadr and the Fall of Iraq*.
72. The Sadrist movement has won a plurality of vote in the last Iraqi elections (at the time of writing) of October 2021: 10 percent of the votes, which translated into the largest parliamentary bloc of 73 seats (out of 329).
73. See Iran's call for dialogue in the midst of the latest inter-Shiʻa clashes.
74. Thurber, "Militias as Sociopolitical Movements," 905.
75. Ibid., 912–93.
76. International Crisis Group, "Iraq's Paramilitary Groups," 4.
77. Haddad, "Hashd."
78. Ibid.
79. International Crisis Group, "Iraq's Paramilitary Groups," 6.
80. The Law of the Popular Mobilisation Units Commission Number 40 for the Year 2016, Ministry of Justice, 5 January 2017. Cited in International Crisis Group, "Iraq's Paramilitary Groups," 6.
81. Article 9 of the Iraqi Constitution.
82. Haddad, "Hashd."
83. Ibid.
84. The complex and multifaceted nature of militias makes this very label somewhat blunt to capture their modus operandi and overall societal reach. See Thurber, "Militias as Sociopolitical Movements."
85. The Sadrist movement, for instance, developed a network of societal services that competed with (or flat out replaced) the official state welfare, in most cases lacking or simply missing. Health clinics, schools, mosques, unemployment subsidies, garbage collection, and even police patrolling of Shiʻa neighborhoods. See Cockburn, *Muqtada al-Sadr and the Fall of Iraq*, and International Crisis Group, "Iraq's Civil War, the Sadrist and the Surge."
86. International Crisis Group, "Iraq's Paramilitary Groups," 9.
87. International Crisis Group, "Iraq: Evading the Gathering Storm."
88. International Crisis Group, "Déjà Vu All Over Again," 4.
89. Haddad, "Hashd."
90. Gengler, "Understanding Sectarianism in the Persian Gulf."
91. Thurber, "Militias as Sociopolitical Movements," 901.

References

Abrahamian, Ervand. *Khomeinism: Essays on the Islamic Republic*. Berkeley: University of California Press, 1993.

Akbarzadeh, Shahram, and James Barry. "State Identity in Iranian Foreign Policy." *British Journal of Middle Eastern Studies* 43, no. 4 (2016): 613–29.

Al-Sayyid Ali Al-Husseini Al-Sistani, official website. "Advice and Guidance to the Fighters on the Battlefields." February 12, 2015. https://www.sistani.org/english/archive/25036/.

Amanat, Abbas. "Iranian Identity Boundaries: A Historical Overview." In *Iran Facing Others*, edited by Abbas Amanat and Farzin Vejdani, 1–33. New York: Palgrave Macmillan, 2012.

Arjomand, Said Amir. *The Turban for the Crown: The Islamic Revolution in Iran*. Studies in Middle Eastern History. New York: Oxford University Press, 1988.

Buzan, Barry, Ale Wæver, and Jaap de Wilde. *Security: A New Framework for Analysis*. Boulder, CO: Lynne Rienner, 1998.

Chehabi, Houchang E. "Iran and Iraq: Intersocietal Linkages and Secular Nationalisms." In *Iran Facing Others*, edited by Abbas Amanat and Farzin Vejdani, 193–218. New York: Palgrave Macmillan, 2012.

Chubin, Shahram, and Charles Tripp. *Iran and Iraq at War*. London: Routledge, 2019.

Cockburn, Patrick. *Muqtada al-Sadr and the Fall of Iraq*. Vol. 2. London: Faber and Faber, 2015.

Gengler, Justin. "Understanding Sectarianism in the Persian Gulf." In *Sectarian Politics in the Persian Gulf*, edited by Lawrence G. Potter, 31–66. Oxford: Oxford University Press, 2014.

Glombitza, Olivia. "Islamic Revolutionary Ideology and Its Narratives: The Continued Relevance of the Islamic Republic's Ideology." *Third World Quarterly* 43 (2022): 1156–1175.

Haddad, Fanar. "The Hashd: Redrawing the Military and Political Map of Iraq." Middle East Institute April 9, 2015.

———. *Sectarianism in Iraq: Antagonistic Visions of Unity*. Oxford: Oxford University Press, 2014.

———. "Sectarian Relations and Sunni Identity in Post-Civil War Iraq," In *Sectarian Politics in the Persian Gulf*, edited by Lawrence G. Potter, 67–115. Oxford: Oxford University Press, 2014.

———. *Shia-Centric State-Building and Sunni Rejection in Post 2003 Iraq*. Vol. 7. Washington, DC: Carnegie Endowment for International Peace, 2016.

Haynes, Jeffrey. "Religion and Foreign Policy Making in the USA, India and Iran: Towards a Research Agenda." *Third World Quarterly* 29, no. 1 (2008): 143–65.

International Crisis Group. "Déjà Vu All Over Again: Iraq's Escalating Political Crisis." Report no. 126, Middle East & North Africa, July 30, 2012.

———. "Iraq: Evading the Gathering Storm." Briefing no. 70, Middle East & North Africa, August 29, 2019.

———. "Iraq's Civil War, the Sadrist and the Surge." Report no. 70, Middle East & North Africa, February 7, 2008.

———. "Iraq's Paramilitary Groups: The Challenge of Rebuilding a Functioning State." Report no. 188, Middle East & North Africa, July 30, 2018.

———. "Shiite Politics in Iraq. The Role of the Supreme Council." Report no. 70, Middle East & North Africa, November 15, 2007.

Ismael, Tareq Y. *The Rise and Fall of the Communist Party of Iraq*. New York: Cambridge University Press, 2008.

Jabar, Faleh. *The Shi'ite Movement in Iraq*. London: Saqi, 2003.

Katzman, Kenneth. "Iran's Foreign and Defense Policies." Congressional Research Service Report R44017. Washington, DC, last updated January 11, 2021.

Khomeini, Ruhollah, and Hamid Algar. *Islamic Government: Governance of the Jurist*. Tehran: Institute for Compilation and Publication of Imam Khomeini's Works, International Affairs Department, 2005.

Kotinsly, Joseph E. "Brave New World Order: The Supreme Council for Islamic Revolution in Iraq and the Rise of Iraqi Shī'ī Identity Politics." *Journal of the Middle East and Africa* 13, no. 1 (2022): 49–65.

Martin, Vanessa. *Creating an Islamic State: Khomeini and the Making of a New Iran*. London: I. B. Tauris, 2000.

Matin-Asgari, Afshin. "The Academic Debate on Iranian Identity." In *Iran Facing Others*, edited by Abbas Amanat and Farzin Vejdani, 173–92. New York: Palgrave Macmillan, 2012.

Mousavian, Seyed Hossein, and Mohammad Reza Chitsazian. "Iran's Foreign Policy in the Middle East: A Grand Strategy." *Middle East Policy* 27, no. 3 (2020): 99–114.

Nakash, Yitzhak. *The Shi'is of Iraq*. Princeton, NJ: Princeton University Press, 2018.

Nasr, Vali. "All Against All: The Sectarian Resurgence in the Post-American Middle East." *Foreign Affairs* 101, no. 1 (2022).

———. *The Shia Revival: How Conflicts within Islam Will Shape the Future*. New York: Norton, 2006.

Nye, Joseph. "Get Smart: Combining Hard and Soft Power." *Foreign Affairs* 88, no. 4 (2009): 160–63.

———. "Soft Power and American Foreign Policy." *Political Science Quarterly* 119, no. 2 (2004): 255–70.

Potter, Lawrence G., ed. *Sectarian Politics in the Persian Gulf*. Oxford: Oxford University Press, 2014.

Robertson, Roland. "Globalisation or Glocalisation?" *Journal of International Communication* 1, no. 1 (1994): 33–52.

Sadjapour, Karim. "Iran's Hollow Victory: The High Price of Regional Dominance." *Foreign Affairs* 101, no. 2 (2022).

Simon, Roger. *Gramsci's Political Thought: An Introduction*. London: Lawrence and Wishart, 2015.

Swyngedouw, Erik, and Kevin Cox. "Neither Global nor Local: 'Glocalization' and the Politics of Scale." In *Spaces of Globalization: Reasserting the Power of the Local*, edited by K. R. Cox, 137–166. New York: Guilford Press, 1997.

Thurber, Ches. "Militias as Sociopolitical Movements: Lessons from Iraq's Armed Shia Groups." *Small Wars & Insurgencies* 25, no. 5–6 (2014): 900–923.

Tripp, Charles. *A History of Iraq*. Cambridge: Cambridge University Press, 2002.

Visser, Reidar. "Other People's Maps." *Wilson Quarterly* 31, no. 1 (2007): 64–68.

Walt, Stephen M. *Revolution and War*. Ithaca, NY: Cornell University Press, 2013.

Zarif, Mohammad Javad. "What Iran Really Wants: Iranian Foreign Policy in the Rouhani era." *Foreign Affairs* 93, no. 3 (2014).

MASSIMO RAMAIOLI is Assistant Professor and Coordinator at the School of Humanities and Social Sciences, Al-Akhawayn University in Ifrane. Previously he was Assistant Dean at the School of Arts, Humanities and Social Sciences and Assistant Professor in the Social Development and Policy Program at Habib University. His main research interests are contentious politics, political Islam, Gramscian theory, and international relations theory. He is a regular contributor for *Nuovo Mondo Economico*, an online publication of the Centro Studi Einaudi of Turin, Italy, and a research fellow at the German Institute for Global and Area Studies.

7

COMMUNAL CONFLICTS AND RADICALIZATION INTO NONJIHADI VIOLENT EXTREMISM IN NIGERIA
The Case of Southern Kaduna

Gbemisola Abdul-Jelil Animasawun

INTRODUCTION

From 1999 to 2012, no less than 700 incidences of communal conflicts had caused over 15,000 deaths accompanied by tens of thousands of displacements in Nigeria.[1] Based on official statistics of the Federal Government of Nigeria (FGN), by 2010, 1.2 million people had been internally displaced owing to religious and ethnic conflict, and at least 13,500 deaths had resulted from religious and ethnic conflicts.[2] Out of 677 incidents of mass atrocities in 2020, 207 came from clashes between farmers and herders.[3] In the first nine months of 2021, 8,000 people were killed as a direct result of various conflicts.[4] These figures must be taken as conservative estimates because there are no comprehensive monitoring systems for conflict fatalities in Nigeria.[5] The nonexistence of a proper accounting system for conflict-fatalities is consistent with known government perception of violent conflicts and such fatalities as indictment on its incapacity to maintain peace and security. The other reason is that many more people die from injuries sustained during clashes after initial counts. As John Campbell and Matthew Page rightly note, "Nigeria's most serious and widespread security challenges and perhaps its least understood: communal violence . . . is often used to describe land disputes involving farmers and herdsmen or between rival ethnic communities."[6]

These conflicts are driven by (counter)narratives and (counter)claims of rights to natural resources (i.e., land and water) and political positions based on autochthony as well as the religionization and ethnicization of civic activities such as elections. Often framed as indigene-settler, in most cases, such conflicts conflate ethnic and religious identities in the mobilization of sentiments and violence that substantially account for the fragility of intergroup relations in Nigeria's Fourth Republic that came into being in 1999.[7] These conflicts have led to the proliferation of ethnic militias that also perform vigilante duties headlined by groups like the Oodua People's Congress in the Yoruba Southwest, the Bakassi Boys in the Southeast, and the Egbesu Boys in the Niger delta, among others, especially in the early days of the Fourth Republic. In a way, there has been a continuous flow and proliferation of conflicts in Nigeria. As Jason Quinn, Madhav Joshi, and Erik Melander have argued, "the historiographies of armed groups show that the choices of rebel groups to initiate a fight, continue a fight, or give up a fight are often influenced by what happened with the groups that came before them."[8]

Military deployments and judicial commissions of inquiry have become lids on communal conflicts instead of conscious efforts to address the conflict drivers.[9] Too often, mutual demonization of the ethnic and religious *other* fester alongside communally felt sense of deprivation and denial. However, the deployment of the military merely restores order in many instances without conscious postconflict peacebuilding initiatives, and when such efforts are initiated, they are hardly seen to logical conclusions. The success recorded in the postconflict peacebuilding process in Ife-Modake conflict,[10] for example, stands in contrast to what played out in many other conflict-affected states like Plateau, Kaduna, Taraba, Kwara, Kogi, Benue, and Nasarrawa, where judicial commissions of inquiry became another source of conflicts.[11] Therefore, the peace in many of these communities remains fragile with intermittent violence generating scores of fatalities from reciprocal violence that do not make the headlines except in rare instances, such as when President Olusegun Obasanjo declared a state of emergency on May 18, 2004.

Not paying attention to the changes and continuities that characterize communal conflicts, prolonged exposure to them, and how they serve as breeding contexts for both homegrown and global terrorism is a knowledge gap with significant policy implications.[12] In Nigeria, the global war on terror has been approached by scholars and policymakers largely as a jihadi issue. This has been informed by the monstrousness of Boko Haram and its breakaway factions—Jama'atu Ahl al-Sunnah li al Da'wati wa al-Jihad (JAS), which is independent; Jama'atu Ansarul Muslimina fi Biladis al-Sudan (Ansaru), which is affiliated to al-Qaeda; and Islamic State West Africa Province (ISWAP), which is affiliated to ISIS.[13]

However, Zamfara and Kaduna states, both in Nigeria's Northwest, are examples of places where prolonged exposure to communal conflicts have incubated criminality and radicalization into violent extremism and insurgency in both the jihadi (Zamfara) and nonjihadi contexts (Southern Kaduna) that are largely local but also feed into globalized terrorism. In Zamfara state, what was initially a communal conflict between the Hausa sedentary farmers and the nomadic Fulani has mutated from conflict to the jihadization of banditry in Zamfara state and the entire Northwest.[14] The conditions that radicalize into violent extremism at the individual and group level loom large in the narratives of the conflicts in Southern Kaduna.[15] This is because all parties to the conflict see themselves as victims of state neglect, deprived of security and justice, at-risk of predatory and biased security personnel, and subjected to institutionalized discrimination based on their religious and ethnic identities.

Therefore, both the Hausa versus Fulani conflict in Zamfara and the Southern Kaduna autochthons and Fulani conflicts depict the potency of communal conflicts to radicalize persons and communities into (non)jihadi violent extremism and terrorism. They also have potentials for exploitation by groups like al-Qaeda that have demonstrated adroitness in hyphenating the local and the global by manipulating local problems for radicalizing persons and communities.[16] Despite this reality, academic and policy exploration has been reticent of a "plural and reflexive theorization" of how communal conflicts radicalize into (non)jihadi violent extremism.[17] This reticence has informed this chapter, which answers the question: Why is the Southern Kaduna conflict radicalizing persons and communities into (non)jihadi violent extremism?

The study is based on expert interview and review of media and secondary sources. After a review of relevant literature and reports in the media, respondents were purposively selected based on having coherent emic perspectives of the conflict. In-depth interviews were conducted with the chair of the Christian Association of Nigeria (CAN) in Kaduna, the president of the Southern Kaduna People's Union (SOKAPU), a leading figure of the Fulani community, a close aide of the Kaduna state governor, security agents, and civil society actors. Using the Ns model (needs of communities and individuals, narratives, networks of violence, and neglect),[18] this chapter shows the manifestation of the global in the local based on how communal conflicts radicalize persons and communities into violent extremism.

The rest of the chapter continues with an inquest into the meanings and trajectories of communal conflicts based on the relevant literature. This is followed by using empirical instances to show the similarities in communal conflicts and radicalization into violent extremism through a glocalization frame. This is followed by the section on the Southern Kaduna crisis as one of such communal conflicts. The conclusion posits that case-specific knowledge of the vulnerabilities of actors and victims of communal conflicts should be prioritized for preventing and countering violent extremism because of its implications for localized individual and mass radicalization into violent extremism.

COMMUNAL CONFLICTS: MEANINGS AND TRAJECTORIES

Communal conflicts are "intense, sudden, though not necessarily wholly unplanned, lethal attacks by civilian members of one ethnic group on civilian members of another ethnic group, the victims chosen because of their group membership."[19] Thus, what puts one at risk or protects one in the context of communal conflicts is one's identity. This is especially true in communities where protracted communal conflicts have led to the territorialization of neighborhoods or the ghettoization of security whereby individuals of certain identities are secure only in specific areas.[20] This is the case in parts of Nigeria like Plateau and Kaduna, where communal conflicts play out in the binaries of indigene-settler, farmer-herder, and Christian-Muslim.

For precision, nonstate-actor violent communal conflicts in Africa can be categorized into two types.[21] These are communal conflicts between distinct ethnic or religious communities and inter/intra conflicts between gangs/militias, which also do not threaten the state. It should be noted that sometimes militias and gangs can be associated, and even represent, an ethnic or religious community in their conflict with another community. In such cases, communal conflicts provide a convergence of civil and violent nonstate actors. This is because civil actors sometimes tacitly endorse, fail to condemn or clearly justify violent acts by violent nonstate actors because of shared ethnic or religious identity.[22]

Unlike insurgents aiming at state power, the actors in a communal conflict are often two feuding nonstate groups organized along shared communal identities.[23] Communal identity in such instances is derived from subjective identifications, such as common history, religion, and claims of autochthony and culture. Therefore, it is a conflict between two distinct communities that do not directly or indirectly aim to unseat an incumbent or to abolish or curtail state power and the victims and actors are primarily civilians.

In contrast to insurgencies, the weapons used in communal conflicts are mostly kitchen knives, cudgels, and small and light arms. Militias and gangs involved in communal conflicts may use military tactics and arms. When deaths from communal conflicts exceed a thousand, it is no longer a communal conflict but a communal war.[24] According to some measures, battle deaths must be up to twenty-five in one calendar year before an incident is considered a violent communal conflict.[25] Communal conflicts can be one-sided, when a major or stronger community embarks on a cleansing or pogrom against a weaker community, or dyadic, when two equally strong communities are pitched against each other.[26]

Communal conflicts can be localized, nationalized, and transnationalized.[27] Localized communal conflicts are boundary- and sometimes resource-based conflicts whose escalations are geographically limited to the locale of the conflict, such as the conflicts between Aguleri and Umuleri in Anambra state and Offa and Erin-Ile in Kwara state.[28] Communal conflicts can be nationalized in instances where the issue in dispute affects members of the community residing in different parts of the country, such as the sharia crisis in Nigeria in 2000, which strained Christian-Muslim relations beyond Zamfara state where Sharia was implemented. The Southern Kaduna conflict has been transnationalized because it has attracted deliberations in the UK Parliament due to its links to terrorism.[29] It should be noted that nationalized and transnationalized communal conflicts have very high propensities to lead to civil wars. Communal conflicts often use glocalization by adapting global practices into local settings to mobilize diaspora remittances and crowdfunding for conflict logistics.[30]

The grievances in communal conflicts are often around resources (e.g., arable and grazing land) and identity (e.g., religion and ethnicity) that are used as the basis to exclude a specific group from access to common goods. This makes arid and semiarid regions of the Sahel and countries like Kenya, Nigeria, and Sudan prone to communal conflicts; climate-related shocks and attendant contestations over land, water, and other natural resources that provide means of livelihood, especially in rural communities, are especially common and acute in these areas. A credence to this is Nigeria's North Central geopolitical zone, an area that is regarded as the country's food basket due to its fertile soil but that has also been compared as the country's Middle East because of the spate of communal conflicts in the area, which are driven by fierce competition for rapidly depleting natural resources; the scuffling over these declining resources has informed the discursive framing of these clashes as indigene-settler and farmer-herder conflicts.[31] The phenomenon is in line with expert predictions that extreme warming will increase the risk of climate-related insecurity (e.g., half a degree Celsius rise in local temperature will lead to 10–20 percent rise in deadly conflicts). Fortunately, climate-related conflicts and insecurity are preventable if they are given proper policy attention.[32]

In addition, (neo)patrimonial networks, especially ethnic- or religious-based electoral politics, escalate (and even cause) communal conflicts. For instance, in states like Kaduna and Plateau, two of the most affected in Nigeria, the ethnicization and religionization of political patronage has been a constant trigger of indigene-settler violence.[33] Also, state bias, insensitivity, and exclusionary policies can precipitate communal conflicts. Unlike separatist insurgencies, which are typically between the national army and insurgents, government involvement in communal conflicts is often in the form of deployment of the state's security asset for the purpose of maintaining order, even when a side in the conflict perceives state bias as the cause of the conflict.

Government's actions or inactions can constitute causes of communal conflict. This is because sometimes the state can be perceived to be (in)advertently supporting a side in the conflict. In Nigeria, the military is often perceived as the militia of the Hausa-Fulani oligarchy, which often rules the country.[34] The state can also be a third party by deploying its security assets to stop violence, support or initiate a peace process, or conduct an inquiry into specific episodes of clashes—and sometimes a combination of all these. In some instances, policies are initiated by the government, such as the anti–open grazing law in some states, which was a response to farmer-herder conflicts. Nonstate actors also seek agency and take positions in communal conflicts. For instance, the Offa Descendants Union and the Erin-Ile Progressive Union consistently maintain diametrically opposed positions on boundary disputes. Similarly, the Miyetti Allah, the Middle-Belt Forum, and the SOKAPU have different views on farmer-herder conflicts.[35]

Generally, there is some tardiness and reluctance by national and international state actors as well as the media to get involved in communal conflicts because of the assumption that these conflicts pose no threat to the government and are often restricted to rural areas. In reality, communal conflicts can be politically significant, especially when they involve issues of political representation, land rights, and access to economic opportunities.[36] An example of this is the politicization of the decision of all the governors in the South to enact laws that will prohibit open grazing, which has been interpreted as a direct attack against the North even though some northern governors have expressed support for the ban on open grazing. It is also important to note that communal conflicts are largely shaped by horizontal inequalities (i.e., social, economic, political, and cultural) based on ethnic or religious identity.[37] Therefore, violence can be prevented or accelerated depending on the way people see the government or the power equation between the conflicting parties.[38]

The mutation and escalation of communal conflicts can take two paths: a civil war or a protracted secessionist quest. Both of these can radicalize into violent extremism and attract global attention if humanitarian crises worsen. By ignoring the potential mutation and escalation of communal conflicts, violence becomes endemic and recurrent.[39] Furthermore, the initial legitimacy conferred on armed nonstate actors posturing as defenders of their communities can provide pathways to their emergence as Big Men—"informal political and/or economic actors situated in social space"—who become subversive of national security and peaceful coexistence, as has been the case in Nigeria.[40]

Shared Features of Communal Conflicts and Violent Extremism

The US Agency for International Development defines violent extremism as "advocating, engaging in, preparing, or otherwise supporting ideologically motivated or justified violence to further social, economic or political objectives."[41] Indeed, this is already playing out in communities with prolonged exposure to violent conflicts across Nigeria especially in the North Central and Northeast regions.

A shared feature of communal conflicts and violent extremism is the instrumentalization of (counter)narratives, which are "(re)collections and (re)constructions of events which happen in sequence, with characters that can cause changes neatly contained within an identifiable beginning, middle and end."[42] Communal groups locked in conflicts consciously construct and promote narratives that serve their purposes and imagined ends. As in well-polished creative works, the narratives have characters, settings, (projected) outcomes, and a plot. Moreover, they have an introduction, a middle, and an end with a call to action.[43] This is done in a way that gives each narrative probability and fidelity.[44] Narrative probability is aimed at giving coherence, believability, and plausibility. Narrative fidelity is done by shoring up the truth features of the narrative so that it would ring true to the intended audience. For instance, one of the narratives of the Boko Haram is that human suffering happens because of sinfulness and disobedience to the words of Allah; therefore, replacing the Nigerian state with an Islamic state would end suffering and usher in a good life. By citing corruption and poverty, such narratives sound plausible, and by invoking verses of the Holy Quran, it rings true to the intended audience. A similar use of narratives is found among communities locked in protracted conflicts where the ethnic or religious other is depicted as the cause of the group's suffering and emancipation is hinged on either exterminating the other or exiting the shared space.

In overcoming the challenge of space and boundaries, communal conflict entrepreneurs and (non)jihadi extremists glocalize their cause through social media (counter)narratives of grievances that might resonate with distant audiences. In states like Plateau, Zamfara, and Kaduna, such use of narratives has framed the ethnic and religious *other* as the problem and dogmatic loyalty to the in-group is absolute. In descending into violent extremism, communal conflict entrepreneurs and jihadists rely on glocal practices and (social)media for demonizing the other, seeking pity, and justifying resort to violence.[45]

For both groups, violence is also framed as legitimate and unavoidable in the pursuit of set goals. A standard feature of violent extremism is forceful propaganda that aims to elevate the status of one group while excluding or dominating the other.[46] In communities with protracted conflicts, violence is used for self-defense and preservation of ancestral land and privileges. Radicalization and recruitment are often directed and sometimes mediated through elites, social influencers and warlords who emerge out of conflicts. They function as soldiers of the communities in the fight for protection and control of resources, and often gain legitimacy by the absence of state authority or the state's inability to protect the community. Unlike jihadi extremists, they are often stationary and localized within the territories of the communities they represent.[47] Radicalization and recruitment are often locally clandestine, but they are now glocalized through social media platforms and the internet at large. To show the threats of violent extremism from communal conflicts in Nigeria, a breakdown of community-based militias, excluding jihadist groups, is provided in table 7.1.

Table 7.1 shows the names of community-based armed groups (excluding jihadist groups), the incidents of violent attacks, and the fatalities as sourced from Armed Conflict Location and Event Data Project (ACLED) from May 31, 2018, to May 31, 2020. In total, nineteen groups were involved in armed violence during the period. Out of these, only three groups are not connected to any ethnic identity, which are: Aye Cult Militia, Black-Axe Student Militia, and Icelander Cult Militia. Collectively, these three groups account for only 3.6 percent of all the incidents of violent attacks. All the other groups are linked to an ethnic group. According to an ACLED reports, "communal and ethnic militia activity has driven an increase in violence targeting civilians in 2022. Overall civilian targeting increased by 45% throughout the first six months of 2022 compared to the same period last year, with more than 2,300 reported civilian fatalities. Communal and ethnic militias were responsible for nearly half of these incidents."[48]

While community armed groups are not entirely the same as jihadists (e.g., Boko Haram, Ansaru and ISWAP), they do share some similarities. All of them are violent, recruit through narratives, shame those who refuse

Table 7.1 Community-based armed groups, violent attacks, and fatalities in Nigeria (May 2018–May 2020)

Number	Group name	Violent attacks	Fatalities	Percentage of violent attack incidents
1.	Fulani ethnic militia	418	1,479	43.6
2.	Zamfara communal militia	87	846	9.1
3.	Unidentified cult militia	47	75	4.9
4.	Unidentified communal militia	31	92	3.2
5.	Tiv ethnic militia	29	86	3.0
6.	Jukun ethnic militia	19	55	2.0
7.	Aye cult militia	15	45	1.6
8.	Ebira ethnic militia	14	31	1.5
9.	Black Axe student militia	13	23	1.4
10.	Katsina communal militia	8	33	0.8
11.	Yansakai militia	8	72	0.8
12.	Icelander cult militia	6	21	0.6
13.	Adara ethnic militia	5	66	0.5
14.	Agila communal militia	5	26	0.5
15.	Bassa ethnic militia	5	28	0.5
16.	Izzi ethnic militia	5	6	0.5
17.	Nasarawa communal militia	5	10	0.5
18.	Yagba communal militia	5	15	0.5
19.	Others (with fewer than 5 incidents each)	234	621	24.4
	Total	959	3,630	100.0

Source: Armed Conflict Location and Event Data Project (ACLED). Accessed June 24, 2020.

to join them, use tactics of terrorism, and sometimes rely on criminality for funding. In making use of terror, both violent jihadi groups and community-based violent groups rely on common factors for attracting, mobilizing, and indoctrinating people into violent extremism.[49] The common factors are: (a) ideology, (b) affiliation, (c), identity, (d) moral emotions, and (e) globalizing grievances. The pathways to violent jihadi and community-based violent extremism are similar—they all rest on social, economic, or political deprivations; developing resentment about these deprivations; attributing these deprivations to an ethnic or religious *other*; and stereotyping and demonizing the *other* as an enemy to be attacked.[50]

Also, the combatants affiliated with violent jihadi groups and community-based violent groups share certain features. For instance, both have foot soldiers who get mobilized for kinetic activities. In both cases, these are mostly young males, including foreign fighters.[51] The other category of combatants comprises rationalizers and defenders of community violence in print and on social media. These kinds of combatants rely heavily on glocalization and media techniques using tools ranging from opinion pieces in newspapers to social media posts and videos on WhatsApp, YouTube, Facebook, Clubhouse, and Twitter, where radicalization and hate messages are churned out regularly. These kinds of media campaigns serve similar functions to the newspaper tigers during the Nigerian civil war.[52]

Another common property that drives communal conflict is the agency of youths. Given the increasing share of the youth population and the youth dimensions of peacebuilding, the agency of youths in shaping social stability and crisis cannot be discounted.[53] Youth are susceptible to ethnic, religious, political, and other identity schisms in their communities. When raised within a context of tense intergroup relations, youths are likely to become creators, defenders, and reinventors of conflict narratives, especially when they are convinced that their emancipation lies in doing so. Their agency in both communal conflicts and violent extremism has been buoyed by social media outlets, where they are often recruited and radicalized.[54] Youth have been targeted for recruitment by various kinds of extremist groups, including jihadists, white supremacists, ethnic extremists, and far-right groups.[55] In the context of communal conflicts, most militias are constituted mainly by male youths.

Nigeria's Fourth Republic has been in persistent conflict because of the protracted confrontation among state, nonstate, and individual actors using violence to achieve political, religious, and other ideological ends.[56] This has created a context wherein violence gets instrumentalized for a range of intents, including religious fundamentalism and ethnicity, even in what might be seen as peacetime. In this context, people learn to hate and kill the perceived other in a manner akin to Amartya Sen's description of Hindu-Muslim riots in India.[57] Similar issues are playing out in Nigerian communities with prolonged exposure to violence, especially in the North Central and Northwest regions.

The legitimation of nonstate violence by communities creates avenues for criminality with rogue actors. This has been the case in communities where members of vigilantes and militias have been involved in human rights abuses and criminal acts, such as taking hostage, smuggling, and robbery.[58] These protracted and recurrent conflicts are often in remote communities and inconclusive in most instances because they stop without an outright victory or peace process. This has been attributed to calculated violence of neglect by the state, wherein governments deliberately choose not to intervene in certain issues if it would not yield political or electoral gains. Another factor seen as responsible for the cyclical pattern of communal conflict is the limited capacity and presence of the state, as evident in places where communal conflicts have led to the active presence of community-based violent groups functioning as ethnic militias and vigilantes.[59]

Southern Kaduna: From Communal Conflict to Nonjihadi Violent Extremism

There are two accounts of the origin of Southern Kaduna.[60] Some claim that it became an official designation after the creation of Katsina state from the old Kaduna state in 1987. The other account holds that Southern Kaduna emerged in 1907 as an administrative change by the British colonial rulers owing to frequent revolts, beginning in 1901, against Muslim-controlled Zaria by an amalgam of Christian ethnic groups. So, it emerged as a "socio-political identity encapsulating the struggle against the Muslim Hausa-Fulani hegemony, particularly on matters of religion, politics, and culture."[61]

Southern Kaduna is situated in the southern hemisphere of Kaduna state and made up of more than fifty ethnic groups, including the Hausa and Fulani populations. Out of the twenty-three local government areas (LGAs) in Kaduna state, eight are in Southern Kaduna. These are Kajuru, Zagon-Kataf, Jema'a, Kaura, Kagarko, Chikun, Kachia, and Jaba. Socio-climatically, Southern Kaduna has been a point of convergence for both agrarian and nomadic populations and a trading hub for centuries. With the influx of various populations, it has acquired an ethnically diverse character and evolved in traditional governance from the time of the Zazzau Emirate to postcolonial Nigeria. The recurrent violence in Southern Kaduna is driven by contrasting claims of belonging based on two "diametrically opposed ideological views and dispositions of belonging."[62] On one side are the non-Hausa and non-Fulani indigenous ethnic-groups who are largely Christians and considered to be the autochthons (i.e., Gbagyi, Adara, Ham, Atyap, Bajjuu, and Agworok), and on the side are Indigenous-nomadic people, who are mainly Fulani and Muslim.

In reality, Southern Kaduna is not an isolated case of insecurity in the morass of insecurity in Kaduna state that have made local and international headlines even before the Fourth Republic.[63] Spatially, the northern senatorial zone of the state is the epicenter of the militant Shi'ite movement led by Ibrahim El Zakzaky. Hard and soft targets have not been spared in the urban parts of the central senatorial zone of the state. The peri-urban communities are fast becoming Ansarustanized going by the presence of the al-Qaeda affiliate Ansaru, which is hibernating in Kuyello district of Birnin Gwari LGA. There, this group has consistently been recruiting, integrating, and consolidating ties with communities in what is left of the environs through marriages with the locals, provision of agricultural and economic support to locals, and even protection from other terror groups.[64] This has been elaborated in many media reports ascribed to Shehu Balarabe, the House of Representatives member representing Birnin-Gwari and Giwa who revealed that many inhabitants have fled the area because the Ansaru group, led by Mallam Abba, has been there since 2012 when they broke away from the Shekau faction of Boko Haram; a fact that was officially corroborated by the state governor Mallam Nasir El-Rufai, and communicated to then-president Muhammadu Buhari.[65] While the preceding speaks of the consolidation of militant jihadi extremism, it only tells a part of the story because the southern senatorial axis of the state features the brutality of the larger Nigerian Christian-Muslim cum indigene-settler conflict that has made the area a killing field from the spate of sporadic clashes between the self-described autochthons and the Fulani.[66] Indeed, the culmination of the disparate forms of conflicts in Kaduna state qualifies it as a frontline state—a state where a substantial part of everyday life is in the throes of both state and nonstate violence.[67]

Communal Violence and Violent Extremism

From 1946 to 1966, the oppressive character of the emirate system headed by Fulani rulers presiding over predominantly non-Fulani communities was the main cause of violent clashes between the Fulani and the Kataf, Atyap, and other autochthonous communities of Southern Kaduna.[68] To date, the relationship between the two remains tenuous as ethnic and religious identities are instrumentalized to mobilize for violence and to identify targets in the series of clashes over property rights and freedom of religion. Since the 1980s, the growing influence of both evangelical Christianity and fundamentalist Islam in Southern Kaduna has become an exacerbator of the long-standing distrust between the two groups.[69] Christian and Muslim leaders are aware of the spike in religious aggressiveness and intolerance because both sides consistently exchange bitter words in the name of God. Over time, every sphere and space of (in)formal interaction between the two groups became a conflict context. The spontaneity of prolonged violence at the slightest trigger attests to the susceptibility of Southern Kaduna to violent extremism.

There are many instances of prolonged violence, which were triggered by fairly minor communal issues. For instance, the violence between Muslim students and their Christian colleagues in March 1987 broke out after a Christian revival on the premises of Kaduna State College of Education. The conflict quickly provided a basis for violent mobilization along ethnoreligious lines in the wider community leading to loss of lives and belongings.[70] In June 1988, the religious undertones of the disputed outcome of the Students' Union election at Ahmadu Bello University in Zaria became violent and spilled into the wider Southern Kaduna. In 1992 and 1998, there were major episodes of violence in Zango-Kataf, Kaduna North, and Kafanchan. Despite the lull in violence, renewed violent conflicts erupted again in 2000 during the two waves of the Sharia crisis (February 21–25 and May 22–23).[71]

In Kaduna, Southern Kaduna became the epicenter of the 2011 postelection violence. Between April and November 2011, organized raids and reprisals as well as lone attacks akin to acts of lone-wolf terrorism were reported across Southern Kaduna, especially in Zonkwa, Zaria, and Kafanchan.[72] Furthermore, persons described as Fulani extremists were accused of torching the residence of a reverend father in Anchuna, Ikulu Chiefdom, in Zangon Kataf in April 2011. In August 2011, there were several attacks on Indigenous ethnic groups believed to have been perpetrated by Fulanis. These include the attack on Gwong communities in Angwan Yaro and Yuli in Kussom in Jema'a LGA, an attack on Angwan Rana communities in Bitaro District of Jaba LGA, and the attacked on Fadia Bakut near Zonkwa. Between November 4 and 8, 2011, there were several attacks in Zangon Kataf, Bajju Chiefdom, and Kafanchan that have been attributed to Fulani militias. In one of the attacks, a church holding a vigil was attacked and a village head and his wife killed. On November 9, there were reprisal attacks on Fulani residents in Kafanchan, Jema'a, and Zangon Kataf. Fulani were again alleged to have engaged in a rampage in Kukum Dutse (Kagoro Chiefdom) on December 11, 2011. On March 15, 2012, ten Christians, including a pastor, were killed in Chikum LGA in what police describe as a reprisal attack.[73]

There was some reduction of violence in the area until 2016, when the conflict resumed with unprecedented coordination of attacks, a disregard for minors and outright brutality, which are all features of Mary Kaldor's new war.[74] Since then, the Miyetti Allah Cattle Breeders Association of Nigeria (MACBAN), which is a Fulani organization, has been consistent in alleging that the Atyap and other ethnic groups in Southern Kaduna are determined to exterminate them. They point out that some attacks occurred over days without any help from the government. One such case was in Kajuru LGA in July 2017, during which fifty-four Fulanis were killed and fifteen went unaccounted for; additionally, numerous cows were killed as part of the attack.[75] Attacks against Fulanis and their cattle continued well into 2022. On January 1, 2022, sixteen cows were shot dead by persons believed to be Kagoro youths, and twenty-two cows went missing during the attack. According to a press statement by MACBAN, on January 24, 2022, two Fulani herders were gruesomely killed in Kisaga village. One of them (twenty-year-old Ya'u Abubakar) was beheaded by people believed to be Kataf youths, while the corpse of the other (thirty-year-old Adamu Usman) was not found for several days. During these attacks, the houses of Fulanis were torched. On January 22, 2022, eight cows belonging to Alhaji Momarwa died from water poisoning in Zunuruk village in Jema'a LGA. On January 25, 2022, Aminu Dahiru was killed in the same village, and the forty-one the cows he was tending were also attacked. On the same day, Kagoro youths severely injured Abubakar and Adamu Para. Another gruesome event was the lynching of nineteen-year-old Zakari Laulo on January 29, 2022, in Gankon village of Gora District while he was rearing his cows. His attackers were believed to be armed Atyap people. On January 31, 2022, Aminu Ahmad also went missing while looking after his cattle in Kagoro. Twelve cows belonging to a Fulani businessman also went missing in Kagoro on February 2, 2022.

The radicalization into violent extremism that has been ongoing was manifested again in Godogodo, Jema'a LGA, where there were clashes between the Fulani and their neighbors (October 15 to 17, 2016). According to one account, in the "heat of the attack by herdsmen, an angry mob, reportedly attacked some herders in the area, killing 14 people."[76] These attacks flared into other areas of Southern Kaduna.[77] According to SBM Intelligence, by 2020 life had become "truly difficult for residents of Southern Kaduna. Aside from the obvious economic and social consequences of the coronavirus pandemic, the area (has) continued to experience incessant violence, killings, and displacement of residents."[78] Since 2020, Kaduna state, and particularly Southern Kaduna, had drifted from being a frontline state, where social life has been militarized owing to the frequency of violent conflicts, to a Hobbesian state, where the government is not able to maintain social order.

The escalation of conflict that has occurred in Southern Kaduna since 2016 speaks to the glocalization model of radicalization into violent extremism. If the Southern Kaduna conflicts are analyzed just through the prism of indigene-settler conflict, radicalization would be linear and phased. However, if the apparent politicization and religionization of the conflict for electoral (dis)advantages are factored in, along with the socioeconomic and environmental factors, the conflict can be seen as multidimensional with contextual realities radicalizing persons and communities into violent extremism.[79]

Using the Ns framework, the following section presents how narratives, needs, networks of violence, and state neglect have radicalized persons and communities into violent extremism in Southern Kaduna.

Conflict (Counter)Narratives and Radicalization Into Violent Extremism

The continuous "warring with words" by parties involved in violent conflicts in Southern Kaduna attests to the potency of (counter)narratives as a conflict-making tool.[80] Key actors, including the Kaduna State government, SOKAPU, CAN, and MACBAN have constructed and aligned conflict (counter)narratives to justify their (in)actions and to demonize the other. The (counter)narratives of SOKAPU and CAN have been consistently aligned in contradistinction to those of MACBAN and sometimes to those of the Kaduna state government. Given that the root and remote causes of the conflict are already well-documented, this section examines how (counter)narratives of the conflict have been radicalizing persons and communities into violent extremism.

First, the author of this chapter was able to assess the various narratives of the conflict based on interviews with stakeholders from SOKAPU and CAN; the coherence of their narrative's introduction, middle, and conclusion indicate inadvertent radicalization into violent extremism. For SOKAPU, the governor of Kaduna, Mallam Nasir El-Rufai, and then-president of Nigeria, Muhammadu Buhari, are both Fulani Muslims who are bent on not just protecting their Fulani kinsmen but also determined to displace the original owners of the land in Southern Kaduna in the overall interest of their kinsmen's cattle business and Islam. Therefore, the autochthons who are sedentary farmers should do all they can to resist and protect themselves.[81] Equally, the aligned narratives of MACBAN and the Fulani in Southern Kaduna has radicalizing potentials. They contend that the Atyap and all other ethnic groups in Southern Kaduna are bent on exterminating the Fulani and their cattle. This is based on misinformation and indoctrination to hate Fulani pastoralists and that is why they attack them at the flimsiest instance, even when they, as conatives, have equal rights to land and its resources. Therefore, violent actions carried out in self-defense are legitimate.[82]

Discernibly, the (counter)narratives from both sides in the conflict legitimize violence. Ontologically, this indicates the onset of radicalization because one of the fundamental needs of the individual is communal recognition and quest for significance which in this case has been tied to been seen as capable of defending oneself and community, even if it goes against the law.[83] This resonates with previously expressed views that the framing of conflicts by elites is critical to the mobilization of communities either for peace or violence as observed in Nigeria and Côte d'Ivoire.[84] This is because elites' framing and mobilization of communities for violence often stems from a sense of loss of ability to exert influence on state authorities.[85] So, exclusion and marginalization from the state informs their construction and instrumentalization of narratives to mobilize their communities. This speaks to the multiplicity of the usages of conflict (counter)narratives, as has been the case in Southern Kaduna. In Southern Kaduna, narratives have been central as they constitute the pillars of radicalization into violent extremism, namely, narratives, need, network, and neglect. Narratives feed into needs, neglect, and networks to activate violent extremism.

Needs of Individuals and Communities: Recognition and Security

The reciprocal violence that defined the conflict has been at a huge cost to both sides. This provides a valid basis to describe them as communities in *need*, at the individual and communal levels, which cannot be understated in the context of lone and mass radicalization into violent extremism in the respective communities. One of the needs of the autochthons of Southern Kaduna is recognition by the state government. According to President of SOKAPU Honorable Jonathan Asake, "after several letters written to the Governor were unacknowledged, we felt unwelcomed." Thereafter, Asake did not mince words in stating the stance of the autochthons of Southern Kaduna: "The Scriptwriter for the violence, the person that kept inciting the Fulanis all through to attack the People of Southern Kaduna is no other person than the Governor of Kaduna State. I have said this at International Media. I gave this kind of interview at Swiss club in Geneva. So, it is not something that I am hiding, he wrote a beautiful script that is now manifesting."[86] A bolder demonstration of nonrecognition and insensitivity to Southern Kaduna as a community of Christian majority was when the governor picked a female Muslim as his running mate and eventual deputy governor in 2019. The Christian majority's feeling of underrepresentation in the government and lack of protection from all forms of attacks on their people, land, identities, and institutions has legitimized self-help, that is, justifying the use of violence in self-defense and growing agitations for the creation of their own state. They believe that they will be safer and better protected in a state where they constitute both ethnic and religious majority. According to Asake, SOKAPU "asked for Gurara State during the 2014 CONFAB. This is because it is very clear that we want to stay, we want to cohabit with people, but they hate us with passion."[87]

The Fulani trace contemporary problems to the postelection violence of 2011, which has worsened their sense of security to underscore their *need* for security. A respondent from MACBAN lamented how lack of security has imperiled the Fulani at the individual and communal levels while radicalizing many into violent extremism. As the respondent notes, "the misery arising from the recent stealing and killing of cattle can be likened to what we suffered in 1983 during a disease outbreak which led many to suicide but now loss of cattle is pushing many into violence." Furthermore, he identified the Fulani's need for understanding from their neighbors and especially sections of the Nigerian media that have profiled them as terrorists by failing to distinguish the Fulani who have settled and lived amicably in Southern Kaduna (i.e., the Kacherere) from the Bororo Fulani, who are constantly on the move. This lumping together of Fulani people creates insecurity for Fulani identity across the country.

Network of Violent Youths

As shown in table 7.2, all sides in the conflict own community-based armed groups. The swelling membership of community-based violent groups in the area has been ascribed to the growing influx of youths from nearby states with similar conflict experiences. Specifically, Tarok youths from Plateau, Taraba, and Nasarawa and the Eggon from Benue and Nasarawa are believed to be jointly launching coordinated attacks and reprisals on Fulani communities in the area.

Indeed, connections can be drawn between the proliferation of these groups and the narratives of the Southern Kaduna autochthons. As the SOKAPU president stated, "I was on the AIT programme Kakaki where I told them that Southern Kaduna should take all available legal means in accordance with domestic and international instruments to protect and defend itself. I have repeated it when we were holding a meeting with the governor, traditional rulers, stakeholders and so on in Southern Kaduna where the governor was seated to my right."[88] While not accepting responsibility for attacks unleashed on sleeping communities by allegedly marauding Fulanis from other parts of West Africa, all respondents of Fulani extraction alluded to and justified the widespread possession of arms because of the need to defend themselves and their cattle. Besides the listed community-based armed groups, individuals exploiting the conflict for lone-actor terrorism and banditry have emerged.[89] According to a security operative in the state, two examples of such people are Zidane, whose real name is Joshua and who is an autochthon of Southern Kaduna, and Black, who is a Fulani.[90]

Table 7.2 Community-based armed groups, incidents of violence and fatalities in southern Kaduna (May 2018–May 2020)

Number	Group	Violent incidents	Fatalities	Percentage of incidents
1.	Fulani ethnic militia	49	339	68.1
2.	Unidentified communal militia	6	28	8.3
3.	Adara ethnic militia	5	66	6.9
4.	Giwa communal militia	3	0	4.2
5.	Hausa ethnic militia	2	57	2.8
6.	Bakira communal militia	1	14	1.4
7.	Buruku communal militia	1	4	1.4
8.	Kaduna communal militia	1	4	1.4
9.	Kujeni communal militia	1	0	1.4
10.	Kwaru communal militia	1	2	1.4
11.	Tsonje communal militia	1	3	1.4
12.	Zamfara communal militia	1	11	1.4
	Total	72	528	100.0

Source: Armed Conflict Location and Event Data Project (ACLED).

Attraction to networks of violence occur against the backdrop of "marginality and dissension, provocative actions by state security forces and escalated conflict," which are present in Southern Kaduna.[91] According to Honorable Asake "security officials often arrest people holding machetes and cutlasses in their houses after surviving attacks rather than chasing the fleeing perpetrators. So, the victims are normally the ones that get arrested, brought to Kaduna, incarcerated, and humiliated."[92] The proliferation of networks in Southern Kaduna shows that (in)advertent bias by security agents in conflict contexts can lead to communal endorsement of self-help that would morph into networks of violence.

State Neglect

Calculated state neglect as a response to crises by many African countries, which is not peculiar to communal conflict, is another N with implications for radicalization. When the state neglects communal conflicts, scholars reason that it is calculated because in most instances such conflicts are localized and their protraction does not directly hinder the conduct of state business even when they breach public peace. Therefore, governments neglect these disputes until they become humanitarian crises that receive global attention, often through social media. This is typical of places where state decay has occurred and where the state has become a "contested leviathan"—that is, places with security structures that are disputed, compromised, and lacking in authority and capacity to protect the citizens. Within the emergent hybrid security context and decaying state, contested leviathans can only negotiate order due to loss of capacity and legitimacy.[93] So, neglecting communal conflicts in such instances is calculated to save the state from embarrassments.

Conclusion

Even though the African Union in 2013 adopted the Master Roadmap of Practical Steps to Silence Guns by the year 2020,[94] communal conflicts are still major causes of avoidable deaths in the glocalized security landscape of Africa.[95] However, because they typically generate lower fatalities than jihadi terrorism, attention to them has not been deliberate and sustained, despite their negative impacts on domestic and regional security and their potential to fuse into global violent extremist networks. Nigeria's contemporary communal conflicts, although mostly localized, also reflect global patterns of radicalization into violent (non)jihadi extremism. For example, the conflict in Zamfara state has turned many communities there into poaching and radicalizing grounds for Boko Haram and other jihadi groups. Other localized communal conflicts like those in Southern Kaduna are also radicalizing persons and communities into violent extremism. All of these have created a glocalized security situation for Nigeria and other countries.

The Southern Kaduna conflict has shown that communal conflicts are not static, and they are potent in radicalizing persons and communities into violent extremism with implications for lone-wolf and group-based terrorist attacks that can be jihadi or nonjihadi operations within and outside of Nigeria. The Ns—that is, (counter)narratives, needs of affected individuals and communities, networks of violent youths, and state neglect—all interact in ways that radicalize groups into violent extremism, turning local conflicts into glocalized security problems.

Notes

1. Lewis, "Managing Conflict in Nigeria," 32.
2. Campbell, *Nigeria*, 9.
3. Global Rights, "Mass Atrocities Tracking."
4. *Economist*, "Insurgency, Secessionism and Banditry Threaten Nigeria."
5. Pavesi, "Tracking Conflict-Related Deaths."
6. Campbell and Page, *Nigeria*, 122.
7. Lewis, *Theaters of War*.
8. Quinn, Joshi, and Melander, "One Dyadic Peace Leads to Another?," 863–75.
9. Rogers, *Irregular War*.
10. Obasanjo, *My Watch*.

11. Animasawun, *(Non)Implementation of Commissions of Enquiry Reports on Communal Conflicts and Challenge of Relapse in Nigeria.*
12. Odozi, and Oyelere, "Violent Conflict Exposure in Nigeria and Economic Welfare."
13. Bukarti, *It's a Bit Tricky.*
14. Barnett, Rufa'i, and Abdulaziz, "Northwestern Nigeria"; Nagarajan, "Analysis of Violence and Insecurity in Zamfara."
15. Allan et al., "Drivers of Violent Extremism"; Kruglanski, Bélanger, and Gunaratna, *Three Pillars of* Radicalization.
16. Turner, *Religious Ideology and the Roots of the Global Jihad.*
17. Ajil, *Politico-Ideological Violence*, 35.
18. Chabal, *Africa.*
19. Horowitz, "Group Loyalty and Ethnic Violence."
20. Madueke, "From Neighbours to Deadly Enemies"; Hills, *Policing Post-Conflict Cities.*
21. Duursma, "Non-State Conflicts, Peacekeeping, and the Conclusion of Local Agreements."
22. Bah, "Civil Non-State Actors in Peacekeeping and Peacebuilding in West Africa"; Idler and Forest, "Behavioral Patterns among (Violent) Non-State Actors."
23. Brosche, "Causes of Communal Conflicts."
24. Krause, "Stabilization and Local Conflicts."
25. Sundberg, Eck, and Joakim, "Introducing the UCDP Non-State Conflict Dataset."
26. Krause, "Stabilization and Local Conflicts."
27. Durusma, "Non-State Conflicts, Peacekeeping, and the Conclusion of Local Agreements"; Lake and Rothchild, "Containing Fear."
28. Institute for Peace & Conflict Resolution, *2016 Strategic Conflict Assessment of Nigeria.*
29. UK House of Lords, "Nigeria."
30. Khondker, "Globalisation to Glocalisation."
31. Okpeh, "Inter-Group Migrations, Conflicts and Displacements in Central Nigeria."
32. Ghani and Marley, "Climate Change Doesn't Have to Stoke Conflict Politics Matter More Than the Environment When It Comes to War and Peace."
33. Bah, *Breakdown and Reconstitution.*
34. Agbaje, "Historical Antecedent of Ethnic Militias in Nigeria."
35. This assessment is based on many press releases issued by ethnic associations.
36. Krause, *Resilient Communities Non-Violence, and Civilian Agency in Communal War.*
37. Fukuda-Parr, Langer, and Mine, "Introduction."
38. Elfversson, "Providing Security or Protecting Interests?"
39. Guelke, *Politics in Divided Societies.*
40. Utas, "Introduction"; Obadare, "How Asari Dokubo Became a Big Man"; Adebanwi, "Becoming a Big Man in Africa."
41. United States Agency for International Development, "Development Response to Violent Extremism and Insurgency."
42. Carthy et al., "Protocol."
43. Baker, "Narratives and Evidence."
44. Baker, "Narratives of Terrorism and Security."
45. Proctor, Keith. *Social Media and Conflict.*
46. Bak, Tarp, and Liang, "Defining the Concept of Violent Extremism."
47. Morten, "Mali."
48. Raleigh, "Nigeria Mid-Year Update."
49. Monahan, "Violence Risk Assessment."
50. Dawson, "Clarifying the Explanatory Context for Developing Theories of Radicalization."

51. Chu and Braithwaite, "Impact of Foreign Fighters on Civil Conflict Outcomes."
52. Adebanwi, *Nation as Grand Narrative*.
53. Ismail and Olonisakin, "Why Do Youth Participate in Violence in Africa?"; Berents and McEvoy-Levy, "Theorising Youth and Everyday Peace(building)."
54. James, *Disconnected Youths, New Media, and the Ethics Gap*.
55. Uba and Bosi, "Explaining Youth Radicalism as a Positioning of the Self at Opposite Extremes."
56. Rangelov and Kaldor, "Persistent Conflict," 195.
57. Sen, " Threats to Secular India," 5–23.
58. Felbab-Brown, *Vigilante Groups and Militias in Southern Nigeria*.
59. Merz, "Less Conflict, More Peace?"
60. Abioro, "Persistent Conflict and Perceived Post-Conflict Peacebuilding in Southern Kaduna Region of Nigeria."
61. Abioro, "Persistent Conflict and Perceived Post-Conflict Peacebuilding in Southern Kaduna Region of Nigeria," 122.
62. Mainangwa, "Crisis of Belonging and Ethnographies of Peacebuilding in Kaduna, Nigeria."
63. Major conflicts in Kaduna state include the 1987 Kafanchan conflict, the sharia clashes of 2000, the 2015 clash between Shiites and the Nigerian army, the postelection violence of 2011, intermittent clashes between communities, and terrorist attacks by Boko Haram on both hard and soft targets in an ongoing counterterrorism operation in the state.
64. Olaoye, "Journey to Ansarustan."
65. *Premium Times*. "Exclusive"; Hassan-Wuyo, "El-Rufai Confirms Presence of Ansaru Terrorists in Kaduna."
66. Amuta, "From Kabul to Kaduna"; Justice Research Institute, "Tackling the Inter-Ethnic Conflict in Southern Kaduna."
67. D. Hoffmann, "Frontline Anthropology Research in a Time of War."
68. Whitaker, *Politics of Tradition*.
69. Craft, "Churches, Mosques Feel Flames of Religious Violence in North Nigeria."
70. Bonnat, "Contemporary Ethnic and Religious Crises in Kaduna State."
71. L. Hoffmann, "Violence in Southern Kaduna Threatens to Undermine Nigeria's Democratic Stability."
72. Hewit, "One-Man War"; Bonnat, "Contemporary Ethnic and Religious Crises in Kaduna State."
73. Ewang, "Multiple Killings in Nigeria's Kaduna State."
74. Kaldor, *New & Old Wars Organised in a Global Era*.
75. Tukur, "54 of Our Members Killed in Recent Southern Kaduna Violence—Fulani Community."
76. *This Day*, "Bloody Attack on Southern Kaduna."
77. SBM Intelligence. "Critical Look at the Southern Kaduna Crisis."
78. SBM Intelligence, "Kaduna Crisis—A Bird's Eye View."
79. McCauley and Moskalenko, "Understanding Political Radicalization."
80. Adebanwi, *Nation as Grand Narrative*, 122.
81. Based on interviews conducted in Kaduna with SOKAPU president and chair of CAN, Kaduna state, March 22, 2020, and April 7, 2019.
82. Based on interviews conducted in Kaduna with an aide of the state governor in his office (May 6, 2020), a security operative in his office (May 7, 2020), and a member of the MACBAN (May 9, 2020).
83. Beelmann, "Social-Developmental Model of Radicalization."
84. McCauley, *Logic of Ethnic and Religious Conflict in Africa*.
85. Ibid.

86. Interview with SOKAPU president, April 7, 2020 in his chambers in Zaria.
87. Ibid.
88. Ibid.
89. Schubert, "Challenge of Community-Based Armed Groups."
90. Interview with SOKAPU president, April 7, 2020, in his chambers.
91. Lewis, "Managing Conflict in Nigeria," 1.
92. Interview with SOKAPU president, April 7, 2020, in his chambers.
93. Bah, *State Decay*; Luckham and Kirk, "Two Faces of Security in Hybrid Political Orders."
94. Alusala and Paneras, "Silencing the Guns by 2020."
95. Palik, Rustad, and Methi, *Conflict Trends*.

References

Abioro, Tunde. "Persistent Conflict and Perceived Post-Conflict Peacebuilding in Southern Kaduna Region of Nigeria." *Polish Political Science Yearbook* 50 (2021): 121–31.

Adebanwi, Wale. "Becoming a Big Man in Africa: Subalternity, Elitism and Ethnic Politics in Nigeria." African Studies Workshop, 2022. https://africa.harvard.edu/event/african-studies-workshop-featuring-wale-adebanwi.

———. *Nation as Grand Narrative: The Nigerian Press and the Politics of Meaning*. Rochester, NY: University of Rochester Press, 2016.

Agbaje, Adigun. "The Historical Antecedent of Ethnic Militias in Nigeria." In *Urban Violence, Ethnic Militias, and the Challenge of Democratic Consolidation in Nigeria*, edited by Tunde Babawale, 20–39. Lagos: Malthouse Press, 2003.

Ajli, Ahmed. "Politico-Ideological Violence: Zooming in on Grievances." *European Journal of Criminology* 19, no. 2 (2022): 304–21.

Allan, Harriet, Andrew Glazzard, Sasha Jesperson, S. Reddy-Tumu, and Emily Winterbotham. "Drivers of Violent Extremism: Hypotheses and Literature Review." Royal United Services Institute, London, 2015.

Alusala, Nelson, and Riana Paneras. "Silencing the Guns by 2020—Ambitious but Essential." Institute for Security Studies, March 14, 2018. https://issafrica.org/iss-today/silencing-the-guns-by-2020-ambitious-but-essential.

Amuta, Chidi. "From Kabul to Kaduna." *ThisDay*, August 29, 2021 https://www.thisdaylive.com/index.php/2021/08/29/from-kabul-to-kaduna/.

Animasawun, Gbemisola. "Everyday People, Autochthony, and Indigene-Settler Crises in Lagos Commodity Markets." *African Conflict & Peacebuilding Review* 6, no. 1 (2016): 24–44.

———. *(Non)Implementation of Commissions of Enquiry Reports on Communal Conflicts and Challenge of Relapse in Nigeria*. Presentation at the National Institute for Policy and Strategic Studies, Kuru, Nigeria, 2021.

Bah, Abu Bakar. *Breakdown and Reconstitution: Democracy, the Nation-State, and Ethnicity in Nigeria*. Lanham, MD: Lexington Books, 2005.

———. "Civil Non-State Actors in Peacekeeping and Peacebuilding in West Africa." *Journal of International Peacekeeping* 17, no. 3–4 (2013): 313–36.

———. "State Decay: A Conceptual Frame for Failing and Failed States in West Africa." *International Journal of Politics, Culture, and Society* 25, no. 1–3 (2012): 71–89.

Bak, Mathias, Kristopher Nilaus Tarp, and Christina Schori Liang. "Defining the Concept of Violent Extremism: Delineating the Attributes and Phenomenon of Violent Extremism." Geneva Paper 24/19. Geneva Center for Security Policy, 2019.

Baker, Mona. " Narratives and Evidence—Which Stories about COVID-19 did We Believe and Why? London School of Economics and Political Science blog, May 25, 2022. https://blogs.lse.ac.uk/impactofsocialsciences/2022/05/25/narratives-and-evidence-which-stories-about-covid-19-did-we-believe-and-why/.

———. "Narratives of Terrorism and Security: 'Accurate' Translations, Suspicious Frames." *Critical Studies on Terrorism* 3, no. 3 (2010): 347–64.

Barnett, James, Murtala Ahmed Rufa'i, and Abdul-Aziz Abdulaziz. "Northwestern Nigeria: A Jihadization of Banditry, or a "Banditization" of Jihad?" *Combating Terrorism Center at West Point* 15, no. 1 (2022): 46–67.

Beelmann, Andreas. "A Social-Developmental Model of Radicalization: A Systematic Integration of Existing Theories and Empirical Research." *International Journal of Conflict and Violence* 14, no. 1 (2020): 1–14.

Berents, Helen, and Siobhan McEvoy-Levy. "Theorising Youth and Everyday Peace(building)." *Peacebuilding* 3, no. 2 (2015): 115–25.

Bonnat, Zwahu. "Contemporary Ethnic and Religious Crises in Kaduna State." *Vanguard*, June 24, 2012. https://www.vanguardngr.com/2012/06/contemporary-ethnic-and-religious-crises-in-kaduna-state/.

Brosche, Johan. "Causes of Communal Conflicts: Government Bias, Elites and Conditions of Cooperation." Development Dissertation Brief no. 6. 2015.

Bukarti, Bulama. *It's a Bit Tricky: Exploring ISIS's Ties with Boko Haram*. Program on Extremism. George Washington University, 2022. https://extremism.gwu.edu/isis-ties-with-boko-haram.

Campbell, John. *Nigeria: Dancing on the Brink*. Washington, DC: Rowman and Littlefield, 2013.

Campbell, John, and Matthew Page. *Nigeria: What Everyone Needs to Know*. Oxford: University Press, 2018.

Carthy, Sarah, Colm Doody, Dennis O'Hora, and Kiran Sarma. "Protocol: Counter-narratives for the Prevention of Violent Radicalisation; A Systematic Review of Targeted Interventions." *Campbell System Review* 14, no. 1 (2018): 1–23.

Chabal, Patrick. *Africa: The Politics of Suffering and Smiling*. London: Zed Books, 2009.

Chu, Tifany, and Alex Braithwaite. "The Impact of Foreign Fighters on Civil Conflict Outcomes." *Research and Politics* 4, no. 3 (2017): 1–7.

Craft, Scott. "Churches, Mosques Feel Flames of Religious Violence in North Nigeria." *Los Angeles Times*, July 18, 1987, https://www.latimes.com/archives/la-xpm-1987-07-18-me-594-story.html.

Dawson, Lorne. "Clarifying the Explanatory Context for Developing Theories of Radicalization: Five Basic Considerations." *Journal for Deradicalization*, no. 18 (2019): 146–84.

Desrosiers, Marie-Eve. "Reframing Frame Analysis: Key Contributions to Conflict Studies." *Ethnopolitics* 11, no. 1 (2012): 1–23.

Duursma, Allard. "Non-State Conflicts, Peacekeeping, and the Conclusion of Local Agreements." *Peacebuilding* 10, no. 2 (2022): 138–55.

Economist. "Insurgency, Secessionism and Banditry Threaten Nigeria." October 23, 2021. https://www.economist.com/leaders/2021/10/23/insurgency-secessionism-and-banditry-threaten-nigeria.

Elfversson, Emma. "Providing Security or Protecting Interests? Government Interventions in Violent Communal Conflicts in Africa." *Journal of Peace Research* 52, no. 6 (2015): 791–805.

Ewang, Anietie. "Multiple Killings in Nigeria's Kaduna State." Human Rights Watch, July 31, 2020. https://www.hrw.org/news/2020/07/31/multiple-killings-nigerias-kaduna-state.

Felbab-Brown, Vanda. *Vigilante Groups and Militias in Southern Nigeria*. New York: United Nations University, 2019.

Fukuda-Parr, Sakiko, Arnim Langer, and Yoichi Mine. "Introduction: Disentangling the Linkages between Horizontal Inequalities and Political Institutions." In *Preventing Violent Conflicts in Africa Inequalities, Perceptions, and Institutions*, edited by Yoichi Mine, Frances Stewart, Sakiko Fukuda-Parr, and Thandika Mkandawire, 1–7. New York: Palgrave MacMillan, 2013.

Ghani, Tarek, and Robert Marley. "Climate Change Doesn't Have to Stoke Conflict Politics Matter More Than the Environment When It Comes to War and Peace." *Foreign Affairs*, September 28, 2020. https://www.foreignaffairs.com/articles/ethiopia/2020-09-28/climate-change-doesnt-have-stoke-conflict.

Global Rights. "Mass Atrocities Tracking." 2020 report. https://www.globalrights.org/ng/wp-content/uploads/2021/02/Mass-Atrocities-report-2020.pdf.

Guelke, Adrian. *Politics in Divided Societies*. Cambridge: Polity, 2012.

Hassan-Wuyo, Ibrahim. "El-Rufai Confirms Presence of Ansaru Terrorists in Kaduna." *Vanguard Metro*, May 19, 2022. https://www.vanguardngr.com/2022/05/el-rufai-confirms-presence-of-ansaru-terrorists-in-kaduna/.

———. "Southern Kaduna Killings: Atyap Bent on Exterminating Us—Miyetti Allah." *Vanguard News*, February 8, 2022. https://www.vanguardngr.com/2022/02/southern-kaduna-killings-atyap-bent-on-exterminating-us-miyetti-allah/.

Hewit, Steve. "'One-Man War': A History of Lone-Actor Terrorism in Canada, 1868–2018." Working paper 2021-01, Canadian Network for Research on Terrorism, Security and Society, 2021.

Hills, Alice. *Policing Post-Conflict Cities*. London: Zed Books, 2010.

Hoffmann, Danny. "Frontline Anthropology Research in a Time of War." *Anthropology Today* 19, no. 3 (2003): 9–12.

Hoffmann, Leena. "Violence in Southern Kaduna Threatens to Undermine Nigeria's Democratic Stability." Chatham House, February 15, 2017. https://www.chathamhouse.org/2017/02/violence-southern-kaduna-threatens-undermine-nigerias-democratic-stability.

Horowitz, Donald. "Group Loyalty and Ethnic Violence." In *Violent Conflict in the 21st Century Causes, Instruments, & Mitigation*, edited by Charles Hermann, Harold K. Jacobson, and Anne S, Moffat, 89–110. Chicago: American Academy of Arts and Sciences, 1999.

Idler, Annette, and James Forest. "Behavioral Patterns among (Violent) Non-State Actors: A Study of Complementary Governance." *Stability: International Journal of Security & Development* 4, no. 1 (2015): 1–19.

Institute for Peace & Conflict Resolution. *2016 Strategic Conflict Assessment of Nigeria*. 2017. Accessed November 6, 2021. https://www.undp.org/sites/g/files/zskgke326/files/migration/ng/Strategic-Conflict-Assessment-of-Nigeria-2016.pdf.

Institute for Security Studies. "Ansaru's Comeback in Nigeria Deepens the Terror Threat." ISS Today, June 1, 2022. https://issafrica.org/iss-today/ansarus-comeback-in-nigeria-deepens-the-terror-threat.

Ismail, Olawale, and Funmi Olonisakin. "Why Do Youth Participate in Violence in Africa? A Review of Evidence." *Conflict, Security and Development* 21, no. 3 (2021): 371–99.

James, Carrie. *Disconnected Youths, New Media and the Ethics Gap*. Cambridge: Massachusetts Institute of Technology, 2014.

Justice Research Institute. "Tackling the Inter-Ethnic Conflict in Southern Kaduna: An Executive Summary Report on the Analysis of the Conflict to understand the Source, Scope and Issues." 2019. Ford Foundation. Accessed August 14, 2022. http://www.justiceresearchinstitute.org/wp-content/uploads/2019/11/Tackling-Inter-Ethnic-Conflict-in-Southern-Kaduna.pdf.

Kaldor, Mary. *New & Old Wars Organised in a Global Era*. Cambridge: Polity, 2012.

Khondker, Habibul. "Globalisation to Glocalisation: A Conceptual Exploration." *Intellectual Discourse* 13, no. 2 (2005): 181–99.

Krause, Jana. *Resilient Communities Non-Violence and Civilian Agency in Communal War*. Cambridge: Cambridge University Press, 2018.

———. "Stabilization and Local Conflicts: Communal and Civil War in South Sudan." *Ethnopolitics* 18, no. 5 (2019): 478–93.

Kruglanski, Arie, Jocelyn Bélanger, and Rohan Gunaratna. *The Three Pillars of Radicalization: Needs, Narratives, and Networks*. Oxford: Oxford University Press, 2019.

Lake, David, and Donald Rothchild. "Containing Fear: The Origins and Management of Ethnic Conflict." *International Security* 21, no. 2 (1996): 41–75.

Lakhani, Suraj. "Radicalisation as a Moral Career: A Qualitative Study of how People become Terrorists in the United Kingdom." PhD diss., Cardiff University, 2013.

Lewis, Peter. "Managing Conflict in Nigeria." Wilson Center, Washington, DC, 2012. https://www.wilsoncenter.org/sites/default/files/media/documents/event/Lewis%20Presentation.pdf.

Luckham, Robin, and Tom Kirk. "The Two Faces of Security in Hybrid Political Orders: A Framework for Analysis and Research." *Stability: International Journal of Security and Development* 2, no. 2 (2013): article 44.

Madueke, Kingsley. "From Neighbours to Deadly Enemies: Excavating Landscapes of Territoriality and Ethnic Violence in Jos, Nigeria." *Journal of Contemporary African Studies* 36, no. 1 (2018): 87–102.

Mainangwa, Benjamin. "The Crisis of Belonging and Ethnographies of Peacebuilding in Kaduna, Nigeria." PhD diss., University of Manitoba, 2019.

McCauley, Clark, and Sophia Moskalenko. "Understanding Political Radicalization: The Two-Pyramids Model." *American Psychologist* 72, no. 3 (2017): 205–16.

McCauley, John. *The Logic of Ethnic and Religious Conflict in Africa*. Cambridge: Cambridge University Press, 2018.

Merz, Sebastian. "Less Conflict, More Peace? Understanding Trends in Conflict Persistence." *Conflict, Security and Development* 12, no. 3 (2012): 201–26.

Miller-Idriss, Cynthia. *The Extreme gone Mainstream: Commercialization and Far-Right Youth Culture in Germany*. Princeton, NJ: Princeton University Press, 2018.

Moghaddam, Fathali. "The Staircase to Terrorism: A Psychological Exploration." *American Psychologist* 60, no. 2 (2005): 161–69.

Monahan, John. "Violence Risk Assessment." In *Handbook of Psychology*, 2nd ed., edited by Irving B. Weiner, 541–55. Hoboken, NJ: John Wiley and Sons, 2013.

Morten, Boas. "Mali: Islam, Arms and Money." In *Africa's Insurgents Navigating an Evolving Landscape*, edited by Morten Boas and Kevin C. Dunn, 135–56. Boulder, CO: Lynne Rienner, 2017.

Nagarajan, Chitra. "Analysis of Violence and Insecurity in Zamfara." 2020. Accessed September 7, 2021. https://chitrasudhanagarajan.wordpress.com/2020/05/15.

Obadare, Ebenezer. "How Asari Dokubo Became a Big Man." *Premium Times*, August 7, 2013. https://www.premiumtimesng.com/opinion/142397-how-asari-dokubo-became-a-big-man-by-ebenezer-obadare.html.

Obasanjo, Olusegun. *My Watch*. Vol. 2, *Political and Public Affairs*. Lagos: Prestige, 2014.

Odozi, John Chiwuzulum, and Ruth Uwaifo Oyelere. "Violent Conflict Exposure in Nigeria and Economic Welfare." Discussion Paper Series No. 12570, Institute of Labor Economics, 2019. https://docs.iza.org/dp12570.pdf.

Okpeh, Ochayi Okpeh, Jr. "Inter-Group Migrations, Conflicts and Displacements in Central Nigeria." In *Population Movements, Conflicts and Displacements in Nigeria*, edited by Toyin Falola and Okpeh Ochayi Okpeh, 1–19. Trenton, NJ: Africa World Press, 2008.

Olaoye, Wole. "Journey to Ansarustan." *Premium Times*, August 14, 2022. https://www.premiumtimesng.com/opinion/548608-journey-to-ansarustan-by-wole-olaoye.html.

Oosterom, Marjoke, and Sha Pam Dung. "Commissions of Inquiry in Plateau State, Nigeria." Institute of Development Studies Working Paper No. 531, 2019. https://opendocs.ids.ac.uk/opendocs/bitstream/handle/20.500.12413/14640/WP531_online.pdf?sequence=1&isAllowed=y.

Palik, Júlia, Siri Aas Rustad, and Fredrik Methi. *Conflict Trends: A Global Overview, 1946–2019*. Oslo: Peace Research Institute Oslo (PRIO), 2020.

Pavesi, Irene. "Tracking Conflict-Related Deaths." Briefing Paper, March 2017. Swiss Agency for Development and Cooperation. https://www.smallarmssurvey.org/sites/default/files/resources/SAS-BP2-conflict-deaths.pdf.

Premium Times. "Exclusive: El-Rufai to Buhari; Boko Haram Puts North-west at Risk of 'Total Darkness.'" August 12, 2022. https://www.premiumtimesng.com/news/headlines/548276-exclusive-el-rufai-to-buhari-boko-haram-puts-north-west-at-risk-of-total-darkness.html.

Proctor, Keith. *Social Media and Conflict: Understanding Risks and Resilience; An Applied Framework for Analysis*. Washington, DC: Mercy Corps. https://www.mercycorps.org/sites/default/files/2021-08/Assessing-Digital-Conflict-Risks-Resilience-073021.pdf.

Quinn, Jason, Madhav Joshi, and Erik Melander. "One Dyadic Peace Leads to Another? Conflict Systems, Terminations, and Net Reduction in Fighting Groups." *International Studies Quarterly* 63, no. 4 (2019): 863–75.

Raleigh, Clionadh. "Nigeria Mid-Year Update: Multiple Security Threats Persist around the Country." 10 Conflicts to Worry about in 2022. ACLED. Accessed September 1, 2024. https://acleddata.com/10-conflicts-to-worry-about-in-2022/nigeria/mid-year-update/.

Rangelov, Lavor, and Mary Kaldor. "Persistent Conflict." *Conflict, Security and Development* 12, no. 3 (2012): 193–99.

Rogers, Paul. *Irregular War: The New Threat from the Margins*. London: I. B. Taurus, 2016.

SBM Intelligence. "A Critical Look at the Southern Kaduna Crisis." Analysis Reports, February 7, 2017. https://www.sbmintel.com/2017/02/a-critical-look-at-the-southern-kaduna-crisis/.

———. "The Kaduna Crisis—A Bird's Eye View." Anayslis Reports, October 31, 2018. https://www.sbmintel.com/2018/10/the-kaduna-crisis-a-birds-eye-view/.

Schuberth, Moritz. "The Challenge of Community-Based Armed Groups: Towards a Conceptualization of Militias, Gangs, and Vigilantes." *Contemporary Security Policy*, 36, no. 2 (2015): 296–320.

Sen, Amartya. "The Threats to Secular India." *Social Scientist* 21, no. 3/4 (1993): 5–23.

Sundberg, Ralp, Kristine Eck, and Joakim Kreutz. "Introducing the UCDP Non-State Conflict Dataset." *Journal of Peace Research* 49, no. 2 (2012): 351–62.

This Day. "The Bloody Attack on Southern Kaduna." Politics. Accessed September 1, 2024. https://www.thisdaylive.com/index.php/2016/10/23/the-bloody-attack-on-southern-kaduna/.

Tukur, Sani. "54 of Our Members Killed in Recent Southern Kaduna Violence—Fulani Community." *Premium Times*, July 23, 2017. https://www.premiumtimesng.com/news/headlines/237816-54-members-killed-recent-southern-kaduna-violence-fulani-community.html.

Turner, John. *Religious Ideology and the Roots of the Global Jihad: Salafi Jihadism and International Order*. London: Palgrave Macmillan, 2014.

Uba, Katrin, and Lorenzo Bosi. "Explaining Youth Radicalism as a Positioning of the Self at Opposite Extremes." *Politics* 42, no. 1 (2022): 128–45.

UK House of Lords. "Nigeria." *Hansard* 792 (June 28, 2018). https://hansard.parliament.uk/lords/2018-06-28/debates/B694EEEC-7D52-4FBB-97E9-20C52519C332/Nigeria.

United States Agency for International Development. "The Development Response to Violent Extremism and Insurgency: Putting Principles into Practice." September 2011. https://www.usaid.gov/sites/default/files/2022-05/VEI_Policy_Final.pdf.

Utas, Mats. "Introduction: Bigmanity and Network Governance in African Conflicts." In *African Conflicts and Informal Power: Big Men and Networks*, edited by Mats Utas, 1–34. London: Zed Books, 2012.

Whitaker, Sylvester. *The Politics of Tradition: Continuity and Change in Northern Nigeria, 1946–1966*. Princeton, NJ: Princeton University Press, 1970.

GBEMISOLA ABDUL-JELIL ANIMASAWUN is a Professor at the Center for Peace and Strategic Studies, University of Ilorin. He was a 2019 African Studies Association (ASA) scholar and has over a decade experience in researching (f)actors, relationships, and issues shaping conflict, violent extremism, peace, and security in local, transnational, and global contexts. Gbemisola links research, policy, and practice as a trainer, facilitator, and consultant to national institutions and development agencies. He has been a recipient of distinguished academic grants including Residencies and Fellowships at the University of Oxford, Harvard University, and the Kofi Annan International Peacekeeping Center (KAIPTC).

8

THE YAM BETWEEN TWO BOULDERS

India, China, and the Glocalization
of Contention in Nepal

Ches Thurber

Introduction

The Cold War era experienced a wave of civil wars, fueled by proxy battles between the United States and the Soviet Union as well as liberation movements against colonial occupation.[1] By the mid-1990s, the frequency of armed insurgencies was in decline.[2] Aspiring rebel outfits could no longer rely on the great powers to provide needed money, guns, and training, while the system of formal imperialism was largely over. Political violence did not end, but its patterns transformed. At the local level, armed groups, often fueled by local natural resources, took advantage of weak states and ungoverned territory to pursue both financial as well as political goals. These conflicts often featured especially high rates of civilian victimization.[3] At the local level, new framings of the global order, from the "responsibility to protect" (R2P) to the global war on terror, became a new normative, or at least discursive, basis for transnational intervention in civil conflicts.[4]

But while terrorist groups, criminal networks, and "new wars" were capturing the attention of global policymakers, the world experienced a rapid increase in another form of contentious politics: civil resistance. Civil resistance refers to a strategy of confronting the state through primarily unarmed tactics, such as mass protests, strikes, and boycotts. Campaigns employing this strategy proved capable of toppling dictators from Ferdinand Marcos in the Philippines to Augusto Pinochet in Chile.[5] Even when civil resistance movements were met with massive state repression, as in Myanmar in 1988 and China's Tiananmen Square in 1989, they demonstrated the ability to pose an existential threat to powerful regimes. The wave of protests across Eastern and central Europe in 1989 and 1990 further showed the power of this form of popular uprising and established a model that would become frequently replicated elsewhere around the globe.[6] Indeed, since 1980, civil resistance campaigns have been the most common form of mass dissent, occurring more frequently than violent insurgencies.[7] They have been roughly twice as effective in achieving regime change as their armed counterparts and have been a leading driver of the spread of democracy.[8] In other cases, such as Syria after 2011 and Ukraine after 2014, they have escalated to violent conflicts that triggered great power intervention.

The phenomenon of civil resistance must therefore be central to our understanding of glocalized security in the post–Cold War world. Glocalization theory has examined the interplay of transnational and domestic forces in the context of social movements.[9] But it has overlooked civil resistance campaigns that pursue maximalist political objectives such as regime change or secession. Meanwhile, scholarship on contemporary transnational security has focused almost exclusively on armed forms of conflict, ignoring the role of unarmed movements both as a force for political change in their own right as well as an alternative to, and sometimes precipitant of, violent conflict.

This chapter seeks to expand the theoretical scope of the concept of glocalized security to evaluate the role of global and regional security dynamics in shaping local resistance movements. It asks two questions that parallel those motivating the larger issues of glocalized security: How does the fusion of domestic issues with external interests shape the initiation and tactics of contentious mobilization? And from this, How can peacebuilding processes better encourage the use of nonviolent tactics as an alternative to violence? To answer these questions, the chapter examines several cases of resistance movements in Nepal with special attention to the roles played by the two major powers in the region: India and China. Nepalis often liken their geopolitical dilemma of being a small country surrounded by two much larger and more powerful nations to that of being "a yam between two boulders."[10] And indeed, as local movements in Nepal have repeatedly mobilized, first in struggles for democratization and later in pursuit of greater equality for marginalized groups, the rivalry between the two larger neighbors has driven interventions in Nepal's domestic politics.

This chapter explicitly does not attempt to present Nepal as a "typical" case, nor does it claim to be systematically testing theory through tightly controlled case comparisons. In fact, it is Nepal's somewhat exceptional history of both domestic contention and regional politics that makes it especially well-suited for the task of generating new insights. It offers a unique opportunity to evaluate the varied impacts of global and regional dynamics on local mobilization over time, bounded by the common context of a single country. The theoretical ideas advanced from this inquiry may be further tested through subsequent research.

Drawing from the Nepali cases, this chapter advances four main arguments about the glocal dimensions of contentious politics. First, the availability of external support impacts local actors' decisions about whether to engage in resistance as well as what tactics to employ. Second, nonmaterial forms of external support, such as mediation, organizing, and symbolic gestures, can be more important for civil resistance campaigns than material support. Third, foreign intervention can backfire, especially in the context of campaigns that involve ethnic or other salient social divisions. Finally, the availability of external support is in large part influenced by regional and global politics as rivalries among larger powers shape the incentives and risks of fomenting instability in the periphery.

While this study is inductive in nature, for the purpose of expositional clarity, it will begin with a theoretical discussion of what we know from existing research—and what we still do not know—about the relationship between global and regional dynamics and local collective action. It will then discuss Nepal through a series of five contentious episodes. Each episode will highlight how the global and regional order shaped the availability of support for resistance movements in Nepal and how the nature and availability of support, in turn, affected the timing, tactics, and outcomes of mobilization. The chapter concludes with an assessment of what Nepal tells us about civil resistance as a form of glocalized security and the implications of these findings for peacebuilding strategies.

Civil Resistance As a form of Glocalized Security

Numerous anecdotal examples suggest a prominent role for external actors in civil resistance campaigns. In South Africa, biting sanctions from the international community forced the apartheid government into negotiations with Nelson Mandela and the African National Congress.[11] UN intervention and trusteeship after the massacre of protesters at Dilli fostered the independence of East Timor. And US support for civil society organizations in the countries of the post-Soviet bloc built a foundation for the "color revolution" movements of the early 2000s.[12] This seemingly crucial role of foreign involvement has driven even world leaders, such as Russia's Vladimir Putin and China's Xi Jinping, to talk of civil resistance not as an organic expression of popular will but a geopolitical tool leveraged primarily by the United

States and the West. They have been joined by scholars from leftist, postcolonial, and, to some degree, realist traditions who similarly see such campaigns as an instrument for the expansion of neoliberalism.[13] According to this perspective, where once the CIA overthrew adversaries and installed client regimes by way of funding guerrilla insurgencies and inciting military coups, it now achieves the same ends by fomenting "nonviolent" uprisings.

These examples highlight the necessity of viewing the civil resistance through a framework of glocalized security. However, in evaluating the glocal dimensions of civil resistance, scholarship has emphasized the primacy of domestic over international factors. There is a consensus on the importance of locally rooted social networks, intergroup unity, and power in numbers.[14] But research on the role of external support has produced weak or mixed findings.[15] In some individual cases, such as those mentioned previously, foreign support was clearly crucial. In many others, however, it appears not to have played a determinative role. Further still, in some cases foreign support can undermine a movement, associating the resistance with "foreigners" and enemies of the national identity. In other aspects, civil resistance scholarship has not yet tackled important dynamics. For example, scholarship on the glocalized dimensions of civil war have systematically evaluated the role of global orders on modes of political violence. Stathis Kalyvas and Laia Balcells examine the decline of foreign sponsorship after the end of the Cold War.[16] Others emphasize the end of colonial rule and the particular security challenges facing the leaders of postcolonial states.[17] Meanwhile, more recent security framings, such as the concept of R2P and the global war on terror have been cited as drivers of global intervention in intrastate conflicts.[18]

This section examines the existing literature on the international dynamics of civil resistance along three dimensions: the impact of material support, backlash against foreign intervention, and the opportunities presented by global and regional rivalries. It seeks to identify theoretical gaps where the subsequent Nepal case studies may be able to make particular contributions.

Material Incentives

Civil resistance scholarship has distinguished two ways in which external actors intervene in conflicts in support of unarmed protesters. First, they may provide direct support or sponsorship to the resistance movement. Second, they can sanction or otherwise try to impose costs on the target regime. Interestingly, neither appears to be significantly correlated with the success of resistance movements.[19] While international support might seem at first glance to be an unalloyed boost for popular resistance, a deeper examination of the strategic dynamics of such campaigns reveals why the benefits to movements might be limited. Foreign direct support to movements, for example, in the form of financial assistance, is likely to only have marginal utility. While violent insurgency requires guns and munitions that are both financially costly and sometimes difficult to obtain, civil resistance movements rely on leveraging deeply rooted social networks that cannot easily be bought.

External sanctions can impose costs on a state being targeted by a civil resistance campaign, pressuring them to grant concessions to the protesters or limiting their willingness to engage in brutal repression that might trigger greater sanctions. However, scholarship on sanctions generally finds their effectiveness to be limited for reasons that are likely to apply equally in contexts of civil resistance.[20] First, it can be difficult to create a set of sanctions that really impose severe costs on a target state. Second, states targeted by sanctions can frequently find alternative economic and diplomatic partners with which to do business. Finally, state leaders can often leverage sanctions to rally nationalism that increases their population's willingness to endure any economic costs created.

The focus on state sponsorship and sanctions overlooks other key ways in which international involvement impacts the trajectories of civil resistance. First, expectations of external support influence whether dissidents decide to initiate a campaign, as well as their decision to embrace or reject the use of armed force. These dynamics unfold before a civil resistance campaign even gets off the ground. Second, foreign actors can provide important non-material support to campaigns that have been overlooked by prior studies. For example, they can serve as mediators and help build coalitions among dissident factions. Wendy Pearlman shows how organizational unity is crucial for nonviolent strategies of resistance.[21] They can also offer symbolic forms of support that shift expectations and spark protest cascades.[22] Each of these dynamics will be explored further in the case studies from Nepal that follow.

Backlash to Foreign Intervention

Several cases suggest that external support for civil resistance campaigns not only is unhelpful but also can actually harm resistance movements. It can unintentionally offer a lifeline to a regime under threat, allowing state leaders to reframe the conflict. Rather than the people seeking change from a corrupt and illegitimate regime, the state can portray the uprising as the machination of foreign forces who are trying to dominate the nation. Sharon Nepstad, for example, highlights how such dynamics unfolded, leading to the failure of movements in Panama and Kenya.[23]

When is such backlash likely to occur? The analytic lens of glocalization can help us better understand the ways in which foreign involvement is likely to be received. At the local level, the presence of social cleavages can make it easier for regimes to try to pit members of different social groups against each other. They can portray the minority group as a "fifth column" that is allied with the country's enemies in an effort to fracture the nation.[24]

At the global level, legacies of colonial domination or preexisting narratives about foreign meddling will enable regimes to portray international support as a form of foreign bullying. Furthermore, global political dynamics can make external intervention backfire when it triggers additional intervention by a geopolitical rival. For example, Nepstad shows that in Panama, US sanctions against the Noriega government prompted Nicaragua, Cuba, and Libya to all offer assistance to the regime.[25] When is such "balancing" through foreign sponsorship most likely to occur? The answer is likely dependent on global and regional power structures.

Regional Rivalries

A glocalized approach to the study of security demands attention to the role of global and regional political rivalries in conditioning the prevalence and form of armed intrastate conflicts. But again, prior scholarship has focused almost exclusively on the impacts of great power conflicts on violent forms of contention.[26] No similar analysis of global and regional power dynamics has been conducted within scholarship on civil resistance. The civil resistance literature has identified some parallel global trends in the incidence and effectiveness of unarmed campaigns. The 1980s witnessed a dramatic rise in the frequency of civil resistance campaigns, a trend that accelerated again after the 2011 Arab Spring. Surprisingly, the past decade has also seen a dramatic decline in the rate at which these campaigns have succeeded in achieving their political goals.[27] Scholars have suggested these trends might be the product of strategic emulation by movements, strategic learning by regimes confronting these movements, and the use of social media as a tool to catalyze mobilization.[28] But little attention has been paid to how changes in global and regional political dynamics could be affecting the initiation and outcomes of civil resistance campaigns.

This stands in stark contrast to how some world leaders see the situation. After the Cold War, the United States spent considerable resources investing in civil society organizations, particularly in the former states of the Soviet Union and Yugoslavia. This funding helped lay the groundwork for a series of "color revolutions" in Serbia, Georgia, Kyrgyzstan, and Ukraine in the early 2000s. For example, the United States provided millions of dollars in grants to Otpor, the organization that led the campaign to overthrow Slobodan Milošević in Serbia.[29] From Russia's perspective, these investments were not altruistic efforts to promote peoples' desires for democratic governance but rather deliberate attempts to overthrow regimes allied with Moscow and replace them with ones pliant to US interests.[30]

This perspective from the vantage point of policymakers and world leaders suggests that the status of regional rivalries, especially under conditions of at least regional (if not global) bipolarity, is likely to influence the availability of external sponsorship to movements, thus conditioning both the incidence and the mode of resistance campaigns. These dynamics will be explored in the case studies from Nepal, as changes in the Sino-Indian relationship shape the options available to local resistance movements.

A Glocalized Analysis of Civil Resistance in Nepal

This chapter now turns to an analysis of five episodes of contention in Nepal to gain greater insights into civil resistance as a form of glocalized security. Nepal's unique history allows us to examine multiple episodes within the bounds of a single country. Over the course of seventy years, dissident movements in Nepal mobilized in pursuit of democracy as well as to redress ethnic, religious, class, regional, and caste-based inequalities. Meanwhile, as the country lies sandwiched between the great powers of India and China, the dynamics of that regional political rivalry shaped external interventions into Nepal's domestic conflicts. Meanwhile, the impact of these global forces was conditioned by local dynamics on the ground, specifically the social composition and networks of the resistance movement.

For India, the goal has consistently been to ensure a government in Nepal that was firmly allied with Delhi. In service of this end, it has alternately used the "carrot" of support for the regime when it shows loyalty to India and the "stick" of supporting dissident movements to either coerce compliance from the regime or simply replace it. China showed only moderate interest in politics within Nepal over the course of the latter twentieth century. Its primary interest was ensuring that Nepal would not serve as a haven for Tibetan activists. But as China's power has grown in the twenty-first century, it has shown increased interest in shaping politics in Kathmandu and challenging India's influence.

The first case examined in this chapter illustrates how an offer of material support from Indian premier Jawaharlal Nehru helped drive a group of former Gandhian acolytes to take arms in their effort to bring democracy to Nepal after their initial efforts at replicating Gandhian nonviolent tactics failed. The second explores how, after the Sino-Indian war of 1962, India cut off support for prodemocracy dissidents in Nepal, forcing them into a long period of relative dormancy. The third and fourth cases, the 1990 Jana Andolan (People's Movement) and the 2006 Jana Andolan II (sometimes called the Loktantra Andolan, or Movement for Democracy), demonstrate the power of nonmaterial support to movements. In both cases, Indian government representatives helped midwife a coalition of ideologically disparate political parties that formed a unified front for civil resistance against the Nepali government. The fifth case examines a 2015 protest movement by the Madhesi people of southern Nepal for greater political autonomy, known as the Madhes Andolan (Madhesi People's Movement). In this case, India intervened on the protesters' behalf with a blockade of fuel shipments. However, this intervention backfired, allowing the Nepali government to consolidate popular support by rallying nationalist sentiment against foreign interference in local affairs. The case also featured Nepal's first successful appeal to Beijing, as a rising China demonstrated a new willingness to confront India through proxy battles in Nepal.

Nehru's Offer and the 1950 Anti-Rana Revolt

In 1947, a delegation from the underground Nepali National Congress (NC) political party met secretly in Delhi with Indian premier Jawaharlal Nehru. Since the mid-nineteenth century, Nepal had been ruled by a noble family, the Ranas, who banned schooling and restricted travel in an effort to maintain political control. The NC leaders largely came from families that had fled political persecution under the Ranas and settled in India. Some had even participated as activists in Gandhi's campaigns for Indian home rule from the British. Now, having seen India gain its independence, this group of exiles hoped to use similar nonviolent tactics in their ancestral home of Nepal to overthrow the Rana regime and establish a democratic government.

The NC delegation sought to leverage their close connections with Indian leaders to get advice and support for their movement. Securing a meeting with none other than Prime Minister Jawaharlal Nehru was an astounding moral victory, which they hoped would lead to material benefits. India's main aim was to secure loyal regimes in its "near-abroad," especially along the border with China. By supporting a revolution in Nepal, it hoped to secure a government that would be pliant to its interests for decades to come.

As the delegation laid out their plans to use a strategy of nonviolent resistance in Nepal, Nehru's response to the delegation was shocking. "What nonsense is this Gandhism?" Nehru exclaimed, "Do some clandestine activity in which there will be invisible support from us."[31] By "clandestine activity," Nehru meant that the NC should turn to arms. If it did, India could provide far greater assistance than if the NC relied on unarmed tactics alone.

At first, the NC was reluctant to follow Nehru's advice. Instead, they organized at a jute mill in the border city of Biratnagar, hoping that a local labor action could serve as a spark for a nationwide uprising.[32] This strategy, to mobilize around local economic grievances as a springboard for national political demonstration, came straight from the Gandhian playbook. However, it did not achieve the desired results. While the strike garnered some remarkable support, it failed to catalyze the type of nationwide uprising necessary to pose an existential threat to the Rana regime. State forces were able to suppress the strike, killing twenty-five protesters, and arresting several key leaders of the NC.[33] The NC turned again to Nehru, who negotiated a settlement between the NC and the Ranas and secured the release of the arrested leaders.[34]

By now the NC was willing to reconsider Nehru's proposal of an armed strategy. They began training fighters, with India providing weapons, expertise, and safe harbor. On November 11, 1950, they launched their first raid across the border. Over the next two months, they captured several border towns, while New Delhi threatened to seize Rana family assets in India.[35] On January 8, 1951, the Ranas agreed to accept a restoration of Nepal's traditional monarch, King Tribhuvan, with a cabinet composed of both Rana and NC leaders.[36] Tribhuvan, meanwhile, committed to the NC leaders that he would call for a constituent assembly to draft a new constitution for Nepal.

This case shows how foreign support can impact the initiation and strategy of uprisings. While Nehru's offer cannot be singled out as the reason the NC abandoned nonviolence, it is clear that the NC would not have been able to turn to guerrilla insurgency were it not for Indian support. The case also shows that while direct material support is crucial for a violent strategy, nonmaterial support might be more useful for a strategy of civil resistance. During the NC's experiment with nonviolence, the most useful assistance from India came in the form of mediation that secured some minor concessions from the regime. Finally, the case illustrates India's desire as a new regional power to exert its influence on its weaker neighbors and to intervene in domestic uprisings to help secure regional allegiance. But India's involvement would not always take the form of bolstering resistance movements. In the decades that followed, India switched between supporting dissidents and supporting the government, depending on how its geopolitical interests aligned with Nepal's domestic politics. The next case shows how India came to withdraw support for the NC to gain stronger relations with the monarch in a time of rising tensions with China.

The Sino-Indian War and the
Withdrawal of Support for Dissent

Less than ten years after the fall of the Rana regime, the NC found itself once again excluded from political power. King Tribhuvan fell ill before making good on his promise to hold a constituent assembly, and his son Mahendra was not inclined to cede the powers of the monarchy. Parliamentary elections were held in 1957, and the NC became the leading party in government. But in 1960, King Mahendra leveraged his substantial popularity within the military to carry out a royal coup, dissolving parliament and seizing full political control.[37]

The NC immediately attempted to make plans to resist the royal takeover and restore at least partially democratic government in Nepal. As in 1949, the NC spoke of using nonviolent methods to restore democracy, but its weak social networks made mass mobilization impossible.[38] In India, Nehru was once again willing to lend his support. While supportive of democracy and perhaps still loyal to Nepali friends who had helped in India's own struggle, Nehru had geopolitical concerns as well. The king had recently signed a new deal with China extending a road from Tibet into Nepal. As tensions between India and China began to escalate, Nehru wanted to ensure a government in Kathmandu that was responsive to New Delhi, not to Beijing.[39] With Indian support, the NC assembled a modest rebel army of three thousand fighters and again launched guerrilla raids from across the Indian border. But this time, they were far less effective in threatening the regime, posing only a "nuisance" to the Royal Nepali Army.[40]

Dynamics shifted again in 1962 when the Sino-Indian War broke out. India reversed course on its policy toward Nepal. Rather than placing its bets on revolution to bring new leaders to power in Kathmandu, it turned to a less risky strategy of reconciliation with the king. Its support for the rebels gave it a powerful bargaining chip in its diplomacy with the royal regime. In exchange for foreign policy loyalty from Kathmandu, New Delhi cut off support for the NC guerrillas, effectively ending the minor insurgency. In the years that followed, some factions of the NC continued to fight, hijacking an airplane and attempting a few very small-scale attacks. But without arms and money from India, these efforts were short-lived and ineffective. The NC became largely dormant, at least in terms of active resistance. It resigned itself to underground organization, hoping to slowly build strength so that, at some future point, it could continue its fight for democratic reform when conditions were more favorable.[41]

This episode highlights again how foreign support can enable domestic conflict and is especially instrumental in the conduct of armed methods of resistance. It also illustrates another reason why armed strategies are often preferable for foreign sponsors. Not only does the supply of arms make a resistance movement especially dependent on the sponsor, it allows the sponsor to change course relatively quickly by cutting off that supply. Finally, the episode reveals how the availability of foreign support changed with shifts in regional security dynamics. The imminent threat posed by the Sino-Indian war required India to solidify relationships with an established regime on its border rather than foment instability.

Mediating for Resistance: The 1990 Jana Andolan

During its years as an underground political party, the NC maintained its commitment to the idea that a democratically elected government should be restored in Nepal. However, it lacked the means to engage in active resistance against the now absolute monarchy. Instead, the NC focused on building its strength through clandestine organization.[42] It attempted several protests and strikes in the late 1970s and 1980s, achieving some noteworthy gains, but it failed to pose a serious threat to the monarchy. From this experience, NC leaders concluded that they would need to ally with other groups to pose a credible challenge.[43] At the same time, several communist political parties were undergoing a parallel process of development. Previously fragmented into numerous factions due to minor differences in ideological doctrine, the various communist groups began a process of gradual merger while at the same time using professional and identity-based fronts to expand their organizational infrastructure.[44]

Meanwhile, in the late 1980s, India once again changed its position regarding its support for the regime in Kathmandu. In an effort to diversify its foreign relations away from singular reliance on India, King Birendra (who succeeded Mahendra in 1972) began reaching out to China. In 1985, Nepal signed an arms deal with Beijing. To New Delhi, this was an unacceptable violation of the tacit agreement it had reached with the monarchy during the 1960s, when it withdrew support for the NC insurgents in exchange for Kathmandu's unwavering allegiance.[45] India's initial response was to turn to informal sanctions: it blocked the shipment of goods, especially fuel, across the border into Nepal. But then it turned to supporting contentious mobilization in Nepal, albeit through different means than it had thirty and forty years prior.

In August 1989, nine Indian parliamentarians traveled to Kathmandu to attend a summit of opposition political parties.[46] The goal was to forge a coalition between the NC and the leftist parties that could mount an effective civil resistance campaign against the king. The efforts were successful. Between February and April 1990, the political parties engaged in a united campaign of protests and strikes that became known as the Jana Andolan. With the economy ground to a halt, tens of thousands of Nepalis in the streets, and the international community sympathetic with the protesters, King Birendra was forced to agree to the legalization of political parties and to the drafting of a new constitution that would give a freely elected parliament substantial political powers.

The case of the 1990 Jana Andolan once again highlights how regional political rivalries shaped the availability of external support for dissident mobilization. After decades of refusing to support democratic activists in Nepal, India changed its stance when it saw Kathmandu attempt to develop closer ties with China. The message sent was clear: India viewed Nepal as within its sphere of influence and was prepared to inflict massive costs on Nepali governments that tried to pivot toward Beijing.

However, there are several notable differences in *how* India was willing to support dissident movements between the mid- and late twentieth century. Whereas previously India had supported guerrilla insurgency in Nepal, now it favored uprising based on unarmed mass mobilization. The global wave of such protest movements in 1989 may have influenced this decision. The success of such campaigns in Eastern Europe and central Asia proved that such a strategy could be highly effective, and perhaps without the risk of violence that could spill over into India. The 1990 Jana Andolan in Nepal may be considered one of the pivotal early cases whereby international actors transitioned away from sponsoring insurgencies and toward supporting civil resistance movements as a more normatively appropriate and strategically effective tool to achieve geopolitical goals.

The case also shows the important role played by nonmaterial forms of support. The decisive factor in the Jana Andolan was the ability of the NC and the leftist parties to set aside ideological differences and historical rivalries to cooperate in a unified effort to restore a party-based parliamentary system. India's efforts to help mediate those discussions proved important in that effort. Furthermore, the symbolism of India's support for the movement was valuable as well. India's close ties with the Royal Nepali Army combined with its clear support for the protesters limited the king's ability to quash the movement through violent repression. Indian support also added further credibility to the movement, which increased expectations for success and encouraged greater popular participation.

Transition to Nonviolence: The 2006 Jana Andolan II

Only six years after the Jana Andolan, Nepal experienced another uprising, this time in the form of a Maoist guerrilla insurgency. While Nepal had transitioned to a constitutional monarchy where an elected parliament and government held substantial political power, many Nepalis felt that the country was nevertheless dominated by a small group of privileged elites. For example, the three most dominant groups, known as Bahuns, Chhetris, and Newars, constituted about a third of the country's population, but held roughly 80 percent of positions in government.[47] The Maoists seized on these grievances, calling for communist revolution as the only means of addressing the country's deeply rooted inequalities.

Nepal's Maoists had little to no support from abroad, relying almost exclusively on their ability to mobilize local ethnic and class grievances and to seize weapons from local police stations.[48] The Maoists reportedly hoped to receive support from China due to shared ideological tenets, but Beijing had no interest in sponsoring the rebels.[49]

There were also numerous allegations that India was helping the Maoists. At times during the conflict, Maoist leaders appeared to easily be able to cross the border into India. Even some Indian officials concede that they may have received assistance from Indian intelligence services to be able to enter India.[50] But at the same time that the intelligence services may have been helping secure safe passage for leaders, the Indian government (especially the Ministry of Defense) was providing the Royal Nepali Army with heavy weaponry, especially helicopters, that was crucial in stemming the Maoist advances.

India's largest role in the conflict came at the end, as it hosted and mediated negotiations that led the Maoists to transition from an armed struggle to civil resistance. In a gruesome palace massacre in 2001, the crown prince, Dipendra, killed King Birendra and numerous other members of the royal family, including himself. This shocking event and the succession of the more authoritarian King Gyanendra sparked discussions between the mainstream political parties and the Maoists about a possible partnership and path to peace. These early discussions, however, were unsuccessful, as the political parties were unwilling to scrap the constitution that had been produced in the aftermath of the 1990 Jana Andolan.[51]

In 2005, India intervened, bringing the Maoists and political parties together in New Delhi for a series of meetings. This produced a document known as the "12-Point Agreement" in which the political parties agreed to Maoist demands for a new constitution, while the Maoists embraced electoral democracy as the political system through which future disputes would be resolved. Meanwhile, the Maoists agreed to cease armed attacks and join the political parties in an unarmed campaign of resistance against the monarchy. A few months later, when the Maoists launched some armed attacks that the political parties believed to be counterproductive, the Maoists and political parties met again in New Delhi to recommit to a strategy of unarmed mobilization.

Accounts vary as to how heavy-handed Indian involvement was in these negotiations. The principal actors, both Nepali and Indian, claim that India only provided "good offices" for the Maoists and political parties to discuss, while others, especially critics of the deal, suggest that India drafted the agreement in its entirety and imposed it on the Nepali factions. Also raising suspicions was the fact that while more moderate Maoist leaders who supported compromise moved freely between Nepal and India, several more radical leaders who were suspicious of the negotiations were arrested as they tried to cross the border.[52] What is not in doubt, however, is that India played a crucial role in facilitating the formation of a coalition that allowed both greater mobilization and greater nonviolent discipline, ultimately yielding a successful outcome for the campaign. After the coalition of Maoists and political parties sustained a general strike of only nineteen days in April 2006, the king was forced to read a statement drafted by the dissident movement, agreeing to their demands to reinstate parliament. This kick-started a political process that led to the formal signing of the Comprehensive Peace Agreement (CPA) to end the civil war, elections for a Constituent Assembly to draft a new constitution with the goal of addressing the country's social and political inequalities, and the formal dissolution of all the monarch's political powers.

By mediating the dialogue among the dissident factions, India not only helped them achieve a unified coalition but also once again provided valuable symbolic support for the movement. The coalition between the formerly irreconcilable political parties and the Maoists changed Nepalis' outlook on the conflict in that it led them to believe that a peace deal could be reached to end the war. This encouraged greater participation in the campaign.[53] Meanwhile, India's close ties with the Royal Nepali Army once again limited the regime's ability to engage in repression. In a critical moment late in the campaign, the army chief of staff reportedly told the king that he could not rely on the army to suppress the movement with overwhelming force.[54]

The 2006 Jana Andolan II episode did reveal one potential risk to foreign sponsors of civil resistance movements. Two weeks into the protests, the king offered to restore the elected government and parliament in exchange for an end to protest. India was supportive of such a compromise, and even the Maoists and political parties themselves were seriously considering the offer. But at this point, the campaign had taken a life of its own, and the protesters in the streets were unwilling to go home with only such modest reforms. A few days later, the king was forced to capitulate entirely, paving the way for a new constitution that would strip him of all political power. Thus, unlike sponsoring armed insurgency, when India was able to quickly reverse course by cutting off the flow of weapons, support for the civil resistance campaigns offered India limited control over the trajectories and outcomes of domestic politics in Nepal.

Turning to China: The 2015 Madhes Andolan

The second Jana Andolan was successful in restoring democratic politics and advanced the process that led to the CPA, which ended the country's decade-long civil war. The CPA, however, left many core issues from the conflict unresolved. Instead, it called for the creation of an elected constituent assembly that would draft a new constitution for the country. The most controversial of these issues were related to social identity as well as the federal structure of the new system. Many minority groups advocated for a high degree of decentralization as well as district borders that reflected the traditional homelands of their group. These groups often found support from the United Nations and international development agencies, highlighting the glocalized processes of postconflict peacebuilding.[55]

The Constituent Assembly, first elected in 2008, struggled to make progress on these issues, failing to garner the supermajority of votes needed to pass a constitution. As the assembly was deadlocked, several organizations representing minority social groups returned to the streets to try to apply political pressure through protests, strikes, and boycotts. The frequency of the protests and the disruption they caused led to fatigue among Nepali citizens, especially those belonging to privileged groups. Political elites began to criticize ethnic advocacy organizations for stalling the constitution-writing process and threatening the "social fabric" of the country.[56]

In the aftermath of a horrific earthquake, Nepal finally passed a constitution in September 2015. But many of the compromises reached to secure its adoption ran counter to the wishes of the organizations representing marginalized groups. Especially controversial were provisions regarding who was eligible for birthright citizenship as well as the boundaries of the new federal districts. In the south of the country, along the border with India, a protest movement emerged from the Madhesi community.[57] The uprising, known as the Madhes Andolan (i.e., Madhesi People's Movement), escalated to violence as protesters attacked police officers and the police responded with lethal violence. An estimated forty Nepalis were killed. India may have had a humanitarian interest in the rights of the Madhesis, as the Madhesis historically have had strong ties with communities across the border in India. But they may also have wished to see Nepal's southern federal districts changed to be better positioned to exert political influence at the local level.

One of the most coercive tactics used by protesters was the implementation of a blockade of fuel shipments from India. While the Indian government denied any role in the blockade, the Nepali government believed India to be responsible. Indeed, it is unlikely that protesters would have been able to implement such a blockade for nearly five months without at least tacit Indian support. The tactic was similar to what India had done previously in 1989. But whereas that earlier blockade encouraged dissidents to take action against the regime, the 2015 blockade sparked a widespread backlash. Nepalis suffered from long gas lines and higher prices on all goods and resorted to burning wood to heat homes and hospitals as an alternative to petroleum.[58] Nepali prime minister K. P. Oli leveraged the suffering to rally nationalist sentiment, criticize the movement, and blame India for interfering in Nepal's domestic affairs.

Oli also turned to China for support. He found Beijing far more willing than it had in the past to confront India in Nepal. China and Nepal signed an agreement that provided Nepal with a third of the oil it was losing from the blockade.[59] The government in Kathmandu also passed an amendment to address some of the grievances raised by the protesters: southern regions were allocated a greater number of parliamentary seats, and Madhesis were added to a list of historically marginalized groups that are guaranteed a quota of government jobs. Madhesi advocacy organizations largely condemned the amendment as inadequate as they did not change the new federal districts or citizenship provisions. However, India saw the amendment as an opportunity to cut its losses and end the blockade. The movement effectively ended in February 2016. Less than a month later, Prime Minister Oli traveled to Beijing, representing a new stage in Nepal's relations with its regional neighbors.

What explains the different outcomes between India's restriction of fuel imports in 1989 versus 2014? Economic coercion against a democratic regime may have been viewed as less legitimate by Nepalis. Furthermore, a decade of political stalemate and frequent political mobilizations may have rendered the public less sympathetic to more "civil resistance." But the biggest difference appears to be in the social identity of the protesters. Because the Madhes Andolan came from a minority community, and especially one that was often prejudicially viewed as closer to Indian than Nepali national identity, it allowed Kathmandu to delegitimize the protest by framing it as a foreign attack on national sovereignty. Similar "meddling" in Nepal's internal affairs by India did not produce nearly the same backlash when it was done in support of movements that were led by elite groups.

Even with the popular backlash to India's intervention, the financial pressure of the blockade still might have been enough to coerce more significant concessions from Kathmandu. But a change in regional balance of power gave the Nepali government another way out. As China's economic might has grown, so too has its willingness to exert political influence in South Asia and beyond. By 2015, Beijing no longer felt compelled to recognize Nepal as within India's sphere of influence. It saw the blockade as an opportunity to forge a new relationship with Kathmandu. India appeared to realize that its efforts had backfired, both in terms of popular support and geopolitics. But by the time it ended the blockade, the damage had already been done. Nepali leaders had seized an opportunity not only to gain relief from the fuel shortages but also to realize a decades-old foreign policy ambition of playing Beijing against New Delhi to gain more favorable diplomatic outcomes. Rather than simply be beholden to New Delhi, Nepal's political leaders now believed they could pursue a dual strategy, building relationships with both India and China.[60]

In the years since the 2015 Madhes Andolan, Nepal has furthered its efforts to build a relationship with China. In 2017, it signed an agreement to build a rail corridor to Nepal as part of the Chinese "Belt and Road Initiative." And while India remains Nepal's primary trading partner, China is now its top source of foreign direct investment. China clearly seeks to develop economic ties with Nepal, but a critical question is whether Beijing will seek to support dissident movements in Nepal to gain political leverage, similar to how India has done. A preliminary answer may have come in early 2022 as the Nepali parliament considered ratification of a $500 million development package from the United States. China denounced the package as a threat to Nepal's security, sovereignty, and prosperity. Meanwhile, over ten thousand protesters massed outside the parliament in opposition to the deal. The protests were spearheaded by two Nepali communist parties that had previously supported the proposal and that have close ties to Beijing, leading some analysts to conclude that the demonstrations were promoted by China.[61]

Conclusion

The episodes from Nepal's dissident mobilizations for democracy and equality offered four key insights into the relationship between global and regional security orders and local collective action. First, foreign sponsorship does not simply impact the outcomes of civil resistance campaigns: it shapes whether they occur at all. India's offer of arms in 1950 made it possible for the NC to abandon nonviolence in favor of guerrilla insurgency. Later, India's mediation was critical in forging political alliances that made the 1990

Jana Andolan possible and convinced the Maoists to lay down their arms in favor of joining a nonviolent movement. India's roles in 1990 and 2006 highlight a second insight: that for civil resistance, forms of nonmaterial support, such as organizing alliances, may be more important than funding or sanctions against the target regime. Third, the case of the 2015 Madhes Andolan shows that the social composition of a campaign may condition the impact of foreign support. India's support of the majority-led movement in 1990 significantly bolstered that movement, but when it intervened on behalf of the Madhesi minority in 2015, it produced backlash as the regime was able to use the intervention to rally nationalist sentiment against the movement. India's intervention in 2015 also backfired in that it prompted China to intervene on behalf of the Nepali government. This highlights a fourth and final insight: the way in which regional strategic rivalries shape the availability of support for movements. Such regional power rivalries further fuse the domestic with the global order in a deeply glocalized manner. With the entry of China into Nepalese domestic affairs, Nepal becomes a deeply glocalized geopolitical space for India and China with profound impacts on peace and security in Nepal.

These four insights highlight the way in which a paradigm of glocalization can help advance our understanding of contentious politics. The rivalry between India and China, and those countries' desires to foster compliant allies in their near-abroad, drove first New Delhi and then Beijing to intervene in domestic uprisings within Nepal. In doing so, they shaped local actors' decision-making about whether to mobilize as well as what tactics to use. They also shaped the regime's calculus about whether and how to respond to dissidents, which greatly impacted peace and security in Nepal. But it would be a mistake to view contentious politics in Nepal as simply driven by powerful outside actors. It is how those actors interacted with local social networks and organizing structures that informed the trajectories of resistance campaigns and, ultimately, whether to fight or make peace. Even the highly coercive act of India blockading fuel imports in 2015 could not help the Madhesi minority achieve their political goals; in fact, the powerful intervention likely undermined their efforts. Intervention by helping to forge coalitions among diverse local actors appears to be a far more effective tactic. As such, it provides a model for how international actors can constructively engage in non-militant forms of peacebuilding.[62]

In this vein, this chapter also pushes the field of international peace and security, and the study of glocalized security, to incorporate the study of resistance movements that employ primarily unarmed tactics. It represents an alternative to both armed force as well as traditional peacebuilding strategies for aggrieved populations seeking major political change. Where power asymmetries between groups can limit the effectiveness of dialogue and mediation-based approaches to conflict transformation, civil resistance can serve as a form of "constructive conflict" for oppressed groups.[63] But these campaigns can sometimes escalate to violence and even spark militarized international intervention, as we have seen in Syria and Ukraine. The rising frequency of civil resistance campaigns creates a need for scholars and policymakers to consider interventions (or noninterventions) that can reduce the likelihood of violence. Doing so requires understanding both the global pressures as well as the local roots that shape the trajectories of contentious mobilization.

Notes

1. Fearon and Laitin, "Ethnicity, Insurgency, and Civil War," 75–90.
2. Human Security Centre, *Human Security Report 2005*.
3. Kaldor, *New and Old Wars*; Kalyvas and Balcells, "International System and Technologies of Rebellion," 415–29.
4. Kaldor, "Decade of the War on Terror and the 'Responsibility to Protect'"; Bah, *International Security and Peacebuilding*.
5. Ackerman and Kruegler, *Strategic Nonviolent Conflict*.
6. Kuran, "Now Out of Never," 7–48.
7. Chenoweth, "Future of Nonviolent Resistance," 71.
8. Chenoweth and Stephan, *Why Civil Resistance Works*; Ackerman and Karatnycky, *How Freedom Is Won*; Pinckney, *From Dissent to Democracy*.
9. Köhler and Wissen, "Glocalizing Protest," 942–51.
10. Chaturvedi and Malone, "Yam between Two Boulders," 287–312.
11. Martin, *Justice Ignited*.
12. To be clear, the relative importance of external versus local factors in each of these cases is contested. They are highlighted simply as cases where foreign involvement has received high levels of scholarly, policymaker, and media attention.
13. Gelderloos, *How Nonviolence Protects the State*.
14. Thurber, *Between Mao and Gandhi*; Pearlman, *Violence, Nonviolence, and the Palestinian National Movement*; DeNardo, *Power in Numbers*.
15. Chenoweth and Stephan, *Why Civil Resistance Works*.
16. Kalyvas and Balcells, "International System and Technologies of Rebellion," 415–29.
17. Fearon and Laitin, "Ethnicity, Insurgency, and Civil War," 75–90; Harkness, *When Soldiers Rebel*; Roessler, *Ethnic Politics and State Power in Africa*.
18. Schmidt, *Foreign Intervention in Africa*; Wheeler, *Saving Strangers*.
19. Chenoweth and Stephan, *Why Civil Resistance Works*.
20. Pape, "Why Economic Sanctions Do Not Work," 90–136.
21. Pearlman, *Violence, Nonviolence, and the Palestinian National Movement*.
22. Kuran, "Now Out of Never," 7–48.
23. Nepstad, *Nonviolent Revolutions*, 134.
24. Mylonas and Radnitz, *Enemies Within*.
25. Nepstad, *Nonviolent Revolutions*, 134.
26. Howard and Stark, "How Civil Wars End," 127–71; Posen, "Civil Wars & the Structure of World Power," 167–79.

27. Chenoweth, "Future of Nonviolent Resistance," 69–84.
28. Beissinger, "Structure and Example in Modular Political Phenomena," 259–76; Burrows and Stephan, *Is Authoritarianism Staging a Comeback?*; Tufekci, *Twitter and Tear Gas*.
29. Chenoweth and Stephan, *Why Civil Resistance Works*, 54.
30. Nikitina, "'Color Revolutions' and 'Arab Spring' in Russian Official Discourse," 87–104.
31. Koirala, *Role in Revolution*, 187.
32. Gautam, *Nepali Congress*, 54.
33. Uprety, *Political Awakening in Nepal*, 125.
34. Misra, *B.P. Koirala*, 45.
35. Whelpton, *History of Nepal*, 72.
36. Maharjan, "Nepali Congress," 280.
37. Brown, *Political History of Nepal*, 39; Joshi and Rose, *Democratic Innovations in Nepal*, 390.
38. Baral, *Opposition Politics in Nepal*, 68; Misra, *B.P. Koirala*, 83; Thurber, *Between Mao and Gandhi*, 65.
39. Whelpton, *History of Nepal*, 99.
40. Brown, *Political History of Nepal*, 39.
41. Thurber, *Between Mao and Gandhi*, 67.
42. Ibid., 66–67.
43. Ogura, *Kathmandu Spring*, 3.
44. Hachhethu, *Party Building in Nepal*, 48–50.
45. Whelpton, *History of Nepal*, 113.
46. Brown, *Political History of Nepal*, 115.
47. Routledge, "Nineteen Days in April: Urban Protest and Democracy in Nepal," 1283.
48. Thapa and Sijapati, *A Kingdom under Siege*, 29.
49. Upreti, "Maoist Insurgency in Nepal: Nature, Growth and Impact," 225.
50. Muni, "Bringing the Maoists Down from the Hills: India's Role," 313–31.
51. Adhikari, *Bullet and the Ballot Box*, 169.
52. Muni, "Bringing the Maoists Down from the Hills: India's Role," 313–31.
53. Routledge, "Nineteen Days in April: Urban Protest and Democracy in Nepal," 1279–99.
54. Dixit, "Spring of Dissent," 120. Retired general Balananda Sharma confirmed in an interview with the author (Kathmandu, July 2013) that other senior military officers held similar understandings of this conversation.
55. Bogati and Thurber, *From the Hills to the Streets to the Table*; Huang, *Wartime Origins of Democratization*.
56. Bogati and Thurber, *From the Hills to the Streets to the Table*, 36.
57. Madhesi refers to a collective identity group of people living in the southern plains region. Many share common language and familial ties with groups across the border in India.
58. Ghosh, "Anger against India over Blockade Snowballs in Nepal."
59. *Kathmandu Post*, "Nepal Inks Historic Oil Agreement with China."
60. Upadhyay, "Nepal, Between the Dragon and the Elephant."
61. Wagle, "Behind the Anti-MCC Protests."
62. Paris, *At War's End*.
63. Dudouet, *Powering to Peace*; Dudouet, *Nonviolent Resistance and Conflict Transformation in Power Asymmetries*.

References

Ackerman, Peter, and Adrian Karatnycky. *How Freedom Is Won: From Civic Resistance to Durable Democracy*. Washington, DC: Freedom House, 2005.

Ackerman, Peter, and Christopher Kruegler. *Strategic Nonviolent Conflict: The Dynamics of People Power in the Twentieth Century.* Westport, CT: Praeger, 1994.

Adhikari, Aditya. *The Bullet and the Ballot Box: The Story of Nepal's Maoist Revolution.* London: Verso, 2014.

Bah, Abu Bakarr, ed. *International Security and Peacebuilding: Africa, the Middle East, and Europe.* Bloomington: Indiana University Press, 2017.

Baral, Lok Raj. *Opposition Politics in Nepal.* Lalitpur, Nepal: Himal Books, 2006.

Beissinger, Mark R. "Structure and Example in Modular Political Phenomena: The Diffusion of Bulldozer/Rose/Orange/Tulip Revolutions." *Perspectives on Politics* 5, no. 2 (2007): 259–76.

Bogati, Subindra, and Ches Thurber. *From the Hills to the Streets to the Table: Civil Resistance and Peacebuilding in Nepal.* Washington, DC: ICNC Press, 2021.

Brown, T. Louise. *A Political History of Nepal.* London: Routledge, 1996.

Burrows, Mathew, and Maria J. Stephan, eds. *Is Authoritarianism Staging a Comeback?* Washington, DC: Atlantic Council, 2015.

Chaturvedy, Rajeev Ranjan, and David M. Malone. "A Yam between Two Boulders: Nepal's Foreign Policy Caught between India and China." In *Nepal in Transition: From People's War to Fragile Peace*, edited by David M. Malone, Sebastian von Einsiedel, and Suman Pradhan, 287–312. Cambridge: Cambridge University Press, 2012.

Chenoweth, Erica. "The Future of Nonviolent Resistance." *Journal of Democracy* 31, no. 3 (2020): 69–84.

Chenoweth, Erica, and Maria J. Stephan. *Why Civil Resistance Works: The Strategic Logic of Nonviolent Conflict.* New York: Columbia University Press, 2011.

DeNardo, James. *Power in Numbers: The Political Strategy of Protest and Rebellion.* Princeton, NJ: Princeton University Press, 1985.

Dixit, Kanak Mani. "The Spring of Dissent: People's Movement in Nepal." *India International Centre Quarterly* 33, no. 1 (2006): 113–25.

Dudouet, Veronique. *Nonviolent Resistance and Conflict Transformation in Power Asymmetries.* Berlin: Berghof Research Center for Constructive Conflict Management, 2008.

———. *Powering to Peace: Integrated Civil Resistance and Peacebuilding Strategies.* Washington, DC: International Center on Nonviolent Conflict, 2017.

Fearon, James D., and David D. Laitin. "Ethnicity, Insurgency, and Civil War." *American Political Science Review* 97, no. 1 (2003): 75–90.

Gautam, Rajesh. *Nepali Congress.* New Delhi, India: Adroit, 2005.

Gelderloos, Peter. *How Nonviolence Protects the State.* Cambridge: South End Press, 2007.

Ghosh, Bishwanath. "Anger against India over Blockade Snowballs in Nepal." *Hindu*, December 26, 2015. https://www.thehindu.com/news/national/Anger-against-India-over-blockade-snowballs-in-Nepal/article60516686.ece.

Hachhethu, Krishna. *Party Building in Nepal: Organization, Leadership and People.* Kathmandu: Mandala Book Point, 2002.

Harkness, Kristen A. *When Soldiers Rebel: Ethnic Armies and Political Instability in Africa.* Cambridge: Cambridge University Press, 2018.

Howard, Lise Morjé, and Alexandra Stark. "How Civil Wars End: The International System, Norms, and the Role of External Actors." *International Security* 42, no. 3 (Winter 2017/18): 127–71.

Huang, Reyko. *The Wartime Origins of Democratization: Civil War, Rebel Governance, and Political Regimes.* Cambridge: Cambridge University Press, 2016.

Human Security Centre. *Human Security Report 2005: War and Peace in the 21st Century.* New York: Oxford University Press, 2006.

Joshi, Bhuwan Lal, and Leo E. Rose. *Democratic Innovations in Nepal.* Berkeley: University of California Press, 1966.

Kaldor, Mary. "A Decade of the War on Terror and the 'Responsibility to Protect.'" In *Global Civil Society 2012: Ten Years of Critical Reflection*, edited by Mary Kaldor, Henrietta L. Moore, Sabine Selchow, and Tamsin Murray-Leach, 88–109. London: Palgrave Macmillan, 2012.

———. *New and Old Wars: Organized Violence in a Global Era*. Malden, MA: Polity, 1999.

Kalyvas, Stathis N., and Laia Balcells. "International System and Technologies of Rebellion: How the End of the Cold War Shaped Internal Conflict." *American Political Science Review* 104, no. 3 (2010): 415–29.

Kathmandu Post. "Nepal Inks Historic Oil Agreement with China." October 29, 2015. https://kathmandupost.com/miscellaneous/2015/10/29/nepal-inks-historic-oil-agreement-with-china.

Köhler, Bettina, and Markus Wissen. "Glocalizing Protest: Urban Conflicts and the Global Social Movements." *International Journal of Urban and Regional Research* 27, no. 4 (2003): 942–51.

Koirala, M.P. *A Role in Revolution*. Lalitpur, Nepal: Jagadamba Prakashan, 2008.

Kuran, Timur. "Now Out of Never: The Element of Surprise in the East European Revolution of 1989." *World Politics* 44, no. 1 (1991): 7–48.

Maharjan, Pancha N. "The Nepali Congress: Party Agency and Nation Building." In *Political Parties in South Asia*, edited by Subrata Mitra, Mike Enskat, and Clemens Spiess, 276–300. Westport, CT: Praeger, 2004.

Martin, Brian. *Justice Ignited: The Dynamics of Backfire*. Lanham, MD: Rowman and Littlefield, 2007.

Misra, Shashi P. *B.P. Koirala: A Case Study in Third World Democratic Leadership*. Bhubaneswar, India: Konark, 1985.

Muni, S. D. "Bringing the Maoists Down from the Hills: India's Role." In *Nepal in Transition: From People's War to Fragile Peace*, edited by Sebastian von Einsiedel, David M. Malone, and Suman Pradhan, 313–31. Cambridge: Cambridge University Press, 2012.

Mylonas, Harris, and Scott Radnitz, eds. *Enemies Within: The Global Politics of Fifth Columns*. Oxford: Oxford University Press, 2022.

Nepstad, Sharon Erickson. *Nonviolent Revolutions: Civil Resistance in the Late 20th Century*. Oxford: Oxford University Press, 2011.

Nikitina, Yulia. "The 'Color Revolutions' and 'Arab Spring' in Russian Official Discourse." *Connections* 14, no. 1 (2014): 87–104.

Ogura, Kiyoko. *Kathmandu Spring: The People's Movement of 1990*. Lalitpur, Nepal: Himal Books, 2001.

Pape, Robert A. "Why Economic Sanctions Do Not Work." *International Security* 22, no. 2 (1997): 90–136.

Paris, Roland. *At War's End: Building Peace after Civil Conflict*. Cambridge: Cambridge University Press, 2004.

Pearlman, Wendy. *Violence, Nonviolence, and the Palestinian National Movement*. Cambridge: Cambridge University Press, 2011.

Pinckney, Jonathan. *From Dissent to Democracy: The Promise and Perils of Civil Resistance Transitions*. New York: Oxford University Press, 2020.

Posen, Barry R. "Civil Wars & the Structure of World Power." *Daedalus* 146, no. 4 (October 1, 2017): 167–79.

Roessler, Philip. *Ethnic Politics and State Power in Africa*. Cambridge: Cambridge University Press, 2016.

Routledge, Paul. "Nineteen Days in April: Urban Protest and Democracy in Nepal." *Urban Studies* 47, no. 6 (2010): 1279–99.

Schmidt, Elizabeth. *Foreign Intervention in Africa: From the Cold War to the War on Terror*. Cambridge: Cambridge University Press, 2013.

Thapa, Deepak, and Bandita Sijapati. *A Kingdom under Siege: Nepal's Maoist Insurgency, 1996 to 2004*. Kathmandu: The Printhouse, 2003.
Thurber, Ches. *Between Mao and Gandhi: The Social Roots of Civil Resistance*. Cambridge: Cambridge University Press, 2021.
Tufekci, Zeynep. *Twitter and Tear Gas: The Power and Fragility of Networked Protest*. New Haven, CT: Yale University Press, 2017.
Upadhyay, Akhilesh. "Nepal, Between the Dragon and the Elephant." *New York Times*, November 6, 2015. https://www.nytimes.com/2015/11/07/opinion/nepal-china-india-dragon-elephant-blockade.html.
Upreti, B.C. "The Maoist Insurgency in Nepal: Nature, Growth and Impact." *South Asian Survey* 13, no. 1 (March 2006): 35–50.
Uprety, Prem R. *Political Awakening in Nepal*. New Delhi: Commonwealth Publishers, 1992.
Wagle, Achyut. "Behind the Anti-MCC Protests." *Kathmandu Post*, September 14, 2021.
Wheeler, Nicholas J. *Saving Strangers: Humanitarian Intervention in International Society*. Oxford: Oxford University Press, 2000.
Whelpton, John. *A History of Nepal*. Cambridge: Cambridge University Press, 2005.

CHES THURBER is Associate Professor of Political Science at Northern Illinois University. He is author of *Between Mao and Gandhi: The Social Roots of Civil Resistance*. His research examines international conflict, security, peacebuilding, and global governance.

9

CONCLUSION

Glocalized Security, Intersectionality, and a Sociology of International Peace and Security

Abu Bakarr Bah

INTRODUCTION

Indeed, this book addresses the all too familiar issues of domestic and external drivers of conflict and how they feed into international peace and security issues.[1] In doing so, it develops the concept of glocalized security by drawing on critiques of the notion of globalization both in terms of its conceptual limitations and limited use in peace and security studies. Yet, a deeper reading of the studies in this book and the concept of glocalized security leads to a new frontier in the area of peace and security studies. This frontier I refer to as the sociology of international peace and security. While there are very few formulations of a sociology of international peace and security in the extant literature,[2] there is a rich tradition of intersectionality in sociology and related disciplines.[3] It is this idea of intersectionality in the study of (social) order that connects sociology to international peace and security issues. In addition to the rich cases the contributors to this volume discuss and the development of the notion of glocalized security, the works in this book force us to rethink how disciplines that have largely been marginal in international peace and security studies, notably sociology, can provide new theoretical and methodological insights into international peace and security issues. Sociology is, traditionally, the study of social order, as is most evident in the orthodox organic and system theories in sociology. In many ways, international peace and security, too, is about order, albeit through the lens of interstate relations. The issue of order necessitates a discourse of conflicts, notably their nature and causes. In sociology, the discourses of conflicts have been anchored on the levers of oppression in society—issues such as class, race, ethnicity, religion, and gender. When these forms of oppression become persistent and acute, they turn into structural violence under conditions of negative peace.[4] In political science and its cognate disciplines of international relations (IR) and international law, conflicts in interstate relations have been framed through the prism of international security and law. Order becomes a proxy for peace and security within a country, regionally, and globally. However, the study of order necessitates a discourse of the drivers of conflicts. In this work, we build on the extant discourses of conflict drivers to arrive at a sociology of international peace and security through the concept of glocalized security and its embeddedness in the intersectionality of domestic and external conflict drivers.

Based on the notion of glocalized security, the sociology of international peace and security leads us not to a bifurcated account of the domestic and the external drivers of conflicts or a bland discussion of the nature of conflicts, but to the emergence of new security dynamics that are glocal in their roots and forms. In this book, we ask two sociologically inspired questions: How does the fusion of domestic issues and interests with external ones generate new security situations that further undermine international peace and security? Moreover, how can the domestic issues and interests be disentangled from the external issues and interests in the efforts to resolve violent conflicts? We study cases and issues that have emerged as problematic for human security, state security, and the regional and international order in countries such as Afghanistan, Iraq, Azerbaijan, Somalia, Nigeria, Ukraine, Nepal, and North Korea. In all of these places, domestic levers of oppression have fused with external interests and ideologies of order to produce armed conflicts and security problems that are glocal in their roots and forms. The all too familiar concepts of order in political science and IR, such as ungoverned spaces, sovereignty, international law, human security, new wars, the global war on terror, and military interventions, take sociological shape through familiar sociological ideas about discrimination and structural violence based on class, ethnicity, race, religion, and nationalism, which can benefit the way we understand conflict drivers, domestically and globally.

GLOCALIZED SECURITY AND THE SOCIOLOGY OF INTERNATIONAL PEACE AND SECURITY

Traditionally, the interdisciplinary study of (international) order has two strands: peace studies and security studies. While peace studies has attracted diverse disciplines, such as anthropology, sociology, psychology, journalism, and education, security studies has largely remained within political science and its related disciplines of IR and international law. Peace studies mostly focuses on conflicts within countries, probing not only the nature of violence but also the root causes of violence, the nature of structural violence and negative peace, and the various modes of conflict resolution, healing, and peace building.[5] In contrast, security studies has mostly been about how the stability and external policies of states relate to the national (security) interests of other countries, regionally and internationally, under realist and normative security policy frames.[6] Glocalized security is anchored in both peace studies and security studies and points to the possibility of a sociology of international peace and security that can capture the intersection of domestic and external conflict drivers and the new security dynamics that emerge from the dialectical connections of the domestic and the external. Peace studies from the classic works of Johan Galtung to the more contemporary works on peacekeeping and peace building, especially in Africa, has produced historically grounded works that are rich in sociological, anthropological, psychological, historical, political, and economic analyses.[7] A common foci among these works is their focus on issues that are grounded in domestic realities, even when they implicate the international system through the frames of colonialism, capitalism, global liberal governance, human security, and human development. Security studies has also evolved from the study of superpower relations to focus on civil wars, regional conflicts, and the threats to the national (security) interests of other countries and the global liberal order through works anchored on notions of liberalism, realism, collective security, and military humanitarianism. Key among these are issues of national interest, such as geopolitics, terrorism, natural resources, human security, and forced migration.[8] In both peace studies and security studies, international law and agencies, notably through the United Nations system, have been instrumentalized to respond to conflicts through peacekeeping, peace building, and global war on terror frames.[9] The sociology of international peace and security brings together these domestic and international variants to the study of order that we see in peace studies and security studies.

The study of (social) order is inherent in sociology as most evident in the works of organic theorists and structural functionalists, such as Emile Durkheim and Talcott Parson.[10] Even in the works of Karl Marx and Max Weber, social order is a central theme, albeit approached differently. While structural functionalists see order through a normative morality built around maintaining the status quo, conflict theorists see the problem of order through the social injustices that cause conflicts, which make change a necessity for social order.[11] In the developmentalist works of Max Weber and critical theory too, order is central. In those works, order is examined through the process of rationalization, most notably the bureaucratic machine. Order takes a dialectical form as societies deal with the contradictions of freedom and oppression within organized capitalism.[12] In the postmodernist works, order takes an even more multidimensional form rooted in technology and the very nature of (post)modern society. As Michel Foucault notes, order is produced through a discipline blockade based on corporal punishment or through the disciplinary machine of the system of generalized surveillance.[13]

Perhaps, what is less known is the way sociologists study order at the international level. For this, an important starting point are studies of the global nature of capitalism, especially through the works of Immanuel Wallerstein, and postmodernist critiques of capitalism. Wallerstein's world system theory captures the sociological understanding of the international system and interstate relations through the capitalist mode of the world system and the struggles for hegemony. In Wallerstein's work, military power is fused with economic power through industrialization and control of financial markets. Order rests on maintaining the world capitalist system and a reliable system of international division of labor, where countries take their place within the core, semi-periphery or periphery—or risk being ostracized.[14] Wallerstein's works examine both the normative and conflict dimension of international order to not only show how the world capitalist system works but also note its social injustices through various modes of colonial and capitalist exploitations. Wallerstein's understanding of order is tied to a globality frame that foreshadows more recent discourses of globalism through postmodern and globalization theories in sociology and cognate disciplines.

As in Wallerstein's works, postmodern and globalization theories show the ambivalences of international order. Capitalism not only dictates the parameters of order within countries and among countries but also produces mixed results in terms of improving human well-being and fostering social justice.[15] The shortcomings of the global order manifest in various forms of domestic conflict drivers that can have implications well beyond the countries that are directly plagued by violence.[16] Indeed, sociological studies of order fit neatly with peace studies, even when they are not explicitly labeled as peace studies. However, globalization in its various forms opens a sociological angle into security studies as seemingly domestic conflicts and forms of disorder in developing countries have increasingly large effects on Western countries and the world capitalist system in general, especially through international terrorism and forced migration. Under these conditions, issues of peace and conflict become glocal and further align with the security narrative.

Indeed, security too has emerged as a sociological issue. However, extant sociological studies of security tend to be micro or country focused as opposed to exploring a sociology of security through an international lens. Perhaps the sociology of security first emerged in studies of nationalism, especially under the totalitarian regimes in Europe. Issues of nationalism and ideologies of collective security and cultural preservation against those framed as others led to varying forms of securitization under totalitarian regimes.[17] Some of the early studies are the critical theory works that emerged in the context of capitalist and communist totalitarianism in Europe. Critical theorists such as Hannah Arendt, Herbert Marcuse, and Antonio Gramsci examined the bureaucratization of ideology through the machinery of state security.[18] In these settings, security became framed as nationalism, which eventually led to interstate wars. More recently, immigration and the application of homeland security policies have emerged as security discourses within sociology.[19] Other sociological works have focused on the micro elements of conflict resolution on issues ranging from labor disputes to high-stakes diplomacy.[20] Sociology also contributes to security studies through studies of the nature of violence, the social causes of violent conflicts, and peace building.[21]

Despite some of the efforts to interject sociology into security studies,[22] a sociology of international peace and security is still lacking because sociological works hardly focus on the interstate issues associated with violence. However, sociology provides a useful way for understanding international peace and security through the study of the drivers of violent conflicts that not only threaten order within countries but also generate regional and international disorders.[23] The strength of sociology lies in not only its studies of global capitalism but also the intersectionality perspective that is embedded in sociology. Indeed, studies of peace and security are laden with the domestic and external causes of conflict.[24] Unfortunately, domestic and external drivers of conflict are often bifurcated as different theories focus on different kinds of conflict drivers. Our works seize on this bifurcation to accentuate the intersectionality of domestic and external conflict drivers and the new conflict dynamics that emerge from the intersection of the local and the global. As such, we approach violent conflicts through the notion of glocalized security, which is informed by the sociological discourse and critiques of globalization as well as the sociological notion of intersectionality.

GLOZALIZED SECURITY: THE INTERSECTIONALITY OF DOMESTIC AND EXTERNAL CONFLICT DRIVERS

Globalization provides a useful entry point into the issue of order not only because of its disruptive sides that feed into conflict drivers but also because of the interconnectedness that it generates among countries. Global interconnections dovetail with international security issues, notably in facilitating the logistics of wars, the flow of refugees, trade disruptions, the shaping of morality and human rights, and the expansion of national interests. As we already note in this book, extant theories on globalization are wide ranging. Starting with works in economics on corporate and trade expansions, globalization theory now encompasses issues such as migration, cultural fusion, human rights, and security—from environmental threats to wars—all coming from diverse disciplines. However, globalization theory swipes everything into a global homogeneity in ways that are biased toward Western histories, cultures, and political, economic and social priorities. As Tom Friedman notes, globalization flattens everything, but that flattening is more of a smashing of everything into the prevailing Western global liberal governance, as if it will be the end of history.[25] As such, globalization theory faces a problem not only because of its limited use in security studies but also its privileging of Western interests and experiences over those of others, especially the Global South. In addition to pointing out globalization's Eurocentric nature, critiques of globalization theory note its continued resistance to, and the increasing importance of, the local, especially in the non-Western world, and the way the global and local intersect in ways that produce new realities, which can be referred to as the glocal.[26] This intersectionality, which is increasingly a manifest reality, has been a lacuna in globalization theory. Interestingly, intersectionality has a rich tradition in sociology. A sociological reading into globalization would note the intersection of the global and the local and accentuate the glocal. We see this in the critiques of the notion of globalization, especially in the works of Roland Robertson and Ulrich Beck.[27] The glocal is a form of intersectionality that provides a new way of understanding the domestic and external drivers of conflicts. As such, a sociology of international peace and security can be framed as glocalized security precisely because of the intersection of the domestic and the external drivers of conflicts.

Unfortunately, domestic and external conflict drivers are accentuated differently across theories, which reinforces the bifurcation of conflict drivers.[28] Liberal peace, for example, often points to the absence of democracy as a major source of conflict as oppression and patrimonialism generate conflict and armed struggles for democracy.[29] However, these issues are framed as domestic problems of governance ignoring the external factors that make democracy and good governance difficult to attain in war-torn countries, especially postcolonial multiethnic states. On the other hand, system theories point to colonialism and neocolonialism as root causes of violent conflicts.[30]

In these works, wars are seen as externally conditioned or instigated, which minimizes issues of domestic oppression. Even works on natural resources, either by way of resource curse or resource scarcity,[31] tend to miss the glocalized nature of security issues as they focus on the political economy of war or the localized impacts of environmental issues. The global war on terror has also emerged as a way of theorizing conflicts. Indeed, there are growing connections between the local and the global in the way terrorism operates and in counterterrorism efforts. However, those interconnections tend to focus more on the logistics, modalities, and ideologies of war, instead of the causes of terrorism warfare. The global war on terror often demonizes Islamist insurgencies for their mode of violence without properly addressing the domestic and external oppressions that result in jihadism.[32] In a similar way, works on human security and the new war discourses generally focus too much on the nature of violence and its immorality and violation of international human rights law without properly addressing the causes of war.[33] In regional security complex theory, we see a similar problem in that the nature of security threat and the national interests of states supersede the root causes of conflicts, which often stem from varying forms of domestic and external injustices.[34] In all of these theories, the intersectionality of domestic and external conflict drivers is often missed, making them skewed toward reducing conflicts to domestic or external causes or simply bypassing the causes of conflict and reducing wars to the immoralities of their form of violence or the threat to the interests of states. But by failing to address the intersectionality of the forms of violence and the causes of violence, and even more the intersectionality of domestic and external drivers of conflicts, efforts to resolve conflicts often fail to lead to sustainable peace that can be a foundation for positive peace. It is this intersectionality gap that we address in this book through the notion of glocalized security and in the process open the door to a sociology of international peace and security.

Indeed, the works in this book abundantly show the intersectionality of the domestic and external drivers of the conflicts that have emerged as regional and international security issues. The violent conflicts in Afghanistan, Iraq, Ukraine, Nagorno-Karabakh, Somalia, Nigeria, and Nepal all assumed regional and international significance. Similarly, the nuclear confrontation between the United States and North Korea as well as Iran are major international security issues. In all of these cases, the sociological notion of intersectionality as first deployed in C. Wright Mills's notion of the sociological imagination and further developed in feminist critiques, such as the work of Patricia Hill Collins,[35] points to a way in which the glocal can be anchored in sociological understanding of the drivers of conflict. Of course, intersectionality in sociology should not just be limited to issues within a single society or the traditional levers of oppression—race, class, ethnicity, religion, and gender.[36] In that sense, intersectionality is a concept as opposed to a matrix of social issues. The task of the sociology of international peace and security is to take this sociological notion of intersectionality into the global, and more importantly into the critiques of globalization, and pin intersectionality into glocalized security. This will then provide a novel way of understanding international peace and security through the intersection of the domestic and external conflict drivers and the new conflict dynamics that is produced in that dialectic, far beyond the way different levels of international relations has been framed.[37] Building on the idea of intersectionality, each chapter in this book shows the glocalized nature of conflicts that have become significant domestic, regional, and international security problems.

Chapter 2 provides a broad picture of the issue of glocalized security by examining how major and emerging powers seek and deploy military power. It examines the intersectionality and the glocality of conflicts through nationalism and the competition for power among major and emerging global powers. In discussing the wars in Afghanistan, Iraq, and Ukraine, the chapter shows how each of these wars has been driven by domestic and external factors and the new war dynamics that emerge in the form of terrorism warfare or hyperproxy war. The national interests of the United States and its Western allies become entangled in wars that are also tied to domestic issues of governance and oppression. In the process, these wars took domestic and external forms as terrorism warfare and hyperproxy war became central to the national security interests of the countries themselves and major powers. Similarly, the confrontation between the United States and North Korea over nuclear weapons fused geopolitics with issues of domestic governance as North Korea's political system became a central issue in its form of acceptable defense arsenal. Domestically, the development of nuclear weapons was a way for the state to boost regime pride and assure the people of the regime's capacity to protect the country, while the totalitarian nature of the regime meant other states viewed it as an aggressive pariah that could not be trusted with nuclear weapons. Furthermore, the chapter shows how external wars and conflicts are fused with domestic narratives of national security that feed into nationalism within major and emerging power countries. In the end, the chapter shows how major powers get involved in conflicts, how they maintain domestic support for their participation in external conflicts, and how civil wars get transformed by the involvement of major powers, such as the case of Russia and the United States in Ukraine. In all of these conflicts, traditional theories of realism, liberal peace, and collective security fail to capture the intersections of domestic and external factors in the conflicts and the way military power is sought and deployed.

Chapter 3 provides a detailed examination of the glocalized nature of the war(s) in Afghanistan. It shows both the domestic and the external drivers that have fueled wars in Afghanistan before and after the 9/11 terrorist attacks on the United States and the subsequent US invasion of Afghanistan. On the one hand are the local issues of governance, including ethnic and regional marginalization, and on the other hand are the interests of various countries within the region and far beyond. Afghanistan's location, history, and domestic instabilities became anchors for the interests of countries such as Pakistan, India, Iran, Russia, United States, Qatar, Saudi Arabia, and China. External actors find Afghanistan's insecurities as threats to their national (security) interests or as opportunities to further their geopolitical interests, which aggravate domestic conflicts and the involvement of other powers. Overall, Afghanistan became a web of contradictory external interests that fed into antagonistic domestic ethnic, political, and economic interests, which constantly undermine peace. In the process, the conflict in Afghanistan has taken the forms of insurgencies for social and political justice, geopolitical proxy wars, and terrorism warfare. In totality, Afghanistan shows the limitations of extant theories based on liberal peace, regional security complex and human security because issues of domestic governance, geopolitics and terrorism all intersect in Afghanistan's long history of ongoing war. In fact, the whole Taliban phenomenon captures the glocalized nature of the Afghan conflict. As we know, the Taliban is a deeply local movement that is focused on local issues of culture, religion, and governance. Yet the Taliban has evoked a lot of international reactions, including ostracization and military invasion. Understanding how the Taliban came to be at the center of international security for over two decades requires a glocalized security approach to the Afghan conflict.

In chapter 4, we see how a local conflict in Azerbaijan became international with major geopolitical significance. Clearly, the conflict in Nagorno-Karabakh is local at its roots. Fundamentally, it is an ethnic conflict between Armenians and Azerbaijanis over marginalization, space, and belonging within Azerbaijan. Nagorno-Karabakh turned into an international conflict right when Armenia and Azerbaijan became independent countries during the disintegration of the Soviet Union, and it morphed into a geopolitical conflict as Russia, Turkey, and Western powers sought to assert influence in the Caucasus region. The stakes in the conflict further increased as Turkey saw an opportunity to enhance its national interests and international prestige by militarily intervening in support of Azerbaijan, which also fed into Turkish domestic politics. With these goals in mind, Turkey saw Nagorno-Karabakh as both a geopolitical and a domestic issue. Similarly, both Armenia and Azerbaijan externalized the conflict in Nagorno-Karabakh. Armenia internationalized the conflict by not only claiming that ethnic Armenians in Nagorno-Karabakh could secede and join it but also seeking military and political support from Western powers for its annexation of Nagorno-Karabakh. Azerbaijan also internationalized the conflict by actively seeking and welcoming Turkish military support and intervention. In the end, the war in Nagorno-Karabakh became an ongoing conflict over ethnic marginalization and a geopolitical issue where Turkey, Russia, and Western powers all tried to gain influence, control, and prestige. Clearly, conventional theories such as liberal peace, regional security complex, and human security do not fully capture the causes or nature of the conflict in Nagorno-Karabakh, which has now become a glocalized security issue.

As explained in chapter 5, we see a similar issue in Somalia. War started in Somalia as a result of domestic political oppression and poor governance. However, the war took a regional and global significance as Somalia became a failed stated where terrorists and criminal networks thrived along with Islamist and non-Islamist insurgents fighting against domestic and external oppressions. As Somalia disintegrated, it became perceived as an ungoverned space that needed to be placed under global liberal governance. However, external interventions by Western and regional powers under the United Nations, the African Union, and various global war on terror military humanitarianism doctrines pushed Somalia into further chaos as terrorism warfare became injected into the war in Somalia. Kenya found itself entangled in the Somali civil war in part because of its huge ethnic Somali population and in part due to its military intervention, which generated further terrorism in Kenya. The Somali civil war came to be characterized by the typical features of new wars—liberal peace, human security, and regional security complex—but none of these theories captures all the elements of the conflict because of its glocalization. Not surprisingly, efforts to restore peace to Somalia through peacekeeping missions or insistence on multiparty elections all failed to lead to sustainable peace. Even Kenya's involvement in Somalia raises questions about the intersection of Kenya's national security interest and the security interests of the major powers at the center of the global war on terror. For Kenya, Somalia became a glocalized security situation precisely because it was protecting broader regional and international security interests while framing its involvement as a national security imperative.

Like Somalia, Iraq too became a space where domestic issues of governance intersect with geopolitics on a much bigger scale as it involved the United States and Iran. Iraq has been a site of contestation between Iran and Western powers even before the 2003 US invasion of Iraq. As we see in chapter 6, the Shi'ite and Kurdish struggles for proper political representation have been long-standing issues in Iraq. However, the Shi'ite cause attracted Iran into Iraqi politics as Iran positioned itself as guardian of Shi'a Islam. Iran's involvement in Iraq in support of the Shi'a has two phases—first, as a war against Saddam Hussein's Ba'athist regime and, later, as a proxy war against the United States during its occupation of Iraq (2003–11). Iran's involvement in Iraq is deeply domestic as it deploys its ideological lever as guardian of the Shi'ites against the Sunni Arabs. At the same time, there is a strong geopolitical component as Iran positioned itself as bulwark against Western intrusions in the region. Both of these found anchors in Iraq as Shi'ites played the double role of leading an insurgency against domestic oppression and the resistance against US occupation. In the process, Iran too played a double role as a stabilizer at times and a destabilizer at others. Overall, neither the Iran-Iraq War nor the civil wars, insurgencies, or terrorism warfare that plague Iraq can be fully understood through a bifurcation of domestic and external conflict drivers or liberal peace. Similarly, neither human security nor regional security complex provides a holistic understanding of the violent conflicts in Iraq. Iraq fits perfectly well into the glocalized security frame as the intersection of domestic and external drivers generated an entirely different breed of war in which a superpower was battling insurgents and a regional power under conditions of terrorism warfare and a proxy war.

Nigeria also shows the intersection of the local and the global through radicalization into violent extremism and the global war on terror. As we see in chapter 7, conflicts over autochthony and landownership among local communities in Kaduna became amplified and transformed in the context of jihadism and the global war on terror that have been waged in Nigeria. Relatively minor local conflicts quickly have become absorbed into the existing modes of extremism, a recurring scenario that has generated deeper concerns for national security from the Nigerian state and opportunities for outsiders enmeshed in the global war on terror to meddle in Nigerian security issues. In the process, common conflicts that have always existed in Kaduna and the Middle Belt region of Nigeria more broadly have quickly accelerated into national and international security issues because of the fusion of domestic and global ideologies of jihadism and terrorism. Local conflicts over land and ethnicity quickly became branded as terrorism, feeding into the global war on terror narrative.

A central issue in the Nigerian case is ideology, both in its local and global variants. Locally, ideologies of ethnic belonging and religious purity germinate into radicalization as they blend with grievance-fueled violent extremism and domestic religious radicalism, such as that practiced by Boko Haram. Internationally, ideologies of global jihadism from al-Qaeda and ISIS as well as the ideologies of the global war on terror and global liberal governance dovetail with discourses of state security and the international order. In that context, the resolution of local conflicts are either misdiagnosed or simply appropriated by state security and global antiterrorism measures. In the process, local conflicts in Nigeria unwittingly slipped into international security issues in ways that the security priorities of local communities do not flow well with those of the Nigerian state or external partners in the global war on terror. Conflicts over land and autochthony in Kaduna got lumped with many other conflicts in the Sahel and Lake Chad regions, creating a giant glocalized security situation that runs across Africa. Of course, the conflicts in Kaduna are tied to issues of political marginalization, poor governance, environmental distress, and human security, which are often the entry points for liberal peace, resource scarcity, and human security discourses. However, none of these captures the intersection of local grievances with ideology at the local and global level as well as the glocalized security approach does.

The sociology of international peace and security is really brought home in the study on Nepal in chapter 8. Nepal's conflict is deeply anchored in structural violence based on ethnicity, class, and ideology—which are all common conflict issues in conventional sociology. However, Indian and Chinese interests became critical determinants of the nature of the conflict, which gravitated between a nonviolent social movement and an armed struggle. The government of Nepal and the insurgents all sought support from India and China as they tried to gain or retain power. Fundamentally, the conflict in Nepal was a struggle for democracy as various antigovernment forces fought the government to end class and ethnic oppression. In the process, insurgents also gravitated toward radical ideologies, notably communism, for which they were branded as terrorists—a label that was deployed to frame a domestic conflict as an international security issue. In essence, the trajectories of the struggle are shaped by the kinds of support India and China were willing to provide in line with their geopolitical interests. Due to the geopolitical considerations of China and India, the Nepalese struggle for democracy fluctuated between an armed struggle and nonviolent resistance. Overall, while the causes of the conflict are domestic, the nature of the conflict and its duration was conditioned by external factors. Moreover, the conflict tapped into extant frames of international security, most notably, democracy, revolution, and terrorism. For the insurgents, their struggle is part of the revolutionary struggles for democracy in the developing world, while for the government, the insurgents were part of global communist movements and terrorists.

Conclusion

In the end, this book asks questions that are increasingly becoming important and urgent as international security issues unfold in numerous civil war situations. Conflicts are increasingly not just domestic or external but both, and in transformative ways. Even more, the nature of conflicts has been significantly transformed from what they used to be during the Cold War period—notably as conflicts that hardly affected the major powers even when those powers participate in the proxy wars. With this transition in mind, we ask: How does the fusion of domestic issues and interests with external ones generate new security situations that further undermine international peace and security? This question is examined in conjunction with the problem of disentangling domestic issues and interests from the external ones so as to resolve violent conflicts. As such, the book focused on cases and issues that have emerged as problematic for human security, state security, and the regional and international order, notably in Afghanistan, Iraq, Azerbaijan, Somalia, Nigeria, Ukraine, Nepal, and North Korea. Overall, this book makes three important contributions to the literature: (a) case studies of some of the most contentious and challenging conflicts across various regions, (b) the concept of glocalized security, and (c) the sociology of international peace and security.

First, the rich historical cases in this book bring up three critical elements in our understanding of international security: (a) national interests, (b) terrorism, and (c) intersectionality. These are issues that cut across cases and show how conflicts become glocalized. Through the framings of national interests, we see how domestic political issues got entangled in external interests fueling more war. This is most evident in the way emerging and major powers seek and deploy military power through nationalistic narratives. In addition to the nuclear confrontation between the United States and North Korea, we see this issue of national (security) interest in the wars in Ukraine, Afghanistan, Iraq, Nagorno-Karabakh, Somalia, and Nepal. In all of these cases, external actors have fused their national interests into the conflicts, making them either active participants or enablers of the wars. The cases also clearly show how terrorism and the global war on terror became a central issue in international security. This is most evident in Afghanistan, Iraq, Somalia, and Nigeria, which are all characterized by terrorism warfare and an expansive global war on terror. Even in Nagorno-Karabakh and Ukraine, where the wars largely remain conventional, we see frames of terrorism in practice. In many ways, the glocal nature of wars lies in the intersectionality of conflict drivers. In all the cases, there are domestic and external issues driving the wars. Overall, the cases not only are individually rich but also show the intersectionality of international security issues.

The second element that clearly emerges from the book is the notion of glocalized security, which has been developed and deployed throughout the chapters. By drawing on the discourses and critiques of globalization theory, the book neatly shows the global and local nature of international security. This adds conceptual depth by not only bringing globalization discourses into international security but also using regionally and globally significant security issues to show the limitations of globalization theory. Glocalized security then becomes a conceptualization of the growing fusion of domestic and external drivers of conflicts and the transformation of contemporary security issues.

Finally, the book takes us to a new frontier, which I refer to as the sociology of international peace and security. Indeed, the notion of glocalized security is inspired by the sociological notion of intersectionality. Sociological studies of (social) order can be useful in understanding international peace and security as the global and local are continuously fused. However, for sociology to extend from its focus on domestic order to international order, it needs to deploy both the concepts of globalization and intersectionality into international security issues. This book is a step in that direction. It has developed the concept of glocalized security, shown the importance of intersectionality in the way we understand conflict drivers, and examined numerous cases where the conflicts are truly glocal. All of these should be a good place to start as we bring sociological thinking into international peace and security issues.

Notes

1. Bah, *African Security*; Bah, *International Security and Peacebuilding*.
2. Stampnitzky, "Toward a Sociology of 'Security,'" 631–33; Wæver, "Towards a Political Sociology of Security Studies," 649–58.
3. Mills, "Promise," 3–24; Romero, *Introducing Intersectionality*; Carastathis, *Intersectionality*; Collins and Bilge *Intersectionality*.
4. Collins, *Black Feminist Thought*; Oliver and Shapiro, *Black Wealth/White Wealth*; Bonilla-Silva, *Racism without Racists*; Galtung, "Violence, Peace, and Peace Research," 167–91; Galtung, "Cultural Violence," 291–305.
5. Galtung, "Structural Theory of Imperialism," 59–108; Galtung, "Cultural Violence," 291–305; Kaldor, *New and Old Wars*; Autesserre, *Peaceland*; Bah, *International Security and Peacebuilding*; Bah and Emmanuel, *International Statebuilding in West Africa*.

6. Buzan et al. *Regions and Powers*; Duffield, *Global Governance and the New Wars*; Lake, "Regional Hierarchy," 35–58; Adler and Greve, "When Security Community Meets Balance of Power," 59–84; Waltz, *Man, the State, and War*; Waltz, *Theory of International Politics*.

7. Galtung, "Violence, Peace, and Peace Research," 167–91; Prunier, *Africa's World War*; Paris, *At War's End*; Bah, "Contours of New Humanitarianism," 3–26; Bah and Emmanuel, *International Statebuilding in West Africa*.

8. Buzan et al. *Regions and Powers*; Charbonneau, "Climate of Counterinsurgency and the Future of Security in the Sahel," 97–104; Collier and Hoeffler, "On Economic Causes of Civil War," 563–73; Duffield, *Global Governance and the New Wars*; Bah, *International Security and Peacebuilding*; Glasius and Kaldor, *Human Security Doctrine for Europe*; Posen, "Security Dilemma and Ethnic Conflict," 27–47; Adebajo, *Building Peace in West Africa*; Bah and Emmanuel, "Migration Cooperation between Africa and Europe."

9. Boutros-Ghali, "Agenda for Peace"; Brahimi, "Report of the Panel on United Nations Peace Operations"; Annan, "Two Concepts of Sovereignty," 49–50; Bah and Emmanuel, "Positive Peace and the Methodology of Costing Peacebuilding Needs: The Case of Burundi," 299–318.

10. Durkheim, *Elementary Forms of the Religious Life*; Durkheim, *Division of Labor in Society*; Parsons, *Social Systems and the Evolution of Action Theory*; Parsons, *Structure of Social Action*.

11. Tucker, *Marx-Engels Reader*; DuBois, *Gift of Black folk*.

12. Gerth, Weber, and Mills, *From Max Weber*; Weber, *Protestant Ethic and the Spirit of Capitalism*; Weber, *Economy and Society*; Habermas, *Legitimation Crisis*; Offe, *Contradictions of the Welfare State*.

13. Foucault, *Discipline and Punishment*.

14. Wallerstein, *Capitalist World-Economy*; Wallerstein, "Globalization or the Age of Transition?," 249–65; Wallerstein, *Historical Capitalism with Capitalist Civilization*.

15. Beck, *What Is globalization?*; Beck, Sznaider, and Winter, *Global America?*; Baudrillard, *Gulf War Did Not Take Place*; Tonkiss, *Contemporary Economic Sociology*.

16. McGrew and Poku, *Globalization, Development and Human Security*; Duffield, *Global Governance and the New*.

17. Neumann, *Behemoth*; Mann, *Fascists*.

18. Arendt, *Origins of Totalitarianism*; Marcuse, *One-Dimensional Man*; Simon, *Gramsci's Political Thought*.

19. Bah, "Racial Profiling and the War on Terror," 76–100; Harris, *Profiles in Injustice*; Welch, "Race, Ethnicity, and the War on Terror"; Ramsay, Cozine, and Comiskey, *Theoretical Foundations of Homeland Security*.

20. Simmel, "Sociology of Conflict," 490–525; Bramsen, *Micro-Sociology of Peace and Conflict*; Trimikliniotis, "Sociology of Reconciliation," *Current Sociology* 61, no. 2 (2013): 244–64.

21. Moore, *Social Origins of Dictatorship and Democracy*; Tilly, "Coercion, Capital, and European States, AD 990–1990"; Foucault, *Discipline and Punishment*; Malešević, *Sociology of War and Violence*; Bah, "State Decay and Civil War," 199–216; Bah, "Contours of New Humanitarianism," 3–26.

22. Stampnitzky, "Toward a Sociology of 'Security,'" 631–33; Wæver, "Towards a Political Sociology of Security Studies," 649–58; Buzan and Hansen, "Beyond the Evolution of International Security Studies?," 659–67.

23. Bah and Emmanuel, *International Statebuilding in West Africa*.

24. Bah, *African Security*.

25. Friedman, *World Is Flat*; Francis, *End of History and the Last Man*.

26. Sassen, *Global City*; Köhler and Wissen, "Glocalizing Protest," 942–51; Kjeldgaard and Askegaard. "Glocalization of Youth Culture," 231–47; Giulianotti and Robertson, "Globalization of Football," 545–68.

27. Robertson, "Globality and Modernity," 153–61; Robertson, "Globalisation or Glocalisation?," 33–52; Robertson, "Glocalization," 25–44; Robertson and White, "What Is Globalization," 54–66; Beck, *What Is Globalization?*
28. Bah, *African Security.*
29. Jackson and Rosberg, *Personal Rule in Black Africa*; Bah and Bangura, "Landholding and the Creation of Lumpen Tenants in Freetown," 1289–305; Bayart, *State in Africa*; Bah, "Changing World Order and the Future of Democracy in Sub-Saharan Africa," 3–12; Bratton and Van de Walle, *Democratic Experiments in Africa.*
30. Davidson, *Black Man's Burden*; Mazrui, "Blood of Experience," 28–34; Mazrui, *Africa's International Relations*; Said, *Orientalism.*
31. Babatunde, "Environmental Insecurity and Poverty in the Niger Delta: A case of Ilaje," 36–59; Turner et al., "Livelihood Transitions and the Changing Nature of Farmer–Herder Conflict in Sahelian West Africa," 183–206; Collier and Hoeffler, "On Economic Causes of Civil War," 563–73.
32. Varin, "No Opportunity Lost," 141–57; Bah, *International Security and Peacebuilding*; Njoku, "Merchants of Terror," 83–107; Ladan, "Transnational Terrorism Revisited," 105–26; Nwankpa, "Understanding the Local-Global Dichotomy and Drivers of the Boko Haram Insurgency," 43–64; Mamdani, "Good Muslim, Bad Muslim," 766–75.
33. Kaldor, *New and Old Wars*; Duffield, *Global Governance and the New Wars.*
34. Kelsen, "Collective Security and Collective Self-Defense under the Charter of the United Nations," 783–96; Kupchan and Kupchan, "Promise of Collective Security," 52–61; Buzan et al., *Regions and Powers.*
35. Mills, "Promise," 3–24; Collins, *Black Feminist Thought*; Collins and Bilge, *Intersectionality.*
36. Romero, *Introducing Intersectionality*; Carastathis, *Intersectionality*; Oliver and Shapiro, *Black Wealth/White Wealth*; Bonilla-Silva, *Racism without Racists*; Galtung, "Violence, Peace, and Peace Research," 167–91; Galtung, "Cultural Violence," 291–305.
37. Buzan et al. *Regions and Powers*; Wallerstein, *Capitalist World-Economy*; Bah, *African Security*; Waltz, *Man, the State, and War*; Waltz, *Theory of International Politics.*

References

Adebajo, Adekeye. *Building Peace in West Africa: Liberia, Sierra Leone, and Guinea-Bissau.* Boulder, CO: Lynne Rienner, 2002.
Adler, Emanuel, and Patricia Greve. "When Security Community Meets Balance of Power: Overlapping Regional Mechanisms of Security Governance." *Review of International Studies* 35, no. 1 (2009): 59–84.
Annan, Kofi A. "Two Concepts of Sovereignty." *Economist* 18, no. 9 (1999): 49–50.
Arendt, Hannah. *The Origins of Totalitarianism.* Boston: Houghton Mifflin Harcourt, 1973.
Autesserre, Sverine. *Peaceland: Conflict Resolution and the Everyday Politics of International Intervention.* Cambridge: Cambridge University Press, 2014.
Babatunde, Abosede Omowumi. "Environmental Insecurity and Poverty in the Niger Delta: A case of Ilaje." *African Conflict and Peacebuilding Review* 7, no. 2 (2017): 36–59.
Bah, Abu Bakarr, ed. *African Security: Local Issues and Global Connections.* Athens: Ohio University Press, 2024.
———. "Changing World Order and the Future of Democracy in sub-Saharan Africa," *Proteus: A Journal of Ideas* 21, no. 1 (Spring 2004): 3–12.
———. "The Contours of New Humanitarianism: War and Peacebuilding in Sierra Leone." *Africa Today* 60, no. 1 (2013): 3–26.
———, ed. *International Security and Peacebuilding: Africa, the Middle East, and Europe.* Bloomington: Indiana University Press, 2017.

———. "Racial Profiling and the War on Terror: Changing Trends and Perspectives." *Ethnic Studies Review* 29, no. 1 (2006): 76–100.

———. "State Decay and Civil War: A Discourse on Power in Sierra Leone." *Critical Sociology* 37, no. 2 (2011): 199–216.

Bah, Abu Bakarr, and Ibrahim Bangura. "Landholding and the Creation of Lumpen Tenants in Freetown: Youth Economic Survival and Patrimonialism in Postwar Sierra Leone." *Critical Sociology* 49, no. 7–8 (2023): 1289–305.

Bah, Abu Bakarr, and Nikolas Emmanuel. *International Statebuilding in West Africa: Civil Wars and New Humanitarianism in Sierra Leone, Liberia, and Côte d'Ivoire*. Bloomington: Indiana University Press, 2024.

———. "Migration Cooperation between Africa and Europe: Understanding the Role of Incentives." In *Oxford Research Encyclopedia of International Studies*. Oxford University Press, published online September 15, 2022. DOI: https://doi.org/10.1093/acrefore/9780190846626.013.735.

———. "Positive Peace and the Methodology of Costing Peacebuilding Needs: The Case of Burundi." *Administrative Theory & Praxis* 43, no. 3 (2020): 299–318.

Baudrillard, Jean. *The Gulf War Did Not Take Place*. Sydney, Australia: Power, 2012.

Bayart, Jean-François. *The State in Africa: The Politics of the Belly*. Cambridge: Polity, 2009.

Beck, Ulrich. *What Is Globalization?* Hoboken, NJ: John Wiley and Sons, 2018.

Beck, Ulrich, Natan Sznaider, and Rainer Winter, eds. *Global America? The Cultural Consequences of Globalization*. Liverpool: Liverpool University Press, 2003.

Bonilla-Silva, Eduardo. *Racism without Racists: Color-Blind Racism and the Persistence of Racial Inequality in the United States*. Lanham, MD: Rowman and Littlefield, 2006.

Boutros-Ghali, Boutros. "An Agenda for Peace: Preventive Diplomacy, Peacemaking and Peace-Keeping: Report of the Secretary-General Pursuant to the Statement Adopted by the Summit Meeting of the Security Council on 31 January 1992." New York: United Nations.

Brahimi, Lakhdar. "Report of the Panel on United Nations Peace Operations." A/55/305 S/2000/809. New York: United Nations, 2000.

Bratton, Michael, and Nicholas Van de Walle, *Democratic Experiments in Africa: Regime Transitions in Comparative Perspective*. Cambridge: Cambridge University Press, 1997.

Bramsen, Isabel. *The Micro-Sociology of Peace and Conflict*. Cambridge: Cambridge University Press, 2023.

Buzan, Barry, and Lene Hansen. "Beyond the Evolution of International Security Studies?" *Security Dialogue* 41, no. 6 (2010): 659–67.

Buzan, Barry and Ole Wæver. *Regions and Powers: The Structure of International Security*. Cambridge: Cambridge University Press, 2003.

Carastathis, Anna. *Intersectionality: Origins, Contestations, Horizons*. Lincoln: University of Nebraska Press, 2016.

Charbonneau, Bruno. "The Climate of Counterinsurgency and the Future of Security in the Sahel." *Environmental Science and Policy* 138 (2022): 97–104.

Collier, Paul, and Anke Hoeffler. "On Economic Causes of Civil War." *Oxford Economic Papers* 50, no. 4 (1998): 563–73.

Collins, Patricia Hill. *Black Feminist Thought: Knowledge, Consciousness, and the Politics of Empowerment*. London: Routledge, 2002.

Collins, Patricia Hill, and Sirma Bilge *Intersectionality*. Cambridge: Polity, 2016.

Davidson, Basil. *The Black Man's Burden: Africa and the Curse of the Nation-State*. New York: Times Press, 1993.

DuBois, W. E. B. *The Gift of Black folk: The Negroes in the Making of America*. Garden City, NY: Square One, 2009.

Duffield, Mark. *Global Governance and the New Wars: The Merging of Development and Security*. London: Zed Books, 2014.

Durkheim, Emile. *The Division of Labor in Society*. New York: Free Press, 1964.
———. *The Elementary Forms of the Religious Life*. London: George Allan and Unwin, 1915.
Foucault, Michel. *Discipline and Punishment: The Birth of the Prison*. New York: Vintage, 1989.
Friedman, Thomas L. *The World Is Flat: A Brief History of the Twenty-First Century*. Updated and expanded ed. New York: Macmillan, 2006.
Fukuyama, Francis. *The End of History and the Last Man*. New York: Free Press, 1992.
Galtung, Johan. "Cultural Violence." *Journal of Peace Research* 27, no. 3 (1990): 291–305.
———. "A Structural Theory of Imperialism." In *Imperialism*, 59–108. London: Routledge, 2023.
———. "Violence, Peace, and Peace Research." *Journal of Peace Research* 6, no. 3 (1969): 167–91.
Gerth, Hans Heinrich, and Wright Mills. *From Max Weber: Essays in Sociology*. London: Routledge, 2013.
Giulianotti, Richard, and Roland Robertson. "The Globalization of Football: A Study in the Glocalization of the 'Serious Life.'" *British Journal of Sociology* 55, no. 4 (2004): 545–68.
Glasius, Marlies, and Mary Kaldor. *A Human Security Doctrine for Europe*. London: Routledge, 2005.
Habermas, Jurgen. *Legitimation Crisis*. Boston, MA: Beacon Press, 1975.
Harris, David A. *Profiles in Injustice: Why Racial Profiling Cannot Work*. New York: New Press, 2003.
Jackson, Robert H., and Carl Gustav Rosberg, *Personal Rule in Black Africa: Prince, Autocrat, Prophet, Tyrant*. Berkley: University of California Press, 1982.
Kaldor, Mary. *New and Old Wars: Organised Violence in a Global Era*. Hoboken, NJ: John Wiley and Sons, 2013.
Kelsen, Hans. "Collective Security and Collective Self-Defense under the Charter of the United Nations." *American Journal of International Law* 42, no. 4 (1948): 783–96.
Kjeldgaard, Dannie, and Søren Askegaard. "The Glocalization of Youth Culture: The Global Youth Segment as Structures of Common Difference." *Journal of Consumer Research* 33, no. 2 (2006): 231–47.
Köhler, Bettina, and Markus Wissen. "Glocalizing Protest: Urban Conflicts and the Global Social Movements." *International Journal of Urban and Regional Research* 27, no. 4 (2003): 942–51.
Kupchan, A. Charles, and Clifford A. Kupchan. "The Promise of Collective Security." *International Security* 20, no. 1 (1995): 52–61.
Ladan, Usman. "Transnational Terrorism Revisited: Is Boko Haram an al-Qaeda Affiliate?" *African Conflict and Peacebuilding Review* 12, no. 1 (2022): 105–26.
Lake, David A. "Regional Hierarchy: Authority and Local International Order." *Review of International Studies* 35, no. 1 (2009): 35–58.
Malešević, Siniša. *The Sociology of War and Violence*. Cambridge: Cambridge University Press, 2010.
Mamdani, Mahmood. "Good Muslim, Bad Muslim: A Political Perspective on Culture and Terrorism." *American Anthropologist* 104, no. 3 (2002): 766–75.
Mann, Michael. *Fascists*. Cambridge: Cambridge University Press, 2004.
Marcuse, Herbert. *One-Dimensional Man: Studies in the Ideology of Advanced Industrial Society*. London: Routledge, 2013.
Mazrui, Ali A. *Africa's International Relations: The Diplomacy of Dependency and Change*. London: Routledge, 2019.
———. "The Blood of Experience: The Failed State and Political Collapse in Africa." *World Policy Journal* 12, no. 1 (1995): 28–34.
McGrew, Anthony G., and Nana K. Poku, eds. *Globalization, Development and Human Security*. Cambridge: Polity, 2007.
Mills, C. Wright. "The Promise." In *The Sociological Imagination*, 3–24. Oxford: Oxford University Press, 1959. http://people.uncw.edu/levyd/soc105/Mills,%20the%20Promise.PDF.

Moore, Barrington, Jr. *Social Origins of Dictatorship and Democracy: Lord and Peasant in the Making of the Modern World*. Boston: Beacon Press, 1966.

Neumann, Franz Leopold. *Behemoth: The Structure and Practice of National Socialism, 1933–1944*. Lanham, MD: Rowman and Littlefield, 2009.

Njoku, Emeka Thaddues, "Merchants of Terror: Neo-Patrimonialism, Counterterrorism Economy, and Expansion of Terrorism in Nigeria." *African Conflict & Peacebuilding Review* 10, no. 2 (2020): 83–107.

Nwankpa, Michael. "Understanding the Local-Global Dichotomy and Drivers of the Boko Haram Insurgency." *African Conflict & Peacebuilding Review* 10, no. 2 (2020): 43–64.

Offe, Claus. *Contradictions of the Welfare State*. Edited by John Keane. Cambridge, MA: MIT Press, 1984.

Oliver, Melvin, and Thomas Shapiro. *Black Wealth/White Wealth: A New Perspective on Racial Inequality*. London: Routledge, 2013.

Paris, Roland. *At War's End: Building Peace after Civil Conflict*. Cambridge: Cambridge University Press, 2004.

Parsons, Talcott. *Social Systems and the Evolution of Action Theory*. New York: Free Press, 1977.

———. *The Structure of Social Action*. New York: Free Press, 1949.

Posen, Barry R. "The Security Dilemma and Ethnic Conflict." *Survival* 35, no. 1 (1993): 27–47.

Prunier, Gérard. *Africa's World War: Congo, the Rwandan Genocide, and the Making of a Continental Catastrophe*. New York: Oxford University Press, 2008.

Ramsay, James. D., Keith Cozine, and John Comiskey, eds. *Theoretical Foundations of Homeland Security: Strategies, Operations, and Structures*. London: Routledge, 2020.

Robertson, Roland. "Glocalization: Time-Space and Homogeneity-Heterogeneity." *Global Modernities* 2, no. 1 (1995): 25–44.

———. "Globalisation or Glocalisation?" *Journal of International Communication* 1, no. 1 (1994): 33–52.

———. "Globality and Modernity." *Theory, Culture and Society* 9, no. 2 (1992): 153–61.

Robertson, Roland, and Kathleen E. White. "What Is Globalization." In *Blackwell Companion to Globalization*, edited by George Ritzer, 54–66. Malden, MA: Blackwell Publishing, 2007.

Romero, Mary. *Introducing Intersectionality*. Hoboken, NJ: John Wiley and Sons, 2017.

Said, Edward. *Orientalism: Western Concepts of the Orient*. New York: Pantheon, 1978.

Sassen, Saskia. *The Global City: New York, London, Tokyo*. Princeton, NJ: Princeton University Press, 2013.

Simon, Roger. *Gramsci's Political Thought: An Introduction*. London: Lawrence and Wishart, 2015.

Simmel, Georg. "The Sociology of Conflict." *American Journal of Sociology* 9, no. 4 (1904): 490–525.

Stampnitzky, Lisa. "Toward a Sociology of 'Security.'" *Sociological Forum* 28, no. 3 (2013): 631–33.

Tilly, Charles. *Coercion, Capital, and European States, AD 990–1990*. Hoboken, NJ: Wiley-Blackwell, 1992.

Tonkiss, Fran. *Contemporary Economic Sociology: Globalization, Production, Inequality*. London: Routledge, 2006.

Trimikliniotis, Nicos. "Sociology of Reconciliation: Learning from Comparing Violent Conflicts and Reconciliation Processes." *Current Sociology* 61, no. 2 (2013): 244–64.

Tucker, Robert C., ed. *The Marx-Engels Reader*. New York: W. W. Norton, 1978.

Turner, Matthew D., et al., "Livelihood Transitions and the Changing Nature of Farmer-Herder Conflict in Sahelian West Africa," *Journal of Development Studies* 47, no. 2 (2011): 183–206.

Varin, Caroline. "No Opportunity Lost: The ISWAP Insurgency in the Changing Climate of Lake Chad Region." *African Conflict & Peacebuilding Review* 10, no. 2 (2020): 141–57.

Wæver, Ole. "Towards a Political Sociology of Security Studies." *Security Dialogue* 41, no. 6 (2010): 649–58.
Wallerstein, Immanuel. "Globalization or the Age of Transition? A Long-Term View of the Trajectory of the World-System." *International Sociology* 15, no. 2 (2000): 249–65.
———. *Historical capitalism with capitalist civilization*. London: Verso, 1995.
———. *The Capitalist World-Economy*. Cambridge: Cambridge University Press, 1979.
Waltz, Kenneth Neal. *Man, the State, and War: A Theoretical Analysis*. New York: Columbia University Press, 2001.
———. *Theory of International Politics*. Long Grove, IL: Waveland Press, 2010.
Weber, Max. *The Protestant Ethic and the Spirit of Capitalism*. London: Routledge, 2013.
———. *Economy and Society*. Berkeley: University of California Press, 2013.
Welch, Kelly. "Race, Ethnicity, and the War on Terror." In *Oxford Research Encyclopedia of Criminology and Criminal Justice*. Oxford University Press, published online July 29, 2019. DOI: https://doi.org/10.1093/acrefore/9780190264079.013.335.

ABU BAKARR BAH is Presidential Research Professor of Sociology and Chair of the Department of Sociology at Northern Illinois University. He is Editor in Chief of *African Conflict & Peacebuilding Review*, African Editor for *Critical Sociology*, and Founding Director of the Institute for Research and Policy Integration in Africa (IRPIA). His works include *International Statebuilding in West Africa* (with Nikolas Emmanuel, Bloomington: Indiana University Press, 2024), *African States* (Alany, NY: SUNY Press, 2025), *African Security* (Athens: Ohio University Press, 2024), *Post-Conflict Institutional Design* (London: Zed Books, 2020), *International Security and Peacebuilding* (Bloomington: Indiana University Press, 2017), and *Breakdown and Reconstitution* (Lanham, MD: Lexington Books, 2005). His articles have been published in top journals such as *African Affairs*; *Administrative Theory & Praxis*; *Critical Sociology*; *Journal of International Peacekeeping*; *International Journal of Politics, Culture, and Society*; and *Africa Today*. Bah has been an invited speaker at major institutions such as Stanford University, the University of Illinois at Urbana Champaign, the University of South Florida, Virginia Commonwealth University, the Global Center for Pluralism (Canada), the Social Science Research Council (New York), the US State Department, ETH (Switzerland), the University of Nairobi (Kenya), Laikipia University (Kenya), Renmin University (China), and Sant'Anna School of Advanced Studies (Italy).

INDEX

Afghanistan, 1, 4, 7, 10, 12, 13, 14, 15, 16, 26, 35, 36–37, 38, 39, 40, 41, 56–57, 69–70, 71, 72–73, 73–74, 75, 76, 77, 78–79, 80–81, 82–83, 83–84, 85–86, 86–87, 87–88, 88–89, 89–90n32, 90n35, 103, 124, 126, 128, 223, 228, 229, 230, 234–35
African National Congress, 201
African Union (AU), 135, 190, 231
African Union Mission in Somalia (AMISOM), 122, 125, 127, 130, 131, 132, 135, 142n24
African Union Peace and Security Council, 125
Aliyev, İlham, 102, 107, 108–9
al-Qaeda, 16–17, 25, 35, 36, 37, 38, 41, 69, 70–71, 72, 73, 74–75, 76, 78, 79, 80, 88, 124, 163, 173, 174, 183, 233
Al-Shabaab, 122, 123, 124–25, 126, 127, 130, 131, 132, 133–34, 134–35, 136, 137–38, 139, 140
American exceptionalism, 39, 42, 47, 55
AQIM (al-Qaeda in the Islamic Maghreb), 37
armed conflict, 8, 48, 223
Armed Conflict Location and Event Data Project (ACLED), 179
armed drones/unmanned aerial vehicles (UAVs), 106, 107, 108, 111, 112
Armenia, 1, 11, 13, 14, 16, 97, 98, 99–100, 101, 102, 103, 104, 105, 106–7, 107–8, 108–9, 111, 112, 152, 230, 231
Azerbaijan, 1, 11, 13, 14, 97, 98, 99–100, 100–101, 102–3, 104–5, 105–6, 107, 108, 109, 110, 111, 112, 223, 230–31, 234

Bush, George H. W., 39–40, 75
Bush, George W., 37, 38–39, 40, 41, 42, 75
Bush doctrine, 36, 37, 38, 39, 42

China, 6, 10, 11, 14, 17, 25, 28, 32, 33, 34, 45, 46–47, 48, 53, 54, 69, 70, 71, 74, 77, 78–79, 80, 81, 83, 84, 88, 96, 199–200, 200–201, 205, 206, 207, 208, 209, 210, 211, 214, 215, 216, 230, 233
Christian Association of Nigeria (CAN), 174, 186
civil resistance, 199–200, 201–2, 203, 204, 205, 206, 207, 209, 210, 211, 212, 213, 214, 215, 216–17
civil war, 1, 6, 7, 8, 10, 36, 41, 56, 86, 97–98, 105, 108, 111, 122, 123, 130, 133, 157, 162, 176–77, 181, 199, 202, 212, 213, 224, 229, 231, 232, 234
class, 13, 14, 43, 73, 157, 205, 211, 223, 228–29, 233
Cold War, 1, 7, 9–10, 24, 51, 55, 72, 86, 99, 140, 141, 166n5, 199, 202, 204, 234
collective security system (CSS), 121, 122–23, 125, 127–28, 129, 130, 131, 132, 134, 135, 136–37, 139, 140, 141
collectivism, 128–29, 130, 134, 139–40
colonialism, 6, 224, 227
communal violence, 16, 172
conflict, 8, 9, 10, 12, 13, 14, 15, 16, 24, 25, 26, 27, 35, 36, 39–40, 43, 44, 45, 46, 48, 52, 54, 70, 74, 83, 84, 86, 87, 88, 95–96, 97, 100–101, 102, 103, 104–5, 106, 107, 108, 109, 110, 122, 123, 126, 128, 129–30, 134, 135–36, 140, 141, 152, 156, 157, 158, 160, 166n5, 181, 182, 186–87, 188, 189, 190, 192n63, 199, 202, 203, 204, 208–9, 211, 212, 213, 217, 235; causes of, 2–3, 226; conflict zones, 2; ethnic conflict, 99–100, 172–73, 230; studies of, 2, 233–34; types of, 6–7, 11, 56–57, 77, 94, 98, 111–12, 205, 222–23, 224, 225, 229–30, 230–31, 233. *See also* indigene-settler; violence
conflict drivers, 4, 13, 14, 56, 173, 223, 225, 226–27, 228, 229, 232, 235

243

conflict resolution, 94, 98, 100, 224, 226
Côte d'Ivoire, 1, 186–87
counterinsurgency, 38
counterterrorism, 74, 82, 130, 134, 135, 141, 192n63, 228

Democratic Republic of Congo, 1, 8, 130
domestic issues, 2, 4, 13, 26, 43, 47, 56–57, 71, 87, 128, 200, 223, 229, 232, 234
domestic security, 48, 70, 71, 87–88, 127, 131, 133–34, 152

East Turkestan Islamic Movement (ETIM), 69–70, 78, 80, 83, 88
Erdoğan, Recep Tayyip, 97, 98, 105, 106, 109, 110, 111, 112
ethnic conflict, 99, 172, 230
ethnicity, 2, 12, 105, 168n47, 176, 181, 223, 227–28, 232, 233
external issues, 1, 2, 4, 13, 56, 223, 235

foreign policy, 83, 84, 88, 94, 95, 96, 97, 98, 102, 104, 105, 106, 108, 109, 110–11, 112, 149, 150, 151, 153, 154, 155, 167n9, 167n10, 167n12, 167n13, 208, 215
Fulani, 8, 174, 180, 182, 183, 184–85, 186, 187, 188, 189

geopolitics, 1–2, 7, 47, 49–50, 51, 57, 215, 224, 229, 230, 232
global liberal governance, 7, 15, 224, 227, 231, 233
global-local, 121
glocalization, 3, 4–5, 26–27, 70, 71, 74–75, 88, 96, 111, 121, 122, 123, 128, 130, 149, 174, 176, 181, 185, 200, 204, 216, 231
glocalized security, 2, 3, 4, 5, 6, 7, 8, 9, 10, 12–13, 14–15, 16, 26, 35, 43, 47, 48, 55, 56, 57, 70, 74, 88, 128, 139, 149, 150, 163, 166, 190, 200, 201, 202, 205, 216, 222, 223, 224, 226, 227, 228, 229, 230, 231, 232, 233, 234, 235
guerrillas, 73, 76, 82, 202, 207, 208, 210, 215

Hausa, 174, 182, 189
Hausa-Fulani, 177, 182
hegemony, 14, 15, 16, 25, 26, 51, 150, 152, 155, 166, 182, 225
Horn of Africa, 122, 124, 125, 126, 127, 130, 131, 132, 134, 136, 140

ideological vector, 11–12, 149, 150, 151, 152, 153, 155, 157, 158–59, 160, 161, 162, 164, 165, 166, 167n9, 167n13, 167n15

India, 10, 11, 14, 17, 25, 32, 34, 48, 53, 54, 69, 71–72, 76, 80, 82, 86–87, 181, 200, 205–6, 206–7, 208, 209, 210, 211, 212, 213, 214, 215–16, 218n57, 230, 233
indigene-settler, 173, 175, 176–77, 183, 185
individual security system, 139
insurgency, 11, 78, 81, 123, 140, 156–57, 163, 165–66, 173–74, 203, 207, 208, 210, 213, 215, 232
international prestige, 95, 96, 97, 98, 99, 108, 109, 111–12
international security, 1, 2, 3, 4, 5, 6, 9, 11, 13, 15, 24–25, 26–27, 31, 32, 33, 35, 39, 43, 47, 48, 52, 55, 56, 71, 76, 87–88, 99, 127, 128, 132, 139, 140, 165, 223, 226, 228, 229, 230, 231, 232, 233–34, 235
International Security Assistance Force, 76
intersectionality, 2–3, 5, 10, 13, 14, 222, 223, 226, 227, 228–29, 234, 235
intervention, 1–2, 4, 6–7, 8, 10–11, 12–13, 14, 15, 16, 39, 70, 74, 94, 95, 97, 98, 105, 111, 121, 122, 124, 127, 128, 131–32, 133–34, 134–35, 136, 138, 139, 140, 141, 150, 153, 199, 200, 201, 202, 204, 205, 206, 214, 216, 217, 223, 231
Iran, 6, 10, 11–12, 13–14, 16, 25, 32, 34, 40, 43, 47, 53, 54, 56, 57, 69, 71, 72–73, 73–74, 77, 80, 81, 85–86, 97, 102, 148–49, 149–50, 151, 152, 153, 154, 155–56, 156–57, 158, 159, 160, 161–66, 167n18, 168n41, 228, 230, 232
Iran-Iraq War, 149, 156, 232
Iraq, 1, 4, 7, 10, 11–12, 12–13, 13–14, 15, 16, 26, 35, 36, 38, 39–40, 40–41, 41–42, 43, 56–57, 74, 96, 97, 128, 148, 149–50, 151, 152, 153, 155, 156, 157, 158, 159, 160, 161, 162–63, 163–64, 165–66, 167n18, 167n30, 168n41, 168n47, 168n48, 168n57, 169n72, 223, 228, 229, 232, 234–35
Islamic State in Iraq and Syria (ISIS), 25, 35, 37, 42, 97, 148, 157–58, 163–64, 165, 173, 233
Islamic State—Khorasan (ISKP), 69, 74, 78, 79–80, 86
Islamic Supreme Council of Iraq (ISCI), 161, 162

Jamiat Ulama-e-Islam (JUI-F), 73, 89–90n32
jihad, 72, 76, 84, 86, 89–90n32
jihadi, 125, 163, 165, 173–74, 179, 180, 181, 183, 190
jihadism, 14, 42, 71, 75, 228, 232, 233
jihadists, 85, 179, 181

Kenya, 8, 10–11, 12, 13, 14, 36, 122, 123, 124, 125, 126–27, 130, 131, 132, 133–35, 136–37, 138–39, 140, 141, 142n23, 176, 203, 231

Kenya Defense Force (KDF), 125, 126, 127, 131–32, 133, 135, 136, 137, 138
Kurdistan Workers' Party (PKK), 97, 106, 110

Latin America, 7–8, 9
liberalism, 7, 35, 42, 48, 51, 54, 55–56, 224
Liberia, 1, 7, 8
Libya, 1, 4, 6, 7, 32, 35, 97, 98, 105, 106, 108, 111, 128, 204
Libyan National Army (LNA), 98
localization, 128, 149–50

Mali, 1, 4, 7, 8, 128
military power, 10, 13, 16, 24, 25–26, 31–32, 32–33, 34–35, 43, 45, 56, 95–96, 225, 229–30, 234
militias, 75, 136, 149, 150, 151, 157, 161, 162, 163, 164–65, 166, 169n84, 173, 175, 179, 181–82, 184
Minsk Group, 100–101, 108, 109
Miyetti Allah Cattle Breeders Association of Nigeria (MACBAN), 177, 184, 185, 186, 188

Nagorno-Karabakh, 7, 10, 11, 12, 13, 14, 16, 95, 97, 98, 99, 100, 101, 103, 104, 105, 106, 107–8, 110, 111, 112, 228, 230, 231, 234, 235
national interest, 2, 6, 10, 11, 12, 13, 14, 17, 24, 25, 27, 29, 30, 31, 56, 95, 108, 129, 134, 136, 224, 227, 228, 229, 230–31, 234
nationalism, 10, 14, 24, 26, 27–28, 29, 30, 31, 34–35, 38–39, 42, 47, 48, 51, 54, 55, 56, 72, 105, 162, 164, 203, 223, 226, 229
national security, 1–2, 6, 7, 10, 11, 12, 13, 14, 16–17, 24, 26, 27, 29–30, 31, 32, 34–35, 36, 37, 39, 42, 44, 48, 49, 54, 55, 56–57, 70, 103, 121, 122–23, 131, 132, 133, 135–36, 137, 139, 140, 178, 229, 231, 232
nation-state, 6, 27, 35, 139, 149, 159
necessary evil, 133–34, 136, 140
Nepal, 7, 10, 11, 12, 14, 15, 17, 200–201, 202, 203, 205–6, 207, 208, 209, 210–11, 212, 213–14, 215, 216, 223, 228, 233, 234
Nepali National Congress (NC), 206–7, 208, 209, 210, 215
neocolonialism, 227
neoliberalism, 15, 25, 40, 202
Nigeria, 1, 4, 8, 10, 11, 12, 13, 15, 74, 128, 129–30, 172, 173–74, 175, 176–77, 178, 179, 180, 181, 182, 183, 184, 186–87, 188, 190, 192n63, 223, 228, 232, 233, 234–35
nonviolence, 207, 215
North Atlantic Treaty Organization (NATO), 17, 25, 32, 52, 103, 127, 129, 141

North Korea, 16, 25, 26, 32, 33, 34, 40, 43, 44–45, 46–48, 54, 56, 57, 223, 228, 229, 234
nuclear weapons, 10, 13, 14, 16, 17, 25, 26, 27, 28, 31–33, 34, 35, 40, 43, 44–45, 46, 47, 49, 53, 54, 55, 56, 228, 229, 234

Organization for Security and Co-operation in Europe (OSCE), 100–101, 105, 107, 108

Pakistan, 10, 14, 25, 32, 34, 36, 37, 48, 69, 71–72, 72–73, 73–74, 75, 76, 77, 78–79, 80, 81, 82–83, 85, 86–87, 88, 89–90n32, 230
Pashinyan, Nikol, 107
peace, 2–3, 4, 5, 6, 8, 11, 14–15, 16, 26, 44, 69, 70, 75, 77, 81, 82–83, 87, 88, 109, 110, 121, 122, 124, 125, 127, 128, 129, 130, 132, 133, 134, 136, 141, 172, 173, 177, 182, 186–87, 189, 211, 212, 216, 222, 223–24, 225, 226, 227, 228, 229–30, 231, 232, 233, 234, 235; negative peace, 87, 88, 223, 224; positive peace, 70, 88, 228; sustainable peace, 4, 14–15, 81, 88, 128, 133, 228, 231
peace and security architecture, 5, 26, 121, 122, 125, 136
People's Defense Units (PYD/YPG), 97
protests, 45, 199, 200, 209–10, 212, 213, 215
Putin, Vladimir, 50, 51, 52, 53, 54, 107, 201–2

radicalization, 12, 173–74, 175, 179, 181, 185, 186, 187, 189, 190, 232, 233
regional politics, 153, 200–201
repression, 159, 168n57, 199–200, 203, 210, 212
resistance, 4, 12, 16, 26, 31, 36–37, 41, 48, 50, 53, 54–55, 72, 73, 74, 124, 125–26, 200, 201, 202–3, 205, 206, 207, 208–9, 211, 216, 227, 232, 233; civil, 199–200, 201–2, 202, 203, 204, 205, 206, 207, 209, 210, 211, 212, 213, 214, 215, 216, 217
responsibility to protect (R2P), 1–2, 7, 199, 202
Revolutionary Schi'a, 155
Russia, 1, 6, 10, 11, 14, 16, 17, 25, 26, 28, 32, 33, 43, 45, 48, 49–53, 54–55, 56–57, 69, 70, 71, 72–73, 74, 77, 80, 81, 84, 95, 96–97, 99, 100, 101–2, 103, 104, 106, 107, 108, 109, 129, 201–2, 205, 229–30, 231

Sadrist movement, 161–62, 166, 169n72, 169n85
Shi'a uprising, 158, 159, 168n48
Shi'ism, 149–50, 153, 154, 155, 156, 157, 160, 166, 166n2, 167n18, 168n53
Sierra Leone, 1, 8
sociological imagination, 3, 228

Index 245

sociology, 2–3, 222, 223–24, 225, 226, 227, 228–29, 233, 234, 235; sociology of international peace and security, 2, 222, 223, 224, 226, 227, 228, 229, 233, 234, 235

Somalia, 1, 4, 7, 8, 10, 11, 12, 13, 14, 15, 35, 74, 122, 123, 124–25, 126–27, 128, 130, 131–32, 133, 134, 135, 136–37, 138, 140, 142n23, 223, 228, 231, 232, 234–35

Southern Kaduna, 12, 173–74, 174–75, 176, 182, 183, 184, 185, 186, 187, 188, 189, 190

Southern Kaduna People's Union (SOKAPU), 174, 177, 186, 187, 188

South Korea, 32, 43, 44, 45, 46, 47, 48

sovereignty, 16, 29, 48, 49, 52, 54, 55, 58n24, 102–3, 105, 140, 214, 215, 223

Supreme Council for Islamic Revolution in Iraq (SCIRI), 161–62

Syria, 1, 4, 7, 35, 41, 74, 97, 98, 105, 106, 108, 111, 128, 166, 200, 217

Taliban, 35, 36–37, 38, 69, 70, 71, 73, 74, 75, 76, 77, 78, 79–80, 81–82, 82–83, 84–87, 88, 89–90n32, 230

Tehrik e Taliban Pakistan (TTP), 69, 70–71, 78, 80, 82, 83, 88

terrorism, 1, 2, 8, 10, 12–13, 24–25, 26, 35, 40, 41, 53, 56, 69–70, 70–71, 74, 77, 78, 80, 83, 84, 87, 96–97, 121, 122, 123, 126, 130–31, 133, 134, 138, 140, 141, 173–74, 176, 179–80, 184, 188, 190, 224, 225, 228, 229, 230, 231, 232, 233–34, 234–35; terrorism warfare, 2, 8, 12, 13, 24–25, 26, 41, 53, 228, 229, 230, 231, 232, 234–35

Treaty on the Non-Proliferation of Nuclear Weapons (NPT), 31, 32, 33, 34, 39, 43, 44, 49

Turkey, 6, 10, 11, 16, 53, 54, 77, 95, 97–98, 99, 101, 102–3, 104–5, 105–6, 107, 108, 109, 110, 111, 112, 230–31

Ukraine, 1, 4, 7, 12, 17, 26, 32, 33, 43, 48, 49–53, 54–55, 56–57, 74, 84, 95, 96–97, 104, 128, 129, 199, 200, 204, 216, 223, 228, 229, 234–35

United Nations, 46, 89n28, 127, 129, 135, 139, 213, 224, 231

United Nations Agency for Refugees, 132

United Nations High Commissioner for Refugees, 100

United Nations Operations in Somalia I (UNOSOM 1), 124, 126

United Nations Security Council (UNSC), 32, 125

United States, 2, 6, 12, 14, 16, 24, 28, 31, 34, 35–36, 37, 38, 39, 40–41, 42, 44, 45, 47, 70, 73, 75, 76, 77, 79, 80–81, 81–82, 86, 87, 88, 100, 101, 109, 123, 124, 134, 136, 142n23, 148, 167n35, 199, 215, 228, 230, 232; invasion of Iraq, 12, 40, 156, 157, 231; military, 25; nuclear weapons, 25, 26, 32–33, 46. *See also* Ukraine; war on terror

unnecessary entanglement, 133–34, 136, 137, 138, 140, 141

violence, 6, 7, 10, 11, 12, 13–14, 16, 29, 69, 87, 141, 158, 160, 164, 165, 172, 173, 174, 177, 178, 179, 181, 182, 183, 184, 185, 186–87, 188, 189, 192n63, 199, 200, 202, 210, 213, 217, 223, 224, 225, 226, 228, 233; structural violence, 223, 224, 233

violent extremism, 12, 14, 83, 173–74, 175, 177–78, 179–80, 180–81, 183, 185, 186, 187, 188, 190, 232, 233

war on terror, 1–2, 7, 8, 10–11, 12, 13, 14, 16–17, 25, 26, 27, 35, 38, 39, 40, 41, 42, 43, 56, 73, 75, 76, 77, 81, 124, 130, 131–32, 134, 135–36, 139, 140, 173, 199, 202, 223, 224, 228, 231, 232, 233, 234–35

Yemen, 1, 4, 35, 74, 128, 166

ABU BAKARR BAH is Presidential Research Professor of Sociology and Chair of the Department of Sociology at Northern Illinois University. He (with Nikolas Emmanuel) is author of *International Statebuilding in West Africa: Civil Wars and New Humanitarianism in Sierra Leone, Liberia, and Côte d'Ivoire* (Bloomington: Indiana University Press, 2024). He is editor of *Post-Conflict Institutional Design: Democracy and Peacebuilding in Africa* (London: Zed Books, 2022) and *International Security and Peacebuilding: Africa, the Middle East, and Europe* (Bloomington: Indiana University Press, 2017) and founding editor of *African Conflict & Peacebuilding Review*.

For Indiana University Press

Tony Brewer, *Artist and Book Designer*
Anna Garnai, *Production Coordinator*
Sophia Hebert, *Assistant Acquisitions Editor*
Samantha Heffner, *Marketing and Publicity Manager*
Katie Huggins, *Production Manager*
David Miller, *Lead Project Manager/Editor*
Bethany Mowry, *Acquisitions Editor*
Dan Pyle, *Online Publishing Manager*
Leyla Salamova, *Artist and Book Designer*